D1275693

THE WORKS
OF
SIR JOHN SUCKLING

THE WORKS OF
SIR JOHN SUCKLING

IN PROSE AND VERSE

EDITED, WITH INTRODUCTION AND NOTES
BY

A. HAMILTON THOMPSON, M.A.

NEW YORK
RUSSELL & RUSSELL · INC
1964

FIRST PUBLISHED IN 1910
REISSUED, 1964, BY RUSSELL & RUSSELL, INC.
BY ARRANGEMENT WITH ROUTLEDGE & KEGAN PAUL, LTD.
L. C. CATALOG CARD NO: 64—15042

PRINTED IN THE UNITED STATES OF AMERICA

CONTENTS

INTRODUCTION

THE *Fragmenta Aurea* of Sir John Suckling were published in 1646, four years after their author's death, 'by a friend to perpetuate his memory.' A second edition followed in 1648, and in 1658 a third edition contained an additional collection of poems and letters and the unfinished tragedy of *The Sad One.* The success of these volumes was aided doubtless by the reputation for high accomplishment and ready wit which Suckling had enjoyed, by the part which he had taken in the public affairs of a critical epoch, by his sudden disappearance, and the mystery which attended his death. He belonged to a family whose chief estates lay at Woodton, in Norfolk, and Barsham, in Suffolk, in the neighbourhood of Bungay and Beccles. His father, Sir John Suckling, became Secretary of State in 1622; his mother was a sister of Lionel Cranfield, who in 1622 was created Baron Cranfield of Cranfield and Earl of Middlesex; and he himself was born in February, 1608-09, at Cranfield's house at Whitton, between Twickenham and Hounslow. He was entered at Trinity College, Cambridge, in 1623, and in 1627, the year of his father's death, was admitted to Gray's Inn. He succeeded to his father's estates, and appears to have spent the time between 1627 and 1630, when he received knighthood, in travelling abroad. His letters bear evident testimony to the fact that he joined the contingent of English soldiers who served in the army of Gustavus Adolphus during the Thirty Years' War; he was certainly with them during the winter of 1631-32, and, although his indications of his movements are very slight, they seem to point to his presence at the battle of Breitenfeld. He certainly returned to London in May, 1632, and seems to have spent the greater part of his time there for the next seven or eight years, a prominent figure among men of fashion at Court and a distinguished amateur of letters. His poems throw a considerable amount of light upon his occupations and friendships during this period, while his letters give us a somewhat closer insight into his personal character. The anecdotes given by Aubrey are founded, like many of Aubrey's statements, on a not necessarily accurate reminiscence of casual gossip ; they testify, however, to certain qualities which may be gathered from the internal evidence of his writings—his versatile and mercurial temperament, and his tendency to ostentation. His expensive production of *Aglaura*, probably at the end of 1637, excited some comment, and the folio edition of the play, with its wide margins and slender channel of type, was referred to with satire in some lines by Richard Brome. When in 1639 he raised a troop for the first Scottish war of Charles I., their extravagant accoutrements were much ridiculed. Aubrey quotes a lampoon by Sir John Mennes, which reflected on Suckling's courage during the campaign. However, if the surface of Suckling's life at this time was unpromising, there can be little doubt that he read widely and wisely, and that his expressed cynicism was often contradicted by a prudent kindliness of heart and a thoughtfulness which was not a leading characteristic of the society in which he moved. His letter of advice to a foolish and selfish cousin, though written in the tone of a man of the world, does not conceal a genuine anxiety for his correspondent. His friendship with men like John Hales, and the fact that he could spare time from his amusements to write his *Account of Religion*, are evidence of qualities far removed from the conventional libertinage of many of his lyrics and some of his letters ; while if, as is possible, the *Account of Religion* was thrown off merely in order to astonish his friends with his versatility, at any rate his letter to Henry Jermyn shows that the expedition to Scotland had awakened in him a serious interest in public affairs and a far-seeing concern for the King's safety. He fell a victim to his politics. In May, 1641, he took an active part in the plot for rescuing Strafford from the Tower. He escaped to France, and died at Paris in 1642, either by taking poison, or, according to another tradition, by the malice of a manservant, who placed an open razor in his boot.

In the various branches of literature in which Suckling worked he was professedly an amateur, cultivating literary society, bestowing upon it the casual inspiration of his wit, but abstaining from any regular apprenticeship to literature. As a natural result, his poetry suffers from a striking irregularity of execution. Many of the verses printed in the present volume are little better than doggerel, and if the doggerel is sometimes clever, it is often very much the reverse. The *Sessions of the Poets* (to give it its earliest title), which won for its author considerable fame as a wit, and produced a crop of imitations, has much of Suckling's casual happiness of phrase, and hits off with terse criticism the more conspicuous attributes of the persons who take part in the contest described. But, beyond the amusement aroused by it at the time, and its historical interest for us to-day, it is of no intrinsic poetical value. Suckling approached verse in a condescending spirit, treating it as a pastime, or as an accomplishment within reach of a gentleman, but unsuited to absorb too much of his time and power. He attached himself to no school of poetry in particular. Some of his friends, Carew, for instance, were nominal disciples of Jonson. Suckling's poetry, save for a few epigrammatic pieces and an imitation, written half in burlesque, of a famous song by Jonson, retains little trace of Jonson's influence. He spoke rather scornfully of the poet's notorious boastfulness in the *Sessions of the Poets*, and caricatured him with a light touch in *The Sad One*. His inclinations led him rather in the direction which had been pointed so forcibly by Donne. The strong, if artificial, style of Donne, with its elaborately pursued metaphors, and its explosive violence of statement, had leavened most of the non-dramatic poetry of Suckling's age. Such poems as *Love's World*, a collection of similes by which the lover proves that he and his passion reflect the universe and its elements in detail, or the *Farewell to Love*, with its gruesome imagery of death's-heads and worms, and the lover's declaration—

'A quick corse, methinks, I spy
In every woman,'

are thoroughly in the ingenious and far-fetched manner of Donne. The opening of the third of the set of verses, entitled 'Sonnets,' is practically borrowed from Donne's fine lines:

'I long to talk with some old lover's ghost,
Who died before the god of love was born.'

Less directly imitated, but still an immediate effect of the type of simile for which Donne was responsible in English poetry—the simile worked up with care from the physical and mechanical science of the day—is the description of the clock in lover's hearts, to which are devoted the lines beginning, 'That none beguiled be by Time's quick flowing.' In the spirit of Donne, but with a more graceful command of phrase, are the lines,

''Tis now, since I sat down before
That foolish fort, a heart,'

with their close description of the siege and its abandonment.

However, if Suckling made his most ambitious attempts in this fashionable style, he did not achieve his greatest successes in it. It is the chief characteristic of the poets of the school of Donne that their artificiality, if the paradox is admissible, is a spontaneous part of their nature. They are naturally involved in expression and diffuse in thought; their style seems to be naturally hard and monotonous. Few of them possessed that force of imagination which, in Donne's case, survived, if it did not always conquer, the tortures to which it was submitted by its owner. The fervent piety of George Herbert redeems much of the triviality which marks its outpourings; but, beyond question, his frame of mind, in which the highest aspirations translated themselves into quaint plays on words and out-of-the-way analogies from Nature, was no artistic pose, but a natural mood. Suckling, in his 'metaphysical' excursions, stands outside the group which indulged in poetical distortions of wit, pious or profane. He may be dull, he is frequently barren, but he is never involved. His idea is clear to himself, and if he elaborates it, he does so without raising a cloud of words and confused images round it for his readers. ‘ ’Tis now since I sat down ’ may recall Donne's favourite figures of thought ; but its ready ease and smoothness, its conciseness of phrase, are very different from Donne's ponderousness and jerkiness, amid which effects are achieved, either by a sudden and apparently accidental digression into short-lived melody, or by a piece of forcible abruptness that arrests the attention and remains fast in the memory. Suckling is clear and easy with no apparent effort. There is no depth of feeling in his poetry ; he evidently prided himself on its absence. The deep emotions of the poet were no part of the equipment of a gentleman. In depth of abstract thought, too, he is deficient. Donne's least graceful verses usually have the merit that their thought, while not always profound, is at least novel. Suckling's thought was commonplace, and had little fertility. Again and again, in his plays and letters, we find old ideas re-used from his poems without more alteration than a careless memory admits. His *Account of Religion by Reason*, a prose pamphlet written during a holiday at Bath, or West Kington, is a clever performance, with a comparative grace and clearness of style that, from the point of view of purely literary merit, place it somewhat in advance of most of the prose of Suckling's age. But its treatment of its subject—a man of the world's apology for Christianity—is merely a light résumé of arguments commonly advanced by other writers; and little original thought has come into being from the perusal of the ‘ cart-load of books ’ which, as Aubrey tells us, Suckling brought down to Bath with him. His ready and superficial intelligence of abstract subjects was consistent with real earnestness and foresight where practical issues were at stake. The letter already alluded to, addressed to Henry Jermyn, and evidently intended for the eye of Charles I., discusses with great clearness and wisdom the proper attitude of the King to Parliament, and the advisability of the surrender of Strafford. Suckling eventually clave whole-heartedly to the royal cause, and Strafford's liberty was the rock on which he made shipwreck ; but it seems clear that his subsequent actions must have been in defiance of his better judgment, and that his end, whatever its manner, was probably hastened by the hopelessness of the cause which he longed to serve. At any rate, the type of intellect which the letter shows was not a type which would be freely employed on the minute intricacies of fancy so dear to Donne and his followers.

It follows that, where Suckling excels as a poet, we find him dealing with concrete subjects, or using imagery with which he is practically familiar. This is the merit of a lyric like ''Tis now since I sat down,' in which the details of the simile are so perfectly adjusted to the subject of the poem. Suckling's obvious cynicism where affairs of the heart were concerned expresses itself at once in verse. 'Why so pale and wan, fond lover?' is a happy impromptu in which the natural Suckling declares himself without reserve. When he turns to hymn constant love in 'O! for some honest lover's ghost,' he is writing conventionally and uneasily, and the conclusion of the poem, with its airy disclaimer of the possible rewards of earthly fidelity, is arrived at with evident relief. Similarly, beside the *Ballad upon a Wedding*, the dialogue on the same subject between Suckling and his friend Bond is awkward and uninteresting. The ballad itself finds Suckling in a thoroughly congenial mood. He has no longer to forage for similes 'far-fetched and dear-bought,' but speaks as a plain person dealing directly with facts. Putting himself in the position of a countryman come up to town, free to adopt the simple imagery of a country life which he evidently loved, his imagination comes into play unforced, and his task of simple description is at once enlivened by the exquisite pictures which imagination in these happy circumstances suggests. It is not that these pictures are peculiarly Suckling's own: the Easter sunshine had already been the chief motive of George Herbert's loveliest and most natural lyric, and other writers had found analogies between fresh beauty and the Catherine pear, but no one had made these allusions with so little elaboration or with so thoroughly pictorial an effect. Here, at his best, Suckling is akin to Herrick, equalling him in the delicacy of line with which his pictures are drawn, but giving no hint of that gentle philosophy, so susceptible to the beauty and pleasure of the moment, while so apprehensive of its fleeting rapture, which gives Herrick's verse its never-failing charm.

In the pretty lyric, 'Love, Reason, Hate,' Suckling again approaches Herrick. He is thoroughly at home in the rustic game which his abstract qualities play, and here, just as in ''Tis now since I sat down,' the real subject of the poem is exactly suited by the image employed.

In the adoption of natural and concrete imagery, then, unhampered by the demands of artifice and ingenuity, Suckling's inborn directness of intellect finds its way to expression most readily, and the chief characteristic of that expression is its happy simplicity of phrase. It was, however, the great drawback to his poetic gift that he felt himself bound, as a fashionable amateur, to follow the latest fashion. We could exchange many of his 'metaphysical' ventures for more lyrics like 'Love, Reason, Hate,' or the *Ballad upon a Wedding*, with their 'music made of morning's merriest heart.' But if in lyric poetry he hastened to be in the mode without much serious thought, it is evident that as a dramatist he took himself more seriously, and had a real desire to excel. Contemporary traditions record the trouble which he took to bring *Aglaura* before the public notice; the play was acted with the unusual addition of scenery, and the cost of the dresses was borne by the author. The plays, one and all, display Suckling's debt to Shakespeare, and the lighter passages are marked by free satirical allusions to the affectations and politics of the day, which give these dramas a definite historical interest. The comedy of *The Goblins*, too, has a very effective centre in the company of outlaws, in whose disguise the secret of the plot is contained. No individual character, however, can lay any real claim to life. The verse-scenes are written in the loosest of that loose blank verse in which the Stewart dramatists abused the free licence of their predecessors, and, in spite of occasional passages of eloquence, are seldom free from tediousness. Excessive complication of plot, as in *Aglaura*, is further obscured by Suckling's inability to keep distinctly before us the motives which animate his characters, and the characters suffer further from that apparent instability of purpose and liability to sudden change of conviction which mark the epoch of Fletcher's and Massinger's influence, and lessen the psychological value of drama, even where plot and character are handled with some individuality. Suckling's failures are more conspicuous, in that he is always pointing us to his models. The influence of the character of Hamlet is perceptible in the discontent of Brennoralt. Hamlet, probably seen through the medium of Vendice in Tourneur's *Revenger's Tragedy*, is again responsible for the hero of *The Sad One*. *Aglaura*, the most ambitious and complicated of the tragedies, is reminiscent of Beaumont and Fletcher's *Maid's Tragedy*, not merely in the hero's reverence for royalty, but in the position of the heroine with regard to her lover and the King. The dramatic strength of the *Maid's Tragedy* resides in the guilt of Evadne, and her vengeance on the seducer who has ruined her life. Aglaura, on the contrary, is innocent; her would-be seducer is murdered by others, while she murders her lover by mistake—a confusion in slaughter by which the tragic horror of Beaumont and Fletcher's play is totally missed. When, after the Restoration, the last act of the *Maid's Tragedy* was altered to avoid the reflections raised by the murder of the guilty King, the effect of the play was spoiled. In Suckling's alternative last act of *Aglaura*, written at an earlier date, with a similar purpose, the change leaves every reader tranquil, unless here and there one may be found who delights in mechanical carnage on the stage. It is impossible to feel much lively interest in the conduct of a plot whose characters go through their evolutions so tamely.

In the present edition the text of the early editions of the *Fragmenta Aurea* has been carefully collated. Its contents, with one or two additions, such as that of the *Cantilena Politica-Jocunda*, are those of the 1646 edition with the additions introduced in 1658. These have been reprinted in as close accordance with the original editions as is permitted by the use of modern spelling. In the plays, the prose-scenes, printed in the early and modern editions alike as though written in blank verse, have been arranged as prose for the first time. The verse-scenes in the early editions are printed very irregularly, and in modern editions have been subjected to much alteration, in which it is often difficult to recognize the likeness to blank verse that presumably dictated such radical departures from the text. The present editor has endeavoured to reproduce where possible the suggestions of the early texts as to the scansion of these scenes, but where, as is often the case, those suggestions are wanting, and the printing of the lines is merely arbitrary, he has arranged the lines in the closest likeness to blank verse that their hasty construction, confused by the constant elision of final vowels and the smaller and more usual monosyllables, and by the frequent use of half-lines in exclamatory passages, may be allowed to bear. In the notes an endeavour has been made to connect the poems and letters as far as possible with Suckling's life and the history of his day, and to trace his allusions to contemporary, and, where necessary, to earlier literature. Here and there allusion has been made to some of the more valuable comments signed 'W. W.,' which are written in a copy of the 1658 edition of the poems, and have been assigned to Wordsworth. These comments, from internal evidence alone, cannot be the work of Wordsworth, although the volume in which they occur seems to have belonged to him, and to contain notes which are his.

Mr. Carew Hazlitt, in his edition of Suckling's works for the *Library of Old Authors*, included a certain amount of new matter, notably two letters, one of which, addressed to Davenant, was printed from MS. Ashmole 826, f. 101, and the other to Sir Henry Vane, from S. P. Dom. Chas. I., vol. ccxvi., p. 6. The second of these is printed as an Appendix to the present volume, from a copy of the original made by the editor. In addition to these, an Appendix to Mr. Hazlitt's edition contains four satires on Suckling, three of which deal with his flight to France, and an anonymous elegy on his death. It is apparent that, while Suckling's somewhat riotous life and conversation excited the enmity of Puritans, his ostentation, of which examples already have been given, made him ridiculous in the eyes of less bigoted contemporaries. At the same time it is impossible to doubt that beneath a gay and careless exterior he possessed sound practical sense, and that his ambition to excel as an amateur wit only too often concealed a high, if somewhat fragile, poetic gift, which on happy occasions rose superior to an atmosphere not a little hostile to its full development.

Fragmenta Aurea.

A Collection of all

THE

Incomparable Peeces,

WRITTEN

By Sir JOHN SVCKLING.

And publiſhed by a Friend to perpetuate his memory.

Printed by his owne Copies.

LONDON,
Printed for *Humphrey Moſeley*, and are to be ſold at his ſhop, at the Signe of the Prin-ces Armes in St *Pauls* Churchyard.
MDCXLVI.

TO THE READER

WHILE Sucklin's name is in the forehead of this book, these Poems can want no preparation. It had been a prejudice to posterity they should have slept longer, and an injury to his own ashes. They that convers'd with him alive and truly (under which notion I comprehend only knowing gentlemen, his soul being transcendent, and incommunicable to others but by reflection) will honour these posthume Idœas of their friend ; and, if any have liv'd in so much darkness, as not to have known so great an ornament of our age, by looking upon these Remains with civility and understanding, they may timely yet repent, and be forgiven.

In this age of paper-prostitutions a man may buy the reputation of some authors into the price of their volume ; but know, the name that leadeth into this Elysium is sacred to Art and Honour ; and no man that is not excellent in both is qualified a competent judge. For, when knowledge is allowed, yet education in the censure of a gentleman requires as many descents as goes to make one ; and he that is bold upon his unequal stock to traduce this name or learning, will deserve to be condemned again into ignorance his original sin, and die in it.

But I keep back the ingenuous reader by my unworthy preface. The gate is open ; and thy soul invited to a garden of ravishing variety. Admire his wit, that created these for thy delight ; while I withdraw into a shade, and contemplate who must follow.

POEMS,

&c.

Written by

Sir JOHN SUCKLING.

Printed by his owne Copy.

The Lyrick Poems were ſet in Muſick by Mr. *Henry Lawes*, Gent. of the Kings Chappel, and one of His Maieſties Private Muſick.

POEMS

ON NEW-YEAR'S DAY, 1640. TO THE KING

I

AWAKE, great sir, the sun shines here,
Gives all your subjects a New-Year ;
Only we stay till you appear,
For thus by us your power is understood,
He may make fair days, you must make them good.
Awake, awake,
And take
Such presents as poor men can make ;
They can add little unto bliss
Who cannot wish.

2

May no ill vapour cloud the sky,
Bold storms invade the sovereignty,
But gales of joy, so fresh, so high,
That you may think Heav'n sent to try this year
What sail, or burthen, a king's mind could bear.
Awake, awake, etc.

3

May all the discords in your state
(Like those in music we create)
Be govern'd at so wise a rate,
That what would of itself sound harsh, or fright,
May be so temper'd that it may delight.
Awake, awake, etc.

4

What conquerors from battles find,
Or lovers when their doves are kind,
Take up henceforth our master's mind,
Make such strange rapes upon the place, 't may be
No longer joy there, but an ecstasy.
Awake, awake, etc.

5

May every pleasure and delight,
That has or does your sense invite,
Double this year, save those o' th' night:
For such a marriage-bed must know no more
Than repetition of what was before.
Awake, awake,
And take
Such presents as poor men can make;
They can add little unto bliss
Who cannot wish.

LOVING AND BELOVED

I

There never yet was honest man
That ever drove the trade of love;
It is impossible, nor can
Integrity our ends promove;
For kings and lovers are alike in this,
That their chief art in reign dissembling is.

2

Here we are lov'd, and there we love;
Good nature now and passion strive
Which of the two should be above,
And laws unto the other give.
So we false fire with art sometimes discover,
And the true fire with the same art do cover.

3

What rack can fancy find so high?
Here we must court, and here engage,
Though in the other place we die.
O, 'tis torture all, and cosenage!
And which the harder is I cannot tell,
To hide true love, or make false love look well.

4

Since it is thus, god of desire,
Give me my honesty again,
And take thy brands back, and thy fire;
I'm weary of the state I'm in:
Since (if the very best should now befall)
Love's triumph must be Honour's funeral.

1

If when Don Cupid's dart
Doth wound a heart,
We hide our grief
And shun relief,
The smart increaseth on that score ;
For wounds unsearcht but rankle more.

2

Then if we whine, look pale,
And tell our tale,
Men are in pain
For us again ;
So, neither speaking doth become
The lover's state, nor being dumb.

3

When this I do descry,
Then thus think I :
Love is the fart
Of every heart ;
It pains a man when 'tis kept close,
And others doth offend when 'tis let loose.

A SESSION OF THE POETS

A session was held the other day,
And Apollo himself was at it, they say,
The laurel that had been so long reserv'd,
Was now to be given to him best deserv'd.
And

Therefore the wits of the town came thither,
'Twas strange to see how they flocked together,
Each strongly confident of his own way,
Thought to gain the laurel away that day.

There was Selden, and he sate hard by the chair ;
Wenman not far off, which was very fair ;
Sands with Townsend, for they kept no order ;
Digby and Shillingsworth a little further.
And

There was Lucan's translator too, and he
That makes God speak so big in 's poetry ;
Selwin and Waller, and Bartlets both the brothers ;
Jack Vaughan and Porter, and divers others.

The first that broke silence was good old Ben,
Prepared before with canary wine,
And he told them plainly he deserved the bays,
For his were called works, where others were but plays.

And

Bid them remember how he had purg'd the stage
Of errors, that had lasted many an age,
And he hoped they did not think the *Silent Woman*,
The *Fox* and the *Alchemist*, outdone by no man.

Apollo stopt him there, and bade him not go on,
'Twas merit, he said, and not presumption
Must carry 't, at which Ben turned about,
And in great choler offer'd to go out:

But

Those that were there thought it not fit
To discontent so ancient a wit;
And therefore Apollo call'd him back again,
And made him mine host of his own New Inn.

Tom Carew was next, but he had a fault
That would not well stand with a laureat;
His muse was hide-bound, and th' issue of 's brain
Was seldom brought forth but with trouble and pain.

And

All that were present there did agree,
A laureat muse should be easy and free,
Yet sure 'twas not that, but 'twas thought that, his grace
Consider'd, he was well he had a cup-bearer's place.

Will. Davenant, asham'd of a foolish mischance
That he had got lately travelling in France,
Modestly hoped the handsomeness of 's muse
Might any deformity about him excuse.

And

Surely the company would have been content,
If they could have found any precedent;
But in all their records either in verse or prose,
There was not one laureat without a nose.

To Will. Bartlet sure all the wits meant well,
But first they would see how his snow would sell:
Will. smil'd and swore in their judgments they went less,
That concluded of merit upon success.

Suddenly taking his place again,
He gave way to Selwin, who straight stept in,
But, alas ! he had been so lately a wit,
That Apollo hardly knew him yet.

Toby Mathews (pox on him !), how came he there ?
Was whispering nothing in somebody's ear ;
When he had the honour to be nam'd in court,
But, sir, you may thank my Lady Carlisle for 't :

For had not her care furnisht you out
With something of handsome, without all doubt
You and your sorry Lady Muse had been
In the number of those that were not let in.

In haste from the court two or three came in,
And they brought letters (forsooth) from the Queen ;
'Twas discreetly done, too, for if th' had come
Without them, th' had scarce been let into the room.

Suckling next was call'd, but did not appear,
But strait one whisper'd Apollo i' th' ear,
That of all men living he cared not for 't,
He loved not the Muses so well as his sport ;

And prized black eyes, or a lucky hit
At bowls, above all the trophies of wit ;
But Apollo was angry, and publiquely said,
'Twere fit that a fine were set upon 's head.

Wat Montague now stood forth to his trial,
And did not so much as suspect a denial ;
But witty Apollo asked him first of all,
If he understood his own pastoral.

For, if he could do it, 'twould plainly appear
He understood more than any man there,
And did merit the bays above all the rest,
But the Monsieur was modest, and silence confest.

During these troubles, in the court was hid
One that Apollo soon mist, little Cid ;
And having spied him, call'd him out of the throng,
And advis'd him in his ear not to write so strong.

Then Murray was summon'd, but 'twas urg'd that he
Was chief already of another company.

Hales set by himself most gravely did smile
To see them about nothing keep such a coil ;
Apollo had spied him, but knowing his mind
Passed by, and call'd Falkland that sate just behind.

But

He was of late so gone with divinity,
That he had almost forgot his poetry,
Though to say the truth (and Apollo did know it)
He might have been both his priest and his poet.

At length who but an Alderman did appear,
At which Will. Davenant began to swear ;
But wiser Apollo bade him draw nigher,
And when he was mounted a little higher,

He openly declared that it was the best sign
Of good store of wit, to have good store of coin ;
And without a syllable more or less said,
He put the laurel on the Alderman's head.

At this all the wits were in such a maze
That for a good while they did nothing but gaze
One upon another : not a man in the place
But had discontent writ in great in his face.

Only the small poets cheer'd up again,
Out of hope, as 'twas thought, of borrowing ;
But sure they were out, for he forfeits his crown,
When he lends any poets about the town.

LOVE'S WORLD

In each man's heart that doth begin
To love, there's ever fram'd within
A little world, for so I found,
When first my passion reason drown'd.

Instead of earth unto this frame, *Earth*
I had a faith was still the same ;
For to be right it doth behoove
It be as that, fixt and not move ;

Yet as the earth may sometime shake
(For winds shut up will cause a quake),
So, often jealousy and fear,
Stol'n into mine, cause tremblings there.

My Flora was my sun, for as *Sun*
One sun, so but one Flora was :
All other faces borrowed hence
Their light and grace, as stars do thence.

My hopes I call my moon, for they, *Moon*
Inconstant still, were at no stay ;
But, as my sun inclin'd to me,
Or more or less were sure to be :

Sometimes it would be full, and then
O ! too, too soon decrease again ;
Eclipst sometimes, that 'twould so fall
There would appear no hope at all.

My thoughts, 'cause infinite they be, *Stars*
Must be those many stars we see ;
Of which some wand'red at their will, *Fixed*
But most on her were fixed still. *Planets*

My burning flame and hot desire *Elements*
Must be the element of fire, *of fire*
Which hath as yet so secret been,
That it as that was never seen :

No kitchen fire, nor eating flame,
But innocent, hot but in name ;
A fire that's starv'd when fed, and gone
When too much fuel is laid on.

But as it plainly doth appear,
That fire subsists by being near
The moon's bright orb, so I believe
Ours doth, for hope keeps love alive.

My fancy was the air, most free *Air*
And full of mutability,
Big with chimeras, vapours here
Innumerable hatcht as there.

The sea's my mind, which calm would be, *Sea*
Were it from winds (my passions) free ;
But out alas ! no sea I find
Is troubled like a lover's mind.

Within it rocks and shallows be,
Despair and fond credulity.

But in this world it were good reason
We did distinguish time and season ;
Her presence then did make the day,
And night shall come when she's away.

Long absence in far-distant place *Winter*
Creates the winter ; and the space
She tarried with me, well I might
Call it my summer of delight. *Summer*

Diversity of weather came
From what she did, and thence had name ;
Sometimes sh' would smile—that made it fair ;
And when she laught, the sun shin'd clear.

Sometimes sh' would frown, and sometimes weep,
So clouds and rain their turns do keep ;
Sometimes again sh' would be all ice,
Extremely cold, extremely nice.

But soft, my Muse ! the world is wide,
And all at once was not descri'd :
It may fall out some honest lover
The rest hereafter will discover.

SONNETS

I

1

Dost see how unregarded now
That piece of beauty passes ?
There was a time when I did vow
To that alone ;
But mark the fate of faces ;
The red and white works now no more on me
Than if it could not charm, or I not see.

2

And yet the face continues good,
And I have still desires,
Am still the selfsame flesh and blood,
As apt to melt
And suffer from those fires ;
O ! some kind power unriddle where it lies,
Whether my heart be faulty, or her eyes ?

3

She every day her man does kill,
And I as often die ;
Neither her power, then, nor my will
Can questioned be,
What is the mystery ?
Sure Beauty's empires, like to greater states,
Have certain periods set, and hidden fates.

II

I

Of thee, kind boy, I ask no red and white,
To make up my delight ;
No odd becoming graces,
Black eyes, or little know-not-whats in faces ;
Make me but mad enough, give me good store
Of love for her I court :
I ask no more,
'Tis love in love that makes the sport.

2

There's no such thing as that we beauty call,
It is mere cosenage all ;
For though some long ago
Lik'd certain colours mingled so and so,
That doth not tie me now from choosing new :
If I a fancy take
To black and blue,
That fancy doth it beauty make.

3

'Tis not the meat, but 'tis the appetite
Makes eating a delight,
And if I like one dish
More than another, that a pheasant is ;
What in our watches, that in us is found ;
So to the height and nick
We up be wound,
No matter by what hand or trick.

III

I

O ! for some honest lover's ghost,
Some kind unbodied post
Sent from the shades below !
I strangely long to know,
Whether the nobler chaplets wear,
Those that their mistress' scorn did bear,
Or those that were us'd kindly.

2

For whatsoe'er they tell us here
To make those sufferings dear,
'Twill there I fear be found,
That to the being crown'd
T' have loved alone will not suffice,
Unless we also have been wise,
And have our loves enjoy'd.

3

What posture can we think him in,
That here unlov'd again
Departs, and 's thither gone
Where each sits by his own ?
Or how can that elysium be,
Where I my mistress still must see
Circled in others' arms ?

4

For there the judges all are just,
And Sophonisba must
Be his whom she held dear,
Not his who lov'd her here :
The sweet Philoclea, since she died,
Lies by her Pirocles his side,
Not by Amphialus.

5

Some bays, perchance, or myrtle bough,
For difference crowns the brow
Of those kind souls that were
The noble martyrs here ;
And if that be the only odds
(As who can tell ?) ye kinder gods,
Give me the woman here.

TO HIS MUCH HONOURED THE LORD LEPINGTON, UPON HIS TRANSLATION OF MALVEZZI, HIS 'ROMULUS' AND 'TARQUIN'

It is so rare and new a thing to see
Ought that belongs to young nobility
In print, but their own clothes, that we must praise
You as we would do those first shew the ways
To arts or to new worlds. You have begun;
Taught travell'd youth what 'tis it should have done:
For 't has indeed too strong a custom been
To carry out more wit than we bring in.
You have done otherwise, brought home, my lord,
The choicest things fam'd countries do afford:
Malvezzi by your means is English grown,
And speaks our tongue as well now as his own.
Malvezzi, he whom 'tis as hard to praise
To merit, as to imitate his ways.
He does not show us Rome great suddenly,
As if the empire were a tympany,
But gives it natural growth, tells how and why
The little body grew so large and high.
Describes each thing so lively, that we are
Concern'd ourselves before we are aware:
And at the wars they and their neighbours wag'd,
Each man is present still, and still engag'd.
Like a good prospective he strangely brings
Things distant to us; and in these two kings
We see what made greatness. And what 't has been
Made that greatness contemptible again.
And all this not tediously deriv'd,
But like to worlds in little maps contriv'd.
'Tis he that doth the Roman dame restore,
Makes Lucrece chaster for her being whore;
Gives her a kind revenge for Tarquin's sin;
For ravish'd first, she ravisheth again.
She says such fine things after 't, that we must
In spite of virtue thank foul rape and lust,
Since 't was the cause no woman would have had,
Though she's of Lucrece side, Tarquin less bad.
But stay; like one that thinks to bring his friend
A mile or two, and sees the journey's end,
I straggle on too far; long graces do
But keep good stomachs off, that would fall to.

AGAINST FRUITION

STAY here, fond youth, and ask no more ; be wise :
Knowing too much long since lost paradise.
The virtuous joys thou hast, thou wouldst should still
Last in their pride ; and wouldst not take it ill,
If rudely from sweet dreams (and for a toy)
Thou wert wak't ? he wakes himself, that does enjoy.

Fruition adds no new wealth, but destroys,
And while it pleaseth much the palate, cloys ;
Who thinks he shall be happier for that,
As reasonably might hope he might grow fat
By eating to a surfeit ; this once past,
What relishes ? even kisses lose their taste.

Urge not 'tis necessary : alas ! we know
The homeliest thing which mankind does is so ;
The world is of a vast extent, we see,
And must be peopled ; children there must be ;
So must bread too ; but since they are enough
Born to the drudgery, what need we plough ?

Women enjoy'd (whate'er before th' have been)
Are like romances read, or sights once seen :
Fruition's dull, and spoils the play much more
Than if one read or knew the plot before.
'Tis expectation makes a blessing dear ;
Heaven were not heaven, if we knew what it were.

And as in prospects we are there pleas'd most,
Where something keeps the eye from being lost,
And leaves us room to guess ; so here restraint
Holds up delight, that with excess would faint.
They who know all the wealth they have, are poor,
He's only rich that cannot tell his store.

I

THERE never yet was woman made,
Nor shall, but to be curst ;
And O, that I, fond I, should first,
Of any lover,
This truth at my own charge to other fools discover !

2

You, that have promis'd to yourselves
Propriety in love,
Know women's hearts like straw do move,
And what we call
Their sympathy, is but love to jet in general.

3

All mankind are alike to them ;
And, though we iron find
That never with a loadstone join'd,
'Tis not the iron's fault,
It is because near the loadstone it was never brought.

4

If where a gentle bee hath fall'n,
And laboured to his power,
A new succeeds not to that flower,
But passes by,
'Tis to be thought, the gallant elsewhere loads his thigh.

5

For still the flowers ready stand :
One buzzes round about,
One lights, one tastes, gets in, gets out ;
All all ways use them,
Till all their sweets are gone, and all again refuse them.

TO MY FRIEND WILL. DAVENANT, UPON HIS POEM OF 'MADAGASCAR'

What mighty princes poets are ! those things
The great ones stick at, and our very kings
Lay down, they venture on ; and with great ease
Discover, conquer what and where they please.
Some phlegmatic sea-captain would have staid
For money now, or victuals ; not have weigh'd
Anchor without 'em ; thou, Will, dost not stay
So much as for a wind, but go'st away,
Land'st, view'st the country ; fight'st, put'st all to rout,
Before another could be putting out !
And now the news in town is, Dav'nant's come
From Madagascar, fraught with laurel home :
And welcome, Will, for the first time ; but prithee
In thy next voyage bring the gold too with thee.

TO MY FRIEND WILL. DAVENANT, ON HIS OTHER POEMS

Thou hast redeem'd us, Will ; and future times
Shall not account unto the age's crimes
Dearth of pure wit. Since the great lord of it,
Donne parted hence, no man has ever writ
So near him in 's own way : I would commend
Particulars ; but then, how should I end
Without a volume ? Ev'ry line of thine
Would ask (to praise it right) twenty of mine.

I

Love, Reason, Hate, did once bespeak
Three mates to play at barley-break :
Love, Folly took ; and Reason, Fancy ;
And Hate consorts with Pride ; so dance they :
Love coupled last, and so it fell,
That Love and Folly were in hell.

2

They break, and Love would Reason meet ;
But Hate was nimbler on her feet :
Fancy looks for Pride, and thither
Hies, and they two hug together :
Yet this new coupling still doth tell
That Love and Folly were in hell.

3

The rest do break again, and Pride
Hath now got Reason on her side :
Hate and Fancy meet, and stand
Untoucht by Love in Folly's hand :
Folly was dull, but Love ran well ;
So Love and Folly were in hell.

SONG

I

I prithee spare me, gentle boy ;
Press me no more for that slight toy,
That foolish trifle of an heart :
I swear it will not do its part,
Though thou dost thine, employ'st thy power and art.

2

For through long custom it has known
The little secrets, and is grown
Sullen and wise, will have its will,
And, like old hawks, pursues that still
That makes least sport, flies only where 't can kill.

3

Some youth that has not made his story,
Will think perchance the pain's the glory,
And mannerly sit out love's feast:
I shall be carving of the best,
Rudely call for the last course 'fore the rest.

4

And O, when once that course is past,
How short a time the feast doth last!
Men rise away, and scarce say grace,
Or civilly once thank the face
That did invite, but seek another place.

UPON MY LADY CARLISLE'S WALKING IN HAMPTON COURT GARDEN

Dialogue

T. C. J. S.

THOM.

DIDST thou not find the place inspir'd,
And flowers, as if they had desir'd
No other sun, start from their beds,
And for a sight steal out their heads?
Heard'st thou not musick when she talk'd?
And didst not find that, as she walk'd
She threw rare perfumes all about,
Such as bean-blossoms newly out,
Or chafed spices give—— ?

J. S.

I must confess those perfumes, Tom,
I did not smell; nor found that from
Her passing by ought sprung up new:
The flowers had all their birth from you;

For I pass'd o'er the selfsame walk,
And did not find one single stalk
Of any thing that was to bring
This unknown after-after-spring.

THOM.

Dull and insensible, could'st see
A thing so near a Deity
Move up and down, and feel no change ?

J. S.

None and so great were alike strange.
I had my thoughts, but not your way ;
All are not born, sir, to the bay :
Alas ! Tom, I am flesh and blood,
And was consulting how I could
In spite of masks and hoods descry
The parts denied unto the eye :
I was undoing all she wore ;
And, had she walkt but one turn more,
Eve in her first state had not been
More naked, or more plainly seen.

THOM.

'Twas well for thee she left the place ;
There is great danger in that face ;
But, hadst thou view'd her leg and thigh,
And, upon that discovery,
Search'd after parts that are more dear
(As Fancy seldom stops so near),
No time or age had ever seen
So lost a thing as thou hadst been.

TO MR. DAVENANT FOR ABSENCE

WONDER not, if I stay not here :
Hurt lovers, like to wounded deer,
Must shift the place ; for standing still
Leaves too much time to know our ill :
Where there is a traitor eye,
That lets in from th' enemy
All that may supplant an heart,
'Tis time the chief should use some art.

Who parts the object from the sense,
Wisely cuts off intelligence.
O, how quickly men must die,
Should they stand all love's battery !
Persinda's eyes great mischief do :
So do, we know, the cannon too ;
But men are safe at distance still :
Where they reach not, they cannot kill.
Love is a fit, and soon is past ;
Ill diet only makes it last :
Who is still looking, gazing ever,
Drinks wine i' th' very height o' th' fever.

AGAINST ABSENCE

My whining lover, what needs all
These vows of life monastical,
Despairs, retirements, jealousies,
And subtile sealing up of eyes ?
Come, come, be wise ; return again ;
A finger burnt 's as great a pain ;
And the same physick, selfsame art
Cures that, would cure a flaming heart,
Wouldst thou, whilst yet the fire is in,
But hold it to the fire again.
If you, dear sir, the plague have got,
What matter is 't whether or not
They let you in the same house lie,
Or carry you abroad to die ?
He, whom the plague or love once takes,
Every room a pest-house makes.
Absence were good if 't were but sense,
That only holds th' intelligence.
Pure love alone no hurt would do ;
But love is love, and magick too,
Brings a mistress a thousand miles,
And the sleight of looks beguiles,
Makes her entertain thee there,
And the same time your rival here ;
And (O, the devil !) that she should
Say finer things now than she would ;
So nobly fancy doth supply
What the dull sense lets fall and die.

Beauty like man's old enemy, 's known
To tempt him most when he's alone :
The air of some wild o'ergrown wood
Or pathless grove is the boy's food.
Return then back, and feed thine eye,
Feed all thy senses, and feast high :
Spare diet is the cause love lasts ;
For surfeits sooner kill than fasts.

A SUPPLEMENT OF AN IMPERFECT COPY OF VERSES OF MR. WILLIAM SHAKESPEARE'S, BY THE AUTHOR

1

One of her hands one of her cheeks lay under,
Cosening the pillow of a lawful kiss,
Which therefore swell'd, and seem'd to part asunder,
As angry to be robb'd of such a bliss :
The one lookt pale, and for revenge did long,
While t' other blush'd, 'cause it had done the wrong.

2

Out of the bed the other fair hand was
On a green satin quilt, whose perfect white
Lookt like a daisy in a field of grass,*
And shew'd like unmelt snow unto the sight :
There lay this pretty perdue, safe to keep
The rest o' th' body that lay fast asleep.

3

Her eyes, (and therefore it was night), close laid,
Strove to imprison beauty till the morn ;
But yet the doors were of such fine stuff made,
That it broke through, and shew'd itself in scorn,
Throwing a kind of light about the place,
Which turned to smiles still, as 't came near her face.

4

Her beams, which some dull men called hair, divided,
Part with her cheeks, part with her lips, did sport ;
But these, as rude, her breath put by still : some
Wiselier downwards sought, but, falling short,
Curl'd back in rings, and seem'd to turn again
To bite the part so unkindly held them in.

* Thus far Shakespear.

THAT none beguiled be by Time's quick flowing,
Lovers have in their hearts a clock still going ;
For, though time be nimble, his motions
Are quicker
And thicker
Where love hath his notions.

Hope is the main-spring on which moves desire ;
And these do the less wheels, Fear, Joy, inspire :
The balance is Thought, evermore
Clicking
And striking,
And ne'er giving o'er.

Occasion's the hand which still 's moving round,
Till by it the critical hour may be found ;
And, when that falls out, it will strike
Kisses,
Strange blisses,
And what you best like.

1

'TIS now, since I sat down before
That foolish fort, a heart,
(Time strangely spent), a year and more,
And still I did my part,

2

Made my approaches, from her hand
Unto her lip did rise,
And did already understand
The language of her eyes ;

3

Proceeded on with no less art—
My tongue was engineer :
I thought to undermine the heart
By whispering in the ear.

4

When this did nothing, I brought down
Great cannon-oaths, and shot
A thousand thousand to the town ;
And still it yielded not.

5

I then resolved to starve the place
  By cutting off all kisses,
Praising and gazing on her face,
  And all such little blisses.

6

To draw her out, and from her strength,
  I drew all batteries in;
And brought myself to lie at length,
  As if no siege had been.

7

When I had done what man could do,
  And thought the place mine own,
The enemy lay quiet too,
  And smil'd at all was done.

8

I sent to know from whence and where
  These hopes and this relief?
A spy inform'd, Honour was there,
  And did command in chief.

9

March, march, quoth I, the word straight give;
  Let's lose no time, but leave her:
That giant upon air will live,
  And hold it out for ever.

10

To such a place our camp remove,
  As will no siege abide:
I hate a fool that starves her love,
  Only to feed her pride.

UPON MY LORD BROHALL'S WEDDING

Dialogue

S[UCKLING]. B[OND].

S. IN bed, dull man,
When Love and Hymen's revels are begun,
And the church ceremonies past and done?
B. Why, who's gone mad to-day?

S. Dull heretick! thou would'st say,
He that is gone to heaven's gone astray:
Brohall, our gallant friend,
Is gone to church, as martyrs to the fire:
Who marry, differ but i' th' end,
Since both do take
The hardest way to what they most desire.
Nor staid he till the formal priest had done;
But, ere that part was finisht, his begun:
Which did reveal
The haste and eagerness men have to seal,
That long to tell the money.
A sprig of willow in his hat he wore—
The loser's badge and liv'ry heretofore,
But now so ordered, that it might be taken
By lookers-on, forsaking as forsaken:
And now and then
A careless smile broke forth, which spoke his mind,
And seem'd to say she might have been more kind.
When this (dear Jack) I saw,
Thought I,
How weak is lover's law!
The bonds made there (like gipsies' knots) with ease
Are fast and loose, as they that hold them please.
B. But was the fair nymph's praise or power less,
That led him captive now to happiness,
'Cause she did not a foreign aid despise,
But enter'd breaches made by others' eyes?
S. The gods forbid!
There must be some to shoot and batter down,
Others to force and to take in the town.
To hawks (good Jack) and hearts
There may
Be sev'ral ways and arts:
One watches them perchance, and makes them tame;
Another, when they're ready, shews them game.

SIR,
WHETHER these lines do find you out,
Putting or clearing of a doubt;
Whether predestination,
Or reconciling three in one,
Or the unriddling how men die,
And live at once eternally,

Now take you up, know 'tis decreed
You straight bestride the college steed,
Leave Socinus and the schoolmen
(Which Jack Bond swears do but fool men),
And come to town : 'tis fit you show
Yourself abroad, that men may know
(Whate'er some learned men have guess'd)
That oracles are not yet ceas'd.
There you shall find the wit and wine
Flowing alike, and both divine ;
Dishes, with names not known in books,
And less amongst the college-cooks,
With sauce so pregnant that you need
Not stay till hunger bids you feed.
The sweat of learned Johnson's brain,
And gentle Shakespear's eas'er strain,
A hackney-coach conveys you to,
In spite of all that rain can do ;
And for your eighteenpence you sit
The lord and judge of all fresh wit.
News in one day as much w' have here,
As serves all Windsor for a year,
And which the carrier brings to you,
After 't has here been found not true.
Then think what company 's design'd
To meet you here, men so refin'd,
Their very common talk at board
Makes wise or mad a young court-lord,
And makes him capable to be
Umpire in 's father's company :
Where no disputes, nor forc'd defence
Of a man's person for his sense,
Take up the time : all strive to be
Masters of truth, as victory ;
And, where you come, I'd boldly swear
A synod might as eas'ly err.

AGAINST FRUITION

Fie upon hearts that burn with mutual fire !
I hate two minds that breathe but one desire.
Were I to curse th' unhallow'd sort of men,
I'd wish them to love, and be lov'd again.

Love's a camelion, that lives on mere air,
And surfeits when it comes to grosser fare :
'Tis petty jealousies, and little fears,
Hopes join'd with doubts, and joys with April tears,
That crowns our love with pleasures : these are gone
When once we come to full fruition,
Like waking in a morning, when all night
Our fancy hath been fed with true delight.
O, what a stroke 'twould be ! sure I should die,
Should I but hear my mistress once say, ay.
That monster expectation feeds too high
For any women e'er to satisfy ;
And no brave spirit ever car'd for that
Which in down beds with ease he could come at.
She's but an honest whore that yields, although
She be as cold as ice, as pure as snow :
He that enjoys her hath no more to say
But 'Keep us fasting, if you'll have us pray.'
Then, fairest mistress, hold the power you have,
By still denying what we still do crave ;
In keeping us in hopes strange things to see
That never were, nor are, nor e'er shall be.

A BALLAD

Upon a Wedding

I tell thee, Dick, where I have been ;
Where I the rarest things have seen,
O, things without compare !
Such sights again cannot be found
In any place on English ground,
Be it at wake or fair.

At Charing Cross, hard by the way
Where we (thou know'st) do sell our hay,
There is a house with stairs ;
And there did I see coming down
Such folk as are not in our town,
Vorty at least, in pairs.

Amongst the rest, one pest'lent fine
(His beard no bigger though than thine)
Walkt on before the rest :
Our landlord looks like nothing to him :
The King (God bless him !), 'twould undo him,
Should he go still so drest.

At Course-a-Park, without all doubt,
He should have first been taken out
By all the maids i' th' town :
Though lusty Roger there had been,
Or little George upon the Green,
Or Vincent of the Crown.

But wot you what ? the youth was going
To make an end of all his wooing ;
The parson for him staid :
Yet by his leave (for all his haste)
He did not so much wish all past
(Perchance) as did the maid.

The maid—and thereby hangs a tale ;
For such a maid no Whitson-ale
Could ever yet produce :
No grape, that's kindly ripe, could be
So round, so plump, so soft as she,
Nor half so full of juice.

Her finger was so small, the ring
Would not stay on, which they did bring ;
It was too wide a peck :
And to say truth (for out it must)
It lookt like the great collar (just)
About our young colt's neck.

Her feet beneath her petticoat,
Like little mice, stole in and out,
As if they fear'd the light :
But O, she dances such a way !
No sun upon an Easter-day
Is half so fine a sight.

He would have kist her once or twice ;
But she would not, she was so nice,
She would not do 't in sight :
And then she lookt as who should say,
' I will do what I list to-day,
And you shall do 't at night.'

Her cheeks so rare a white was on,
No daisy makes comparison
(Who sees them is undone) ;
For streaks of red were mingled there,
Such as are on a Katherne pear
(The side that's next the sun).

Her lips were red ; and one was thin,
Compar'd to that was next her chin
(Some bee had stung it newly) :
But, Dick, her eyes so guard her face,
I durst no more upon them gaze
Than on the sun in July.

Her mouth so small, when she does speak,
Thou 'dst swear her teeth her words did break,
That they might passage get ;
But she so handled still the matter,
They came as geod as ours, or better,
And are not spent a whit.

If wishing should be any sin,
The parson himself had guilty been
(She lookt that day so purely) ;
And, did the youth so oft the feat
At night, as some did in conceit,
It would have spoil'd him surely.

Just in the nick the cook knockt thrice,
And all the waiters in a trice
His summons did obey :
Each serving-man, with dish in hand,
Marcht boldly up, like our train'd band,
Presented, and away.

When all the meat was on the table,
What man of knife or teeth was able
To stay to be intreated ?
And this the very reason was—
Before the parson could say grace,
The company was seated.

The bus'ness of the kitchen's great,
For it is fit that man should eat ;
Nor was it there deni'd—
Passion o' me, how I run on !
There's that that would be thought upon
(I trow) besides the bride.

Now hats fly off, and youths carouse,
Healths first go round, and then the house :
The bride's came thick and thick ;
And, when 'twas nam'd another's health,
Perhaps he made it hers by stealth ;
(And who could help it, Dick ?)

O'th'sudden up they rise and dance ;
Then sit again and sigh, and glance ;
Then dance again and kiss :
Thus several ways the time did pass,
Whilst ev'ry woman wished her place,
And every man wished his.

By this time all were stol'n aside
To counsel and undress the bride ;
But that he must not know :
But yet 'twas thought he guess'd her mind,
And did not mean to stay behind
Above an hour or so.

When in he came, Dick, there she lay
Like new-fall'n snow melting away
('Twas time, I trow, to part) :
Kisses were now the only stay,
Which soon she gave, as who would say,
God b' w' ye, with all my heart.

But, just as Heav'ns would have, to cross it,
In came the bridemaids with the posset :
The bridegroom eat in spite ;
For, had he left the women to 't,
It would have cost two hours to do 't,
Which were too much that night.

At length the candle's out ; and now
All that they had not done they do :
What that is, who can tell ?
But I believe it was no more
Than thou and I have done before
With Bridget and with Nell.

My dearest rival, lest our love
Should with excentric motion move,
Before it learn to go astray,
We'll teach and set it in a way,
And such directions give unto 't,
That it shall never wander foot.
Know first then, we will serve as true
For one poor smile, as we would do,
If we had what our higher flame
Or our vainer wish could frame.

Impossible shall be our hope ;
And love shall only have his scope
To join with fancy now and then,
And think what reason would condemn :
And on these grounds we'll love as true,
As if they were most sure t' ensue :
And chastly for these things we'll stay,
As if to-morrow were the day.
Meantime we two will teach our hearts
In love's burdens bear their parts :
Thou first shall sigh, and say she's fair ;
And I'll still answer, past compare.
Thou shalt set out each part o' th' face,
While I extol each little grace :
Thou shalt be ravisht at her wit ;
And I, that she so governs it :
Thou shalt like well that hand, that eye,
That lip, that look, that majesty,
And in good language them adore ;
While I want words and do it more.
Yea we will sit and sigh a while,
And with soft thoughts some time beguile ;
But straight again break out, and praise
All we had done before, new-ways.
Thus will we do, till paler death
Come with a warrant for our breath ;
And then, whose fate shall be to die
First of us two, by legacy
Shall all his store bequeath, and give
His love to him that shall survive ;
For no one stock can ever serve
To love so much as she'll deserve.

SONG

I

Honest lover whosoever,
If in all thy love there ever
Was one wav'ring thought, if thy flame
Were not still even, still the same :
Know this,
Thou lov'st amiss ;
And, to love true,
Thou must begin again, and love anew.

2

If when she appears i' th' room,
Thou dost not quake, and are struck dumb,
And, in striving this to cover,
Dost not speak thy words twice over :
Know this,
Thou lov'st amiss ;
And, to love true,
Thou must begin again, and love anew.

3

If fondly thou dost not mistake,
And all defects for graces take,
Persuad'st thyself that jests are broken,
When she hath little or nothing spoken,
Know this,
Thou lov'st amiss ;
And, to love true,
Thou must begin again, and love anew.

4

If when thou appear'st to be within,
Thou lett'st not men ask and ask again ;
And, when thou answer'st, if it be,
To what was ask'd thee, properly :
Know this,
Thou lov'st amiss ;
And, to love true,
Thou must begin again, and love anew.

5

If, when thy stomach calls to eat,
Thou cutt'st not fingers 'stead of meat,
And, with much gazing on her face
Dost not rise hungry from the place :
Know this,
Thou lov'st amiss ;
And, to love true,
Thou must begin again, and love anew.

6

If by this thou dost discover
That thou art no perfect lover,
And, desiring to love true,
Thou dost begin to love anew,
Know this,
Thou lov'st amiss ;
And, to love true,
Thou must begin again, and love anew.

UPON TWO SISTERS

Believe 't, young man, I can as eas'ly tell
How many yards and inches 'tis to hell,
Unriddle all predestination,
Or the nice points we now dispute upon.
Had the three goddesses been just as fair,
. . . . .
It had not been so easily decided ;
And sure the apple must have been divided :
It must, it must ; he's impudent, dares say
Which is the handsomer till one 's away.
And it was necessary it should be so :
Wise Nature did foresee it, and did know,
When she had fram'd the eldest, that each heart
Must at the first sight feel the blind god's dart :
And, sure as can be, had she made but one,
No plague had been more sure destruction ;
For we had lik'd, lov'd, burnt to ashes too,
In half the time that we are choosing now :
Variety and equal objects make
The busy eye still doubtful which to take,
This lip, this hand, this foot, this eye, this face,
The other's body, gesture, or her grace ;
And, whilst we thus dispute which of the two,
We unresolv'd go out, and nothing do.
He sure is happiest that has hopes of either ;
Next him is he that sees them both together.

TO HIS RIVAL

Now we have taught our love to know
That it must creep where 't cannot go,

And be for once content to live,
Since here it cannot have to thrive;
It will not be amiss t' enquire
What fuel should maintain this fire:
For fires do either flame too high,
Or, where they cannot flame they die.
First then (my half but better heart)
Know this must wholly be her part;
(For thou and I, like clocks, are wound
Up to the height, and must move round):
She then, by still denying what
We fondly crave, shall such a rate
Set on each trifle, that a kiss
Shall come to be the utmost bliss.
Where sparks and fire do meet with tinder,
Those sparks mere fire will still engender:
To make this good, no debt shall be
From service or fidelity;
For she shall ever pay that score,
By only bidding us do more:
So (though she still a niggard be)
In gracing, where none 's due, she 's free.
The favours she shall cast on us,
(Lest we should grow presumptuous)
Shall not with too much love be shown,
Nor yet the common way still done;
But ev'ry smile and little glance
Shall look half lent, and half by chance:
The ribbon, fan, or muff that she
Would should be kept by thee or me,
Should not be giv'n before too many,
But neither thrown to 's, when there 's any;
So that herself should doubtful be
Whether 'twere fortune flung 't, or she.
She shall not like the thing we do
Sometimes, and yet shall like it too;
Nor any notice take at all
Of what, we gone, she would extol.
Love she shall feed, but fear to nourish;
For, where fear is, love cannot flourish;
Yet live it must, nay must and shall,
While Desdemona is at all:
But, when she's gone, then love shall die,
And in her grave buried lie.

FAREWELL TO LOVE

1

WELL, shadow'd landskip, fare ye well :
How I have lov'd you none can tell,
At least, so well
As he that now hates more
Than e'er he lov'd before.

2

But, my dear nothings, take your leave :
No longer must you me deceive,
Since I perceive
All the deceit, and know
Whence the mistake did grow.

3

As he, whose quicker eye doth trace
A false star shot to a mark'd place,
Does run apace,
And, thinking it to catch,
A jelly up does snatch :

4

So our dull souls, tasting delight
Far off, by sense and appetite,
Think that is right
And real good ; when yet
'Tis but the counterfeit.

5

O, how I glory now, that I
Have made this new discovery !
Each wanton eye
Inflam'd before : no more
Will I increase that score.

6

If I gaze now, 'tis but to see
What manner of death's-head 'twill be,
When it is free
From that fresh upper skin,
The gazer's joy and sin.

7

The gum and glist'ning, which, with art
And studi'd method in each part,
Hangs down the hair, 't
Looks (just) as if that day
Snails there had crawl'd the hay.

8

The locks, that curl'd o'er each ear be,
Hang like two master-worms to me,
That (as we see)
Have tasted to the rest
Two holes, where they like 't best.

9

A quick corse, methinks, I spy
In ev'ry woman ; and mine eye,
At passing by,
Checks, and is troubled, just
As if it rose from dust.

10

They mortify, not heighten me ;
These of my sins the glasses be :
And here I see
How I have loved before.
And so I love no more.

FINIS

The Laſt Remains of Sr. John Suckling.

Being a Full Collection Of all his

Poems and Letters

which have been ſo long expected, and never till now Publiſhed.

With

The *Licence* and *Approbation* of his Noble and Deareſt Friends.

London :
Printed for *Humphrey Moſeley* at the Prince's Arms in St. *Pauls* Churchyard . 1659.

EDITOR'S NOTE

IN the old editions of *Fragmenta Aurea,* Suckling's letters and other prose works are printed to follow the poems. In the present edition the prose works are printed at the end of the book, after the poems and the dramas; and three pieces, which on later authority have been ascribed to Suckling, and were printed in Mr. Hazlitt's edition of the works, here follow the poems comprised in the *Last Remains.* These three pieces have been re-edited, and the original readings of the *Cantilena Politica-Jocunda* have been restored.

TO THE

MOST HONOURED

AND HIGHLY DESERVING

THE

LADY SOUTHCOT

THOUGH I approach with all humility in presenting these Poems to your ladyship, yet dare I not despair of their acceptation, since it were a kind of felony to offer them to any other. They come to you at so many capacities, that they seem rather to return and rebound back to you, as the famous *Arcadia* was sent to that excellent Lady, who was sister to that great author. Your ladyship best knows, that I now bring the last *Remains* of your incomparable brother, Sir *John Suckling*. And, as here are all the world must ever hope for, so here are nothing else but his, not a line but what at first flow'd from him, and will soon approve itself to be too much his to be alter'd or supplied by any other hand ; and sure he were a bold man had thoughts to attempt it. After which 'twould be high presumption in me to say more, but that

I am

(Madam)

Your Ladyship's most obliged, and

Most obedient humble servant,

HUM: MOSELEY.

THE STATIONER TO THE READER

Among the highest and most refin'd wits of the nation, this gentle and princely poet took his generous rise from the Court, where, having flourish'd with splendour and reputation, he liv'd only long enough to see the sunset of that majesty from whose auspicious beams he derived his lustre, and with whose declining state his own loyal fortunes were obscured. But, after the several changes of those times, being sequestred from the more serene contentments of his native country, he first took care to secure the dearest and choicest of his papers in the several cabinets of his noble and faithful friends ; and, among other testimonies of his worth, these elegant and florid pieces of his fancy were preserved in the custody of his truly honourable and virtuous sister, with whose free permission they were transcribed, and now published exactly according to the originals.

This might be sufficient to make you acknowledge that these are the real and genuine works of Sir John Suckling ; but, if you can yet doubt, let any judicious soul seriously consider the freedom of the fancy, richness of the conceipt, proper expression, with that air and spirit diffus'd through every part ; and he will find such a perfect resemblance with what hath been formerly known, that he cannot with modesty doubt them to be his.

I could tell you further (for I myself am the best witness of it), what a thirst and general inquiry hath been after what I here present you, by all that have either seen or heard of them. And by that time you have read them, you will believe me, who have, now for many years, annually published the productions of the best wits of our own and foreign nations.

H. M.

POEMS

THE INVOCATION

Ye juster Powers of Love and Fate,
Give me the reason why
A lover crost
And all hopes lost
May not have leave to die.

It is but just; and Love needs must
Confess it is his part,
When she doth spy
One wounded lie,
To pierce the other's heart.

But yet if he so cruel be
To have one breast to hate,
If I must live
And thus survive,
How far more cruel 's Fate?

In this same state I find too late
I am; and here 's the grief:
Cupid can cure,
Death heal, I'm sure,
Yet neither sends relief.

To live or die, beg only I:
Just Powers, some end me give;
And traitor-like
Thus force me not
Without a heart to live.

[A POEM WITH THE ANSWER]

Sir J. S.

I

Out upon it! I have lov'd
Three whole days together;
And am like to love three more,
If it prove fair weather.

2

Time shall moult away his wings,
  Ere he shall discover
In the whole wide world again
  Such a constant lover.

3

But the spite on 't is, no praise
  Is due at all to me:
Love with me had made no stays,
  Had it any been but she.

4

Had it any been but she,
  And that very face,
There had been at least ere this
  A dozen dozen in her place.

Sir Toby Matthews

1

Say, but did you love so long?
  In troth, I needs must blame you:
Passion did your judgment wrong,
  Or want of reason shame you.

2

Truth, time's fair and witty daughter,
  Shortly shall discover,
Y' are a subject fit for laughter,
  And more fool than lover.

3

But I grant you merit praise
  For your constant folly:
Since you doted three whole days,
  Were you not melancholy?

4

She to whom you prov'd so true,
  And that very, very face,
Puts each minute such as you
  A dozen dozen to disgrace.

LOVE TURNED TO HATRED

I WILL not love one minute more, I swear,
No, not a minute ; not a sigh or tear
Thou get'st from me, or one kind look again,
Though thou shouldst court me to 't and wouldst begin.
I will not think of thee but as men do
Of debts and sins, and then I'll curse thee too :
For thy sake woman shall be now to me
Less welcome, than at midnight ghosts shall be :
I'll hate so perfectly, that it shall be
Treason to love that man that loves a she ;
Nay, I will hate the very good, I swear,
That's in thy sex, because it doth lie there ;
Their very virtue, grace, discourse, and wit,
And all for thee ; what, wilt thou love me yet ?

THE CARELESS LOVER

1

NEVER believe me, if I love,
Or know what 'tis, or mean to prove ;
And yet in faith I lie, I do,
And she's extremely handsome too :
She's fair, she's wondrous fair,
But I care not who know it,
Ere I'll die for love, I'll fairly forego it.

2

This heat of hope, or cold of fear,
My foolish heart could never bear :
One sigh imprison'd ruins more
Than earthquakes have done heretofore :
She's fair, etc.

3

When I am hungry, I do eat,
And cut no fingers 'stead of meat ;
Nor with much gazing on her face
Do e'er rise hungry from the place :
She's fair, etc.

4

A gentle round fill'd to the brink
To this and t' other friend I drink ;
And when 'tis nam'd another's health,
I never make it hers by stealth :
She's fair, etc.

5

Black-Friars to me, and old Whitehall,
Is even as much as is the fall
Of fountains on a pathless grove,
And nourishes as much my love :
She's fair, etc.

6

I visit, talk, do business, play,
And for a need laugh out a day :
Who does not thus in Cupid's school,
He makes not love, but plays the fool :
She's fair, etc.

LOVE AND DEBT ALIKE TROUBLESOME

This one request I make to him that sits the clouds above,
That I were freely out of debt, as I am out of love.
Then for to dance, to drink and sing, I should be very willing,
I should not owe one lass a kiss, nor ne'er a knave a shilling.
'Tis only being in love and debt that breaks us of our rest ;
And he that is quite out of both, of all the world is blest :
He sees the golden age, wherein all things were free and common ;
He eats, he drinks, he takes his rest, he fears no man nor woman.
Though Crœsus compassed great wealth, yet he still craved more,
He was as needy a beggar still, as goes from door to door.
Though Ovid were a merry man, love ever kept him sad ;
He was as far from happiness as one that is stark mad.
Our merchant he in goods is rich, and full of gold and treasure ;

But when he thinks upon his debts, that thought destroys his pleasure.
Our courtier thinks that he's preferr'd, whom every man envies;
When love so rumbles in his pate, no sleep comes in his eyes.
Our gallant's case is worst of all, he lies so just betwixt them;
For he's in love and he's in debt, and knows not which most vex him.
But he that can eat beef, and feed on bread which is so brown,
May satisfy his appetite, and owe no man a crown;
And he that is content with lasses clothed in plain woollen,
May cool his heat in every place: he need not to be sullen,
Nor sigh for love of lady fair: for this each wise man knows—
As good stuff under flannel lies, as under silken clothes.

SONG

I PRITHEE send me back my heart,
  Since I cannot have thine:
For if from yours you will not part,
  Why then shouldst thou have mine?

Yet now I think on't, let it lie:
  To find it were in vain,
For th' hast a thief in either eye
  Would steal it back again.

Why should two hearts in one breast lie,
  And yet not lodge together?
O love, where is thy sympathy,
  If thus our breasts thou sever?

But love is such a mystery,
  I cannot find it out:
For when I think I'm best resolv'd,
  I then am in most doubt.

Then farewell care, and farewell woe,
  I will no longer pine:
For I'll believe I have her heart
  As much as she hath mine.

TO A LADY THAT FORBADE TO LOVE BEFORE COMPANY

What! no more favours? Not a ribband more,
Not fan nor muff to hold as heretofore?
Must all the little blisses then be left,
And what was once love's gift become our theft?
May we not look ourselves into a trance,
Teach our souls parley at our eyes, not glance,
Not touch the hand, not by soft wringing there
Whisper a love that only yes can hear?
Not free a sigh, a sigh that's there for you?
Dear, must I love you, and not love you too?
Be wise, nice, fair; for sooner shall they trace
The feather'd choristers from place to place,
By prints they make in th' air, and sooner say
By what right line the last star made his way
That fled from heaven to earth, than guess to know
How our loves first did spring, or how they grow.
Love is all spirit: fairies sooner may
Be taken tardy, when they night-tricks play,
Than we. We are too dull and lumpish rather:
Would they could find us both in bed together!

THE GUILTLESS INCONSTANT

My first love, whom all beauties did adorn,
Firing my heart, suprest it with her scorn;
Since like the tinder in my breast it lies,
By every sparkle made a sacrifice.
Each wanton eye can kindle my desire,
And that is free to all which was entire.
Desiring more, by the desire I lost,
As those that in consumptions linger most.
And now my wand'ring thoughts are not confin'd
Unto one woman, but to womankind:
This for her shape I love, that for her face,
This for her gesture, or some other grace:
And where that none of all these things I find,
I choose her by the kernel, not the rind:
And so I hope, since my first hope is gone,
To find in many what I lost in one;
And, like to merchants after some great loss,
Trade by retail, that cannot do in gross.

The fault is hers that made me go astray ;
He needs must wander that hath lost his way :
Guiltless I am ; she doth this change provoke,
And made that charcoal, which to her was oak,
And as a looking-glass from the aspect,
Whilst it is whole, doth but one face reflect ;
But, being crackt or broken, there are grown
Many less faces, where there was but one ;
So love unto my heart did first prefer
Her image, and there placed none but her ;
But, since 'twas broke and martyr'd by her scorn,
Many less faces in her place are born.

LOVE'S REPRESENTATION

LEANING her head upon my breast,
There on love's bed she lay to rest ;
My panting heart rock'd her asleep,
My heedful eyes the watch did keep ;
Then, love by me being harbour'd there,
(No hope to be his harbinger)
Desire his rival kept the door ;
For this of him I begg'd no more,
But that, our mistress to entertain,
Some pretty fancy he would frame,
And represent it in a dream,
Of which myself should give the theme.
Then first these thoughts I bid him show,
Which only he and I did know,
Arrayed in duty and respect,
And not in fancies that reflect :
Then those of value next present,
Approv'd by all the world's consent ;
But, to distinguish mine asunder,
Apparrell'd they must be in wonder.
Such a device then I would have,
As service, not reward, should crave,
Attir'd in spotless innocence,
Not self-respect, nor no pretence :
Then such a faith I would have shown,
As heretofore was never known,
Cloth'd with a constant clear intent,
Professing always as it meant :

And, if love no such garments have,
My mind a wardrobe is so brave,
That there sufficient he may see
To clothe Impossibility.
Then beamy fetters he shall find,
By admiration subt'ly twin'd,
That will keep fast the wanton'st thought,
That e'er imagination wrought:
There he shall find of joy a chain,
Fram'd by despair of her disdain,
So curiously that it can't tie
The smallest hopes that thoughts now spy.
There acts, as glorious as the sun,
Are by her veneration spun,
In one of which I would have brought
A pure, unspotted, abstract thought,
Considering her as she is good,
Not in her frame of flesh and blood.
These atoms then, all in her sight,
I bad him join, that so he might
Discern between true love's creation,
And that love's form that's now in fashion.
Love, granting unto my request,
Began to labour in my breast;
But, with the motion he did make,
It heav'd so high that she did wake,
Blush'd at the favour she had done,
Then smil'd, and then away did run.

SONG

THE crafty boy that had full oft assay'd
To pierce my stubborn and resisting breast,
But still the bluntness of his darts betray'd,
Resolv'd at last of setting up his rest,
Either my wild unruly heart to tame,
Or quit his godhead, and his bow disclaim.

So all his lovely looks, his pleasing fires;
All his sweet motions, all his taking smiles;
All that awakes, all that inflames desires,
All that sweetly commands, all that beguiles,
He does into one pair of eyes convey,
And there begs leave that he himself may stay.

And there he brings me, where his ambush lay,
Secure and careless, to a stranger land ;
And, never warning me, which was foul play,
Does make me close by all this beauty stand :
  Where, first struck dead, I did at last recover,
  To know that I might only live to love her.

So I'll be sworn I do, and do confess
The blind lad's power, whilst he inhabits there ;
But I'll be even with him, ne'ertheless,
If e'er I chance to meet with him elsewhere.
  If other eyes invite the boy to tarry,
  I'll fly to hers as to a sanctuary.

UPON THE BLACK SPOTS WORN BY MY LADY D. E.

MADAM,

I KNOW your heart cannot so guilty be,
That you should wear those spots for vanity ;
Or, as your beauty's trophies, put on one
For every murther which your eyes have done :
No, they're your mourning-weeds for hearts forlorn,
Which, though you must not love, you could not scorn ;
To whom since cruel honour doth deny
Those joys could only cure their misery,
Yet you this noble way to grace them found,
Whilst thus your grief their martyrdom hath crown'd,
Of which take heed you prove not prodigal ;
For, if to every common funeral
By your eyes martyr'd, such grace were allow'd,
Your face would wear not patches, but a cloud.

SONG

IF you refuse me once and think again,
    I will complain.
You are deceiv'd, love is no work of art ;
    It must be got and born,
    Not made and worn,
By every one that hath a heart.

Or do you think they more than once can die,
Whom you deny ;
Who tell you of a thousand deaths a day,
Like the old poets feign
And tell the pain
They met, but in the common way ?

Or do you think 't too soon to yield,
And quit the field ?
Nor is that right ; they yield that first entreat :
Once one may crave for love,
But more would prove
This heart too little, that too great.

O that I were all soul, that I might prove
For you as fit a love
As you are for an angel ; for, I know,
None but pure spirits are fit loves for you.

You are all ethereal ; there 's in you no dross,
Nor any part that's gross.
Your coarsest part is like a curious lawn,
The vestal relics for a covering drawn.

Your other parts, part of the purest fire
That e'er Heaven did inspire,
Makes every thought that is refined by it,
A quintessence of goodness and of wit.

Thus have your raptures reach'd to that degree
In Love's philosophy,
That you can figure to yourself a fire
Void of all heat, a love without desire.

Nor in Divinity do you go less :
You think, and you profess,
That souls may have a plenitude of joy,
Although their bodies meet not to employ.

But I must needs confess, I do not find
The motions of my mind
So purified as yet, but at the best
My body claims in them an interest.

I hold that perfect joy makes all our parts
As joyful as our hearts.
Our senses tell us, if we please not them.
Our love is but a dotage or a dream.

How shall we then agree ? you may descend,
But will not, to my end.
I fain would tune my fancy to your key,
But cannot reach to that obstructed way.

There rests but this, that, whilst we sorrow here,
Our bodies may draw near :
And, when no more their joys they can extend,
Then let our souls begin where they did end.

PROFFERED LOVE REJECTED

It is not four years ago,
I offered forty crowns
To lie with her a night or so :
She answer'd me in frowns.

Not two years since, she meeting me
Did whisper in my ear,
That she would at my service be,
If I contented were.

I told her I was cold as snow,
And had no great desire ;
But should be well content to go
To twenty, but no higher.

Some three months since or thereabout,
She, that so coy had been,
Bethought herself and found me out,
And was content to sin.

I smil'd at that, and told her I
Did think it something late,
And that I'd not repentance buy
At above half the rate.

This present morning early she
Forsooth came to my bed,
And gratis there she offered me
Her high-priz'd maidenhead.

I told her that I thought it then
Far dearer than I did,
When I at first the forty crowns
For one night's lodging bid.

DESDAIN

1

A QUOY servent tant d'artifices
Et serments aux vents iettez,
Si vos amours et vos services
Me sont des importunitez.

2

L'amour a d'autres vœux m'appelle ;
Entendez jamais rien de moy,
Ne pensez nous rendre infidele,
A mi tesmoignant vostre foy.

3

L'amant qui mon amour possede
Est trop plein de perfection,
Et doublement il vous excede
De merit et d'affection.

4

Je ne puis estre refroidie,
Ni rompre un cordage si doux,
Ni le rompre sans perfidie,
Ni d'estre perfide pour vous.

5

Vos attentes son toutes en vain,
Le vous dire est vous obliger,
Pour vous faire espargner vos peines
Des vœux et du temps mesnager.

Englished thus by the Author

1

To what end serve the promises
And oaths lost in the air,
Since all your proffer'd services
To me but tortures are ?

2

Another now enjoys my love,
Set you your heart at rest :
Think not me from my faith to move,
Because you faith protest.

3

The man that doth possess my heart,
Has twice as much perfection,
And does excel you in desert,
As much as in affection.

4

I cannot break so sweet a bond,
Unless I prove untrue :
Nor can I ever be so fond,
To prove untrue for you.

5

Your attempts are but in vain
(To tell you is a favour) :
For things that may be rack your brain ;
Then lose not thus your labour.

LUTEA ALLISON

Si sola es, nulla es

THOUGH you, Diana-like, have liv'd still chaste,
Yet must you not (fair) die a maid at last :
The roses on your cheeks were never made
To bless the eye alone, and so to fade ;
Nor had the cherries on your lips their being,
To please no other sense than that of seeing :
You were not made to look on, though that be
A bliss too great for poor mortality :
In that alone those rarer parts you have,
To better uses sure wise nature gave
Than that you put them to ; to love, to wed,
For Hymen's rights, and for the marriage-bed
You were ordain'd, and not to lie alone ;
One is no number, till that two be one.
To keep a maidenhead but till fifteen,
Is worse than murder, and a greater sin
Than to have lost it in the lawful sheets
With one that should want skill to reap those sweets :
But not to lose 't at all—by Venus, this,
And by her son, inexpiable is ;
And should each female guilty be o' th' crime,
The world would have its end before its time.

PERJURY EXCUSED

Alas, it is too late! I can no more
Love now than I have loved before:
My Flora, 'tis my fate, not I;
And what you call contempt is destiny.
I am no monster, sure: I cannot show
Two hearts; one I already owe;
And I have bound myself with oaths, and vowed
Oft'ner, I fear, than Heaven hath e'er allowed,
That faces now should work no more on me,
Than if they could not charm, or I not see.
And shall I break them? shall I think you can
Love, if I could, so foul a perjur'd man?
O no, 'tis equally impossible that I
Should love again, or you love perjury.

UPON T. C. HAVING THE POX

Troth, Tom, I must confess I much admire
Thy water should find passage through the fire;
For fire and water never could agree:
These now by nature have some sympathy:
Sure then his way he forces, for all know
The French ne'er grants a passage to his foe.
If it be so, his valour I must praise,
That being the weaker, yet can force his ways;
And wish that to his valour he had strength,
That he might drive the fire quite out at length;
For, troth, as yet the fire gets the day,
For evermore the water runs away.

UPON THE FIRST SIGHT OF MY LADY SEYMOUR

Wonder not much, if thus amaz'd I look;
Since I saw you, I have been planet-strook:
A beauty, and so rare, I did descry,
As, should I set her forth, you all, as I,
Would lose your hearts; for he that can
Know her and live, he must be more than man—
An apparition of so sweet a creature,
That, credit me, she had not any feature

That did not speak her angel! But no more
Such heavenly things as these we must adore,
Nor prattle of; lest, when we do but touch,
Or strive to know, we wrong her too too much.

UPON L. M. WEEPING

WHOEVER was the cause your tears were shed,
May these my curses light upon his head:
May he be first in love, and let it be
With a most known and black deformity,
Nay, far surpass all witches that have been,
Since our first parents taught us how to sin!
Then let this hag be coy, and he run mad
For that which no man else would e'er have had;
And in this fit may he commit the thing
May him impenitent to th' gallows bring!
Then might he for one tear his pardon have,
But want that single grief his life to save!
And being dead, may he at heaven venter,
But for the guilt of this one fact ne'er enter.

THE DEFORMED MISTRESS

I KNOW there are some fools that care
Not for the body, so the face be fair;
Some others, too, that in a female creature
Respect not beauty, but a comely feature;
And others, too, that for those parts in sight
Care not so much, so that the rest be right.
Each man his humour hath, and, faith, 'tis mine
To love that woman which I now define.
First I would have her wainscot foot and hand
More wrinkled far than any pleated band,
That in those furrows, if I'd take the pains,
I might both sow and reap all sorts of grains:
Her nose I'd have a foot long, not above,
With pimples embroider'd, for those I love;
And at the end a comely pearl of snot,
Considering whether it should fall or not:
Provided, next, that half her teeth be out,
Nor do I care much if her pretty snout

Meet with her furrow'd chin, and both together
Hem in her lips, as dry as good whit-leather :
One wall-eye she shall have, for that's a sign
In other beasts the best : why not in mine ?
Her neck I'll have to be pure jet at least,
With yellow spots enamell'd ; and her breast,
Like a grasshopper's wing, both thin and lean,
Not to be toucht for dirt, unless swept clean :
As for her belly, 'tis no matter, so
There be a belly, and ——
Yet, if you will, let it be something high,
And always let there be a timpany.
But soft ! where am I now ? here I should stride,
Lest I fall in, the place must be so wide,
And pass unto her thighs, which shall be just
Like to an ant's that's scraping in the dust :
Into her legs I'd have love's issues fall,
And all her calf into a gouty small :
Her feet both thick and eagle-like display'd,
The symptoms of a comely, handsome maid.
As for her parts behind, I ask no more :
If they but answer those that are before,
I have my utmost wish ; and, having so,
Judge whether I am happy, yea or no.

NON EST MORTALE QUOD OPTO

Upon Mrs. A. L.

Thou think'st I flatter, when thy praise I tell,
But thou dost all hyperboles excel ;
For I am sure thou art no mortal creature,
But a divine one, thron'd in human feature.
Thy piety is such, that heaven by merit,
If ever any did, thou shouldst inherit :
Thy modesty is such, that, hadst thou been
Tempted as Eve, thou wouldst have shunn'd her sin :
So lovely fair thou art, that sure Dame Nature
Meant thee the pattern of the female creature :
Besides all this, thy flowing wit is such,
That were it not in thee, 't had been too much
For woman-kind : should envy look thee o'er,
It would confess thus much, if not much more.
I love thee well, yet wish some bad in thee ;
For sure I am thou art too good for me.

HIS DREAM

On a still, silent night, scarce could I number
One of the clock, but that a golden slumber
Had lockt my senses fast, and carried me
Into a world of blest felicity,
I know not how : first to a garden, where
The apricock, the cherry, and the pear,
The strawberry, and plum, were fairer far
Than that eye-pleasing fruit that caus'd the jar
Betwixt the goddesses, and tempted more
Than fair Atlanta's ball, though gilded o'er.
I gaz'd awhile on these, and presently
A silver stream ran softly gliding by,
Upon whose banks, lilies more white than snow
New fall'n from heaven, with violets mixt, did grow ;
Whose scent so chaf'd the neighbour air, that you
Would surely swear that Arabick spices grew
Not far from thence, or that the place had been
With musk prepar'd, to entertain Love's queen.
Whilst I admir'd, the river past away,
And up a grove did spring, green as in May
When April had been moist ; upon whose bushes
The pretty robins, nightingales, and thrushes
Warbled their notes so sweetly, that my ears
Did judge at least the musick of the spheres.
But here my gentle dream conveyed me
Into the place where I most long'd to see,
My mistress' bed ; who, some few blushes past
And smiling frowns, contented was at last
To let me touch her neck ; I, not content
With that, slipt to her breast, thence lower went,
And then—— I awak'd.

UPON A. M.

Yield all, my love ; bur be withal as coy
As if thou knew'st not how to sport and toy :
The fort resign'd with ease, men cowards prove
And lazy grow. Let me besiege my love ;
Let me despair at least three times a day,
And take repulses upon each essay :
If I but ask a kiss, straight blush as red
As if I tempted for thy maidenhead ;

Contract thy smiles, if that they go too far,
And let thy frowns be such as threaten war:
That face which nature sure never intended
Should e'er be marr'd, because 't could ne'er be mended.
Take no corruption from thy grandame Eve;
Rather want faith to save thee, than believe
Too soon; for credit me 'tis true,
Men most of all enjoy when least they do.

A CANDLE

THERE is a thing which in the light
Is seldom us'd; but in the night
It serves the maiden female crew,
The ladies, and the good-wives too.
They use to take it in their hand,
And then it will uprightly stand;
And to a hole they it apply,
Where by its good-will it would die:
It spends, goes out, and still within
It leaves its moisture thick and thin.

THE METAMORPHOSIS

THE little boy, to show his might and power,
Turn'd Io to a cow, Narcissus to a flower;
Transform'd Apollo to a homely swain,
And Jove himself into a golden rain.
These shapes were tolerable, but by th' mass!
He's metamorphos'd me into an ass.

TO B. C.

WHEN first, fair mistress, I did see your face,
I brought, but carried no eyes from the place:
And, since that time, god Cupid hath me led
In hope that once I shall enjoy your bed.
But I despair; for now, alas! I find,
Too late for me the blind does lead the blind.

UPON SIR JOHN LAURENCE'S BRINGING WATER OVER THE HILLS TO MY L. MIDDLESEX HIS HOUSE AT WITTEN

AND is the water come ? sure 't cannot be ;
It runs too much against philosophy :
For heavy bodies to the centre bend ;
Light bodies only naturally ascend.
How comes this then to pass ? The good knight's skill
Could nothing do without the water's will :
Then 'twas the water's love that made it flow ;
For love will creep where well it cannot go.

A BARBER

I AM a barber, and, I'd have you know,
A shaver too, sometimes no mad one though :
The reason why you see me now thus bare
Is 'cause I always trade against the hair.
But yet I keep a state ; who comes to me,
Whos'e'er he is, he must uncover'd be.
When I'm at work, I'm bound to find discourse,
To no great purpose, of great Sweden's force,
Of Witel, and the Burse, and what 'twill cost
To get that back which was this summer lost :
So fall to praising of his Lordship's hair ;
Ne'er so deform'd, I swear 'tis *sans* compare :
I tell him that the King's doth sit no fuller,
And yet his is not half so good a colour ;
Then reach a pleasing glass, that's made to lie,
Like to its master, most notoriously ;
And, if he must his mistress see that day,
I with a powder send him strait away.

A SOLDIER

I AM a man of war and might,
And know thus much, that I can fight,
Whether I am i' th' wrong or right,
Devoutly.

No woman under heaven I fear,
New oaths I can exactly swear ;
And forty healths my brain will bear
Most stoutly.

I cannot speak, but I can do
As much as any of our crew;
And, if you doubt it, some of you
May prove me.

I dare be bold thus much to say:
If that my bullets do but play,
You would be hurt so night and day,
Yet love me.

TO MY LADY E. C. AT HER GOING OUT OF ENGLAND

I MUST confess, when I did part from you,
I could not force an artificial dew
Upon my cheeks, nor with a gilded phrase
Express how many hundred several ways
My heart was tortur'd, nor, with arms across,
In discontented garbs set forth my loss:
Such loud expressions many times do come
From lightest hearts: great griefs are always dumb.
The shallow rivers roar, the deep are still;
Numbers of painted words may shew much skill:
But little anguish and a cloudy face
Is oft put on, to serve both time and place:
The blazing wood may to the eye seem great;
But 'tis the fire rak'd up that has the heat,
And keeps it long. True sorrow's like to wine:
That which is good does never need a sign.
My eyes were channels far too small to be
Conveyers of such floods of misery:
And so pray think; or if you'd entertain
A thought more charitable, suppose some strain
Of sad repentance had, not long before,
Quite emptied for my sins that watery store:
So shall you him oblige that still will be
Your servant to his best ability.

A PEDLAR OF SMALL-WARES

A PEDLAR I am, that take great care
And mickle pains for to sell small-ware:
I had need do so, when women do buy,
That in small wares trade so unwillingly.

L. W.

A looking-glass, will 't please you, madam, buy ?
A rare one 'tis indeed, for in it I
Can shew what all the world besides can't do,
A face like to your own, so fair, so true.

L. E.

For you a girdle, madam ; but I doubt me
Nature hath order'd there's no waist about ye :
Pray, therefore, be but pleas'd to search my pack,
There's no ware that I have that you shall lack.

L. E. L. M.

You, ladies, want you pins ? if that you do,
I have those will enter, and that stiffly too :
It's time you choose, in troth ; you will bemoan
Too late your tarrying, when my pack's once gone.

L. B. L. A.

As for you, ladies, there are those behind
Whose ware perchance may better take your mind :
One cannot please ye all ; the pedlar will draw back,
And wish against himself that you may have the knack.

AN ANSWER TO SOME VERSES MADE IN HIS PRAISE

THE ancient poets and their learned rimes
We still admire in these our later times,
And celebrate their fames. Thus, though they die,
Their names can never taste mortality :
Blind Homer's muse and Virgil's stately verse,
While any live, shall never need a herse.
Since then to these such praise was justly due
For what they did, what shall be said to you ?
These had their helps : they writ of gods and kings,
Of temples, battles, and such gallant things ;
But you of nothing : how could you have writ,
Had you but chose a subject to your wit ?
To praise Achilles, or the Trojan crew,
Shewed little art, for praise was but their due.
To say she's fair that's fair, this is no pains :
He shows himself most poet, that most feigns.

To find out virtues strangely hid in me;
Ay, there's the art and learned poetry!
To make one striding of a barbed steed,
Prancing a stately round—I use indeed
To ride Bat Jewel's jade—this is the skill,
This shows the poet wants not wit at will.
I must admire aloof, and for my part
Be well contented, since you do 't with art.

LOVE'S BURNING-GLASS

Wondering long, how I could harmless see
Men gazing on those beams that fired me,
At last I found it was the crystal, Love,
Before my heart that did the heat improve:
Which, by contracting of those scatter'd rays
Into itself, did so produce my blaze.
Now, lighted by my love, I see the same
Beams dazzle those, that me are wont t' inflame;
And now I bless my love, when I do think
By how much I had rather burn than wink.
But how much happier were it thus to burn,
If I had liberty to choose my urn!
But since those beams do promise only fire,
This flame shall purge me of the dross, Desire.

THE MIRACLE

If thou be'st ice, I do admire
How thou couldst set my heart on fire;
Or how thy fire could kindle me,
Thou being ice, and not melt thee;
But even my flames, light as thy own,
Have hard'ned thee into a stone!
Wonder of love, that canst fulfil,
Inverting nature thus, thy will;
Making ice one another burn,
Whilst itself doth harder turn!

[Εἰ μὲν ἦν μαθεῖν]

Εἰ μὲν ἦν μαθεῖν
Ἃ δεῖ παθεῖν
Καὶ μὴ παθεῖν,
Καλὸν ἦν τὸ μαθεῖν·

Εἰ δὲ δεῖ παθεῖν
Ἃ δεῖ μαθεῖν,
Τὶ δεῖ μαθεῖν;
Χρῆ γὰρ παθεῖν·

Scire si liceret quæ debes subire,
Et non subire, pulchrum est scire:
Sed si subire debes quæ debes scire,
Quorsum vis scire? nam debes subire.

Englished thus

If man might know
The ill he must undergo,
And shun it so,
Then it were good to know:
But, if he undergo it,
Though he know it,
What boots him know it?
He must undergo it.

SONG

When, dearest, I but think of thee,
Methinks all things that lovely be
Are present, and my soul delighted:
For beauties that from worth arise
Are like the grace of deities,
Still present with us, though unsighted.

Thus whilst I sit, and sigh the day
With all his borrowed lights away,
Till night's black wings do overtake me,
Thinking on thee, thy beauties then,
As sudden lights do sleeping men,
So they, by their bright rays awake me.

Thus absence dies, and dying proves
No absence can subsist with loves
That do partake of fair perfection;
Since in the darkest night they may
By love's quick motion find a way
To see each other by reflection.

The waving sea can with each flood
Bathe some high promont that hath stood
Far from the main up in the river :
O, think not then but love can do
As much ; for that's an ocean too,
Which flows not every day, but ever !

THE EXPOSTULATION

Tell me, ye juster deities,
That pity lovers' miseries,
Why should my own unworthiness
Fright me to seek my happiness ?
It is as natural as just
Him for to love, whom needs I must :
All men confess that love's a fire ;
Then who denies it to aspire ?

Tell me, if thou wert fortune's thrall,
Would'st thou not raise thee from the fall,
Seek only to o'erlook thy state
Whereto thou art condemn'd by fate ?
Then let me love my Coridon,
And, by love's leave, him love alone :
For I have read of stories oft,
That love hath wings and soars aloft.

Then let me grow in my desire,
Though I be martyr'd in that fire ;
For grace it is enough for me,
But only to love such as he :
For never shall my thoughts be base,
Though luckless, yet without disgrace :
Then let him that my love shall blame
Or clip love's wings, or quench love's flame.

DETRACTION EXECRATED

Thou vermin slander, bred in abject minds
Of thoughts impure, by vile tongues animate,
Canker of conversation ! couldst thou find
Nought but our love whereon to show thy hate ?
Thou never wert, when we two were alone ;
What canst thou witness then ? thy base dull aid

Was useless in our conversation,
Where each meant more than could by both be said.
Whence hadst thou thy intelligence ; from earth ?
That part of us ne'er knew that we did love.
Or from the air ? Our gentle sighs had birth
From such sweet raptures as to joy did move.
Our thoughts, as pure as the chaste morning's breath,
When from the night's cold arms it creeps away,
Were cloth'd in words and maiden's blush that hath
More purity, more innocence than they.
Nor from the water couldst thou have this tale :
No briny tear hath furrow'd her smooth cheek ;
And I was pleas'd : I pray what should he ail
That had her love, for what else could he seek ?
We short'ned days to moments by love's art,
Whilst our two souls in amorous extasy
Perceiv'd no passing time, as if a part
Our love had been of still eternity.
Much less could have it from the purer fire :
Our heat exhales no vapour from coarse sense,
Such as are hopes, or fears, or fond desires ;
Our mutual love itself did recompense.
Thou hast no correspondency in heaven,
And th' elemental world thou seest is free :
Whence hadst thou then this talking, monster ? even
From hell, a harbour fit for it and thee.
Curst be th' officious tongue that did address
Thee to her ears, to ruin my content :
May it one minute taste such happiness,
Deserving lose 't, unpitied it lament !
I must forbear her sight, and so repay
In grief those hours joy shortened to a dram :
Each minute I will lengthen to a day,
And in one year outlive Methusalem.

SONG

UNJUST decrees, that do at once exact
From such a love as worthy hearts should own
So wild a passion,
And yet so tame a presence
As, holding no proportion,
Changes into impossible obedience.

Let it suffice, that neither I do love
In such a calm observance as to weigh
Each word I say,
And each examin'd look t' approve
That towards her doth move,
Without so much of fire
As might in time kindle into desire.

Or give me leave to burst into a flame,
And at the scope of my unbounded will
Love her my fill—
No superscriptions of fame,
Of honour, or good name;
No thought, but to improve
The gentle and quick approaches of my love.

But thus to throng, and overlade a soul
With love, and then to leave a room for fear
That shall all that control,
What is it but to rear
Our passions and our hopes on high,
That thence they may descry
The noblest way how to despair and die?

A PROLOGUE OF THE AUTHOR'S TO A MASQUE AT WITTEN

Expect not here a curious river fine:
Our wits are short of that—alas the time!
The neat refined language of the court
We know not; if we did, our country sport
Must not be too ambitious: 'tis for kings,
Not for their subjects, to have such rare things.
Besides, though, I confess, Parnassus hardly,
Yet Helicon this summer-time is dry:
Our wits were at an ebb, or very low;
And, to say troth, I think they cannot flow.
But yet a gracious influence from you
May alter nature in our brow-sick crew.
Have patience then, we pray, and sit awhile,
And, if a laugh be too much, lend a smile.

CANTILENA POLITICA-JOCUNDA FACTA POST PRINCIPIS DISCESSUM IN HISPANIAM, 1623

I COME from England into France,
Neither to learn to sing nor dance,
Nor yet to ride nor fence;
Nor yet to see strange things as those,
Which have returned without the nose
They carried out from hence.
But I to Paris rode along,
Just like John Dory in the song,
Upon an holy tide;
For I an ambling nag did get:
I hope he is not paid for yet,
I spurred him on each side.
And to St. Dennis first I came
To see the sights at Notre Dame,
The man that showeth snuffles;
Where who is apt for to believe
May see St. Mary's right-hand sleeve,
And her old pantuffles,
Her breast, her milk, her very gown,
Which she did wear in Bethlehem town,
When in the inn she lay.
That all the world knows is a fable;
For so good clothes ne'er lay in stable
Upon a lock of hay.
Nor carpenter could by his trade
Gain so much coin as to have made
A gain of such rich stuff:
Yet they (poor souls) think, for her credit,
They must believe old Joseph did it,
'Cause he deserved enough.
There is one of the Cross's nails,
Which whoso sees his bonnet vails,
And (if he will) may kneel:
Some say 'twas false, 'twas never so;
But, feeling it, thus much I know,
It is as true as steel!
There is the lanthorn, which the Jews,
When Judas led them forth, did use;
It weighs my weight down-right:

Yet, to believe it, you must think
The Jews did put a candle in 't ;
And then 'twas wonderous light.
There's one saint there did lose his nose,
Another 's head, another 's toes,
An elbow and a thumb.
But, when we had seen these holy rags,
We went to our inn, and took our nags,
And so away did come.
I came to Paris on the Seine :
'Twas wonderous fair, but little clean :
'Tis Europe's greatest town.
How strange it is, I need not tell it,
For all the world may eas'liest smell it,
As they pass up and down.
There's many strange things for to see—
The Palace, the great Gallery ;
Place Royal doth excel ;
The new bridge and the statue there :
At Notre Dame, St. Christopher,
The steeple bears the bell.
For learning the University,
And for old clothes the Frippary—
That house the queen did build ;
St. Innocent, whose teeth devours
Dead corpse in four-and-twenty hours—
And there the king was kill'd.
The Basteen and St. Denis Street ;
The Spital, like to London Fleet ;
The Arsenal, no toy.
But, if you'll see the prettiest thing,
You must go to court, and see the king :
O, 'tis a hopeful boy !
For he by all his dukes and peers
Is reverenced for wit as much as years :
Nor may you think it much ;
For he with little switch can play,
And can make fine dirt-pies of clay—
O, never king made such !
A bird, that can but kill a fly,
Or prates, doth please his Majesty,
'Tis known to every one :
The Duke of Guise gave him a parrot ;
And he had twenty cannons for it,
And a great galleon.

O, that I e'er might have the hap
To get the bird !—within the map
'Tis called the Indian Ruck;
I'd give it him, and look to be
As great and wise as Luenie,
Or else I had hard luck.
Birds round his chamber stands;
And he them feeds with his own hands—
'Tis his humility:
And, if that they want anything,
They may go whistle for their king;
And he'll come presently.
Besides all this he hath a jerk,
Taught him by nature, for to work
In iron with great ease:
Sometimes into his forge he goes,
And there he puffs and there he blows,
And makes both locks and keys:
Which puts a doubt in every one,
Whether he were Mars' or Vulcan's son—
Some few believes his mother;
But yet, let all say what they will,
I am resolved, and will think still,
As much the one as the other.
The people do mislike the youth,
Alleging reasons for a truth,
Mothers should honoured be;
Yet some believes he loves her rather,
As well as she did love his father—
And that's notoriously.
'Tis charity, for to be known,
Loves others' children as his own;
Nor must you think it shame;
Unless that he would greater be
Than was his father Henry,
Whose thoughts ne'er did the same.

VERSES

I AM confirm'd a woman can
Love this, or that, or any other man!
This day she's melting hot;
To-morrow swears she knows you not;

If she but a new object find,
Then straight she's of another mind.
Then hang me, Ladies, at your door,
If e'er I doat upon you more!

Yet still I love the fairsome (why?
For nothing but to please my eye);
And so the fat and soft-skinn'd dame
I'll flatter to appease my flame:
For she that's musical I'll long,
When I am sad, to sing a song.
Then hang me, Ladies, at your door,
If e'er I doat upon you more!

I'll give my fancy leave to range
Through everywhere to find out change:
The black, the brown, the fair shall be
But objects of variety.
I'll court you all to serve my turn,
But with such flames as shall not burn.
Then hang me, Ladies, at your door,
If e'er I doat upon you more!

SIR JOHN SUCKLING'S ANSWER

I TELL thee, fellow, whoe'er thou be,
That made this fine sing-song of me,
Thou art a rhyming sot:
These very lines do thee bewray;
This barren wit makes all men say,
'Twas some rebellious Scot.

But it's no wonder that you sing
Such songs of me who am no king,
When every Blue Cap swears
He'll not obey King James his ba'rn,
That hugs a bishop under his arm,
And hangs them in his ears.

Had I been of your covenant,
You would have call'd me John of Gaunt,
And given me great renown;
But, now I am John for the King,
You say I am but a poor Suckling,
And thus you cry me down.

Well, it's no matter what you say
Of me or mine, that ran away :
I hold it no good fashion
A loyal subject's blood to spill,
When we have knaves enough to kill
By force and proclamation.

Commend me unto Lashly stout,
And all his pedlars him about :
Tell them without remorse
That I will plunder all their packs
Which they have gotten, with the stolen knick-knacks,
With these my hundred horse.

This holy war, this zealous firk
Against the bishops and the kirk,
And its pretended bravery—
Religion, all the world can tell,
Amongst Highlanders ne'er did dwell—
It's but to cloak your knavery.

Such desperate gamesters as you be,
I cannot blame for tutoring me,
Since all you have is down ;
And every boor forgets the plough,
And swears that he'll turn gamester now
And venture for a crown.

AGLAURA.

PRESENTED

At the Private Houſe in *Black-Fryers*, by his Ma-jeſties Servants.

Written by

Sir JOHN SVCKLING.

LONDON,
Printed by T. W. for *Humphrey Moſeley*, and are to be ſold at his ſhop, at the Signe of the Princes Armes in St. *Pauls* Churchyard.
1646.

To Sir IOHN SUTLIN upon his *Aglaura :* First, a bloody Tragedy, then by the said Sir IOHN turn'd to a

COMEDY

WHEN first I read thy Book, methought each word
Seem'd a short Dagger, and each line a Sword.
Where Women, Men; Good, Bad; Rich, Poore—all dy:
That needs must prove a fatal Tragedy.
But when I find, whom I so late saw slain
In thy first Book, in this revive again,
I cannot but with others much admire
In humane shape a more than earthly Fire.
So when Prometheus did inform this Clay,
He stole his Fire from heaven. What shall I say?
First for to Kill, and then to life restore,
This *Sutlin* did: the Gods can do no more.

PROLOGUE

I'VE thought upon 't ; and cannot tell which way
Ought I can say now should advance the play :
For plays are either good or bad : the good
(If they do beg) beg to be understood ;
And, in good faith, that has as bold a sound,
As if a beggar should ask twenty pound.
—Men have it not about them :
Then, gentlemen, if rightly understood,
The bad do need less prologue than the good ;
For, if it chance the plot be lame, or blind,
Ill-cloth'd, deform'd throughout, it needs must find
Compassion—it is a beggar without art :
But it falls out in penny-worths of wit,
As in all bargains else—men ever get
All they can in ; will have London measure,
A handful over, in their very pleasure.
And now ye have 't, he could not well deny 'ee,
And I dare swear he's scarce a saver by ye.

PROLOGUE TO THE COURT

THOSE common passions, hopes, and fears, that still,
The poets first, and then the prologues fill
In this our age, he that writ this, by me
Protests against as modest foolery.
He thinks it an odd thing to be in pain
For nothing else, but to be well again.
Who writes to fear is so : had he not writ,
You ne'er had been the judges of his wit ;
And, when he had, did he but then intend
To please himself, he sure might have his end
Without th' expense of hope ; and that he had
That made this play, although the play be bad.
Then, gentlemen, be thrifty : save your dooms
For the next man or the next play that comes ;
For smiles are nothing where men do not care,
And frowns as little where they need not fear.

TO THE KING

THIS, Sir, to them : but unto Majesty
All he has said before he does deny ;
Yet not to Majesty—that were to bring
His fears to be but for the Queen and King,
Not for your selves ; and that he dares not say.
You are his sovereigns another way :
Your souls are princes, and you have as good
A title that way, as ye have by blood,
To govern ; and here your power's more great
And absolute than in the royal seat.
There men dispute, and but by law obey :
Here is no law at all, but what ye say.

Dramatis Personæ

KING, in love with Aglaura.

THERSAMES, Prince, in love with Aglaura.

ORBELLA, Queen, at first mistress to Ziriff; in love with Ariaspes.

ARIASPES, brother to the King.

ZIRIFF, otherwise Zorannes disguised, Captain of the Guard, in love with Orbella; brother to Aglaura.

IOLAS, a Lord of the Council, seeming friend to the Prince, but a traitor, in love with Semanthe.

AGLAURA, in love with the Prince, but nam'd mistress to the King.

ORSAMES, a young lord anti-Platonic; friend to the Prince.

PHILAN, the same.

SEMANTHE, in love with Ziriff; Platonic.

ORITHIE, in love with Thersames.

PASITHAS, a faithful servant.

IOLINA, Aglaura's waiting-woman.

Courtiers. Huntsmen. Priest. Guard.

SCŒNA, PERSIA.

AGLAURA

ACT I

SCENE I

Enter IOLAS, IOLINA

Iol. MARRIED ? and in Diana's grove ?
Iolin. So was th' appointment, or my sense deceiv'd me.
Iol. Married !
Now, by those powers that tie those pretty knots,
'Tis very fine : good faith, 'tis wondrous fine.
Iolin. What is, brother ?
Iol. Why, to marry, sister ;
T' enjoy 'twixt lawful and unlawful thus
A happiness, steal as it were one's own ;
Diana's grove, sayest thou ? [*Scratcheth his head*
Iolin. That is the place ; the hunt once up, and all
Engaged in the sport, they mean to leave
The company, and steal unto those thickets,
Where there's a priest attends them.
Iol. And will they lie together, think'st thou ?
Iolin. Is there distinction of sex, think you,
Or flesh and blood ?
Iol. True ; but the king, sister !
Iolin. But love, brother !
Iol. Thou sayest well ; 'tis fine, 'tis wondrous fine !
Diana's grove ?
Iolin. Yes, Diana's grove ; but, brother,
If you should speak of this now.
Iol. Why, thou knowest
A drowning man holds not a thing so fast :
Semanthe !

Enter SEMANTHE ; *she sees* IOLAS, *and goes in again*

She shuns me too !
Iolin. The wound [is] fest'red sure,
The hurt the boy gave her, when first she look'd

Abroad into the world, is not yet cur'd.
Iol. What hurt?
Iolin. Why, know you not
She was in love long since with young Zorannes,
Aglaura's brother, and the now queen's betroth'd?
Iol. Some such slight tale I've heard.
Iolin. Slight!
She yet does weep, when she but hears him nam'd,
And tells the prettiest and the saddest stories
Of all those civil wars and those amours,
That, trust me, both my lady and myself
Turn weeping statues still.
Iol. Pish! 'tis not that.
'Tis Ziriff and his fresh glories here have robb'd
Me of her: since he thus appear'd in court,
My love has languished worse than plants in drought.
But time's a good physician. Come, let's in:
The king and queen by this time are come forth.
[*Exeunt*

SCENE II

Enter Serving-men *to* ZIRIFF

1 *Serv.* Yonder's a crowd without, as if some strange sight were to be seen to-day here.

2 *Serv.* Two or three with carbonadoes afore instead of faces mistook the door for a breach, and, at the opening of it, are striving still which should enter first.

3 *Serv.* Is my lord busy? [*Knocks*

Enter ZIRIFF, *as in his study*

1 *Serv.* My lord, there are some soldiers without.
Zir. Well, I will despatch them presently.
2 *Serv.* Th' ambassadors from the Cadusians too.
Zir. Show them the gallery.
3 *Serv.* One from the king.
Zir. Again? I come, I come.
[*Exeunt Serving-men*
Greatness, thou vainer shadow of the prince's beams,
Begot by mere reflection, nourish'd in extremes,
First taught to creep and live upon the glance,
Poorly to fare, till thine own proper strength
Bring thee to surfeit of thyself at last!
How dull a pageant would this states-play seem

To me now, were not my love and my revenge
Mix'd with it !—
Three tedious winters have I waited here,
Like patient chemists, blowing still the coals,
And still expecting when the blessed hour
Would come, should make me master of
The Court Elixir, Power ; for that turns all.
'Tis in projection now ; down, sorrow, down,
And swell my heart no more ! and thou, wrong'd ghost
Of my dead father, to thy bed again,
And sleep securely !
It cannot be long,—for sure fate must,
As it has been cruel, so a while be just. [*Exit*

SCENE III

Enter KING *and* Lords, *the* Lords *entreating for prisoners*

King. I say they shall not live : our mercy
Would turn [to] sin, should we but use it e'er.
Pity and love the bosses only be
Of government, merely for show and ornament.
Fear is the bit that man's proud will restrains,
And makes its vice its virtue.—See it done.

Enter to them QUEEN, AGLAURA, Ladies. *The* KING *addresses himself to* AGLAURA

So early and so curious in your dress, fair mistress ?
These pretty ambushes and traps for hearts,
Set with such care to-day, look like design :
Speak, lady, is't a massacre resolv'd ?
Is conquering one by one grown tedious sport ?
Or is the number of the taken such,
That for your safety you must kill outright ?
Agl. Did none do greater mischief, sir, than I,
Heav'n would not much be troubled with sad story ;
Nor would the quarrel man has to the stars
Be kept alive so strongly.
King. When he does leave 't,
Women must take it up, and justly too,
For robbing of the sex, and giving all to you.
Agl. Their weaknesses you mean and I confess, sir.
King. The greatest subjects of their power or glory.

Such gentle rape thou act'st upon my soul,
And with such pleasing violence dost force it still,
That, when it should resist, it tamely yields,
Making a kind of haste to be undone,
As if the way to victory were loss,
And conquest came by overthrow.

Enter an Express, *delivering a packet upon his knee. The* KING *reads*

Queen [*looking upon a flower in one of the Ladies' heads*]. Pretty!
Is it the child of nature, or of some fair hand?
La. 'Tis as the beauty, madam, of some faces,
Art's issue only.
King. Thersames, this concerns you most. Brought you her picture?
Exp. Something made up for her in haste I have.
[*Presents the picture*
King. If she does owe no part of this fair dower
Unto the painter, she is rich enough.
Agl. A kind of merry sadness in this face
Becomes it much.
King. There is indeed, Aglaura,
A pretty sullenness dress'd up in smiles,
That says this beauty can both kill and save.
How like you her, Thersames?
Ther. As well as any man can do a house
By seeing of the portal: here's but a face;
And faces, sir, are things I have not studied.
I have my duty, and may boldly swear,
What you like best will ever please me most.
King. Spoke like Thersames and my son!
Come: the day holds fair.
Let all the huntsmen meet us in the vale;
We will uncouple there.

[*Exeunt:* ARIASPES *stays behind*

Ari. How odd a thing a crowd is unto me!
Sure, nature intended I should be alone.
Had not that old doting man-midwife Time
Slept when he should have brought me forth, I had
Been so too. [*Studies and scratches his head*
To be born near, and only near, a crown!

Enter IOLAS

Iol. How now, my lord ? What, walking o' th[e] tops
Of pyramids ? Whispering yourself away
Like a denied lover ? come, to horse, to horse !
And I will show you straight a sight shall please you,
More than kind looks from her you dote upon
After a falling out.

Ari. Prithee, what is't ?

Iol. I'll tell you as I go. [*Exeunt*

SCENE IV

Enter Huntsmen *hallooing and whooping*

Hunts. Which way, which way ?

Enter THERSAMES, *with* AGLAURA *muffled*

Ther. This is the grove, 'tis somewhere here within. [*Exeunt*

Enter, dogging of them, ARIASPES, IOLAS

Iol. Gently, gently !

Enter ORSAMES, PHILAN, *a* Huntsman, *two* Courtiers

Hunts. No hurt, my lord, I hope ?

Ors. None, none : thou wouldst have warranted it to another, if I had broke my neck. What ! dost think my horse and I show tricks, that, which way soever he throws me, like a tumbler's boy I must fall safe ? Was there a bed of roses there ? would I were eunuch, if I had not as lief ha' fallen in the state as where I did ! the ground was as hard as if it had been paved with Platonic ladies' hearts, and this unconscionable fellow asks whether I have no hurt ! Where's my horse ?

1 *Court.* Making love to the next mare, I think.

2 *Court.* Not the next, I assure you : he's gallop'd away, as if all the spurs i' th' field were in his sides.

Ors. Why, there it is : the jade's in the fashion too : now h'as done me an injury, he will not come near me ! Well, when I hunt next, may it be upon a starv'd cow, without a saddle too ; and may I fall into a sawpit, and not be taken up but with suspicion of having been private with mine own beast there ! Now I better consider on't too, gentlemen, 'tis but the same thing we do at court : here's every man striving who shall be foremost, and hotly pursuing of what he seldom overtakes ; or, if he does, it's no great matter.

Phi. He that's best hors'd, that is, best friended, gets in soonest; and then all he has to do is to laugh at those that are behind. Shall we help you, my lord?

Ors. Prithee, do. Stay! To be in view's to be in favour, is it not?

Phi. Right; and he that has a strong faction against him, hunts upon a cold scent, and may in time come to a loss.

Ors. Here's one rides two miles about, while another leaps a ditch, and is in before him.

Phi. Where note, the indirect way's the nearest!

Ors. Good again!

Phi. And here's another puts on, and falls into a quagmire, that is, follows the court, till he has spent all; for your court quagmire is want of money—there a man is sure to stick, and then not one helps him out, if they do not laugh at him.

1 *Court.* What think you of him that hunts after my rate, and never sees the deer?

2 *Court.* Why, he is like some young fellow that follows the court, and never sees the king.

Ors. To spur a horse, till he is tired, is——

Phi. To importune a friend till he weary of you.

Ors. For then, upon the first occasion, y'are thrown off, as I was now.

Phi. This is nothing to the catching of your horse, Orsames.

Ors. Thou sayest true: I think he is no transmigrated philosopher, and therefore not likely to be taken with morals. Gentlemen, your help! the next, I hope, will be yours; and then 'twill be my turn. [*Exeunt*

Enter again, married, THERSAMES *and* AGLAURA, *with* Priest

Ther. Fear not, my dear! if, when love's diet was
Bare looks, and those stol'n too, he yet did thrive,
What then will he do now, when every night
Will be a feast, and every day fresh revelry?

Agl. Will he not surfeit, when he once shall come
To grosser fare, my lord, and so grow sick?
And love once sick, how quickly it will die!

Ther. Ours cannot; 'tis as immortal as the things
That elemented it, which were our souls:
Nor can they e'er impair in health for what
These holy rites do warrant us to do,

More than our bodies would for quenching thirst.
Come, let's to horse ; we shall be miss'd ; for we
Are envy's mark, and court eyes carry far.
Your prayers and silence, sir ! [*To the Priest*
[*Exeunt*

SCENE V

Enter ARIASPES, IOLAS

Ari. If it succeed, I wear thee here, my Iolas.
Iol. If it succeed ? will night succeed the day,
Or hours one to another ? is not his lust
The idol of his soul, and was not she
The idol of his lust ? As safely he might
Have stol'n the diadem from off his head,
And he would less have miss'd it.
You now, my lord, must raise his jealousy :
Teach it to look through the false optic, fear,
And make it see all double. Tell him, the prince
Would not have thus presum'd, but that he does
Intend worse yet ; and that his crown and life
Will be the next attempt.
Ari. Right ; and I will urge,
How dangerous 'tis unto the present state
To have the creatures and the followers
Of the next prince, whom all now strive to please,
Too near about him.
Iol. What if the malcontents
That use to come unto him, were discovered ?
Ari. By no means ; for it were in vain to give
Him discontent (which, too, must needs be done),
If they within him gave't not nourishment.
Iol. Well, I'll away first ; for the print's too big,
If we be seen together. [*Exit*
Ari. I have so fraught this bark with hope, that it
Dares venture now in any storm or weather ;
And, if he sink or splits, all's one to me.
' Ambition seems all things, and yet is none,
But in disguise stalks to opinion,
And fools it into faith for everything.'
'Tis not with the ascending to a throne
As 'tis with stairs and steps that are the same :
For to a crown each humour's a degree ;
And, as men change and differ, so must we.
The name of virtue doth the people please,

Not for their love to virtue, but their ease;
And parrot-rumour I that tale have taught.
By making love I hold the woman's grace;
'Tis the court double-key, and entrance gets
To all the little plots. The fiery spirits
My love to arms hath drawn into my faction:
All but the minion of the time is mine,
And he shall be, or shall not be at all.
He that beholds a wing in pieces torn,
And knows not that to heav'n it once did bear
The high-flown and self-lessening bird, will think
And call them idle subjects of the wind;
When he, that has the skill to imp and bind
These in right places, will thus truth discover,
That borrowed instruments do oft convey
The soul to her propos'd intents, and where
Our stars deny, art may supply. [*Exit*

Enter SEMANTHE, ORITHIE, ORSAMES, PHILAN

Sem. Think you it is not then
The little jealousies, my lord, and fears;
Joy mix'd with doubt, and doubt reviv'd with hope,
That crowns all love with pleasure? these are lost,
When once we come to full fruition,
Like waking in the morning, when all night
Our fancy has been fed with some new strange delight.
Ors. I grant you, madam, that the fears and joys,
Hopes and desires, mix'd with despairs and doubts,
Do make the sport in love; [and] that they are
The very dogs by which we hunt the hare;
But, as the dogs would stop and straight give o'er,
Were it not for the little thing before,
So would our passions; both alike must be
Flesh'd in the chase.
Ori. Will you, then, place the happiness but there,
Where the dull ploughman and the ploughman's horse
Can find it out? Shall souls refin'd not know
How to preserve alive a noble flame,
But let it die—burn out to appetite?
Sem. Love's a chameleon, and would live on air,
Physic for agues; starving is his food.
Ors. Why, there it is now! a greater epicure
Lives not on earth. My lord and I have been
In's privy kitchen, seen his bills of fare.

Sem. And how, and how, my lord ?
Ors. A mighty prince,
And full of curiosity ! Hearts newly slain
Serv'd up entire, and stuck with little arrows
Instead of cloves.
Phi. Sometimes a cheek plump'd up
With broth, with cream and claret mingled
For sauce, and round about the dish
Pomegranate kernels, strew'd on leaves of lilies !
Ors. Then will he have black eyes, for those of late
He feeds on much, and for variety
The grey.
Phi. You forget his cover'd dishes
Of jenestrays, and marmalade of lips,
Perfum'd by breath sweet as the bean's first blossoms.
Sem. Rare !
And what's the drink to all this meat, my lord ?
Ors. Nothing but pearl dissolv'd, tears still fresh fetch'd
From lovers' eyes, which, if they come to be
Warm in the carriage, are straight cool'd with sighs.
Sem. And all this rich proportion perchance
We would allow him.
Ors. True : but therefore this
Is but his common diet, only serves
When his chief cooks, Liking and Opportunity,
Are out of the way ; for, when he feasts indeed,
'Tis there where the wise people of the world
Did place the virtues—i' th' middle, madam.
Ori. My lord,
There is so little hope we should convert you ;
And, if we should, so little got by it,
That we'll not lose so much upon't as sleep.
Your lordship's servants. [*Prepare to go*
Ors. Nay, ladies, we'll wait upon you to your chambers.
Phi. Prithee, let's spare the compliment : we shall do no good.
Ors. By this hand, I'll try :
They keep me fasting, and I must be praying.
[*Exeunt*

Scene VI

Aglaura *undressing herself.* Iolina

Agl. Undress me ; is it not late, Iolina ?
It was the longest day this——

Enter Thersames

Ther. Softly, as death
Itself comes on, when it does steal away
The sick man's breath, and standers-by perceive 't not,
Have I trod the way unto these lodgings. How wisely
Do those powers, that give us happiness, order it,
Sending us still fears to bound our joys,
Which else would overflow and lose themselves.
See where she sits,
Like day retir'd into another world.
Dear mine! where all the beauty man admires
In scattered pieces does united lie;
Where sense does feast, and yet where sweet desire
Lives in its longing, like a miser's eye,
That never knew nor saw satiety:
Tell me, by what approaches must I come
To take in what remains of my felicity?

Agl. Needs there any new ones, where the breach
Is made already? you are enter'd here,
Long since, sir, here, and I have giv'n up all.

Ther. All but the fort; and, in such wars as these,
Till that be yielded up, there is no peace
Nor triumph to be made—
Come,
Undo, undo; and from these envious clouds
Slide quick into love's proper sphere, thy bed.
The weary traveller, whom the busy sun
Hath vex'd all day, and scorch'd almost to tinder,
Ne'er long'd for night as I have long'd for this.
What rude hand is that?

[*One knocks hastily. Iolina goes to the door*

Go, Iolina, see, but let none enter——

Iolin. 'Tis Ziriff, sir.

Ther. O!
Something of weight hath fallen out, it seems,
Which in his zeal he could not keep till morning.
But one short minute, dear, into that chamber!

[*Exit Aglaura*

Enter Ziriff

How now? thou start'st as if thy sins had met thee,
Or thy father's ghost; what news, man?

Zir. Such as will send the blood of hasty messages
Unto the heart, and make it call

All that is man about you into council:
Where is the princess, sir?
Ther. Why, what of her?
Zir. The king must have her.
Ther. How?
Zir. The king must have her, sir.
Ther. Though fear of worse makes ill still relish better,
And this look handsome in our friendship, Ziriff,
Yet so severe a preparation
There needed not. Come, come, what is't?
[*Ziriff leads him to the door, and shows him a guard*
A guard!
Thersames, thou art lost,
Betray'd by faithless and ungrateful man,
Out of a happiness.
[*He steps between the door and him, and draws*
The very thought of that
Will lend my anger so much noble justice,
That, wert thou master of as much fresh life as
Thou'st been of villainy, it should not serve,
Nor stock thee out to glory or repent
The least of it!
Zir. Put up, put up! such unbecoming anger
I have not seen you wear before. What, draw
Upon your friend! [*Discovers himself*
Do you believe me right now?
Ther. I scarce believe mine eyes! Zorannes?
Zir. The same; but how preserv'd, or why thus long
Disguis'd, to you a freer hour must speak.
That y'are betray'd, is certain; but by whom,
Unless the priest himself, I cannot guess,
More than the marriage though he knows not of.
If you now send her on this early summons,
Before the sparks are grown into a flame,
You do redeem th' offence, or make it less;
And, on my life, yet his intents are fair;
And he will but besiege, not force affection:
So you gain time. If you refuse, there's but
One way; you know his power and passion.
Ther. Into how strange a labyrinth am I
Now fall'n! what shall I do, Zorannes?
Zir. Do, sir, as seamen that have lost their light
And way: strike sail, and lie quiet a while.
Your forces in the province are not yet

In readiness, nor is our friend Zephines
Arriv'd at Delphos ; nothing is ripe. Besides——
Ther. Good heav'ns ! did I but dream that she was mine ?
Upon imagination did I climb
Up to this height ? Let me then wake and die !
Some courteous hand snatch me from what's to come,
And, ere my wrongs have being, give them end !
Zir. How poor and how unlike the prince is this !
This trifle, woman, does unman us all ;
Robs us so much, it makes us things of pity.
Is this a time to loose our anger in,
And vainly breathe it out, when all we have
Will hardly fill the sail of Resolution,
And make us bear up high enough for action ?
Ther. I have done, sir ; pray chide no more ;
The slave, whom tedious custom has inur'd,
And taught to think of misery as of food,
Counting it but a necessary of life,
And so digesting it, shall not so much as once
Be nam'd to patience, when I am spoken of.
Mark me ; for I will now undo myself
As willingly as virgins give up all
First nights to them they love. [*Offers to go out*
Zir. Stay, sir : 'twere fit Aglaura yet were kept
In ignorance. I will dismiss the guard,
And be myself again. [*Exit*
Ther. In how much worse estate am I in now,
Than if I ne'er had known her ! Privation is
A misery as much above bare wretchedness
As that is short of happiness :
So, when the sun does not appear,
'Tis darker, 'cause it once was here.

Re-enter Ziriff. *Speaks to* Orsames *and others half entered*

Zir. Nay, gentlemen,
There needs no force where there is no resistance :
I'll satisfy the king myself.
Ther. O ! it is well y'are come.
There was within me fresh rebellion,
And reason was almost unking'd again.
But you shall have her, sir. [*Goes out to fetch Aglaura*
Zir. What doubtful combats in this noble youth
Passion and reason have !

Re-enter Thersames, *leading* Aglaura

Ther. Here, sir. [*Gives her and goes out*
Agl. What means the prince, my lord?
Zir. Madam,
His wiser fear has taught him to disguise
His love, and make it look a little rude at parting.
Affairs, that do concern all that you hope
From happiness, this night force him away;
And, lest you should have tempted him to stay,—
Which he did doubt you would, and would prevail—
He left you thus: he does desire by me
You would this night lodge in the little tower,
Which is in my command: the reasons why
Himself will shortly tell you.
Agl. 'Tis strange, but I am all obedience. [*Exeunt*

ACT II

Scene I

Enter Thersames *and* Iolas

Iol. I told him so, sir; urg'd 'twas no common knot,
That to the tying of it two powerful princes,
Virtue and Love, were join'd, and that a greater
Than these two was now engaged in't, Religion.
But 'twould not do; the cork of passion
Buoy'd up all reason so, that what was said
Swam but o' th' top of th' ear, ne'er reach'd the heart.
Ther. Is there no way for kings to show their power,
But in their subjects' wrongs?—no subject neither,
But his own son?
Iol. Right, sir!
No quarry for his lust to gorge on, but
On what you fairly had flown at and taken?
Well, wer't not the king, or wer't indeed not you,
That have such hopes, and such a crown to venture—
And yet, 'tis but a woman.
Ther. How? that *but*
Again, and thou art more injurious
Than he, and wou'lt provoke me sooner!

Iol. Why, sir?
There are no altars yet addrest unto her,
Nor sacrifice. If I have made her less
Than what she is, it was my love to you;
For in my thoughts and here within I hold her
The noblest piece Nature e'er lent our eyes,
And of the which all women else are but
Weak counterfeits, made up by her journeymen.
But was this fit to tell you?
I know you value but too high all that;
And in a loss we should not make things more:
'Tis misery's happiness that we can make
It less by art, through a forgetfulness
Upon our ills. Yet who can do it here,
When every voice must needs, and every face,
By shewing what she was not, shew what she was?
Ther. I'll instantly unto him. [*Draws*
Iol. Stay, sir!
Though't be the utmost of my fortune's hope
To have an equal share of ill with you;
Yet I could wish we sold this trifle, life,
At a far dearer rate than we are like
To do, since 'tis a king's the merchant.
Ther. Ha!
King? Ay, it is indeed; and there's no art
Can cancel that high bond.
Iol. [*To himself*] He cools again.
[*Aloud*] True, sir; and yet, methinks, to know a reason;
For passive nature ne'er had glorious end;
And he that states' preventions ever learn'd,
Knows 'tis one motion to strike and to defend.

Enter Serving-man.

Serv. Some of the lords without, and from the king,
They say, wait you.
Ther. What subtle state-trick now?
But one turn here, and I am back, my lord. [*Exit*
Iol. This will not do: his resolution's like
A skilful horseman; and reason is the stirrup,
Which, though a sudden shock may make it loose,
Yet does it meet it handsomely again.
Stay! it must be some sudden fear of wrong

To her, that may draw on a sudden act
From him, and ruin from the king ; for such
A spirit will not, like common ones, be rais'd
By every spell : 'tis in love's circle only
'Twill appear.

Enter THERSAMES

Ther. I cannot bear the burthen of my wrongs
One minute longer.
Iol. Why ! what's the matter, sir ?
Ther. They do pretend the safety of the state :
Now, nothing but my marriage with Cadusia
Can secure th' adjoining country to it ;
Confinement during life for me, if I
Refuse Diana's nunnery for her :
And at that 'nunn'ry,' Iolas, allegiance
In me, like the string of a watch wound up
Too high, and forc'd above the nick, ran back ;
And in a moment was unravell'd all.
Iol. Now, by the love I bear to justice, that 'nunn'ry'
Was too severe ! When virtuous love's a crime,
What man can hope to 'scape a punishment,
Or who's indeed so wretched to desire it ?
Ther. Right !
Iol. What answer made you, sir !
Ther. None.
They gave me till to-morrow ; and e'er that be,
Or they or I must know our destiny.
Come, friend, let's in ; there is no sleeping now ;
For time is short, and we have much to do. [*Exeunt*

SCENE II

Enter ORSAMES, PHILAN, Courtiers

Ors. Judge you, gentlemen, if I be not as unfortunate as a gamester thinks himself upon the loss of the last stake ; this is the first she I ever swore to heartily ; and, by those eyes ! I think I had continued unperjur'd a whole month ; and that's fair, you'll say.

1 *Court.* Very fair.

Ors. Had she not run mad betwixt !

2 *Court.* How ? mad ? Who ? Semanthe ?

Ors. Yea, yea, mad ; ask Philan else.
People that want clear intervals talk not

So wildly. I'll tell you, gallants; 'tis now,
Since first I found myself a little hot
And quivering 'bout the heart, some ten days since:
A tedious ague, sirs; but what of that?
The gracious glance and little whisper past,
Approaches made from th' hand unto the lip,
I came to visit her, and, as you know, we use,
Breathing a sigh or two by the way of prologue,
Told her that in love's physic 'twas a rule,
Where the disease had birth, to seek a cure.
I had no sooner nam'd love to her, but she
Began to talk of flames, and flames
Neither devouring nor devour'd, of air
And of chameleons.

1 *Court.* O, the Platonics!

2 *Court.* Those of the new religion in love!
Your lordship's merry, troth! how do you like
The humour on't?

Ors. As thou would'st like red hair
Or leanness in thy mistress, scurvily!
'T does worse with handsomeness than strong desire
Could do with impotence—a mere trick
To enhance the price of kisses!

Phi. Surely these silly women, when they feed
Our expectation so high, do but like
Ignorant conjurers, that raise a spirit,
Which handsomely they cannot lay again.

Ors. True, 'tis like some that nourish up young lions, till they grow so great they are afraid of themselves: they dare not grant at last, for fear they should not satisfy.

Phi. Who's for the town? I must take up again.

Ors. This villainous love's as changeable as the philosopher's stone, and thy mistress as hard to compass too!

Phi. The Platonic is ever so: they are as tedious before they come to the point, as an old man fall'n into the stories of his youth.

2 *Court.* Or a widow into the praises of her first husband.

Ors. Well, if she hold out but one month longer, if I do not quite forget I e'er beleaguered there, and remove the siege to another place, may all the curses beguil'd virgins loose upon their perjur'd lovers fall upon me.

Phi. And thou wou'lt deserve 'em all.

Ors. For what?

Phi. For being in the company of those
That took away the prince's mistress from him.

Ors. Peace, that will be redeem'd.
I put but on this wildness to disguise myself;—
There are brave things in hand: hark 'i thy ear.
[*Whispers*

1 *Court.* Some severe plot upon a maidenhead! These two young lords make love, as embroiderers work against a mask, night and day. They think importunity a nearer way than merit, and take women as schoolboys catch squirrels—hunt 'em up and down, till they are weary, and fall down before 'em.

Ors. Who loves the prince fails not——

Phi. And I am one;
My injuries are great as thine, and do
Persuade as strongly.

Ors. I had command to bring thee:
Fail not, and in thine one disguise.

Phi. Why in disguise?

Ors. It is the prince's policy and love; for, if
We should miscarry, some one taken might
Betray the rest, unknown to one another.
Each man is safe in his own valour.

2 *Court.* And what mercers wife are you to cheapen now instead of his silks?

Ors. Troth! 'tis not so well; 'tis but a cousin of thine:
Come, Philan, let's along. [*Exeunt*

SCENE III

Enter QUEEN *alone*

Orb. What is it thus within whispering remorse,
And calls love tyrant? all powers but his
Their rigour and our fear have made divine;
But every creature holds of him by sense—
The sweetest tenure. Yea—but my husband's brother:
And what of that? do harmless birds or beasts
Ask leave of curious Heraldry at all?
Does not the womb of one fair spring
Bring unto the earth many sweet rivers,
That wantonly do one another chase,
And in one bed kiss, mingle, and embrace?
Man (Nature's heir) is not by her will tied

To shun all creatures are allied unto him ;
For then she should shun all : since death and life
Doubly allies all them that live by breath.
The air that does impart to all life's brood
Refreshment, is so near to itself, and to us all,
That all in all is individual.
But how am I sure one and the same desire
Warms Ariaspes ?
For art can keep alive a bedrid love.

Enter Ariaspes

Ari. Alone, madam, and overcast with thought !
Uncloud, uncloud ; for, if we may believe
The smiles of fortune, love shall no longer pine
In prison thus, nor undelivered travail
With throes of fear and of desire about it.
The prince, like to a valiant beast in nets,
Striving to force a freedom suddenly,
Has made himself at length the surer prey :
The king stands only now betwixt, and is
Just like a single tree, that hinders all
The prospect : 'tis but the cutting down of him,
And we——

Orb. Why wouldst thou thus embark into strange seas,
And trouble Fate for what we have already ?
Thou art to me, what thou now seek'st, a kingdom ;
And, were thy love as great as thy ambition,
I should be so to thee.

Ari. Think you you are not, madam ?
As well and justly may you doubt the truths
Tortur'd or dying men do leave behind them.
But then my fortune turns my misery,
When my addition shall but make you less :
Shall I endure that head, that wore a crown,
For my sake should wear none ? First, let me lose
Th' exchequer of my wealth—your love ; nay, may
All that rich treasury you have about you
Be rifled by the man I hated, and I look on !
Though youth be full of sin, and heaven be just,
So sad a doom I hope they keep not for me.
Remember what a quick apostasy he made,
When all his vows were up to heav'n and you.
How, ere the bridal torches were burnt out,
His flames grew weak and sicklier : think on that :

Think how unsafe you are, if she should now
Not sell her honour at a lower rate
Than your place in his bed.
Orb. And would not you prove false, too, then ?
Ari. By this—
And this—love's breakfast ! [*kisses her*] By his feasts, too, yet
To come ! by all the beauty in this face,
Divinity too great to be profan'd !
Orb. O, do not swear by that ;
Cankers may eat that flower upon the stalk
(For sickness and mischance are great devourers) ;
And, when there is not in these cheeks and lips
Left red enough to blush at perjury,
When you shall make it, what shall I do then ?
Ari. Our souls by that time, madam,
Will by long custom so acquainted be,
They will not need that duller trouch-man, Flesh ;
But freely, and without those poorer helps,
Converse and mingle : meantime we'll teach
Our loves to speak, not thus to live by signs ;
And action is his native language, madam.

Enter Ziriff *unseen*

This box but open'd to the sense will do it.
Orb. I undertake I know not what.
Ari. Thine own safety,
Dearest : let it be this night, if thou dost love
Thyself or me. [*Whisper and kiss*
Orb. That's very sudden.
Ari. Not
If we be so, and we must now be wise :
For when their sun sets, ours begin to rise. [*Exeunt*

Ziriff *solus*

Zir. Then all my fears are true, and she is false,
False as a falling star or glowworm's fire.
This devil Beauty is compounded strangely :
It is a subtle point, and hard to know,
Whether it has in it more active tempting,
Or [is] more passive tempted ;
So soon it forces, and so soon it yields.
Good Gods ! she seiz'd my heart, as if from you

She'd had commission to have us'd me so,
And all mankind beside. And see,
If the just ocean makes more haste to pay
To needy rivers what is borrow'd first,
Than she to give where she ne'er took. Methinks
I feel anger, revenge's harbinger,
Chalking up all within, and thrusting out
Of doors the tame and softer passions.
It must be so:
To love is noble frailty; but poor sin,
When we fall once to love, unlov'd again. [*Exit*

Scene IV

Enter King, Ariaspes, Iolas

Ari. 'Twere fit your justice did consider, sir,
What way it took. If you should apprehend
The prince for treason, which he never did,
And which, unacted, is unborn—
At least 'twill be believed so;—lookers-on
And the loud-talking crowd will think it all
But water-colours laid on for a time,
And which, wip'd off, each common eye would see
Strange ends through stranger ways.

King. Think'st thou I will compound with treason then,
And make one fear another's advocate?

Iol. Virtue forbid, sir! but if you would permit
Them to approach the room (yet who would advise
Treason should come so near?) there would be then
No place left for excuse.

King. How strong are they?

Iol. Weak, considering
The enterprise; they are but few in number,
And those few, too, having nothing but
Their resolutions considerable about them:
A troop indeed design'd to suffer what
They come to execute.

King. Who are they are thus weary of their lives?

Iol. Their names I cannot give you;
For those he sent for, he did still receive
At a back door, and so dismist them too:
But I do think Ziriff is one.

King. Take heed!
I shall suspect thy hate to others, not

Thy love to me, begot this service ;—
This treason, thou thyself dost say, has but
An hour's age ; and I can give accompt
Of him beyond that time. Brother, in the little tower,
Where now Aglaura's prisoner, you shall find him.
Bring him along :
He yet doth stand untainted in my thoughts ;
And to preserve him so, he shall not stir
Out of my eyes' command, till this great cloud
Be over.

Iol. Sir, 'twas the prince, who first——

King. I know all that.
Urge it no more ! I love the man ; and 'tis with pain
We do suspect, where we do not dislike.
Thou'rt sure he will have some, and that they will come
To-night ?

Iol. As sure as night will come itself.

King. Get all your guards in readiness ; we will ourself
Disperse them afterwards ; and both be sure
To wear your thoughts within : I'll act the rest. [*Exeunt*

Scene V

Enter Philan, Orsames, Courtiers

2 *Court.* Well, if there be not some great storm towards,
Ne'er trust me ; Whisper (Court-thunder) is in
Every corner, and there has been to-day
About the town a murmuring and buzzing,
Such as men use to make when they do fear
To vent their fears.

1 *Court.* True, and all the statesmen
Hang down their heads, like full-ear'd corn ; two of them,
Where I supp'd, ask'd what time of night it was,
And, when 'twas told them, started, as if they
Had been to run a race.

2 *Court.* The king, too (if
You mark him), doth feign mirth and jollity ;
But, through them both, flashes of discontent
And anger make escapes.

Ors. Gentlemen ! 'tis pity heav'n
Design'd you not to make the almanacs.
You guess so shrewdly by the ill aspects,
Or near conjunctions of the great ones,
At what's to come still, that without all doubt

The country had been govern'd wholly by you,
And plough'd and reap'd accordingly. For me,
I understand this mystery as little
As the new love ; and as I take it, too,
'Tis much about the time that everything
But owls and lovers take their rest. Good-night,
Philan. Away! [*Exit*

1 *Court.* 'Tis early yet ; let's go on the queen's side,
And fool a little ; I love to warm myself,
Before I go to bed ; it does beget
Handsome and sprightly thoughts, and makes our dreams
Half-solid pleasures.

2 *Court.* Agreed. [*Exeunt*

ACT III

Scene I

Enter Prince, Conspirators

Ther. Couldst thou not find out Ziriff ?

1 *Court.* Not speak with him, my lord ; yet I sent in
By several men.

Ors. I wonder Iolas meets us not here, too.

Ther. 'Tis strange, but let's on now howe'er ;
When fortunes, honour, life, and all's in doubt,
Bravely to dare is bravely to get out.

[*Excursions. The Guard upon them*

Ther. Betray'd ! betray'd !

Ors. Shift for yourself, sir, and let us alone ;
We will secure your way, and make our own. [*Exeunt*

Enter the King *and* Lords

King. Follow, lords, and see quick execution done ;
Leave not a man alive.
Who treads on fire, and does not put it out,
Disperses fear in many sparks of doubt. [*Exeunt*

Re-enter Conspirators, *and the* Guard *upon them*

Ors. Stand, friends : an equal party.

[*Fight. Three of the Conspirators fall, and three of the King's side : Orsames and Philan kill the rest. They throw off their disguises.*

Phi. Brave Orsames, 'tis pleasure to die near thee.

Ors. Talk not of dying, Philan ; we will live,
And serve the noble prince again.

We are alone : off, then, with thy disguise,
And throw it in the bushes——
Quick, quick, before the torrent comes upon us !
We shall be straight good subjects ; and I despair not
Of reward for this night's service. So, we two
Now kill'd our friends ! 'tis hard, but 't must be so.

Enter ARIASPES, IOLAS, *two* Courtiers, *part of the* Guard

Ari. Follow, follow !
Ors. Yes, so you may now ; y'are not likely to overtake.
Iol. Orsames and Philan ! how came you hither ?
Ors. The nearest way, it seems; you follow'd, thank you,
As if 't had been through quicksets.
Iol. 'Sdeath, have they all escap'd ?
Ors. Not all :
Two of them we made sure ; but they cost dear :
Look here else.
Ari. Is the prince there ?
Phi. They are both princes,
I think : they fought like princes, I am sure.
[*Iolas pulls off the vizors*
Iol. Stephines and Odiris.
We trifle : which way took the rest ?
Ors. Two of them are certainly hereabouts.
Ari. Upon my life, they swam the river.
Some, straight to horse, and follow o'er the bridge !
[*To Iolas*] You and I, my lord, will search this place a little better.
Ors. Your highness will, I hope, remember who were the men were in——
Ari. O, fear not, your mistress shall know y'are valiant.
Ors. Philan, if thou lov'st me, let's kill them upon the place.
Phi. Fie, thou now art wild indeed ! Thou taught'st me to be wise first, and I will now keep thee so. Follow, follow. [*Exeunt*

SCENE II

Enter AGLAURA *with a lute*

The Prince comes and knocks within

Ther. Madam !
Agl. What wretch is this that thus usurps
Upon the privilege of ghosts, and walks
At midnight ?
Ther. Aglaura !

Agl. Betray me not,
My willing sense, too soon ; yet, if that voice
Be false——
Ther. Open, fair saint, and let me in !
Agl. It is the prince. As willingly as those
That cannot sleep do light——
Welcome, sir. [*Opens*] Welcome above.
[*Spies his sword drawn*
Bless me !
What means this unsheath'd minister of death ?
If, sir, on me quick justice be to pass,
Why this ? Absence, alas ! or such strange looks
As you now bring with you, would kill as soon.
Ther. Softly ! for I, like a hard-hunted deer,
Have only herded here ; and, though the cry
Reach not our ears, yet am I follow'd close :
O my heart ! since I saw thee
Time has been strangely active, and begot
A monstrous issue of unheard-of story :
Sit ; thou shalt have it all ! nay, sigh not :
Such blasts will hinder all the passage.
Dost thou remember how we parted last ?
Agl. Can I forget it, sir ?
Ther. That word of parting was ill-plac'd, I swear.
It may be ominous ; but dost thou know
Into whose hands I gave thee ?
Agl. Yes, into Ziriff's, sir.
Ther. That Ziriff was thy brother, brave Zorannes,
Preserv'd by miracle in that sad day
Thy father fell, and since, thus in disguise
Waiting his just revenge.
Agl. You do amaze me, sir.
Ther. And must do more, when I tell all the story.
The king, the jealous king, knew of the marriage ;
And, when thou thought'st thyself by my direction,
Thou wert his prisoner.
Unless I would renounce all right, and cease
To love thee—O strange and fond request !—immur'd
Thou must have been in some sad place, and lock'd
For ever from Thersames' sight, for ever !
And, that unable to endure, this night
I did attempt his life.
Agl. Was it well done, sir ?
Ther. O no ! extremely ill !
For to attempt and not to act was poor.

Here the dead-doing law (like ill-paid soldiers)
Leaves the side 'twas on to join with power.
Royal villainy now will look so like to justice,
That the times to come and curious posterity
Will find no difference.
Weep'st thou, Aglaura? Come to bed, my love;
And we will there mock tyranny and fate:
Those softer hours of pleasure and delight
That, like so many single pearls, should have
Adorn'd our thread of life, we will at once,
By love's mysterious power and this night's help,
Contract to one, and make but one rich draught
Of all.

Agl. What mean you, sir?

Ther. To make myself incapable of misery,
By taking strong preservatives of happiness:
I would this night enjoy thee.

Agl. Do, sir, do what you will with me;
For I am too much yours to deny the right,
However claim'd; but——

Ther. But what, Aglaura?

Agl. Gather
Not roses in a wet and frowning hour:
They'll lose their sweets then, trust me they will, sir.
What pleasure can love take to play his game out,
When death must keep the stakes?—— [*A noise without*
Hark, sir!
Grave-bringers and last minutes are at hand:
Hide, hide yourself; for love's sake, hide yourself!

Ther. As soon the sun may hide himself as I.
The Prince of Persia hide himself!

Agl. O, talk not, sir; the sun does hide himself,
When night and blackness comes.

Ther. Never, sweet ignorance, he shines in th' other world then;
And so shall I, if I set here in glory.
Enter, ye hasty seekers of life!
[*Opens the door. Enter Ziriff*
Zorannes!

Agl. My brother!
If all the joy within me come not out,
To give a welcome to so dear an object,
Excuse it, sir; sorrow locks up all doors.

Zir. If there be such a toy about you, sister,

Keep 't for yourself, or lend it to the prince:
There is a dearth of that commodity;
And you have made it, sir.
Now,
What is the next mad thing you mean to do?
Will you stay here? when all the court's beset,
Like to a wood at a great hunt, and busy mischief hastes
To be in view, and have you in her power——

Ther. To me all this?
For great grief's deaf, as well as it is dumb,
And drives no trade at all with counsel. Sir,
Why do you not tutor one that has the plague,
And see if he will fear an after-ague-fit;
Such is all mischief now to me, there is none left
Is worth a thought: death is the worst I know;
And that, compar'd to shame, does look more lovely now
Than a chaste mistress set by common woman;
And I must court it, sir?

Zir. No wonder, if
That heav'n forsake us when we leave ourselves:
What is there done should feed such high despair?
Were you but safe——

Agl. Dear sir, be rul'd;
If love be love, and magic too,
As sure it is, where it is true;
We then shall meet in absence, and, in spite
Of all divorce, freely enjoy together
What niggard fate thus peevishly denies.

Ther. Yea: but, if pleasures be themselves but dreams,
What then are the dreams of these to men?
That monster, Expectation, will devour
All that is within our hope or power,
And ere we once can come to show how rich
We are, we shall be poor, shall we not, Zorannes?

Zir. I understand not this.
In times of envious penury, such as these are,
To keep but love alive is fair; we should
Not think of feasting him. Come, sir:
Here in these lodgings is a little door,
That leads unto another; that again
Unto a vault that has his passage under
The little river, opening into the wood;
From thence 'tis but some few minutes' easy business
Unto a servant's house of mine, who, for

His faith and honesty, hereafter must
Look big in story. There you are safe, however;
And, when this storm has met a little calm,
What wild desire dares whisper to itself
You may enjoy, and at the worst may steal.
Ther. What shall become of thee, Aglaura, then?
Shall I leave thee their rage's sacrifice?
And, like dull seamen threaten'd with a storm,
Throw all away I have to save myself?
Agl. Can I be safe, when you are not, my lord?
Knows love in us divided happiness?
Am I the safer for your being here?
Can you give that you have not for yourself?
My innocence is my best guard, and that your stay,
Betraying it unto suspicion, takes away.
If you did love me——
Ther. Grows that in question? then 'tis time to part!
[*Kisses her*
When we shall meet again, heaven only knows;
And, when we shall, I know we shall be old.
Love does not calculate the common way;
Minutes are hours there, and the hours are days;
Each day's an year, and every year an age.
What will this come to, think you?
Zir. Would this were all the ill!
For these are pretty little harmless nothings.
Time's horse runs full as fast, hard-borne and curb'd,
As in his full career, loose rein'd and spurr'd.
Come, come, let's away.
Ther. Happiness such as men, lost in misery,
Would wrong in naming, 'tis so much above them,
All that I want of it, all you deserve,
Heaven send you in my absence!
Agl. And misery, such as witty malice would
Lay out in curses on the thing it hates,
Heaven send me in the stead, if when y'are gone
[*Leads him out, and enters up out of the vault*
I welcome it but for your sake alone. [*Exit*
Zir. Stir not from hence, sir, till you hear from me:
So, good-night, dear prince.
Ther. Good-night, dear friend.
Zir. When next we meet, all this will but advance—
Joy never feasts so high,
As when the first course is of misery. [*Exeunt*

ACT IV

Scene I

Enter three or four Courtiers

1. *Court.* By this light, a brave prince! He made no more of the guard, than they would of a tailor on a masque-night, that has refused trusting before.

2 *Court.* He's as active as he is valiant too. Didst mark him how he stood like all the points o' th' compass, and, as good pictures, had his eyes towards every man?

3 *Court.* And his sword too. All th' other side walk up and down the court now as if they had lost their way, and stare like greyhounds, when the hare has taken the furze.

1 *Court.* Right; and have more troubles about 'em than a serving-man, that has forgot his message, when he's come upon the place.

2. *Court.* Yonder's the king within, chafing and swearing like an old falconer upon the first flight of a young hawk, when some clown has taken away the quarry from her; and all the lords stand round him as if he were to be baited, with much more fear and at much more distance than a country gentlewoman sees the lions the first time. Look, he's broke loose!

Enter King *and* Lords

King. Find him!
Or, by Osiris' self, you are all traitors,
And equally shall pay to justice.
A single man, and guilty too, break through you all!

Enter Ziriff

Zir. Confidence,
Thou paint of women and the statesman's wisdom,
Valour of cowards, and the guilty's innocence,
Assist me now! [*To the king*] Sir, send these starers off.
I have some business will deserve your privacy.

King. Leave us.

Iol. How the villain swells upon us! [*Exeunt Lords*

Zir. Not to punish thought,
Or keep it long upon the rack of doubt,
Know, sir, that, by corruption of the waiting-woman,

The common key of secrets, I have found
The truth at last, and have discover'd all.
The prince, your son, was, by Aglaura's means,
Convey'd last night unto the cypress grove,
Through a close vault that opens in the lodgings.
He does intend to join with Carimania;
But, ere he goes, resolves to finish all
The rites of love, and this night means to steal
What is behind.

King. How good is heav'n unto me,
That, when it gave me traitors for my subjects,
Would lend me such a servant!

Zir. How just, sir, rather,
That would bestow this fortune on the poor;
And, where your bounty had made debt so infinite
That it grew desperate, their hope to pay it——

King. Enough of that! Thou dost but gently chide
Me for a fault that I will mend; for I
Have been too poor and low in my rewards
Unto thy virtue. But to our business:
The question is, whether we shall rely
Upon our guards again?

Zir. By no means, sir.
Hope on his future fortunes, or their love
Unto his person, has so sicklied o'er
Their resolutions, that we must not trust them.
Besides, it were but needless here:
He passes through the vault alone, and I
Myself durst undertake that business,
If that were all; but there is something else
This accident doth prompt my zeal to serve you in.
I know you love Aglaura, sir, with passion,
And would enjoy her; I know besides
She loves him so, that whosoe'er shall bring
The tidings of his death must carry back
The news of hers; so that your justice, sir,
Must rob your hope. But there is yet a way——

King. Here, take my heart; for I have hitherto
Too vainly spent the treasure of my love.
I'll have it coin'd straight into friendship all,
And make a present to thee.

Zir. If any part of this rich happiness
Fortune prepares now for you, shall owe itself
Unto my weak endeavours, I have enough.

Aglaura without doubt this night expects
The prince; and why
You should not then supply his place by stealth,
And in disguise——

King. I apprehend thee, Ziriff;
But there's difficulty.

Zir. Who trades in love must be an adventurer, sir;
But here
Is scarce enough to make the pleasure dearer:
I know the cave: your brother and myself
With Iolas (for those, w'are sure, do hate him),
With some few chosen more, betimes will wait
The prince's passing through the vault: if he
Comes first, he's dead; and, if it be yourself,
We will conduct you to the chamber door,
And stand 'twixt you and danger afterwards.

King. I have conceiv'd of joy, and am grown great;
Till I have safe deliverance, time's a cripple
And goes on crutches. As for thee, my Ziriff,
I do here entertain a friendship with thee,
Shall drown the memory of all patterns past.
We will oblige by turns, and that so thick
And fast, that curious studiers of it
Shall not once dare to cast it up, or say
By way of guess, whether thou or I
Remain the debtors when we come to die. [*Exeunt*

SCENE II

Enter SEMANTHE, ORITHIE, PHILAN, ORSAMES, Lords *and* Ladies

Ori. Is the Queen ready to come out?

Phi. Not yet:
Sure, the king's brother is but newly enter'd.

Sem. Come, my lord, the song then.

Ori. The song.

Ors. A vengeance take this love! it spoils a voice
Worse than the losing of a maidenhead.
I have got such a cold with rising and walking in my shirt a-nights, that a bittern whooping in a reed is better music.

Ori. This modesty becomes you as ill, my lord,
As wooing would us women:
Pray, put's not to't.

Ors. Nay, ladies, you shall find me
As free as the musicians of the woods
Themselves : what I have, you shall not need to call for ;
Nor shall it cost you anything.

SONG

Why so pale and wan, fond lover ?
Prithee, why so pale ?
Will, when looking well can't move her,
Looking ill prevail ?
Prithee, why so pale ?

Why so dull and mute, young sinner ?
Prithee, why so mute ?
Will, when speaking well can't win her,
Saying nothing do't ?
Prithee, why so mute ?

Quit, quit, for shame, this will not move :
This cannot take her.
If of herself she will not love,
Nothing can make her :
The devil take her !

Ori. I should have guess'd, it had been the issue of
Your brain, if I had not been told so.
Ors. A little foolish counsel, madam, I gave
A friend of mine four or five years ago,
When he was falling into a consumption.

Enter QUEEN

Orb. Which of all you have seen the fair prisoner,
Since she was confin'd ?
Sem. I have, madam.
Orb. And how behaves she now herself ?
Sem. As one that had intrench'd so deep in innocence,
She fear'd no enemies, bears all quietly,
And smiles at Fortune whilst she frowns on her.
Orb. So gallant ?
I wonder where the beauty lies, that thus
Inflames the royal blood.
Ori. Faces, madam, are
Like books ; those that do study them know best ;
And, to say truth, 'tis still much as it pleases
The Courteous Reader.

Orb. These lovers sure are like astronomers,
That, when the vulgar eye discovers but
A sky above, studded with some few stars,
Find out, besides, strange fishes, birds, and beasts.
Sem. As men in sickness, scorch'd into a raving,
Do see the devil in all shapes and forms,
When standers-by, wondering, ask where and when,
So they in love; for all's but fever there,
And madness too.
Orb. That's too severe, Semanthe;
But we will have your reasons in the park:
Are the doors open through the gardens?
Lord. The king has newly led the way. [*Exeunt*

Scene III

Enter Ariaspes, *and* Ziriff *with a warrant sealed*

Ari. Thou art a tyrant, Ziriff: I shall die
With joy.
Zir. I must confess, my lord, had but
The prince's ills proved slight, and not thus dangerous
He should have ow'd to me—at least I would
Have laid a claim unto his safety; and,
Like physicians that do challenge right
In nature's cures, look'd for reward and thanks;
But, since 'twas otherwise, I thought it best
To save myself, and then to save the state.
Ari. 'Twas wisely done.
Zir. Safely, I'm sure, my lord! you know 'tis not
Our custom, where the king's dislike once swells
To hate, there to engage ourselves. Court friendship
Is a cable, that in storms is ever cut;
And I made bold with it. Here is the warrant seal'd;
And, for the execution of it, if
You think we are not strong enough, we may
Have Iolas; for him the king did name.
Ari. And him I would have nam'd.
Zir. But is he not too much the prince's, sir?
Ari. He is as lights in scenes at masques:
What glorious show soe'er he makes without,
I, that set him there, know why and how.
But here he is.

Enter IOLAS.

Come, Iolas ; and since the heav'ns decreed
The man, whom thou shouldst envy, should be such
That all men else must do't, be not asham'd
Thou once wert guilty of it ;
But bless them, that they give thee now a means
To make a friendship with him, and vouchsafe
To find thee out a way to love, where well
Thou couldst not hate.
Iol. What means my lord ?
Ari. Here, here he stands that has preserv'd us all ;
That sacrific'd unto a public good
The dearest private good we mortals have,
Friendship ; gave into our arms the prince,
When nothing but the sword, perchance a ruin,
Was left to do it.
Iol. How could I chide my love and my ambition now,
That thrust me upon such a quarrel ?
Here I do vow——
Zir. Hold, do not vow, my lord !
Let it deserve it first, and yet (if Heav'n
Bless honest men's intents) 'tis not impossible.
My lord,
You will be pleas'd to inform him in particulars.
I must be gone.
The King, I fear, already has been left
Too long alone.
Ari. Stay : the hour and place.
Zir. Eleven, under the Terrace Walk ;
I will not fail you there. [*Goes out, returns back again*
I had forgot : 't may be, the small remainder
Of those lost men, that were of the conspiracy,
Will come along with him : 'twere best to have
Some chosen of the guard within our call. [*Exit Ziriff*
Ari. Honest and careful Ziriff! [*Iolas stands musing*
How now, planet-struck ?
Iol. This Ziriff will grow great with all the world.
Ari. Shallow man,
Short-sighteder than travellers in mists,
Or women that outlive themselves, dost thou
Not see that whilst he does prepare a tomb
With one hand for his friend, he digs a grave
With th' other for himself ?

Iol. How so?

Ari. Dost think he shall not feel the weight of this,
As well as poor Thersames?

Iol. Shall we then kill him, too, at the same instant?

Ari. And say the prince made an unlucky thrust.

Iol. Right.

Ari. Dull, dull, he must not die so uselessly.
As when we wipe off filth from any place,
We throw away the thing that made it clean;
So, this once done, he's gone.
Thou know'st
The people love the prince: to their rage something
The state must offer up. Who fitter than
Thy rival and my enemy?

Iol. Rare!
Our witness will be taken.

Ari. Pish! let me
Alone. The giants that made mountains ladders,
And thought to take great love by force, were fools:
Not hill on hill, but plot on plot, does make
Us sit above, and laugh at all below us. [*Exeunt*

Scene IV

Enter Aglaura *and a* Singing Boy

Boy. Madam, 'twill make you melancholy,
I'll sing the prince's song; that's sad enough.

Agl. What you will, sir.

Song

No, no, fair heretic, it needs must be
But an ill love in me,
And worse for thee.

For were it in my power,
To love thee now this hour
More than I did the last;

'Twould then so fall,
I might not love at all.
Love that can flow, and can admit increase,
Admits as well an ebb, and may grow less.

True love is still the same: the torrid zones,
And those more frigid ones,
It must not know;

For love, grown cold or hot,
Is lust or friendship, not
The thing we have :

For that's a flame would die,
Held down or up too high.

Then think I love more than I can express,
And would love more, could I but love thee less.

Agl. Leave me, for to a soul so out of tune,
As mine is now, nothing is harmony :
When once the mainspring, Hope, is fall'n into
Disorder ; no wonder if the lesser wheels,
Desire and Joy, stand still : my thoughts, like bees,
When they have lost their king, wander
Confusedly up and down, and settle nowhere.

Enter ORITHIE

Orithie, fly, fly the room,
As thou wouldst shun the habitations
Which spirits haunt, or where thy nearer friends
Walk after death ! Here is not only love,
But love's plague too, misfortune ; and so high,
That it is sure infectious.
Ori. Madam,
So much more miserable am I this way
Than you, that, should I pity you, I should
Forget myself : my sufferings are such,
That with less patience you may endure
Your own, than give mine audience.
There is that difference, that you may make
Yours none at all, but by considering mine.
Agl. O, speak them quickly then : the marriage-day
To passionate lovers never was more welcome,
Than any kind of ease would be to me now.
Ori. Could they be spoke, they were not then so great.
I love, and dare not say I love ; dare not hope
What I desire, yet still too must desire ;
And, like a starving man brought to a feast,
And made say grace to what he ne'er shall taste,
Be thankful after all, and kiss the hand,
That made the wound thus deep.
Agl. 'Tis hard indeed ;
But, with what unjust scales thou took'st the weight

Of our misfortunes, be thine own judge now.
Thou mourn'st for loss of that thou never hadst;
Or, if thou hadst a loss, it never was
Of a Thersames.
Wouldst thou not think a merchant mad, Orithie,
If thou shouldst see him weep and tear his hair,
Because he brought not both the Indies home?
And wouldst not think his sorrows very just,
If, having fraught his ship with some rich treasure,
He sunk i' th' very port? This is our case.
Ori. And do you think there is such odds in it?
Would heaven we women could as easily change
Our fortunes as, 'tis said, we can our minds.
I cannot, madam, think them miserable,
That have the prince's love.
Agl. He is the man, then.
Blush not, Orithie: 'tis a sin to blush
For loving him, though none at all to love him.
I can admit of rivalship without
A jealousy, nay, shall be glad of it:
We two will sit, and think, and sigh,
And sigh, and talk of love and of Thersames.
Thou shalt be praising of his wit, while I
Admire he governs it so well;
Like this thing said thus, th' other thing thus done;
And in good language him for these adore,
While I want words to do't, yet do it more.
Thus will we do till death itself shall us
Divide; and then whose fate't shall be to die
First of the two, by legacy shall all
Her love bequeath, and give her stock to her
That shall survive; for no one stock can serve
To love Thersames so as he'll deserve.

Enter KING *and* ZIRIFF

King. What, have we here impossibility?
A constant night, and yet within the room
That, that can make the day before the sun!
Silent, Aglaura, too?
Agl. I know not what you say.
Is't to your pity or your scorn I owe
The favour of this visit, sir? for such
My fortune is, it doth deserve them both.
King. And such thy beauty is, that it makes good

All fortunes : sorrow looks lovely here ;
And there's no man that would not entertain
His griefs as friends, were he but sure they'd shew
No worse upon him.
But I forget myself : I came to chide.
Agl. If I have sinn'd so high,
That yet my punishment equals not my crime,
Do, sir.
I should be loth to die in debt to justice,
How ill soe'er I paid the scores of love.
King. And those indeed thou hast but paid indifferently
To me. I did deserve at least fair death,
Not to be murthered thus in private.
That was too cruel, mistress.
And I do know thou dost repent, and wilt
Yet make me satisfaction.
Agl. What satisfaction, sir ?
I am no monster, never had two hearts :
One is by holy vows another's now ;
And, could I give it you, you would not take it :
For 'tis alike impossible for me
To love again, as you love perjury.
O sir, consider what a flame love is !
If by rude means you think to force a light,
That of itself it would not freely give,
You blow it out, and leave yourself i' th' dark.
The prince once gone, you may as well persuade
The light to stay behind, when the sun posts
To th' other world, as me. Alas ! we two
Have mingled souls more than two meeting brooks ;
And, whosoever is design'd to be
The murtherer of my lord (as sure there is
Has anger'd heav'n so far, that 't has decreed
Him to increase his punishment that way),
Would he but search the heart, when he has done,
He there would find Aglaura murther'd too.
King. Thou hast o'ercome me, mov'd so handsomely
For pity, that I will disinherit
The elder brother, and from this hour be
Thy convert, not thy lover.
Ziriff, despatch ! Away ! And he that brings
News of the prince's welfare, look that he have
The same reward we had decreed to him
Brought tidings of his death.

'T must be a busy and bold hand, that would
Unlink a chain the gods themselves have made :
Peace to thy thoughts, Aglaura. [*Exit*

Zir. [*steps back and speaks*]. Whate'er he says, believe
him not, Aglaura ;
For lust and rage ride high within him now :
He knows Thersames made th' escape from hence,
And does conceal it only for his ends ;
For, by the favour of mistake and night,
He hopes t' enjoy thee in the prince's room.
I shall be miss'd, else I would tell thee more ;
But thou mayest guess, for our condition
Admits no middle ways : either we must
Send them to graves, or lie ourselves in dust.
[*Exit. Aglaura stands still and studies*

Agl. Ha !
'Tis a strange act thought puts me now upon ;
Yet sure my brother meant the self-same thing,
And my Thersames would have done't for me :
To take his life, that seeks to take away
The life of life—honour—from me, and from
The world the life of honour—Thersames,
Must needs be something, sure, of kin to justice.
If I do fail, th' attempt howe'er was brave ;
And I shall have at worst a handsome grave. [*Exit*

Scene V

Enter Iolas *on one side,* Semanthe *on the other : she steps back, Iolas stays her*

Iol. What ! are we grown, Semanthe, night and day ?
Must one still vanish, when the other comes ?
Of all that ever love did yet bring forth
(And 't has been fruitful too) this is
The strangest issue.

Sem. What, my lord ?

Iol. Hate, Semanthe.

Sem. You do mistake ; if I do shun you, 'tis
As bashful debtors shun their creditors.
I cannot pay you in the self-same coin,
And am asham'd to offer any other.

Iol. It is ill done, Semanthe, to plead bankrupt,
When with such ease you may be out of debt.

In love's dominions native commodity
Is current payment: change is all the trade,
And heart for heart the richest merchandise.
Sem. 'Twould here be mean, my lord, since mine would prove
In your hands but a counterfeit, and yours in mine
Worth nothing. Sympathy, not greatness, makes
Those jewels rise in value.
Iol. Sympathy? O, teach but yours to love, then;
And two so rich no mortal ever knew.
Sem. That heart would love but ill that must be taught:
Such fires as these still kindle of themselves.
Iol. In such a cold and frozen place as is
Thy breast, how should they kindle of themselves,
Semanthe?
Sem. Ask how the flint can carry fire within!
'Tis the least miracle that love can do.
Iol. Thou art thyself the greatest miracle;
For thou art fair to all perfection,
And yet dost want the greatest part of beauty—
Kindness. Thy cruelty (next to thyself)
Above all things on earth takes up my wonder.
Sem. Call not that cruelty, which is our fate.
Believe me, Iolas, the honest swain,
That from the brow of some steep cliff far off
Beholds a ship labouring in vain against
The boisterous and unruly elements, ne'er had
Less power or more desire to help than I.
At every sigh I die; and every look
Does move; and any passion you will have
But love, I have in store. I will be angry,
Quarrel with destiny and with myself,
That it is no better: be melancholy;
And (though mine own disasters well might plead
To be in chief) yours only shall have place.
I'll pity, and (if that's too low) I'll grieve,
As for my sins, I cannot give you ease.
All this I do; and this I hope will prove,
'Tis greater torment not to love than love. [*Exit*
Iol. So perishing sailors pray to storms, and so
They hear again. So men, with death about them,
Look on physicians, that have given them o'er;
And so they turn away. Two fixed stars,
That keep a constant distance, and, by laws

Made with themselves, must know no motion
Eccentric, may meet as soon as we.
The anger that the foolish sea does show,
When it does brave it out, and roar against
A stubborn rock that still denies it passage,
Is not so vain and fruitless as my prayers.
Ye mighty powers of love and fate, where is
Your justice here ? It is thy part, fond boy,
When thou dost find one wounded heart, to make
The other so ; but, if thy tyranny
Be such, that thou wilt leave one breast to hate ;
If we must live, and this survive,
How much more cruel's fate ? *Exit*

ACT V

Scene I

Enter Ziriff, Ariaspes, Iolas

Iol. A glorious night !
Ari. Pray heav'n it prove so ! Are we not there yet ?
Zir. 'Tis about this hollow. [*Enter the cave*
Ari. How now ! what region are we got into ?
Th' inheritance of night !
Are we not mistaken a turning, Ziriff,
And stept into some melancholy devil's territory ?
Sure 'tis a part of the first Chaos, that would
Endure no change.
Zir. No matter, sir : 'tis as proper for our purpose,
As the lobby for the waiting-woman's.
Stay you here : I'll move a little backward ;
And so we shall be sure to put him past
Retreat. You know the word, if't be the prince.
[*Goes to the mouth of the cave*

Enter King

Here, sir, follow me, all's quiet yet.
King. He's not come, then ?
Zir. No.
King. Where's Ariaspes ?
Zir. Waiting within.
[*He leads him on : steps behind him, gives the false word : they kill the King*

Iol. I do not like this waiting,
Nor this fellow's leaving us.
Ari. This place does put odd thoughts into thee. Then,
Thou art in thine own nature, too, as jealous
As either love or honour.
Come, wear thy sword in readiness, and think
How near we are a crown.
Zir. Revenge! So,
Let's drag him to the light, and search his pockets:
There may be papers there, that will discover
The rest of the conspirators. Iolas,
Your hand! [*Draws out the King's body*
Iol. Whom have we here? the king?
Zir. Yes, and Zorannes
Too. Hallo, ho! [*Enter Pasithas and others*
Unarm them.
D'ye stare?
This for my father's injuries and mine!
[*Points to the King's dead body*
Half love, half duty's sacrifice! this for
The noble prince, an offering to friendship!
[*Runs at Iolas*
Iol. Basely! and tamely—— [*Dies*
Ari. What hast thou done?
Zir. Nothing! kill'd a traitor.
So, away with them, and leave us. Pasithas,
Be only you in call.
Ari. What, dost thou pause?
Hast thou remorse already, murtherer?
Zir. No, fool: 'tis but a difference I put
Betwixt the crimes: Orbella is our quarrel;
And I do hold it fit, that love should have
A nobler way of justice than revenge
Or treason. Follow me out of the wood,
And thou shalt be master of this again:
And then best arm and title take.
[*They go out and enter again*
There! [*Gives him his sword*
Ari. Extremely good! Nature took pains, I swear:
The villain and the brave are mingled handsomely.
Zir. 'Twas fate that took it, when it decreed
We two should meet, nor shall they mingle now:
We are brought together straight to part. [*They fight*
Ari. Some devil, sure, has borrowed this shape. [*Pause*

My sword ne'er stay'd thus long to find an entrance.
Zir. To guilty men all that appears is devil;
Come, trifler, come. [*Fight again. Ariaspes falls*
Ari. Whither, whither,
Thou fleeting coward life? Bubble of time,
Nature's shame, stay a little, stay, till I
Have look'd myself into revenge, and star'd
This traitor to a carcass first!
It will not be—— [*Falls*
The crown,
The crown, too,
Now is lost, for ever lost.
O! ambition's but an *ignis fatuus*,
I see, misleading fond mortality,
That hurries us about, and sets us down
Just—where—we—first—begun—— [*Dies*
Zir. What a great spreading mighty thing this was,
And what a nothing now! how soon poor man
Vanishes into his noontide shadow!
But hopes o'erfed have seldom better done. [*Halloes*

Re-enter PASITHAS

Take up this lump of vanity and honour,
And carry it the back way to my lodging;
There may be use of statesmen when they're dead:
So. For the Citadel now; for in such times
As these, when the unruly multitude
Is up in swarms, and no man knows which way
They'll take, 'tis good to have retreat. [*Exeunt*

Enter THERSAMES

Ther. The dog-star's got up high: it should be late;
And sure by this time every waking ear
And watchful eye is charm'd; and yet methought
A noise of weapons struck my ear just now!
'Twas but my fancy, sure; and, were it more,
I would not tread one step that did not lead
To my Aglaura, stood all his guard betwixt,
With lightning in their hands.
Danger! thou dwarf dress'd up in giant's clothes,
That shew'st far off still greater than thou art,
Go, terrify the simple and the guilty, such
As with false optics still do look upon thee.
But fright not lovers: we dare look on thee

In thy worst shape, and meet thee in them too.
Stay.
These trees I made my mark ; 'tis hereabouts.
Love, guide me but right this night,
And lovers shall restore thee back again
Those eyes the poets took so boldly from thee. [*Exit*

SCENE II

AGLAURA *discovered, with a torch in one hand, and a dagger in the other*

Agl. How ill
This does become this hand : how much the worse
This suits with this ! one of the two should go.
The she within me says, it must be this :
Honour says this ; and honour is Thersames' friend.
What is that she then ? it is not a thing
That sets a price, not upon me, but on
Life in my name, leading me into doubt,
Which, when't has done, it cannot light me out.
For fear does drive to fate ; or fate, if we
Do fly, o'ertakes, and holds us, till or death
Or infamy, or both, doth seize us. [*Puts out the light*
Ha ! would 'twere in again !
Antics and strange misshapes,
Such as the porter to my soul, mine eye,
Was ne'er acquainted with, fancy lets in,
Like a distracted multitude, by some
Strange accident piec'd together !
Fear now afresh comes on, and charges love
Too home. He comes ! he comes !
Woman,
If thou wouldst be the subject of man's wonder,
Not his scorn hereafter, now show thyself.

Enter PRINCE, *rising from the vault ; she stabs him two or three times ; he falls ; she goes back to her chamber*

Sudden and fortunate !
My better angel, sure, did both infuse
A strength, and did direct it.

Enter ZIRIFF

Zir. Aglaura !
Agl. Brother !
Zir. The same.

So slow to let in such a long'd-for guest?
Must joy stand knocking, sister? come, prepare,
Prepare;
The king of Persia's coming to you straight—
The king! mark that.

Agl. I thought how poor the joys you brought with you,
Were in respect of those that were with me.
Joys are our hopes stript of their fears; and such
Are mine: for know, dear brother, the king is come
Already, and is gone. Mark that.

Zir. Is this instinct or riddle? what king? how gone?

Agl. The cave will tell you more——

Zir. Some sad mistake: thou hast undone us all.

[*Goes out, enters hastily again*

The prince, the prince! cold as the bed of earth
He lies upon, as senseless too! death hangs
Upon his lips, like an untimely frost
Upon an early cherry. The noble guest,
His soul, took it so ill that you should use
His old acquaintance so, that neither pray'rs
Nor tears can e'er persuade him back again.

[*Aglaura swoons; he rubs her*

Hold, hold! we cannot sure part thus. Sister! Aglaura!
Thersames is not dead: it is the prince
That calls.

Agl. The prince? where?
Tell me, or I will straight
Go back again into those groves of jessamine
Thou took'st me from, and find him out, or lose
Myself for ever.

Zir. For ever? Ay, there's it!
For in those groves thou talk'st of,
There are so many byways and odd turnings,
Leading unto such wide and dismal places,
That should we go without a guide, or stir
Before heav'n calls, 'tis strongly to be feared,
We there should wander up and down for ever,
And be benighted to eternity.

Agl. Benighted to eternity? What's that?

Zir. Why, 'tis to be benighted to eternity,
To sit i' th' dark, and do I know not what;
Unriddle at our own sad cost and charge
The doubts the learned here do only move.

Agl. What place have murtherers, brother, there ? for, sure,
The murtherer of the prince must have a punishment
That heav'n is yet to make.
Zir. How is religion fool'd betwixt our loves
And fears ! Poor girl, for ought that thou hast done,
Thy chaplets may be fair and flourishing
As his in the Elysium.
Agl. Do you think so ?
Zir. Yes, I do think so.
The juster judges of our actions,
Would they have been severe upon our weaknesses,
Would, sure, have made us stronger. Fie ! those tears
A bride upon the marriage-day as properly
Might shed as thou :
Here widows do't, and marry next day after.
To such a funeral as this there should
Be nothing common.
We'll mourn him so that those, that are alive,
Shall think themselves more buried far than he ;
And wish to have his grave, to find his obsequies :
But stay : the body.
[*Brings up Thersames' body ; she swoons and dies*
Again ! sister, Aglaura !
O, speak once more, once more look out, fair soul.
She's gone—
Irrevocably gone, and winging now
The air like a glad bird broken from some cage.
Poor bankrupt heart, when 't had not wherewithal
To pay to sad disaster all that was
Its due, it broke—would mine would do so too !
My soul
Is now within me, like a well-mettled hawk
On a blind falc'ner's fist : methinks I feel
It baiting to be gone : and yet I have
A little foolish business here on earth
I will despatch. [*Exit*

SCENE III

Enter PASITHAS, *with the body of Ariaspes*

Pas. Let me be like my burthen, if I had not here as lieve kill two of the blood royal for him, as carry one of them ! these gentlemen of high actions are three times as heavy after death, as your private retir'd ones : look if he be not reduc'd to the state of a courtier of the second form now, and cannot stand upon his own legs, nor do anything without help ! Hum ! and what's become of the great prince in prison, as they call it now, the toy within us that makes us talk and laugh and fight. Ay, why, there's it. Well, let him be what he will, and where he will, I'll make bold with the old tenement here. Come, sir, come along. [*Exit*

Enter Ziriff

Zir. All's fast too here—
They sleep to-night i' their winding-sheets, I think ;
There's such a general quiet. O, here's light,
I warrant ;
For lust does take as little rest as care
Or age—courting her glass, I swear. Fie ! that's
A flatterer, madam !
In me you shall see trulier what you are. [*Knocks*

Enter the Queen

Orb. What make you up at this strange hour, my lord ?
Zir. My business is my boldness' warrant, madam.
And I could well afford t' have been without
It now, had heav'n so pleas'd.
Orb. 'Tis a sad prologue.
What follows, in the name of virtue ?
Zir. The king.
Orb. Ay, what of him ? is well, is he not ?
Zir. Yes.
If to be free from the great load we sweat
And labour under here on earth, be to
Be well, he is.
Orb. Why, he's not dead, is he ?
Zir. Yes, madam, slain ; and the prince too.
Orb. How ? where ?
Zir. I know not ; but dead they are.
Orb. Dead ?
Zir. Yes, madam.
Orb. Didst see them dead ?
Zir. As I see you alive.
Orb. Dead !
Zir. Yes, dead.
Orb. Well, we must all die ;

The sisters spin no cables for us mortals ;
They're Thread, and Time, and Chance.
Trust me, I could weep now ;
But wat'ry distillations do but ill
On graves : they make the lodging colder. [*She knocks*
Zir. What would you, madam ?
Orb. Why, my friends, my lord,
I would consult, and know what's to be done.
Zir. Madam, 'tis not so safe to raise the court,
Things thus unsettled : if you please to have——
Orb. Where's Ariaspes ?
Zir. In's dead sleep by this time, I'm sure.
Orb. I know he is not ! find him instantly.
Zir. I'm gone. [*Turns back again*
But, madam, why make you choice of him, from whom,
If the succession meet disturbance, all
Must come of danger ?
Orb. My lord, I am not yet
So wise, as to be jealous : pray, dispute
No further.
Zir. Pardon me, madam, if, before I go,
I must unlock a secret unto you : such a one
As, while the king did breathe, durst know no air——
Zorannes lives !
Orb. Ha !
Zir. And, in the hope of such a day as this,
Has ling'red out a life, snatching, to feed
His almost famished eyes, sights now and then
Of you, in a disguise.
Orb. Strange !
This night is big with miracle.
Zir. If you did love him, as they say you did,
And do so still, 'tis now within your power——
Orb. I would it were, my lord ; but I am now
No private woman. If I did love him once,
(And 'tis so long ago, I have forgot),
My youth and ignorance may well excuse't.
Zir. Excuse it ?
Orb. Yes, excuse it, sir.
Zir. Though I confess I lov'd his father much,
And pity him ; yet, having offer'd it
Unto your thoughts, I have discharg'd a trust ;
And zeal shall stray no further. Your pardon, madam. [*Exit*
Orb. [*Studies*] Maybe 'tis

A plot to keep off Ariaspes' greatness,
Which he must fear, because he knows he hates him.
For these are statesmen, that, when time has made bold
With the king and subject, throwing down all fence
That stood betwixt their power and others' right,
Are on a change ;
Like wanton salmons coming in with floods,
That leap o'er wires and nets, and make their way
To be at the return to every one a prey.

Enter Ziriff *and* Pasithas ; *they throw down the dead body of Ariaspes*

Orb. Ha ! murther'd too ! Treason, treason !
Zir. But such another word, and half so loud,
And th'rt——
Orb. Why ? thou wilt not murther me too,
Wilt thou, villain ?
Zir. I do not know my temper :
[*Discovers himself*
Look here, vain thing, and see thy sins full blown :
There's scarce a part in all this face thou hast
Not been forsworn by, and Heav'n forgive thee for't !
For thee I lost a father, country, friends,
Myself almost ; for I lay buried long :
And, when there was no use thy love could pay
Too great, thou mad'st the principal away.
Had I but staid, and not began revenge,
Till thou hadst made an end of changing, I
Had had the kingdom to have kill'd.
As wantons, ent'ring a garden, take the first
Fair flower they meet, and treasure't in their laps ;
Then, seeing more, do make fresh choice again,
Throwing in one and one, till at the length
The first poor flower, o'ercharg'd with too much weight,
Withers and dies :
So hast thou dealt with me ; and, having kill'd
Me first, I'll kill——
Orb. Hold, hold !
Not for my sake, but Orbella's, sir ! a bare
And single death is such a wrong to justice,
I must needs except against it.
Find out a way to make me long a-dying ;
For death's no punishment : it is the sense,
The pains and fears afore, that makes a death.

To think what I had had, had I had you ;
What I have lost in losing of myself ;
Are deaths far worse than any you can give.
Yet kill me quickly ; for, if I have time,
I shall so wash this soul of mine with tears,
Make it so fine, that you would be afresh
In love with it ; and so perchance I should
Again come to deceive you.
[*She rises up weeping, and hanging down her head*
Zir. So rises day, blushing at night's deformity ;
And so the pretty flowers, blubber'd with dew,
And overwash'd with rain, hang down their heads.
I must not look upon her. [*She goes towards him*
Orb. Were but the lilies in this face as fresh
As are the roses ; had I but innocence
Join'd to their blushes, I should then be bold ;
For, when they went on begging, they were ne'er denied.
'Tis but a parting kiss, sir.
Zir. I dare not grant it.
Orb. Your hand, sir, then ; for that's a part I shall
Love after death (if after death we love),
'Cause it did right the wrong'd Zorannes here.
[*Steps to him, and opens the box of poison ;*
Zorannes falls
Sleep, sleep for ever ; and forgotten too,
All but thy ills, which may succeeding time
Remember, as the seaman does his marks,
To know what to avoid ! May at thy name
All good men start, and bad too ! may it prove
Infection to the air, that people dying of it
May help to curse thee for me !
[*Turns to the body of Ariaspes*
Could I but call thee back as eas'ly now !
But that's a subject for our tears, not hopes !
There is no piecing tulips to their stalks,
When they are once divorc'd by a rude hand ;
All we can do is to preserve in water
A little life, and give, by courteous art,
What scanted nature wants commission for.
That thou shalt have ; for to thy memory
Such tribute of moist sorrow I will pay,
And that so purifi'd by love, that on
Thy grave nothing shall grow but violets
And primroses ; of which, too, some shall be

Of the mysterious number, so that lovers shall
Come hither, not as to a tomb, but to an oracle.
[*She knocks, and raises the Court*

Enter ORITHIE, SEMANTHE, *with other* Ladies *and* Courtiers, *as out of their beds*

Orb. Come, come! help me to weep myself away,
And melt into a grave! for life is but
Repentance' nurse, and will conspire with memory
To make my hours my tortures.
Ori. What scene of sorrow's this? Both dead?
Orb. Dead? Ay,
And 'tis but half death's triumphs this: the king
And prince lie somewhere, just such empty trunks
As these.
Ori. The prince? Then in grief's burthen I
Must bear a part.
Sem. The noble Ariaspes!
Valiant Ziriff, too! [*Weeps*
Orb. Weep'st thou for him, fond prodigal? dost know
On whom thou spend'st thy tears? This is the man
To whom we owe our ills, the false Zorannes,
Disguis'd; not lost, but kept alive by some.

Enter PASITHAS, *surveys the bodies, finds his master*

Incensed power, to punish Persia thus!
He would have kill'd me too; but heav'n was just,
And furnish'd me with means to make him pay
This score of vill'ny, ere he could do more.
Pas. Were you his murth'rer then?
[*Runs to Orbella, kills her, and flies*
Ori. Ah me! the queen!
[*They rub Orbella till she comes to herself*
Sem. How do you do, madam?
Orb. Well; but I was better,
And shall—— [*Dies*
Sem. O, she is gone for ever!

Enter Lords *in their nightgowns*, ORSAMES, PHILAN

Ors. What have we here?
A churchyard? Nothing but silence and grave!
Ori. O, here has been, my lords, the blackest night
The Persian world e'er knew! The king and prince
Are not themselves exempt from this arrest:

But, pale and cold as these, have measur'd out
Their lengths.
Lords. Impossible ! which way ?
Sem. Of that
We are as ignorant as you ;
For, while the Queen was telling of the story,
An unknown villain here has hurt her so,
That, like a sickly taper, she but made
One flash, and so expir'd.
[*Enter some, bearing in Pasithas*
Phi. Here he is ; but no confession.
Ori. Torture must force him then ;
Though 'twill indeed but weakly satisfy
To know, now they are dead, how they did die.
Phi. Come, take the bodies up, and let us all
Go drown ourselves in tears. This massacre
Has left so torn a state, that 'twill be policy,
As well as debt, to weep till we are blind ;
For who would see the miseries behind ?

EPILOGUE

Our play is done; and yours doth now begin:
What different fancies people now are in!
How strange and odd a mingle it would make,
If, ere they rise, 'twere possible to take
All votes!—
But, as when an authentic watch is shown,
Each man winds up and rectifies his own;
So in our very judgments. First there sits
A grave grand jury on it of town wits;
And they give up their verdict: then again
The other jury of the court comes in:
And that's of life and death; for each man sees;
That oft condemns, what th' other jury frees.
Some three days hence, the ladies of the town
Will come to have a judgment of their own.
And, after them, their servants: then the city;
For that is modest, and is still last witty.
'Twill be a week at least yet, ere they have
Resolv'd to let it live, or give't a grave:
Such difficulty there is to unite
Opinion, or bring it to be right.

EPILOGUE FOR THE COURT

SIR,

That the abusing of your ear's a crime,
Above th' excuse any six lines in rhyme
Can make, the poet knows : I am but sent
T' intreat he may not be a precedent ;
For he does think, that in this place there be
Many have done't as much and more than he.
But here's, he says, the difference of the fates :
He begs a pardon after't, they estates.

THE FIFTH ACT OF AGLAURA AS PRESENTED AT THE COURT

Aglaura. Presented at the Court by His Majesties Servants. Written by Sir John Suckling.

PROLOGUE

'Fore love, a mighty session ; and (I fear)
Though kind last 'sizes, 'twill be now severe :
For it is thought, and by judicious men,
Aglaura 'scap't only by dying then.
But 'twould be vain for me now to endear,
Or speak unto my Lords, the Judges here :
They hold their places by condemning still,
And cannot show at once mercy and skill ;
For wit's so cruel unto wit, that they
Are thought to want, that find not want i' th' play.
But, ladies, you who never lik'd a plot,
But where the servant had his mistress got,
And whom to see a lover die it grieves,
Although 'tis in worse language that he lives,
Will like't, w' are confident, since here will be
That, your sex ever lik'd, variety !

PROLOGUE TO THE COURT

'Tis strange, perchance you'll think, that she, that died
At Christmas, should at Easter be a bride:
But 'tis a privilege the poets have,
To take the long-since dead out of the grave.
Nor is this all; old heroes, asleep
'Twixt marble coverlets, and six foot deep
In earth, they boldly wake, and make them do
All they did living here—sometimes more too.
They give fresh life, reverse and alter fate,
And (yet more bold) Almighty-like create,
And out of nothing, only to deify
Reason and Reason's friend, Philosophy:
Fame, honour, valour, all that's great or good—
Or is at least 'mongst us so understood—
They give: heav'n's theirs; no handsome woman dies,
But, if they please, is straight some star i' th' skies.
But O, how those poor men of metre do
Flatter themselves with that that is not true!
And, 'cause they can trim up a little prose,
And spoil it handsomely, vainly suppose
They're omnipotent, can do all those things
That can be done only by Gods and kings!
Of this wild guilt he fain would be thought free,
That writ this play; and therefore (sir) by me
He humbly begs you would be pleas'd to know,
Aglaura's but repriev'd this night; and, though
She now appears upon a poet's call,
She's not to live, unless you say she shall.

AGLAURA

PRESENTED AT THE COURT

ACT V

SCENE I

Enter ZIRIFF, PASITHAS, *and* Guard : *he places 'em and Exit. A state set out*

Enter ZIRIFF, IOLAS, ARIASPES

Iol. A glorious night!
Ari. Pray heav'n it prove so ! Are we not there yet ?
Zir. 'Tis about this hollow. [*They enter the cave*
Ari. How now ! what region are we got into,
Th' inheritance of night !
Have we not mistaken a turning, Ziriff,
And stepp'd into the confines of
Some melancholy devil's territory ?
Iol. Sure, 'tis a part of the first Chaos, that would
Not suffer any change.
Zir. No matter, sir : 'tis as proper for our purpose,
As the lobby for the waiting-woman's.
Stay you here ; I'll move a little backward ;
And so we shall be sure to put him past
Retreat. You know the word, if it be the prince ?
[*Ziriff goes to the door of the cave*

Enter KING

Zir. Here, sir, follow me : all's quiet yet.
King. Is he not come then ?
Zir. No.
King. Where's Ariaspes ?
Zir. Waiting within.
Iol. I do not like this waiting,
Nor this fellow's leaving of us.

Ari. This place does put odd thoughts into thee. Then
Thou art in thine own nature, too, as jealous
As love or honour. Wear thy sword in readiness,
And think how near we are a crown.
Zir. Revenge!
[*Guard seizeth on the King and Ariaspes*
King. Ha! what's this?
Zir. Bring them forth!
[*The guard brings them forth*
Ari. The King!
Zir. Yes, and the prince's friend. [*Discovers himself*
D'you know this face?
King. Zorannes!
Zor. The very same, the wrong'd Zorannes! King,
D'you stare? Away with them, where I appointed.
King. Traitors!
Let me go, villain, thou dar'st not do this.
Zor. Poor counterfeit,
How fain thou wouldst act a king, and art not!
[*To Ariaspes*] Stay you. [*Whispers to the guard*] Unhand him.
Leave us now.
[*Exeunt all but Ariaspes and Ziriff*
Ari. [*aside*]. What does this mean?
Sure he does intend the crown to me!
Zor. We are alone. Follow me out of the wood,
And thou shalt be master of this again;
And then best arm and title take it!
Ari. Thy offer is so noble,
In gratitude I cannot but propound
Gentler conditions; we will divide the empire.
Zor. Now, by my father's soul,
I do almost repent my first intents,
And now could kill thee scurvily, for thinking,
If I'd a mind to rule, I would not rule alone.
Let not thy easy faith, lost man,
Fool thee into so dull a heresy:
Orbella is our quarrel,
And I have thought it fit that love should have
A nobler way of justice than revenge
Or treason. If thou dar'st die handsomely,
Follow me. [*Exeunt, and enter both again*
Zor. There! [*Gives him his sword*

Ari. Extremely good! Nature took pains, I swear:
The villain and the brave are mingled handsomely.
Zir. 'Twas fate that took it, when that it decreed
We two should meet; nor shall they mingle now:
We are but brought together straight to part.
[*They fight*
Ari. Some devil sure has borrowed this shape:
My sword ne'er stay'd thus long to find an entrance.
Zir. To guilty men all that appears is devil;
Come, trifler, come. [*They fight*
Ari. Dog, thou hast it.
Zir. Why, then, it seems my star's as great as his:
I smile at thee.
[*Ariaspes pants, and runs at him to catch his sword*
Thou now wouldst have me kill thee,
And 'tis a courtesy I cannot afford thee.
I have bethought myself, there will be use
Of thee. Pasithas, to the rest with him! [*Exit*
[*Enter Pasithas and two of the Guard: they seize Ariaspes and go out again*

Enter THERSAMES

Ther. The dog-star's got up high: it should be late;
And sure by this time every waking ear
And watchful eye is charm'd: and yet methought
A noise of weapons struck my ear just now.
'Twas but my fancy, sure; and, were it more,
I would not tread one step that did not lead
To my Aglaura, stood all his guard betwixt,
With lightning in their hands.
Danger, thou dwarf dress'd up in giant's clothes,
That show'st far off still greater than thou art,
Go, terrify the simple and the guilty, such
As with false optics still do look upon thee!
But fright not lovers: we dare look on thee
In thy worst shapes, and meet thee in them too.
Stay.
These trees I made my mark: 'tis hereabouts.
Love, guide me but right this night,
And lovers shall restore thee back again
Those eyes the poets took so boldly from thee. [*Exit*

Scene II

A Taper. Table out

Enter Aglaura *with a torch in one hand, and a dagger in the other*

Agl. How ill this does become this hand ! much worse
This suits with this ! one of the two should go.
The she within me says, it must be this :
Honour says, this ; and honour is Thersames' friend.
What is that she then ? is it not a thing
That sets a price, not upon me, but on
Life in my name, leading me into doubt,
Which, when't has done, it cannot light me out ?
For fear does drive to fate ; or fate, if we
Do fly, o'ertakes and holds us, till or death
Or infamy, or both, do seize us. [*Puts out the light*
Ha ! would 'twere in again !
Antics and strange misshapes,
Such as the porter to my soul, mine eye,
Was ne'er acquainted with, fancy lets in,
Like a disrouted multitude, by some
Strange accident piec'd together.
Fear now afresh comes on, and charges love
Too home. He comes, he comes !
[*A little noise below*
Woman,
If thou wouldst be the subject of man's wonder,
Not his scorn hereafter, now show thyself !

Enter Thersames *from the vaults ; she stabs him, as he riseth*

Ther. Unkindly done !
Agl. The prince's voice ! defend it, goodness !
Ther. What art
Thou that thus poorly hast destroy'd a life ?
Agl. O sad mistake ! 'tis he.
Ther. Hast thou no voice ?
Agl. I would I had not, nor a being neither.
Ther. Aglaura ? it cannot be.
Agl. O still believe so, sir !
For 'twas not I indeed, but fatal love.
Ther. Love's wounds us'd to be gentler than these were ;

The pains they give us have some pleasure in them,
And that these have not.

Enter ZIRIFF *with a taper*

O do not say 'twas you ; for that
Does wound again. Guard me, my better angel !
Do I wake ? my eyes (since I was man) ne'er met
With any object gave them so much trouble :
I dare not ask neither to be satisfied,
She looks so guiltily. [*Aside*

Agl. [*to Ziriff*]. Why do you stare and wonder at a thing,
That you yourself have made thus miserable ?

Zir. Good gods, and I o' the party too ! [*Aside*

Agl. Did you not tell me, that the king this night
Meant to attempt mine honour ? that our condition
Would not admit of middle ways, and that we must
Send them to graves, or lie ourselves in dust ?

Zir. Unfortunate mistake ! [*He knocks*] I never did
Intend our safety by thy hands.

Enter PASITHAS

Pasithas,
Go instantly and fetch Andrages from his bed.
How is it with you, sir ?

Ther. As with the besieg'd :
My soul is so beset, it does not know
Whether 't had best to make a desperate sally
Out by this port, or not.

Agl. Sure,
I shall turn statue here !

Ther. If thou dost love me,
Weep not, Aglaura ! All those are drops of blood,
And flow from me.

Zir. Now all the gods defend
This way of expiation !
Thinkest thou thy crime, Aglaura, would be less
By adding to it ?
Or canst thou hope to satisfy those powers,
Whom great sins do displease, by doing greater ?

Agl. Discourteous courtesy !
I had no other means left me than this,
To let Thersames know I would do nothing
To him I would not do unto myself ;
And that thou tak'st away.

Ther. Friend, bring me a little nearer.

I find a kind of willingness to stay,
And find that willingness something obey'd.
My blood, now it persuades itself you did
Not call in earnest, makes not such haste.

Agl. O my dearest lord,
This kindness is so full of cruelty,
Puts such an ugliness on what I have done,
That, when I look upon ['t], it needs must fright
Me from myself, and (which is more insufferable)
I fear, from you.

Ther. Why should that fright thee, which most comforts me?
I glory in it, and shall smile i' th' grave,
To think our love was such, that nothing but
Itself could e'er destroy it.

Agl. Destroy it? can it have ever end? Will you
Not be thus courteous, then, in the other world?
Shall we not be together there as here?

Ther. I cannot tell whether I may or not.

Agl. Not tell?

Ther. No. The gods thought me unworthy of thee here;
And, when thou art more pure, why should I not
More doubt it?

Agl. Because, if I shall be more pure,
I shall be then more fit for you. Our priests
Assure us an Elysium; and can
That be Elysium, where true lovers must
Not meet? Those powers that made our lives, did they
Intend them mortal, would sure have made them of
A coarser stuff, would they not, my lord?

Ther. Pr'ythee, speak still:
This music gives my soul such pleasing business,
Takes it so wholly up, it finds not leisure
To attend unto the summons death does make.
Yet they are loud and peremptory now;
And I can only—— [*Faints*

Agl. Some pitying power
Inspire me with a way to follow him! Heart,
Wilt thou not break of thyself!

Zir. My griefs
Besot me.
His soul will sail out with this purple tide;
And I shall here be found staring after't,

Like a man that's too short o' th' ship, and's left
Behind upon the land. [*She swoons*

Enter ANDRAGES

O, welcome, welcome!
Here lies, Andrages, alas! too great
A trial for thy art.
And. There's life in him:
From whence these wounds?
Zir. O, 'tis no time for story.
And. 'Tis not mortal, my lord: bow him gently,
And help me to infuse this into him.
The soul is but asleep, and not gone forth.
Ther. O, O!
Zir. Hark! the prince does live.
Ther. Whate'er thou art hast given me now a life,
And with it all my cares and miseries.
Expect not a reward: no, not a thanks.
If thou wouldst merit from me (yet who would
Be guilty of so lost an action?),
Restore me to my quietness again;
For life and that are most incompatible.
Zir. Still in despairs! I did not think till now
'Twas in the power of fortune to have robb'd
Thersames of himself. For pity, sir,
And reason, live: if you will die, die not:
Aglaura's murther'd: that's not so handsome; at least
Die not her murther'd and her murtherer too;
For that will surely follow. Look up, sir;
This violence of fortune cannot last ever:
Who knows
But all these clouds are shadows to set off
Your fairer days? If it grows blacker, and
The storms do rise, this harbour's always open.
Ther. What sayest thou, Aglaura?
Agl. What says Andrages?
And. Madam, would heaven his mind would admit
As easy cure as his body will!
'Twas only want of blood; and two hours' rest
Restores him to himself.
Zir. And, by that time,
It may be, Heav'n will give our miseries
Some ease. Come, sir, repose upon a bed;
There's time enough to-day.

Ther. Well,
I will still obey, though I must fear it will
Be with me but as 'tis with tortured men,
Whom states preserve only to rack again. [*Exeunt*

SCENE III

Take off table. Enter ZIRIFF *with a taper*

Zir. All fast too here!
They sleep to-night i' their winding-sheets, I think;
There's such a general quiet. O, here's light,
I warrant you;
For lust does take as little rest as care,
Or age courting her glass, I swear!—Fie! that's
A flatterer, madam,
In me you shall see trulier what you are. [*He knocks*

Enter QUEEN

Orb. What make you up at this strange hour, my lord?
Zir. My business is my boldness' warrant, madam;
And I could well afford t' have been without
It now, had Heav'n so pleas'd.
Orb. 'Tis a sad prologue.
What follows, in the name of virtue?
Zir. The king——
Orb. Ay, what of him. Is well, is he not?
Zir. Yes.
If to be on's journey to the other world
Be to be well, he is.
Orb. Why, he's not dead, is he?
Zir. Yes, madam, dead.
Orb. How? where?
Zir. I do not know particulars.
Orb. Dead!
Zir. Yes, madam.
Orb. Art sure he's dead?
Zir. Madam, I know him as certainly dead,
As I know you too must die hereafter.
Orb. Dead!
Zir. Yes, dead.
Orb. We must all die.
The sisters spin no cables for us mortals;
They're Thread, and Time, and Chance.

Trust me, I could weep now ;
But watery distillations do but ill
On graves, they make the lodging colder. [*She knocks*
Zir. What would you, madam ?
Orb. Why, my friends, my lord,
I would consult, and know what's to be done.
Zir. Madam, 'tis not so safe to raise the court,
Things thus unsettled : if you please to have——
Orb. Where's Ariaspes ?
Zir. In's dead sleep by this time, sure.
Orb. I know he is not. Find him instantly.
Zir. I'm gone. [*Turns back again*
But, madam, why make you choice of him, from whom,
If the succession meet disturbance, all
Must come of danger ?
Orb. My lord, I am not yet
So wise as to be jealous : pray, dispute
No further.
Zir. Pardon me, madam, if, before I go,
I must unlock a secret to you ; such a one
As, while the king did breathe, durst know no air—
Zorannes lives !
Orb. Ha !
Zir. And, in the hope of such a day as this,
Has linger'd out a life, snatching, to feed
His almost famish'd eyes, sights now and then
Of you, in a disguise.
Orb. Strange !
This night is big with miracle.
Zir. If you did love him, as they say you did,
And do so still, 'tis now within your power——
Orb. I would it were, my lord ; but I am now
No private woman. If I did love him once,
(As 'tis so long ago, I have forgot),
My youth and ignorance may well excuse't.
Zir. Excuse it ?
Orb. Yes, excuse it, sir.
Zir. Though I confess I lov'd his father much,
And pity him, yet, having offer'd it
Unto your thoughts, I have discharg'd a trust ;
And zeal shall stray no further. Your pardon, madam.
[*Exit*.
Orb. Maybe, 'tis but
A plot to keep off Ariaspes' greatness,

Which he must fear, because he knows he hates him.
For these great statesmen, that, when time has made bold
With the king and subject, throwing down all fence
That stood betwixt their power and others' right,
Are on a change ;
Like wanton salmons coming in with floods,
That leap o'er wires and nets, and make their way,
To be at the return to every one a prey.

Re-enter Ziriff

Zir. Look here, vain thing, and see thy sins full blown !
There's scarce a part in all this face thou hast
Not been forsworn by, and Heav'n forgive thee for't !
For thee I lost a father, country, friends,
Myself almost ; for I lay buried long :
And, when there was no use thy love could pay
Too great, thou mad'st the principal away.
As wantons, ent'ring a garden, take the first
Fair flower they meet, and treasure't in their laps ;
Then, seeing more, do make fresh choice again,
Throwing in one and one, till at the length
The first poor flower, overcharged with too much weight,
Withers and dies :
So hast thou dealt with me ; and, having kill'd
Me first, I will kill——

Orb. Hold, hold !
Not for my sake, but Orbella's, sir ! a bare
And single death is such a wrong to justice,
I must needs except against it.
Find out a way to make me long a-dying ;
For death's no punishment : it is the sense,
The pains and fears afore, that makes a death.
To think what I had had, had I had you ;
What I have lost in losing of myself ;
Are deaths far worse than any you can give.
Yet kill me quickly ; for, if I have time,
I shall so wash this soul of mine with tears,
Make it so fine, that you would be afresh
In love with it ; and so perchance I should
Again come to deceive you.

[*She rises up weeping, and hanging down her head*

Zir. So rises day, blushing at night's deformity ;
And so the pretty flowers, blubber'd with dew,

And over-wash'd with rain, hang down their heads.
I must not look upon her. [*Queen goes towards him*
Orb. Were but the lilies in this face as fresh
As are the roses; had I but innocence
Join'd to these blushes, I should then be bold;
For when they went a-begging, they were ne'er denied.
'Tis but a parting kiss, sir!

Enter PASITHAS, *and* Two Guards

Zir. I dare not grant it.
Pasithas, away with her! [*Exeunt*

SCENE IV

A bed put out. THERSAMES *and* AGLAURA *on it,* ANDRAGES *by*

Ther. She wak'd me with a sigh,
And yet she sleeps herself, sweet innocence!
Can it be sin to love this shape? and if
It be not, why am I persecuted thus?
She sighs again!
Sleep that drowns all cares, cannot, I see, charm love's.
Blest pillows, through whose fineness does appear
The violets, lilies, and the roses
You are stuff'd withal! to whose softness I owe
The sweet of this repose, permit me to
Leave with you this. [*Kisses them; she wakes*
See, if I have not wak'd her.
Sure I was born, Aglaura, to destroy
Thy quiet!
Agl. Mine, my lord!
Call you this drowsiness a quiet, then?
Believe me, sir, 'twas an intruder I
Much struggled with; and have to thank a dream,
Not you, that it thus left me.
Ther. A dream! What dream, my love?
Agl. I dreamt, sir, it was day;
And the fear you should be found here——

Enter ZIRIFF

Zir. Awake! How is it with you, sir?
Ther. Well,
Extremely well, so well that, had I now

No better a remembrancer than pain,
I should forget I e'er was hurt, thanks to Heav'n
And good Andrages!

Zir. And more than thanks: I hope we yet shall live
To pay him. How old's the night?

And. Far spent, I fear,
My lord.

Zir. I have a cause that should be heard
Yet ere day break, and I must needs entreat
You, sir, to be the judge in't.

Ther. What cause, Zorannes?

Zir. When you have promis'd——

Ther. 'Twere hard I should deny thee anything.
[*Exit Ziriff*
Know'st thou, Andrages, what he means?

And. Nor cannot guess, sirs. [*Draw in the bed*
I read a trouble in his face, when first he left you,
But understood it not.

Re-enter Ziriff, *with* King, Ariaspes, Iolas, Queen, *and* Two *or* Three Guards

Zir. Have I not pitch'd my nets like a good huntsman?
Look, sir, the noblest of the herd are here.

Ther. I am astonished.

Zir. This place is yours. [*Helps him up*

Ther. What wouldst thou have me do?

Zir. Remember, sir, your promise.
I could do all I have to do alone; but justice
Is not justice, unless't be justly done.
Here, then, I will begin; for here began
My wrongs. This woman, sir, was wondrous fair
And wondrous kind—ay, fair and kind; for so
The story runs.
She gave me look for look and glance for glance;
And every sigh like Echo's, was return'd.
We sent up vow by vow, promise on promise,
So thick and strangely multiplied, that sure
We gave the heavenly registers their business,
And other mortals' oaths then went for nothing.
We felt each other's pains, each other's joys;
Thought the same thought, and spoke the very same:
We were the same; and I have much ado
To think she could be ill, and I not be
So too; and after this, all this, sir, she

Was false, lov'd him and him ; and, had I not
Begun revenge, till she had made an end
Of changing, I had had the kingdom to have killed.
What does this deserve ?

Ther. A punishment he best can make,
That suffered the wrong.

Zir. I thank you, sir.
For him I will not trouble you : his life
Is mine—I won it fairly—and his is yours—
He lost it foully to you. To him, sir, now !
A man so wicked that he knew no good,
But so as't made his sins the greater for't.
Those ills, which, singly acted, bred despair
In others, he acted daily, and ne'er thought
Upon them.
The grievance each particular has against him,
I will not meddle with : it were to give him
A long life to give them hearing. I'll only speak
My own : first, then, the hopes of all my youth,
And a reward which Heav'n hath settled on me
(If holy contracts can do anything)
He ravish'd from me, kill'd my father—
Aglaura's father, sir—would have whor'd my sister,
And murthered my friend. This is all ! And now
Your sentence, sir.

Ther. We have no punishment can reach these crimes :
Therefore 'tis justest, sure, to send him, where
They're wittier to punish than we are here ;
And, 'cause repentance oft stops that proceeding,
A sudden death is sure the greatest punishment.

Zir. I humbly thank you, sir.

King. What a strange glass th' have showed me now myself in !
Our sins, like to our shadows, when our day
Is in its glory, scarce appear'd : towards
Our evening how great and monstrous they are !

Zir. Is this all you have to say ? [*Draws*

Ther. Hold !
Now go you up.

Zir. What mean you, sir ?

Ther. Nay, I denied not you.
That all these accusations are just,
I must acknowledge ;
And to these crimes I have but this t'oppose—

He is my father and thy sovereign!
'Tis wickedness, dear friend, we go about to punish;
And, when we have murther'd him,
What difference is there 'twixt him and ourselves,
But that he first was wicked? Thou now wouldst kill
Him, 'cause he kill'd thy father; and when thou'st killed,
Have not I the self-same quarrel?

Zir. Why, sir, you know you would yourself have done it.

Ther. True;
And therefore 'tis I beg his life.
There was no way for me to have redeem'd
Th' intent but by a real saving of it.
If he did not ravish from thee thy Orbella,
Remember that that wicked issue had
A noble parent—love.

[*Be ready, Courtiers and Guard, with their swords drawn at the breasts of the prisoners*

Remember how
He lov'd Zorannes, when he was Ziriff!
There's something due to that.
If you must needs have blood for your revenge,

[*Offers his breast*

Take it here.
Despise it not, Zorannes. [*Zorannes turns away*
The gods themselves,
Whose greatness makes the greatness of our sins,
And heightens 'em above what we can do
Unto each other, accept of sacrifice
For what we do 'gainst them. Why should not you?
And 'tis much thriftier too. You cannot let
Out life there, but my honour goes; and all
The life you can take here, posterity
Will give me back again. See, Aglaura weeps!
That would have been ill rhetoric in me;
But, where it is, it cannot but persuade.

Zir. Th' have thaw'd the ice about my heart: I know
Not what to do.

King. Come down, come down! I will be king again.
There's none so fit to be the judge of this
As I. The life you show'd such zeal to save
I here could willingly return you back;
But that's the common price of all revenge.

Enter Guard, ORSAMES, PHILAN, Courtiers, ORITHIE, SEMANTHE

Iol. Ari. Ha, ha, ha! how they look now!
Zir. Death! what's this?
Ther. Betray'd again!
All th' ease our fortune gives our miseries
Is hope; and that, still proving false, grows part of it.
King. From whence this guard?
Ari. Why, sir, I did corrupt,
While we were his prisoners, one of his own
To raise the court.
Shallow souls, that thought we could not countermine!
Come, sir, y'are in good posture to despatch them.
King. Lay hold upon his instrument. Fond man!
Dost think I am in love with villainy?
All the service they can do me here is but
To let these see the right I do them now
Is unconstrain'd. Then thus I do proceed:
Upon the place Zorannes lost his life
I vow to build a tomb; and on that tomb
I vow to pay three whole years' penitence.
If in that time I find that heaven and you
Can pardon, I shall find again the way
To live amongst you.
Ther. Sir, be not
So cruel to yourself: this is an age.
King. 'Tis now irrevocable. Thy father's lands
I give thee back again, and his commands,
And, with them, leave to wear the tiara
That man there has abus'd. To you, Orbella,
Who, it seems, are foul as well as I,
I do prescribe the self-same physic I
Do take myself; but in another place,
And for a longer time—Diana's nunnery.
Orb. Above my hopes. [*Aside*
King. [*To Ari.*] For you, who still have been
The ready instrument of all my cruelties,
And there have cancell'd all the bonds of brother,
Perpetual banishment! Nor should
This line expire, shall thy right have a place.
Ari. Hell and furies! [*Exit*
King. [*To Zir.*] Thy crimes deserve no less; yet, 'cause
Thou wert Heaven's instrument to save my life,

Thou only hast that time of banishment
I have of penitence.
[*Comes down. Ziriff offers to kiss the King's hand*
Iol. May it be plague and famine here, till I return!
No, thou shalt not
Yet forgive me.
King. Aglaura, thus I freely part with thee,
And part with all fond flames and warm desires.
I cannot fear new agues in my blood,
Since I have overcome the charms thy beauty had:
No other ever can have so much pow'r.
Thersames, thou look'st pale! Is't want of rest?
Ther. No, sir; but that's a story for your ear.
[*They whisper*
Ors. A strange and happy change.
Ori. All joys wait on you ever!
Agl. Orithie, how for thy sake now could I wish
Love were no mathematic point, but would
Admit division, that Thersames might,
Though at my charge, pay thee the debt he owes thee.
Ori. Madam, I lov'd the prince, not myself. Since
His virtues have their full rewards, I have
My full desires.
King. What miracles of preservation have we had!
How wisely have the stars prepar'd you for
Felicity! Nothing endears a good
More than the contemplation of the difficulty
We had to attain to it.
But see, night's empire's out; and a more glorious
Auspiciously does begin. Let us
Go serve the gods, and then prepare for jollity.
This day
I'll borrow from my vows; nor shall it have
A common celebration, since 't must be
A high record to all posterity. [*Exeunt omnes*

EPILOGUE

Plays are like feasts ; and every act should be
Another course, and still variety :
But, in good faith, provision of wit
Is grown of late so difficult to get,
That, do we what we can, we are not able
Without cold meats to furnish out the table.
Who knows but it was needless too ? maybe,
'Twas here as in the coachman's trade ; and he
That turns in the least compass shows most art.
Howe'er, the poet hopes, sir, for his part,
You'll like not those so much, who shew their skill
In entertainment, as who shew their will.

The Goblins

A Comedy.

Presented at the Private House in Black Fryers, by His *Majesties* servants.

WRITTEN

By Sir JOHN SUCKLING.

London,
Printed for *Humphrey Moseley*, and are to be sold at his shop, at the Signe of the Prin-ces Armes in S[t] *Pauls* Churchyard.
MDCXLVI.

PROLOGUE

Wit in a prologue poets justly may
Style a new imposition on a play.
When Shakespeare, Beaumont, Fletcher, rul'd the stage,
There scarce were ten good palates in the age ;
More curious cooks than guests ; for men would eat
Most heartily of any kind of meat.
And then what strange variety ! each play
A feast for epicures, and that each day !
But mark how oddly it is come about,
And how unluckily it now falls out :
The palates are grown higher, number increas'd,
And there wants that which should make up the feast ;
And yet y'are so unconscionable, you'd have
Forsooth of late, that which they never gave ;
Banquets before, and after——
Now pox on him that first good prologue writ !
He left a kind of rent-charge upon wit ;
Which if succeeding poets fail to pay,
They forfeit all their worth ; and that's their play :
Y'have ladies' humours, and y'are grown to that,
You will not like the man, 'less that his boots and hat
Be right ; no play, unless the prologue be
And ep'logue writ to curiosity.
Well, gentles, 'tis the grievance of the place,
And pray consider't, for here's just the case ;
The richness of the ground is gone and spent,
Men's brains grow barren, and you raise the rent.

Dramatis Personæ

PRINCE, in love with Sabrina.
ORSABRIN, brother to the Prince, yet unknown.
SAMORAT, belov'd of Sabrina.
PHILATEL, } brothers to Sabrina.
TORCULAR, }
NASSURAT, } Cavaliers, friends to Samorat.
PELLEGRIN, }
TAMOREN, king of the thieves, disguised in devil's habit.
PERIDOR, ambitious of Reginella, disguis'd in devil's habit.
STRAMADOR, a courtier, servant to the Prince.
ARDELLAN, } formerly servants to Orsabrin's father.
PIRAMONT, }
PHONTREL, servant to Philatel.
SABRINA, beloved by Samorat.
REGINELLA, in love with Orsabrin.
PHEMILIA, Sabrina's maid.

Captain and Soldiers.
Two Judges.
Two Lawyers.
Two Serjeants.
Gaoler.
Constable.
Tailor.
Two Drawers.
Fiddlers.
Clowns and Wenches.
Thieves, disguised in devils' habits, living underground by the woods.
Guard. Attendants.

THE SCENE, FRANCELIA.

THE GOBLINS

ACT I

Scene I

Enter as to a duel, Samorat, Philatel, Torcular

Samorat. But, my lords,
May not this harsh business yet be left undone ?
Must you hate me, because I love your sister ?
And can you hate at no less rate than death ?
Philatel. No, at no less :
Thou art the blaster of our fortunes ;
The envious cloud that darkens all our day.
While she thus prodigally and fondly throws
Away her love on thee, she has not where
Withal to pay a debt unto the Prince.
Samorat. Is this all ?
Torcular. Faith,
What, if in short we do not think you worthy
Of her ?
Samorat. I swear that shall not make a quarrel.
I think so too ;
Have urg'd it often to myself ;
Against myself have sworn't as oft to her.
Pray, let this satisfy.
Philatel. Sure, Torcular, he thinks we come to talk.
Look you, sir. [*Draws*
And, brother, since his friend has fail'd him,
Do you retire.
Torcular. Excuse me, Philatel ;
I have an equal interest in this,
And fortune shall decide it.
Philatel. It will not need ; he's come.

Enter Orsabrin

Orsabrin. Mercury protect me ! what are these ?
The brothers of the highway !

Philatel. A stranger, by his habit.
Torcular. And, by his looks,
A gentleman. Sir, will you make one ?
We want a fourth.
Orsabrin. I shall be robb'd with a trick now !
Samorat. My lords, excuse me !
This is not civil : in what concerns myself,
None but myself must suffer.
Orsabrin. A duel, by this light !——
Now has his modesty and t'other's forwardness warm'd me. [*Goes towards them*
Gentlemen,
I wear a sword, and commonly in readiness.
If you want one, speak, sir : I do not fear
Much suffering. [*To Samorat*
Samorat. Y'are noble, sir ;
I know not how t' invite you to it :
Yet there is justice on my side ; and since
You please to be a witness to our actions,
'Tis fit you know our story.
Orsabrin. No story, sir, I beseech you ;
The cause is good enough as 'tis : it may
Be spoil'd i' th' telling.
Philatel. Come, we trifle then.
Samorat. It is impossible to preserve, I see,
My honour, and respect to her :
And since you know this too, my lord,
It is not handsome in you thus to press me.
But come—— [*Torcular beckons to Orsabrin*
Orsabrin. O ! I understand you, sir. [*Exeunt*
[*Philatel and Samorat fight*
Philatel. In posture still !
[*Samorat receives a slight wound*
O, y'are mortal then, it seems.
Samorat. Thou hast undone thyself, rash man ;
For with this blood thou hast let out a spirit
Will vex thee to thy grave.
[*Fight again ; Samorat takes away Philatel's sword, and takes breath, then gives it him.*
Samorat. I'm cool again.
Here, my lord,
And let this present bind your friendship.
Philatel. Yes, thus—— [*Runs at him*
Samorat. Treacherous and low !

Re-enter ORSABRIN

Orsabrin. I have drill'd my gentleman. I have made as many
Holes in him as would sink a ship royal
In sight of the haven. How now?
[*Samorat upon his knee*
'Sfoot,
Yonder's another going that way too:
Now have I forgot of which side I'm on!
No matter:
I'll help the weakest: there's some justice in that.
Philatel. The villain sure has slain my brother.
If I have any friends above, guide now
My hand unto his heart!
[*Orsabrin puts it by; runs at him. Samorat steps in*
Samorat. Hold, noble youth; destroy me not with kindness!
Men will say he could have kill'd me; and that
In justice should not be. For honour's sake,
Leave us together.
Orsabrin. 'Tis not my business, fighting! [*Puts up*
Th' employment's yours, sir. If you need me,
I am within your call. [*Exit*
Samorat. The gods reward thee!
Now, Philatel, thy worst!
[*They fight again, and close; Samorat forces his sword*

Re-enter ORSABRIN

Orsabrin. Hell and the furies are broke loose upon us!
Shift for yourself, sir.
[*Fly into the woods several ways, pursued by thieves in devils' habits*

Re-enter TORCULAR, *weak with bleeding*

Torcular. It will not be—my body is a jade:
I feel it tire and languish under me.
Those thoughts came to my soul, like screech-owls to
A sick man's window.

Enter Thieves *back again*

Thieves. Here, here!
Torcular. O, I am fetch'd away alive!
[*They bind him and carry him away. Exeunt*

Re-enter Orsabrin

Orsabrin. Now the good gods preserve my senses right,
For they were never in more danger!
I' th' name of doubt, what could this be?
Sure, 'twas a conjurer I dealt withal;
And, while I thought him busy at his prayers,
'Twas at his circle, levying this regiment.
Here they are again!

Re-enter Samorat

Samorat. Friend—Stranger—Noble youth——
Orsabrin. Here, here!
Samorat. Shift, shift the place,
The wood is dangerous: as you love safety,
Follow me. [*Exeunt*

Re-enter Philatel

Philatel. Th' have left the place;
And yet I cannot find the body anywhere.
Maybe, he did not kill him then,
But he recover'd strength, and reach'd the town.
It may be not too. O, that this hour
Could be call'd back again! But 'tis too late;
And time must cure the wound that's given by fate. [*Exit*

Re-enter Samorat *and* Orsabrin

Orsabrin. I' th' shape of lions too, sometimes, and bears?
Samorat. Often, sir.
Orsabrin. Pray, unriddle.
Samorat. The wiser sort
Do think them thieves, which but assume these forms
To rob more powerfully.
Orsabrin. Why does not then
The state set out some forces, and suppress them?
Samorat. It often has, sir, but without success.
Orsabrin. How so?
Samorat. During the time those levies are abroad,
Not one of them appears. There have been,
That have attempted under ground; but of those,
As of the dead, there has been no return.
Orsabrin. Strange!
Samorat. The common people think them
A race of honest and familiar devils;
For they do hurt to none, unless resisted.

They seldom take away, but with exchange ;
And to the poor they often give ; return
The hurt and sick recover'd ;
Reward or punish, as they do find cause.
Orsabrin. How, cause ?
Samorat. Why, sir, they blind still those they take,
And make them tell the stories of their lives ;
Which known, they do accordingly.
Orsabrin. You make me wonder, sir.
How long is't since they thus have troubled you ?
Samorat. It was immediately upon
The great deciding day, fought 'twixt the two
Pretending families, the Tamorens
And the Orsabrins.
Orsabrin. Ha ! Orsabrin ?
Samorat. But, sir, that story's sad and tedious :
W'are ent'ring now the town, a place less safe
Than were the woods, since Torcular is slain.
Orsabrin. How, sir ?
Samorat. Yes.
He was the brother to the Prince's mistress ;
The lov'd one too.
If we do prize ourselves at any rate,
We must embark, and change the clime : there is
No safety here.
Orsabrin. Hum !
Samorat. The little stay we make,
Must be in some dark corner of the town ;
From whence, the day hurried to th' other world,
We'll sally out, to order for our journey.
That I am forc'd to this, it grieves me not ;
But, gentle youth, that you should for my sake——
Orsabrin. Sir,
Lose not a thought on that : a storm at sea
Threw me on land, and now a storm on land
Drives me to sea again.
Samorat. Still noble ! [*Exeunt*

Scene II

Enter Nassurat *and* Pellegrin

Nassurat. Why, suppose 'tis to a wench, you would not go with me, would you ?
Pellegrin. To choose—to choose !

Nassurat. Then there's no remedy.

[*Flings down his hat, unbuttons himself, draws*

Pellegrin. What dost mean ?

Nassurat. Why, since I cannot leave you alive, I will try to leave you dead.

Pellegrin. I thank you kindly, sir, very kindly. Now the Sedgly curse upon thee, and the great fiend ride through thee booted and spurr'd, with a scythe on his neck ! Pox on thee, I'll see thee hang'd first ! 'Sfoot, you shall make none of your fine points of honour up at my charge ! Take your course, if you be so hot : be doing, be doing. [*Exit*

Nassurat. I am got free of him at last. There was no other way : h'as been as troublesome as a woman that would be lov'd, whether a man would or not ; and has watch'd me, as if he had been my creditor's serjeant : if they should have dispatch'd in the meantime, there would be fine opinions of me. I must cut his throat in earnest, if it should be so. [*Exit*

Scene III.

Enter Tamoren *and* Peridor, *with other* Thieves, *and* Torcular

A horn sounds

Thieves. A prize ! A prize ! A prize !

Peridor. Some duel, sir, was fought this morning : this,
Weaken'd with loss of blood, we took ; the rest
Escap'd.

Tamoren. He's fitter for our surgeon than for us ;
Hereafter we'll examine him. [*Again a shout*

Thieves. A prize ! A prize ! A prize !

[*They set them down, Ardellan, Piramont*

Tamoren.

Bring them, bring them, bring them in,
See, if they have mortal sin :
Pinch them as you dance about,
Pinch them, till the truth come out.

Peridor. What art ?

Ardellan. Extremely poor and miserable.

Peridor. 'Tis well, 'tis well, proceed : nobody will
Take that away from me. Fear not. What country ?

Ardellan. Francelia.

Peridor. Thy name ?

Ardellan. Ardellan.
Peridor. And thine ?
Piramont. Piramont.
Peridor. Thy story ?
Ardellan. What story ?
Peridor. Thy life, thy life. [*Pinch him*
Ardellan. Hold, hold : you shall have it. [*He sighs.*]
It was upon
The great defeat given by the Tamorens
Unto the Orsabrins, that the old prince,
For safety of the young, committed him
Unto the trust of Garradan, and some
Few servants more, 'mongst whom I fill'd a place.
Tamoren. Ha ! Garradan ?
Ardellan. Yes.
Tamoren. Speak out, and set me nearer.
So, void the place [*to Attend.*]. Proceed.
Ardellan. We put to sea, but had scarce lost the sight
Of land, ere we were made a prey to pirates :
There Garradan, resisting the first board,
Chang'd life with death ; with him the servants too,
All but myself and Piramont.
Under these pirates ever since
Was Orsabrin brought up ;
And into several countries did they carry him.
Tamoren. Knew Orsabrin himself ?
Ardellan. Oh no, his spirit was too great : we durst
Not tell him anything, but waited for
Some accident might throw us on Francelia ;
'Bout which we hover'd often, and we were near
It now ; but Heaven decreed it otherwise. [*He sighs*
Tamoren. Why dost thou sigh ?
Ardellan. Why do I sigh indeed !
For tears cannot recall him : last night,
About the second watch, the winds broke loose,
And vex'd our ship so long, that it began
To reel and totter, and, like a drunken man,
Took in so fast his liquor, that it sunk
Down i' th' place.
Tamoren. How did you 'scape ?
Ardellan. I bound myself unto a mast, and did
Advise my master to do so ;
For which he struck me only, and said I did
Consult too much with fear.

Tamoren. 'Tis a sad story. Within there!
Let them have wine and fire. But hark you. [*Whispers*

Enter THIEVES, *with a* POET.

Thieves. A prize! A prize! A prize!
Peridor. Set him down.
Poet. And for the blue, [*Sings*
Give him a cup of sack, 'twill mend his hue.
Peridor. Drunk, as I live! [*Pinch him, pinch him.*]
What art?
Poet. I am a poet,
A poor dabbler in rhyme.
Peridor. Come, confess, confess.
Poet. I do confess, I do want money.
Peridor. By the description he's a poet indeed.
Well, proceed. [*Pinch him*
Poet. What d'you mean, pox on you?
Prithee, let me alone.

Some candles here!
And fill us t'other quart, and fill us,
Rogue, drawer, t'other quart.
Some small-beer.
And for the blue,
Give him a cup of sack, 'twill mend his hue.

Tamoren. Set him by, till he's sober.
Come, let's go see our duellist drest. [*Exeunt*

SCENE IV.

Enter TAILOR *and two* SERJEANTS

Tailor. He's something tall; and, for his chin, it has
No bush below: marry, a little wool,
As much as an unripe peach doth wear; just
Enough to speak him drawing towards a man.
Serj. Is he of fury? Will he foin, and give
The mortal touch?
Tailor. O no, he seldom wears
His sword.
Serj. Topo is the word, if he do:
Thy debt, my little myrmidon?
Tailor. A yard and a half, I assure you, without abatement.

Serj. 'Tis well, 'tis wondrous well :
Is he retir'd into this house of pleasure ?
Tailor. One of these he's entered :
'Tis but a little waiting, you shall find me
At the next tavern.
Serj. Stand close ; I hear one coming. [*Exit*

Enter ORSABRIN

Orsabrin. This house is sure no seminary for Lucreces :
Then the matron was so over-diligent ;
And, when I ask'd for meat or drink, she look'd
As if I had mistook myself, and call'd
For a wrong thing.
Well, 'tis but a night ; and part of it I'll spend
In seeing of this town, so famous in
Our tales at sea.

Serj. Look, look ! muffled, and as melancholy after't as a gamester upon loss : upon him, upon him !

Orsabrin. How now, my friends ; why do you use me thus ?

Serj. Quietly ; 'twill be your best way.

Orsabrin. Best way, for what ?

Serj. Why, 'tis your best way, because there will be no other. *Topo* is the word ; and you must along.

Orsabrin. Is that the word ? Why, then, this is my sword. [*Run away*

Serj. Murder, murder, murder ! h'as kill'd the Prince's officer : murder, murder, murder !

Orsabrin. I must not stay, I hear them swarm. [*Exit*

Enter CONSTABLE, People

Constable. Where is he, where is he ?
Serj. Here, here ! Oh, a man-mender, a man-mender !
H' as broach'd me in so many places, all
The liquor in my body will run out.
Constable. In good sooth,
Neighbour, h'as tapp'd you at the wrong end too ;
He has been busy with you here behind,
As one would say ; lend a hand, some of you,
And the rest follow me. [*Exeunt*

Enter ORSABRIN

Orsabrin. Still pursu'd ! which way now ? I see no passage ;

I must attempt this wall. O, a lucky door,
And open ! [*Exit*

Enters again

Where am I now ? A garden, and
A handsome house !
If't be thy will, a porch to't, and I'm made ;
'Twill be the better lodging of the two. [*Goes to the porch*

Enter PHEMILIA

Phemilia. O, welcome, welcome, sir !
My lady hath been in such frights for you.
Orsabrin. Hum ! for me !
Phemilia. And thought you would not come to-night.
Orsabrin. Troth, I might very well have fail'd her. [*Aside*
Phemilia. She's in the gallery, alone i' th' dark.
Orsabrin. Good, very good.
Phemilia. And is so melancholy.
Orsabrin. Hum !
Phemilia. Have you shut the garden doors ?
Come, I'll bring you to her ; enter, enter.
Orsabrin. Yes, I will enter :
He who has lost himself, makes no great venter. [*Exeunt*

ACT II

Scene I

Enter SABRINA, ORSABRIN

Sabrina. Oh, welcome !
Welcome, as open air to prisoners ;
I have had such fears for you.
Orsabrin. She's warm, and soft as lovers' language :
She spoke, too, prettily. Now have I forgot
All the danger I was in. [*Aside*
Sabrina. What have you done to-day, my better part ?
Orsabrin. Kind little rogue !
I could say the finest things to her, methinks ;
But then she would discover me :
The best way will be to fall to quietly. [*Aside. Kisses her*
Sabrina. How now, my Samorat !
What saucy heat hath stol'n into thy blood,

And height'ned thee to this ? I fear you are
Not well.

Orsabrin. 'Sfoot ! 'tis a Platonic :
Now cannot I so much as talk that way neither. [*Aside*

Sabrina. Why are you silent, sir ?
Come, I know you have been in the field to-day.

Orsabrin. How does she know that ? [*Aside*

Sabrina. If you have kill'd my brother, speak : it is
No new thing that true love should be unfortunate.

Orsabrin. 'Twas her brother I kill'd then !
Would I were with my devils again !
I got well [rid] of them : that will be here impossible.

Enter PHEMILIA

Phemilia. Oh, madam, madam, y'are undone !
The garden walls are scal'd : a flood of people
Are entering th' house.

Orsabrin. Good !
Why here's variety of ruin yet. [*Aside*

Sabrina. 'Tis so :
The feet of justice, like to those of time,
Move quick, and will destroy (I fear) as sure.
Oh, sir,
What will you do ? there is no vent'ring forth.
My closet is the safest : enter there,
While I go down and meet their fury, hinder
The search, if possible. [*Exit*

Orsabrin. Her closet ? yea, where's that ?
And, if I could find it, what should I do there ?
She will return. I will venture out. [*Exit*

Enter the PRINCE, PHILATEL, PHONTREL, *Company*, *Music*

Philatel. The lightest airs ; 'twill make them more secure.
Upon my life he'll visit her to-night.
[*Music plays, and sings*

Prince. Nor she nor any lesser light appears :
The calm and silence 'bout the place
Persuades me she does sleep.

Philatel. It may not be :
But hold, it is enough : let us retire.
Behind this pillar, Phontrel, is thy place ;
As thou didst love thy master, show thy care :
You to the other gate ; there's thy ladder. [*Exeunt*

Re-enter Sabrina

Sabrina. Come forth, my Samorat, come forth.
Our fears were false, it was the Prince with music.
Samorat, Samorat! He sleeps:—Samorat!
Or else he's gone to find me out i' th' gallery;
Samorat, Samorat! it must be so. [*Exit*

Re-enter Orsabrin

Orsabrin. This house is full of thresholds and trapdoors.
I have been i' th' cellar, where the maids lie too—
I laid my hand, groping for my way,
Upon one of them, and she began to squeak.
Would I were at sea again i' th' storm!
Oh, a door: though the devil were the porter,
And kept the gate, I'd out.

Enter Samorat

Ha! guarded! taken in a trap?
Nay, I will out, and there's no other but this.
[*Retires and draws, runs at him; another pass, they close*

Samorat. Philatel in ambush, on my life!

Re-enter Sabrina *and* Phemilia *with a light*

Sabrina. Where should he be?
Ha!
Good heavens, what a spectacle is this! my Samorat!
Some apparition, sure!
[*They discover one another by the light, throw away their weapons, and embrace*

Samorat. My noble friend!
What angry and malicious planet govern'd
At this point of time?

Sabrina. My wonder does grow higher.

Orsabrin. That which governs ever: I seldom knew it better.

Samorat. It does amaze me, sir, to find you here:
How enter'd you this place?

Orsabrin. Forc'd by unruly men i' th' street.

Sabrina. Now the mistake is plain.

Orsabrin. Are you not hurt?

Samorat. No; but you bleed.

Orsabrin. I do indeed, but 'tis not here; this is

A scratch : it is within, to see this beauty ;
For by all circumstance it was her brother
Whom my unlucky sword found out to-day.

Sabrina. Oh, my too cruel fancy ! [*Weeps*

Samorat. It was indeed
Thy sword, but not thy fault ; I am the cause
Of all these ills. Why do you weep, Sabrina ?

Sabrina. Unkind unto thyself and me,
The tempest this sad news has rais'd within me
I would have laid with tears, but thou disturb'st me.
O Samorat,
Hadst thou consulted but with love as much
As honour, this had never been.

Samorat. I have no love for thee, that has not had
So strict an union with honour still,
That in all things they were concern'd alike ;
And, if there could be a division made,
It would be found, honour had here the leaner share :
'Twas love that told me 'twas unfit that you
Should love a coward.

Sabrina. These handsome words
Are now as if one bound up wounds with silk,
Or with fine knots, which do not help the cure,
Or make it heal the sooner. O Samorat,
This accident lies on our love like to
Some foul disease which, though it kill it not,
Yet will't destroy the beauty ; disfigure't so,
That 'twill look ugly to the world hereafter.

Samorat. Must then the acts of fate be crimes of men ?
And shall a death he pull'd upon himself
Be laid on others ?
Remember, sweet, how often you have said
It in the face of heaven, that 'twas no love,
Which length of time or cruelty of chance
Could lessen or remove. Oh, kill me not
That way, Sabrina ! This is the nobler.
Take it, and give it entrance anywhere.
[*Kneels, and presents his sword*
But here ; for you so fill that place, that you
Must wound yourself.

Orsabrin. Am I so slight a thing ?
So bankrupt ? So unanswerable in this world
That, being principally in the debt,
Another must be call'd upon, and I

Not once look'd after ?
Madam,
Why d'you throw away your tears on one
That's irrecoverable ?
Sabrina. Why ? Therefore, sir,
Because he's irrecoverable.
Orsabrin. But why on him ? he did not make him so.
Sabrina. I do confess my anger is unjust,
But not my sorrow, sir.
Forgive these tears, my Samorat :
The debts of nature must be paid, though from
The stock of love :
Should they not, sir ?
Samorat. Yes :
But thus the precious minutes pass ; and time,
Ere I have breath'd the sighs due to our parting,
Will be calling for me.
Sabrina. Parting !
Samorat. Oh yes, Sabrina ! I must part,
As day does from the world, not to return
Till night be gone, till this dark cloud be over.
Here to be found were foolishly to make
A present of my life unto mine enemy.
Retire into thy chamber, fair ; there thou
Shalt know all.
Sabrina. I know too much already. [*Exeunt*

Re-enter PHONTREL

Phontrel. Hold rope for me, and then hold rope for him. Why, this is the wisdom of the law now : a prince loses a subject, and does not think himself paid for the loss, till he loses another. Well ! I will do my endeavour to make him a saver ; for this was Samorat. [*Exit*

Scene II

Enter SAMORAT *and* ORSABRIN *bleeding*

Orsabrin. Let it bleed on. You shall not stir, I swear.
Samorat. Now, by the friendship that I owe thee, and
The gods beside, I will.
Noble youth,
Were there no danger in the wound, yet would
The loss of blood make thee unfit for travel.
My servants wait me for direction—

With them my surgeon ; I'll bring him instantly.
Pray, go back. [*Exeunt*

Enter Philatel with Guard

He places them at the door

Philatel. There ! You to the other gate ;
The rest follow me. [*Exeunt*

Re-enter Orsabrin *with* Sabrina

Sabrina. Hark ! a noise, sir !
The tread's too loud to be my Samorat's.

Enter the Searchers *to them*

Searchers. Which way ? which way ?
Sabrina. Some villainy's in hand. Step in here, sir ;
Quick, quick. [*Locks him in her closet*

Re-enter Philatel *and* Guard

They pass over the stage

Philatel. Look everywhere.
[*He dragging out his sister*
Protect thy brother's murderer ?
Tell me, where thou hast hid him !
Or, by my father's ashes, I will search
In every vein thou hast about thee for him.

[Orsabrin (*within the closet*) *bounces thrice at the door : it flies open*

Orsabrin. Ere such a villainy should be, the gods
Would lend unto a single arm such strength,
It should have power to punish an army such
As thou art.
Philatel. O, are you here, sir ?
Orsabrin. Yes, I am here, sir [*Fight*
Philatel. Kill her ! [*Sabrina interposes*
Orsabrin. O, save thyself, fair excellence,
And leave me to my fate.
[*The Guard comes behind him, and catches hold of his arms*
Base !
Philatel. So, bring him ! One !—the other is not far.
[*Exeunt*

Enter Sabrina *with* Phemilia

Sabrina. Run, run, Phemilia, to the garden walls,
And meet my Samorat. Tell him, O tell him—anything.
Charge him, by all our loves,
He instantly take horse and put to sea.
There is more safety in a storm, than where
My brother is. [*Exeunt*

ACT III

Scene I

Enter Peridor *and the other* Thieves

Stramador *is led in : they dance about him and sing*

Thieves. A prize ! A prize ! A prize !

Peridor. Bring him forth, bring him forth.

Welcome, welcome, mortal wight,
To the mansion of the night.
Good or bad, thy life discover ;
Truly all thy deeds declare ;
For about thee spirits hover,
That can tell, tell what they are.
Pinch him, if he speak not true ;
Pinch him, pinch him black and blue.

Peridor. What art thou ?
Stramador. I was a man.
Peridor. Of whence ?
Stramador. The court.
Peridor. Whither now bound ?
Stramador. To my own house.
Peridor. Thy name ?
Stramador. Stramador.
Peridor. O, you fill a place about
His grace, and keep out men of parts, d'you not ?
Stramador. Yes.
Peridor. A foolish utensil of state
Which, like old plate upon a gaudy day,
'S brought forth to make a show, and that is all :
For of no use y'are. Y' had best deny this.
Stramador. O no !
Peridor. Or that you do want wit,
And then talk loud, to make that pass for it.
You think there is no wisdom but in form,
Nor any knowledge like to that of whispers.

Stramador. Right, right!
Peridor. Then, you can hate,
And fawn upon a man at the same time:
And dare not urge the vices of another,
You are so foul yourself.
So the Prince seldom hears truth.
Stramador. O, very seldom.
Peridor. And did you never give his grace odd counsels;
And, when you saw they did not prosper,
Persuade him take them on himself?
Stramador. Yes, yes, often.
Peridor. Get baths of sulphur quick, and flaming oils;
This crime is new, and will deserve it.
He has inverted all the rule of state,
Confounded policy.
There is some reason why a subject
Should suffer for the errors of his prince;
But, why a prince should bear the faults of's ministers,—
None, none at all.—Caldrons of brimstone there!
Thief. Great judge of this infernal place, allow
Him yet the mercy of the court.
Stramador. Kind devil!
Peridor. Let him be boil'd in scalding lead a while,
T'enure and prepare him for the other.
Stramador. O, hear me, hear me!
Peridor. Stay!
Now I have better thought upon't, he shall
To earth again;
For villainy is catching, and will spread.
He will enlarge our empire much;
Then we're sure of him at any time.
So, 'tis enough. Where's our governor? [*Exeunt*

Scene II

Enter Gaoler, Samorat, Nassurat, Pellegrin, *and three others in disguise*

Gaoler. His hair curls naturally: a handsome youth!
Samorat. The same. [*Drinks to him*] Is there no speaking with him?
He owes me a trifling sum.
Gaoler. Sure, sir, the debt is something desperate;
There is no hopes he will be brought to clear
With the world:

He struck me but for persuading him to make
Even with heaven.
He is as surly as an old lion, and
As sullen as a bullfinch.
He never ate since he was taken, gentlemen !
Samorat. I must needs speak with him.
Hark in thy ear.
Gaoler. Not for all the world.
Samorat. Nay, I do but motion such a thing.
Gaoler. Is this the business, gentlemen ? Fare you well.
Samorat. There is no choice of ways then.
[*They run after the Gaoler, draw their daggers, and set on to his breast*
Stir not ! If thou but think'st a noise, or breath'st
Aloud, thou breath'st thy last. So, bind him now.
[*They bind the Gaoler*
Undo quickly, quickly—his jerkin, his hat !
Nassurat. What will you do ? None of these beards will serve ;
There's not an eye of white in them.
Pellegrin. Pull out the silver'd ones in his, and stick
Them in the other.
Nassurat. Cut them, cut them out. The bush will suit
Well enough with a grace still.
[*They put a false beard on the Gaoler, and gag him*
Samorat. Desperate wounds must have desperate cures :
Extremes must thus be serv'd. You know your parts.
[*Exit in the Gaoler's habit*
Nassurat. Fear not : let us alone. [*They sing a catch*

Some drink ! what, boy, some drink !
Fill it up, fill it up to the brink.
When the pots cry clink,
And the pockets chink,
Then 'tis a merry world.

To the best, to the best, have at her ;
And a pox take the woman-hater !—
The Prince of Darkness is a gentleman :
Mahu, Mahu is his name.—

How d'you, sir ?
[*To the Gaoler gagg'd*
You gape, as if you were sleepy.
Good faith, he looks like an *O yes !*

Pellegrin. Or as if he had overstrain'd himself
At a deep note in a ballad.
Nassurat. What think you of an oyster at a low ebb?
Some liquor for him!
You will not be a pimp for life, you rogue,
Nor hold a door to save a gentleman.
You are—pox on him, what he is, Pellegrin?
If you love me, let's stifle him, and say
'Twas a sudden judgment upon him for swearing.
The posture will confirm it.
Pellegrin. We're in excellent humour;
Let's have another bottle, and give out
That Ann, my wife, is dead.
Shall I, gentlemen?
Nassurat. Rare rogue in buckram, let me bite thee.
Before me thou shalt go out wit, and upon
As good terms as some of those in the ballad, too.
Pellegrin. Shall I so? Why then, *foutre for the Guise!*
Saints shall accrue; and ours shall be
The black-ey'd beauties of the time.
I'll tickle you for old ends of plays. [*They sing*

Around, around, around.
Around, around, around.

Somebody's at the door! [*Knocking at the door*
Pr'ythee, pr'ythee: sirrah, sirrah, try thy skill.
Nassurat. Who's there?

Enter a Messenger

Messenger. One Sturgelot a gaoler here?
Nassurat. Such a one there was, my friend, but he's gone
Above an hour ago.
Now did this rogue whisper in his heart, that's a lie;
And for that very reason I'll cut his throat.
Pellegrin. No, pr'ythee now,—for thinking?
Thou shalt not take the pains; the law shall do't.
Nassurat. How, how?
Pellegrin. Marry, we'll write it over, when we're gone,
He join'd in the plot, and put himself into
This posture, merely to disguise it to
The world.
Nassurat. Excellent! Here's to thee for that conceit!
We should have made rare statesmen, we are so witty in our mischief! Another song, and so let's go: it will be time. [*They sing*

A health to the nut-brown lass,
With the hazel eyes : let it pass.
She that has good eyes,
Has good thighs.
Let it pass, let it pass.

As much to the lively grey ;
'Tis as good i' th' night as day :
She that has good eyes,
Has good thighs.
Drink away, drink away.

I pledge, I pledge : what ho ! some wine !
Here's to thine, and to thine !
The colours are divine.

But O the black, the black !
Give me as much again, and let't be sack.
She that has good eyes,
Has good thighs,
And, it may be, a better knack. [*They knock*

Enter a Drawer.

Nassurat. A reckoning, boy. There. [*Pay him.*] Dost hear ? Here's a friend of ours has forgotten himself a little, as they call it : the wine has got into his head, as the frost into his hand ; he is benumbed, and has no use of himself for the present.

Boy. Hum, sir—— [*Smiles*

Nassurat. Prithee, lock the door ; and when he comes to himself, tell him he shall find us at the old place. He knows where.

Boy. I will, sir. [*Exeunt*

SCENE III

Enter ORSABRIN, *in prison*

Orsabrin. To die ! Ay, what's that ?
For yet I never thought on't seriously.
It may be 'tis—hum !—it may be 'tis not, too.

Enter SAMORAT *as the* Gaoler ; *he undoes his fetters*

Ha ! [*As amaz'd*
What happy intercession wrought this change ?
To whose kind prayers owe I this, my friend ?

Samorat. Unto thy virtue, noble youth ;

The gods delight in that as well as prayers.
I am——

Orsabrin. Nay, nay.
Be what thou wilt, I will not question it.
Undo, undo.

Samorat. —thy friend Samorat.

Orsabrin. Ha!

Samorat. Lay by thy wonder, and put on these clothes:
In this disguise thou'lt pass unto the prison gates;
There you shall find one that is taught to know you.
He will conduct you to the corner of the wood;
And there my horses wait us.
I'll throw this gaoler off in some odd place.

Orsabrin. My better angel! [*Exeunt*

Scene IV

Enter Peridor *with the other* Thieves

Peridor. It is e'en
As hard a world for thieves as honest men:
Nothing to be got; no prize stirring.

1st Thief. None, but one with horses,
Who seem'd to stay for some that were to come;
And that has made us wait thus long.

Peridor. A lean day's work, but what remedy?
Lawyers, that rob men with their own consent,
Have had the same. Come, call in our perdues:
We will away—— [*They whistle*

Enter Orsabrin, *as seeking the horses*

Orsabrin. I hear them now; yonder they are.

Peridor. Hallo! Who are these? any of ours?

Thief. No, stand close; they shall be presently.
Yield! yield!

Orsabrin. Again betray'd!
There is no end of my misfortune!
Mischief vexes me like a quotidian;
It intermits a little, and returns,
Ere I have lost the memory of
My former fit——

Peridor. Sentences, sentences!
Away with him,—away with him! [*Exeunt*

Scene V

Enter Gaoler *and* Drawers *over the stage*

Gaoler. I am the gaoler.
Undone, undone ! conspiracy ! a cheat !
My prisoner, my prisoner ! [*Exeunt*

Scene VI

Enter Samorat

Samorat. No men, nor horses ! Some strange mistake !
Maybe, th'are sheltered in the wood. [*Exit*

Scene VII

Enter Peridor *and other* Thieves, *examining the young* Lord Torcular *that was hurt*

Peridor. And, if a lady did but step aside
To fetch a mask or so, you follow'd after still,
As if she had gone proud ? Ha ! Is't not so ?

Torcular. Yes.

Peridor. And, if you were us'd but civilly in a place,
You gave out doubtful words upon't, to make
Men think you did enjoy ?

Torcular. O yes, yes.

Peridor. Made love to every piece of cri'd-up beauty,
And swore the same things over to them.

Torcular. The very same——

Peridor. Abominable !
Had he but sworn new things yet, 't had been tolerable.

[*One of them reads the sum of the confession*

Thief. Let me see, let me see. Hum ! 'Court ladies eight, of which two great ones. Country ladies twelve ; termers all.'

Peridor. Is this right ?

Torcular. Very right.

Thief. Citizens' wives of several trades : he cannot count them.
Chambermaids and country wenches, about thirty , of which
The greater part the night before they were married, or else upon the day !

Peridor. A modest reckoning ! Is this all ?

Torcular. No, I will be just to a scruple.
Peridor. Well said, well said : out with it.
Torcular. Put down two old ladies more.
Peridor. I' th' name of wonder, how could he think of old
In such variety of young ?
Torcular. Alas ! I could never be quiet for them.
Peridor. Poor gentleman !
Well, what's to be done with him now ? Shall he
Be thrown into the caldron with the cuckolds ?
Thief. Or with the jealous ? that's the hotter place.

Peridor. Thou mistakest ; 'tis the same : they go together still. Jealous and cuckolds differ no otherwise than sheriff and alderman : a little time makes the one th' other. What think you of gelding him, and sending him to earth again amongst his women ? 'Twould be like throwing a dead fly into an ant's nest ; there should be such tearing and pulling, and getting up upon him, they would worry the poor thing to death !

1st Thief. Excellent ! Or leave a string, as they do sometimes in young colts. Desire and impotence would be a rare punishment.

Peridor. Fie, fie, the common disease of age ! every old man has it.

Enter TAMOREN *and more* Thieves, *leading* ORSABRIN

A prize, a prize, a prize ! [*Horns blow, brass pots beat on*
Orsabrin. This must be hell, by the noise !
Tamoren. Set him down, set him down : bring forth
The newest rack and flaming pinching-irons.
This is a stubborn piece of flesh : 'twould have broke loose.
Orsabrin. So,
This comes of wishing myself with devils again !
Peridor. What art ?
Orsabrin. The slave of chance ; one of Fortune's fools :
A thing she kept alive on earth to make her sport.
Peridor. Thy name ?
Orsabrin. Orsabrin.
Peridor. Ha ! he that liv'd with pirates ?
Was lately in a storm ?
Orsabrin. The very same.
Tamoren. Such respect as you have paid to me—
[*Whispers with Peridor*

Prepare to revels, all that can be thought on ;
But let each man still keep his shape. *[Exit*
[They unbind him. All bow to him
[Music and a dance]

Orsabrin. Ha ! another false smile of Fortune ?
[They bring out several suits of clothes and a banquet
Is this the place
The gowned clerks do fright men so on earth with ?
Would I had been here before !
Master devil, to whose use are these set out ?
Peridor. To yours, sir.
Orsabrin. I'll make bold to change a little.
[Takes a hat, dresses himself
Could you not
Afford a good plain sword to all this gallantry ?
Peridor. We'll see, sir.
Orsabrin. A thousand times civiller
Than men, and better natur'd !

Enter TAMOREN *and* REGINELLA

Tamoren. All leave the room.
Peridor. I like not this. *[Exeunt*
Tamoren. Cupid, do thou the rest !
A blunter arrow, and but slackly drawn,
Would perfect what's begun :
When young and handsome meet, the work's half done.
[Exit
Orsabrin. She cannot be
Less than a goddess, and't must be Proserpine.
I'll speak to her, though Pluto's self stood by—
Thou beauteous queen of this dark world, that mak'st
A place so like a hell so like a heaven !
Instruct me in what form I must approach thee,
And how adore thee.
Reginella. Tell me what thou art first ; for such a creature
Mine eyes did never yet behold !
Orsabrin. I am that which they name above a man.
I' th' wat'ry elements I much have liv'd ;
Hnd there they term me Orsabrin.
Aave you a name, too ?
Reginella. Why do you ask ?

Orsabrin. Because I'd call upon it in a storm,
And save a ship from perishing sometimes.
Reginella. 'Tis Reginella.
Orsabrin. Are you a woman, too?
I never was in earnest until now.
Reginella. I know not what I am; for like myself
I never yet saw any.
Orsabrin. Nor ever shall.
O! how came you hither? Sure, you were betray'd.
Will you leave this place, and live with such as I am?
Reginella. Why may not you live here with me?
Orsabrin. Yes;
But I'd carry thee where there is a glorious light;
Where all above is spread a canopy,
Studded with twinkling gems,
Beauteous as lovers' eyes; and underneath
Carpets of flow'ry meads to tread on:
A thousand thousand pleasures, which this place
Can ne'er afford thee.
Reginella. Indeed.
Orsabrin. Yes, indeed.
I'll bring thee unto shady walks,
And groves fringed with silver purling streams,
Where thou shalt hear soft-feathered quiristers
Sing sweetly to thee of their own accord.
I'll fill thy lap with early flowers;
And whilst thou bind'st them up mysterious ways,
I'll tell thee pretty tales, and sigh by thee;
Thus press thy hand, and warm it thus with kisses.
Reginella. Will you indeed?

Re-enter TAMOREN *and* PERIDOR *above, with others*

Tamoren. Fond girl! Her rashness
Sullies the glory of her beauty: 'twill make
The conquest cheap, and weaken my designs!
Go part them instantly, and blind him as before.
Be you his keeper, Peridor.
Peridor. Yes, I will keep him.
Orsabrin. Her eyes like lightning shoot into my heart:
They'll melt it into nothing, ere I can
Present it to her! Sweet excellence!

Enter Thieves, *and blind him*

Ha!
Why is this hateful curtain drawn before my eyes?

If I have sinn'd, give me some other punishment :
Let me but look on her still, and double it !
O, whither, whither do you hurry me ? [*Carry him away*

Peridor. Madam, you must in.

Reginella. Ay me ! what's this ?
Must !—— [*Exit*

Enter other Devils

1st Thief. We have had such sport ! Yonder's the rarest poet without, h'as made all his confession in blank verse ; not left a god nor a goddess in heaven, but fetch'd them all down for witnesses. H'as made such a description of Styx and the Ferry, and verily thinks he has past them ! Enquires for the bless'd shades, and asks much after certain British blades ; one Shakespeare and Fletcher : and grew so peremptory at last, he would be carried where they were.

2nd Thief. And what did you with him ?

1st Thief. Mounting him upon a coal-staff, which (tossing him something high) he apprehended to be Pegasus. So we have left him to tell strange lies ; which he'll turn into verse ; and some wise people hereafter into religion. [*Exeunt*

ACT IV

Scene I

Enter Samorat, Nassurat, *and* Pellegrin

Nassurat. Good faith, 'tis wondrous well. We have e'en done
Like eager disputers ; and with much ado
Are got to be just where we were. This is
The corner of the wood.

Samorat. Ha ! 'tis indeed !

Pellegrin. Had we no walking fire,
Nor saucer-ey'd devil of these woods that led us ?
Now am I as weary as a married man after the first week ; and have no more desire to move forwards than a post-horse that has pass'd his stage.

Nassurat. 'Sfoot, yonder's the night too, stealing away with her black gown about her, like a kind wench that had staid out the last minute with a man.

Pellegrin. What shall we do, gentlemen ? I apprehend

falling into this gaoler's hands strangely. He'd use us worse than we did him.

Nassurat. And that was ill enough, of conscience. What think you of turning beggars? Many good gentlemen have done't. Or thieves?

Pellegrin. That's the same thing at court: begging is but a kind of robbing the exchequer.

Nassurat. Look! four fathom and a half O O S in contemplation of his mistress. There's a feast! You and I are out now, Pellegrin. 'Tis a pretty trick, this enjoying in absence! What a rare invention 'twould be, if a man could find out a way to make it real!

Pellegrin. Dost think there's nothing in't, as 'tis?

Nassurat. Nothing, nothing. Didst never hear of a dead Alexander rais'd to talk with a man? Love's a learned conjurer, and with the glass of fancy will do as strange things! You thrust out a hand: your mistress thrusts out another. You shake that hand: that shakes you again. You put out a lip: she puts out hers. Talk to her: she shall answer you. Marry, when you come to grasp all this, it is but air.

Samorat [*as out of his study*]. It was unlucky.
Gentlemen,
The day appears: this is no place to stay in:
Let's to some neighbouring cottage. Maybe,
The searchers will neglect the nearer places;
And this will best advance unto our safety.

Enter Fiddlers

Nassurat. Who are there?

1st Fiddler. Now, if the spirit of melancholy should possess 'em?

2nd Fiddler. Why, if it should, an honourable retreat.

Nassurat. I have the rarest fancy in my head. Whither are you bound, my friends, so early?

1st Fiddler. To a wedding, sir.

Nassurat. A wedding? I told you so. Whose?'

1st Fiddler. A country wench's here hard by, one Erblin's daughter.

Nassurat. Good. Erblin! the very place! to see how things fall out! Hold, here's money for you. Hark you, you must assist me in a small design.

1st Fiddler. Anything.

Samorat. What dost mean?

Nassurat. Let me alone—I have a plot upon a wench.

1st Fiddler. Your worship is merry.

Nassurat. Yes, faith, to see her only. Look you, some of you shall go back to th' town and leave us your coats. My friend and I are excellent at a little instrument; and then we'll sing catches rarely.

Pellegrin. I understand thee not.

Nassurat. Thou hast no more forecast than a squirrel, and hast less wise consideration about thee. Is there a way safer than this? dost think what we have done will not be spread beyond this place with every light? Should we now enter any house thus near the town, and stay all day, 'twould be suspicious: what pretence have we?

Pellegrin. He speaks reason, Samorat.

Samorat. I do not like it.
Should anything fall out, 'twould not look well;
I'd not be found so much out of myself,
So far from home as this disguise would make me,
Almost for certainty of safety.

Nassurat. Certainty! why, this will give it us. Pray let me govern once.

Samorat. Well,
You suffer'd first with me: now 'tis my turn.

Pellegrin. Prithee, name not suffering.

Nassurat. Come, come, your coats! our beards will suit rarely to them. There's more money. Not a word of anything, as you tender——

1st Fiddler. O, sir!

Nassurat. And see you carry't gravely too! Now, afore me, Pellegrin's rarely translated! 'Sfoot, they'll apprehend the head of the bass-viol as soon as thee, thou art so like it! Only, I must confess, that has a little the better face.

Pellegrin. Has it so? Pox on thee, thou look'st like, I cannot tell what.

Nassurat. Why, so I would, fool: th' end of my disguise is to have none know what I am.

Enter a Devil

Look, look, a devil airing himself! I'll catch him like a mole, ere he can get underground.

Pellegrin. Nassurat, Nassurat!

Nassurat. Pox on that noise, he's earth'd! Prithee, let's watch him, and see whether he'll heave again.

Pellegrin. Art mad ?

Nassurat. By this light, three or four of their skins, and we'd rob ! 'Twould be the better way. Come, come, let's go. [*Exeunt*

Enter Captain *and* Soldiers

Captain. Let the horse skirt about this place : we'll make
A search within. [*Exeunt and enter again*
Now disperse :
I' th' hollow of the wood we'll meet again. [*Exit*

Re-enter Samorat, Nassurat, Pellegrin, *and* Fiddlers

Soldiers. Who goes there ? Speak ! O, they are fiddlers !
Saw you no men nor horse i' th' wood to-day
As you came along ?

Nassurat. Speak, speak, rogue.
[*He pulls one of the Fiddlers by the skirt*

1st Fiddler. None, sir.

Soldiers. Pass on. [*Exeunt*

Nassurat. Gentlemen, what say you to th' invention now ? I'm a rogue, if I do not think I was design'd for the helm of state : I am so full of nimble stratagems, that I should have ordered affairs, and carried it against the stream of a faction with as much ease as a skipper would laver it against the wind. [*Exeunt*

Re-enter Captain *and* Soldiers, *meeting*

Captain. What, no news of any ?

Soldiers. No, not a man stirring.

Enter other Soldiers : *they cry*

Soho ! away, away !

Captain. What ? any discovery ?

Soldier. Yes, the horse has staid three fellows, fiddlers they call themselves. There's something in't : they look suspiciously. One of them has offer'd at confession once or twice, like a weak stomach at vomiting ; but 'twould not out.

Captain. A little cold iron thrust down his throat will fetch it up. I am excellent at discovery, and can draw a secret out of a knave with as much dexterity as a barber-surgeon would a hollow tooth. Let's join forces with them. [*Exeunt*

SCENE II

ORSABRIN *discovered in prison, bound*

Orsabrin. Sure 'tis eternal night with me! would this
Were all too!
For I begin to think the rest is true,
Which I have read in books, and that there's more
To follow.

Enter REGINELLA

Reginella. Sure this is he—— [*She unbinds him*

Orsabrin. The pure and first-created light broke through
The chaos thus!
Keep off, keep off, thou brighter excellence,
Thou fair divinity! if thou com'st near,
(So tempting is the shape thou now assum'st),
I shall grow saucy in desire again,
And entertain bold hopes, which will but draw
More and fresh punishment upon me.

Reginella. I see y'are angry, sir: but, if you kill
Me too, I meant no ill. That which brought me hither
Was a desire I have to be with you
Rather than those I live with. This is all,
Believe't.

Orsabrin. With me? O thou kind innocence, witness all
That can punish falsehood, that I could live with thee,
Even in this dark and narrow prison, and think
All happiness confin'd within the walls!
O, hadst thou but as much of love as I!

Reginella. Of love! What's that?

Orsabrin. Why, 'tis a thing that's had, before 'tis known;
A gentle flame, that steals into a heart,
And makes it like one object so, that it scarce cares
For any other delights, when that is present;
And is in pain, when 't's gone; thinks of that alone,
And quarrels with all other thoughts that would
Intrude, and so divert it.

Reginella. If this be love, sure I have some of it.
It is no ill thing, is it, sir?

Orsabrin. O, most divine:
The best of all the gods strangely abound in't;
And mortals could not live without it: it is
The soul of virtue and the life of life.

Reginella. Sure, I should learn it, sir, if you would teach it.

Orsabrin. Alas, thou taught'st it me;
It came with looking thus—

[*They gaze upon one another*

Enter PERIDOR

Peridor. I will no longer be conceal'd, but tell
Her what I am, before this smooth-fac'd youth
Hath taken all the room up in her heart.
Ha!
Unbound!
And, sure, by her! Hell and furies!
What, ho! within there—

Enter other Thieves

Practice escapes?—
Get me new irons to lead him unto death.

Orsabrin. I am so used to this, it takes away
The sense of it; I cannot think it strange.

Reginella. Alas! he never did intend to go.
Use him, for my sake, kindly!
I was not wont to be deni'd. Ah me!
They are hard-hearted all. What shall I do?
I'll to my governor, he'll not be thus cruel. [*Exeunt*

SCENE III

Enter SAMORAT, NASSURAT, *and* PELLEGRIN

Nassurat. 'Tis a rare wench, she i' th' blue stockings: what a complexion she had, when she was warm! 'Tis a hard question of these country wenches, which are simpler, their beauties or themselves. There's as much difference betwixt a town-lady and one of these, as there is betwixt a wild pheasant and a tame.

Pellegrin. Right. There goes such essencing, washing, perfuming, daubing to th' other, that they are the least part of themselves. Indeed, there's so much sauce a man cannot taste the meat.

Nassurat. Let me kiss thee for that. By this light, I hate a woman drest up to her height worse than I do sugar with muscadine: it leaves no room for me to imagine I could improve her, if she were mine. It looks like a jade, with his tail tied up with ribbons, going to a fair to be sold.

Pellegrin. No, no, thou hatest it out of another reason, Nassurat.

Nassurat. Prithee, what's that ?

Pellegrin. Why, th'are so fine, th'are of no use that day.

Nassurat. Pellegrin is in good feeling ! Sirrah, didst mark the lass i' th' green upon yellow, how she bridled in her head, and danc'd a stroke in and a stroke out, like a young fillet training to a pace ?

Pellegrin. And how she kist, as if she had been sealing and delivering herself up to the use of him that came last ; parted with her sweetheart's lips still as unwillingly and untowardly as soft wax from a dry seal ?

Nassurat. True ; and, when she kisses a gentleman, she makes a curtsey, as who should say the favour was on his side. What dull fools are we, to besiege a face three months for that trifle ! Sometimes it holds out longer ; and then this is the sweeter flesh too !

Enter Fiddlers

Fiddler. You shall have horses ready at the time,
And good ones too (if there be truth in drink) ;
And, for your letters, they are there by this.

Samorat. An excellent officer !

Enter Wedding of Clowns

Clown. Tut, tut, tut ! that's a good one, i' faith ! not dance ? Come,
Come, strike up.

[*They dance : in that time enter Soldiers muffled up in their cloaks*

Samorat. Who are those that eye us so severely ?
Belong they to the wedding ?

Fiddlers. I know 'em not.

Clown. Gentlemen, will't please you dance ?

[*Clowns offer their women to them to dance*

Soldier. No, keep your women : we'll take out others here.
Samorat ! if I mistake not !

Samorat. Ha ! betray'd ! [*A bustle*

Clown. How now ! what's the matter ? abuse our fiddlers !

2nd Soldier. These are no fiddlers, fools. Obey the Prince's officers, unless you desire to go to prison too.

Samorat. The thought of what must follow disquiets not

At all ; but tamely thus to be surpris'd
In so unhandsome a disguise. [*They carry him away*

Pellegrin. Is't even so ? Why then
' Farewell the plumed troops and the big wars,
Which made ambition virtue.'

Nassurat. Ay, ay ; let them go, let them go.

Pellegrin. Have you ever a stratagem, Nassurat ? 'Twould be very seasonable. What think you now ? Are you designed for the helm of state ? Can you laver against this tempest ?

Nassurat. Prithee, let me alone : I am thinking for life.

Pellegrin. Yes, 'tis for life, indeed ; would 'twere not !

Clown. This is very strange : let's follow after, and see if we can understand it. [*Exeunt*

Scene IV

Enter Peridor, Orsabrin

Peridor. A mere phantasm, rais'd by art to try thee.

Orsabrin. Good kind devil, try me once more :
Help me to the sight of this phantasm again.

Peridor. Thou art undone.
Wert thou not amorous in th' other world ?
Didst not love women ?

Orsabrin. Who did hate them ?

Peridor. Why, there's it :
Thou thought'st there was no danger in the sin,
Because 'twas common.
Above the half of that vast multitude,
Which fills this place, women sent hither ; and they
Are highliest punished still, that love the handsomest.

Orsabrin. A very lying devil this, certainly !

Peridor. All that had their women with you,
Suffer with us.

Orsabrin. By your friendship's favour, though,
There's no justice in that : some of them
Suffered enough, in all conscience, by 'em there.

Peridor. O, this is now your mirth ;
But when you shall be pinch'd into a jelly,
Or made into a cramp all over, these
Will be sad truths.

Orsabrin. He talks oddly now ; I do not like it. Dost hear ?

Prithee, exchange some of thy good counsel for deeds.
If thou be'st
An honest devil (as thou seem'st to be),
Put a sword into my hand, and help me to
The sight of this apparition again.
Peridor. Well,
Something I'll do for thee, or rather for
Myself. [*Exeunt*

Enter two other Devils

1st Devil. Come, let's go relieve our poet.
2nd Devil. How?
Relieve him? He's released, is he not?
1st Devil. No, no:
Bersat bethought himself at the mouth of the cave,
And found he would be necessary to
Our masque to-night. We have set him with his feet
In a great tub of water, in which he dabbles,
And believes it to be Helicon. There he's contriving
'I th' honour of Mercury, who, I have told him,
Comes this night of a message from Jupiter
To Pluto, and is feasted here by him.

Enter Thieves *with* Poet

Devil. O, they have fetch'd him off!
Poet. —— Querer per solo Querer,
Or he that made the 'Fairy Queen.'
1st Thief. No, none of these:
They are by themselves, in some other place;
But here's he that writ Tamerlane.
Poet. I beseech you,
Bring me to him; there's something in his scene
Betwixt the empresses a little high
And cloudy: I would resolve myself.
1st Thief. You shall, sir.
Let me see—the author of the 'Bold Beauchamps.'
And 'England's Joy.'
Poet. The last was a well-writ piece, I assure you;
A Briton, I take it, and Shakespeare's very way.
I desire to see the man.
1st Thief. Excuse me; no seeing here.
The gods, in compliment to Homer,
Do make all poets poor above, and we,
All blind below. But you shall confess, sir.
Follow. [*Exeunt*

SCENE V

Enter PERIDOR, ORSABRIN

Orsabrin. Ha!
Light and the fresh air again! The place I know too;
The very same I fought the duel in.
The devil was in the right:
This was a mere apparition; but 'twas
A handsome one; it left impressions here,
Such as the fairest substance I shall e'er
Behold will scarce deface. Well, I must resolve;
But what, or where? Ay, that's the question.
The town's unsafe, there's no returning thither:
And then the port—— [*Some Clowns pass over hastily*
Ha! what means the busy haste of these?
[*Calls to one*] Honest friend! dost hear? No. What's the matter, pray?

Clown. Gentlemen, gentlemen!

Orsabrin. That's good satisfaction, indeed!
[*To another*] Prithee,
Good fellow, tell me: what causes all this hurry?

Enter another

Clown. One Samorat is led to prison, sir,
And another gentleman about Lord Torcular.

Orsabrin. Ha! Samorat!
There is no mean nor end of Fortune's malice!
O, 'tis insufferable: I'm made a boy
Whipt on another's back. Cruel! I'll not
Endure 't, by Heaven! He shall die for me:
I will not hold a wretched life upon
Such wretched terms.

Enter TAMOREN, PERIDOR, *and others*

Tamoren. Fly, fly, abroad! Search every place,
And bring him back! Thou hast undone us all
With thy neglect; destroy'd the hopes we had
To be ourselves again. I shall run mad
With anger! Fly, begone! [*Exeunt all but Tamoren*

Enter REGINELLA

My Reginella, what brings you abroad?

Reginella. Dear governor! I have a suit to you.

Tamoren. To me, my pretty sweetness? what?

Reginella. You will deny me, sir, I fear.
Pray let me have the stranger, that came last,
In keeping.
Tamoren. Stranger! Alas! he's gone, made an escape.
Reginella. I fear'd
He would not stay, they us'd him so unkindly.
Indeed, I would have us'd him better; and then
He had been here still. [*She weeps*
Tamoren. Come, do not weep, my girl.
Forget him, pretty pensiveness; there will
Come others every day as good as he.
Reginella. O, never!
I'll close my eyes to all, now he is gone.
Tamoren. How catching are the sparks of love! Still this
Mischance shows more and more unfortunate.
I was too curious: Come, indeed you must
Forget him.
The gallant'st and the goodliest to the eye
Are not the best. Such handsome and fine shapes
As these are ever false and foul within.
Reginella. Why, governor, d'you then put your finest things
Still in your finest cabinets?
Tamoren. Pretty innocence!
No, I do not: you see I place not you there.
Come, no more tears!
Let's in, and have a mate at chess;
'Diversion cures a loss, or makes it less.' [*Exeunt*

ACT V

SCENE I

Enter TAMOREN, PERIDOR, *and other* Thieves

Peridor. Cross'd all the highways, search'd the woods, beat up
And down with as much pain and diligence,
As ever huntsman did for a lost deer.
Tamoren. A race of cripples are y' all, issue of snails;
He could not else have 'scap'd us. Now, what news bring you?

Thief. Sir, we have found him out : the party is
In prison.
Tamoren. How, in prison ?
Thief. For certain, sir.
It seems young Samorat and he
Were those that fought the duel t'other day,
And left our Torcular so wounded there.
For his supposed death was Samorat taken ;
Which when this youth had found,
He did attempt to free him, scaling the wall
By night ; but, finding it impossible,
Next morning did present himself into
The hands of justice, imagining his death,
That did the fact, an equal sacrifice.
Tamoren. Brave Orsabrin !
Thief. Not knowing that the greedy law asks more,
And doth proscribe the accessory as well
As principal.
Tamoren. Just so, i' th' nick ! i' th' very nick of time !
Peridor. He's troubled.
Tamoren. It will be excellent.
Be all in soldiers' habits straight. Where's Torcular ?
Thief. Forthcoming, sir.
Tamoren. How are his wounds ? Will they endure the air ?
Under your gaberdines wear pistols all.
Peridor. What does he mean ?
Tamoren. Give me my other habit and my sword.
I' th' least suspected way haste after me.
Thief. All ?
Tamoren. All but Peridor. I will abroad.
My broken hopes and suff'rings shall have now
Some cure.
Fortune, spite of herself, shall be my friend,
And either shall redress, or give them end.
[*Exeunt all but Peridor*
Peridor. I've found it out : he does intend to fetch
This stranger back, and give him Reginella :
Or else—no, no, it must be that : his anger
And the search declare it—the secret of the prison-house
Shall out, I swear. I'll set all first on fire ;
For middle ways to such an end are dull. [*Exit*

Scene II

Enter Prince, Philatel, *and* Servant

Servant. Since she was refus'd to speak with you, sir, she will
Not look on any ; languishes so fast,
Her servants fear she will not live to know
What does become of him.

Philatel. Sir, 'tis high time you visit her.

Prince. I cannot look upon her and deny her.

Philatel. Nor need you, sir ;
All shall appear to her most gracious.
Tell her, the former part o' th' law must pass ;
But when it comes t' execute, promise her
That you intend to interpose.

Prince. And shall then Samorat live ?

Philatel. O, nothing less !
The censure pass'd,
His death shall follow without noise. 'Tis but
Not owning of the fact, disgracing for a time
A secretary or so—the thing's not new.
Put on forgiving looks, sir ; we are there.

[*The scene changes to Sabrina's chamber*

A mourning silence !
Sister Sabrina !——

Sabrina. Hence, hence, thou cruel hunter after life !
Thou art a pain unto my eyes, as great
As my dear mother had when she did bring
Thee forth ; and, sure, that was extreme, since she
Produc'd a monster.

Philatel. Speak to her yourself :
She's so incens'd against me,
She will not welcome happiness, because
I bring it.

Prince. Fair ornament of grief, why are you troubled ?
Can you believe there's anything within
My power which you shall mourn for ? if you have
Any fears, impart them ; any desires,
Give them a name, and I will give the rest.
You wrong the greatness of my love to doubt
The goodness of it.

Sabrina. Alas ! I do not doubt your love, my lord :

I fear it : 'tis that which does undo me.
For 'tis not Samorat that's prisoner now :
It is the Prince's rival.
O ! for your own sake, sir, be merciful.
How poorly will this sound hereafter,
'The Prince did fear another's merit so ;
Found so much virtue in his rival, that
He was forc'd to murder it, make it away ' !
There can be no addition to you, sir,
By his death : by his life there will ; you get the point
Of honour.
Fortune does offer here what time perchance
Cannot regain ; a handsome opportunity
To show the bravery of your mind.
Prince. This pretty rhetoric
Cannot persuade me, fair, to let your Samorat
Live for my sake : it is enough, he shall
For yours.
Sabrina. Though virtue still rewards itself, yet here
May it not stay for that ! but may the gods
Show'r on you suddenly such happiness,
That you may say, 'My mercy brought me this !'
Prince. The gods no doubt will hear when you do pray
Right ways ; but here you take their names in vain,
Since you can give yourself that happiness
Which you do ask of them.
Sabrina. Most gracious sir,
Do not——
Prince. Hold !
I dare not hear thee speak, for fear thou now
Shouldst tell me what I do tell myself ; that I
Would poorly bargain for thy favours.
Retire, and banish all any fears.
I will be kind and just to thee, Sabrina.
Whatsoe'er thou prov'st to me. [*Exit Sabrina*
Philatel. Rarely acted, sir !
Prince. Ha !
Philatel. Good faith, to th' very life.
Prince. Acted ! No, 'twas not acted.
Philatel. How, sir !
Prince. I was in earnest : I mean to conquer her
This way : the other's low and poor.
Philatel. Ha !

Prince. I told thee 'twould be so before.
Philatel. Why, sir,
You do not mean to save him ?
Prince. Yes, I do.
Samorat shall be released immediately.
Philatel. Sure, you forget I had a brother, sir ;
And one that did deserve justice at least.
Prince. He did ;
And he shall have it.
He that kill'd him shall die ;
And 'tis high satisfaction that. Look not :
It must be so. [*Exeunt*

Scene III

Enter Stramador *and* Peridor

Peridor. No devils, Stramador.
Believe your eyes, to which I cannot be
So lost, but you may call to mind one Peridor.
Stramador. Ha ! Peridor !
Thou didst command that day, in which
The Tamorens fell.
Peridor. I did ; yet Tamoren lives.
Stramador. Ha !
Peridor. Not Tamoren the prince (he fell indeed) ;
But Tamoren his brother, who that day
Led our horse.
Young Reginella too, which is the subject
Of the suit you have engag'd yourself by oath
The Prince shall grant.
Stramador. O, 'tis impossible !
Instruct me how I should believe thee.
Peridor. Why, thus :
Necessity upon that great defeat
Forc'd us to keep the woods, and hide ourselves
In holes, which since we much inlarg'd,
And fortifi'd them in the entrance so,
That 'twas a safe retreat upon pursuit.
Then swore we all allegiance to this Tamoren :
These habits, better to disguise ourselves, we took
At first ; but finding with what ease we robb'd,
We did continue 'em, and took an oath,
Till some new troubles in the state should happen,
Or fair occasion to make known ourselves

Offer itself, we would appear no other.
But come,
Let's not lose what we shall ne'er recover,
This opportunity. [*Exeunt*

SCENE IV

Enter NASSURAT *and* PELLEGRIN, *in prison*

Pellegrin. Nassurat,
You have not thought of any stratagem yet ?

Nassurat. Yes, I have thought.

Pellegrin. What ?

Nassurat. That if you have any accompts with heaven,
They may go on.
This villainous dying's like a strange tune, has run so in my head, no wholesome consideration would enter it. Nothing angers me neither, but that I pass my mistress's window to't.

Pellegrin. Troth, that's unkind! I have something troubles me too.

Nassurat. What's that ?

Pellegrin. The people will say, as we go along, thou art the properer fellow. Then I break an appointment with a merchant's wife ; but who can help it, Nassurat ?

Nassurat. Yea, who can help it indeed ? she's to blame, though, faith, if she does not bear with thee, considering the occasion——

Pellegrin. Considering the occasion, as you say, a man would think he might be borne with. There's a scrivener I should have paid some money to, upon my word ! but——

Enter ORSABRIN, SAMORAT, *and* Prince's Servants *with Samorat's releasement*

Orsabrin. By fair Sabrina's name,
I conjure you not to refuse the mercy
Of the Prince.

Samorat. It is resolv'd, sir. You know my answer.

Orsabrin. Whither am I fallen !
I think, if I should live a little longer,
I should be made the cause of all the mischief
Which should arise to the world. Hither I came
To save a friend, and, by a slight of fortune,
I destroy him. My very ways to good

Prove ills.
Sure, I can look a man into misfortune!
The plague's so great within me, 'tis infectious.
O, I am weary of myself.
Sir, I beseech you, yet accept of it;
For I shall be this way a sufferer
And an executioner too.

Samorat. I beg of thee, no more;
Thou dost beget in me desire to live:
For, when I find how much I am behind
In noble acts of friendship,
I cannot choose but wish for longer time,
That I might struggle with thee for what thou hast
Too clearly now got from me, the point of honour.
O, it is wisdom and great thrift to die!
For who with such a debt of friendship and
Of love, as you and my Sabrina must
Expect from me, could e'er subsist?

Nassurat. They are complimenting; 'sfoot, they make no more of it than if 'twere who should go in first at a door. I think, Pellegrin, as you and I have cast it up, it comes to something more.

Enter Messenger

Messenger. Gentlemen, prepare: the court is sitting.

Samorat. Friends,
This is no time for ceremony; but what
A rack have I within me to see you suffer!
And yet I hope the Prince will let his anger
Die in me, not to take the forfeiture of you.

Nassurat. If he should, Pellegrin and I are resolved, and are ready—all but our speeches to the people; and those will not trouble us much, for we intend not to trouble them. [*Exeunt*

Scene V

Enter Prince, Philatel, *and* Attendants

Prince. Not accept it! Lose this way too!—
What shall I do? he makes advantages
Of mine; and, like a skilful tennis-player,
Returns my very best with excellent design.
It must not be. Bring to the closet here above
The chief o' th' jury: I'll try another way.

[*Exeunt to the gallery above*

Enter Judges, Lawyers, SAMORAT, ORSABRIN, NASSURAT, *and* PELLEGRIN

Nassurat. Of all ways of destroying mankind, the judges have the easiest : they sleep and do it.

Pellegrin. To my thinking now, this is but a solemner kind of puppet-play. How the devil came we to be actors in't ?
So, it begins.

1st Judge. The Prince's counsel, are they ready ?

Lawyer. Here.

Judge. Begin then.

Lawyer. My lords, that this so great and strange——

Samorat. Most reverend judges,
To save th' expense of breath and time, and dull
Formalities of law, I here pronounce myself
Guilty.

[*A curtain drawn : Prince, Philatel, with others, appear above*

Prince. Again he has prevented me !

Samorat. So guilty, that no other can pretend
A share.
This noble youth, a stranger to everything
But gallantry, ignorant in our laws and customs,
Has made perchance in strange severity
A forfeit of himself ; but, should you take it,
The gods, when he is gone, will sure revenge it.
If from the stalk you pull this bud of virtue,
Before't has spread and shown itself abroad,
You do an injury to all mankind ;
And public mischief cannot be private justice.
This man's as much above a common man,
As man's above a beast : and, if the law
Destroys not man for killing of a beast,
It should not here for killing of a man.
O, what mistake 'twould be !
For here you sit to weed the cankers out,
That would do hurt i' th' state, to punish vice ;
And under that you'd root out virtue too.

Orsabrin. If I do blush, 'tis not (most gracious judges)
For anything which I have done ; 'tis for that
This much-mistaken youth hath here deliver'd.
'Tis true (and I confess) I ever had
A little stock of honour, which I still preserv'd :

But that (by leaving me behind alive)
He now most cunningly does think to get from me;
And I beseech your lordships to assist me,
For 'tis most fraudulent all he desires.
Your laws, I hope, are reasonable, else why
Should reasonable men be subject to them?
And then
Upon what grounds is he made guilty now?
How can he be thought accessory
To the killing of a man, that did not know
O' th' fighting with him? Witness all
Those pow'rs which search men's hearts, that I myself,
Until he beckon'd me, knew nothing of it.
If such a thing as sacrifice must be,
Why, man for man's enough; though elder times,
T'appease diviner justice, did offer up
(Whether through gallantry or ignorance)
Vast multitudes of beasts in sacrifice,
Yet numbers of men is seldom heard of.
One single Curtius purg'd a whole state's sin.
You will not say th' offence is now as great;
Or that you ought to be more highly satisfied
Than heaven.

Prince. Brave youths!

Nassurat. Pellegrin, you and I will let our speeches alone.

1st Judge. If that the law were of so fine a web,
As wit and fancy spin it out to here,
Then these defences would be just, and save:
But that is more substantial,
Of another make; and, gentlemen,
If this be all, sentence must pass.

Enter Tamoren *and* Stramador

Tamoren. Orsabrin!

Orsabrin. Ha! who names me there?

Tamoren. A friend. Hear me. I am an officer
In that dark world from whence thou cam'st, sent thus
Disguised by Reginella, our fair queen,
And to redeem thee.

Orsabrin. Reginella! in the midst of all these ills,
How preciously that name does sound!

Tamoren. If thou wilt swear to follow me,
At the instant thou'rt releas'd,
I'll save thee and thy friends in spite of law. [*Aside*

Orsabrin. Doubt not of that.
Bring me where Reginella is, and if
I follow not, perpetual misery follow me!
It cannot be a hell where she appears. [*Aside*

Tamoren. Be confident!

[*He goes out, and returns, bringing* Torcular.

Behold, grave lords, the man
Whose death questioned the life of these,
Found and recover'd by the thieves i' th' woods,
And rescued since by us, to rescue innocence.

Orsabrin. Rare devil!
With what dexterity h'as raised this shape
Up to delude them!

Prince. Ha! Torcular alive!

Philatel. Torcular!
I should as soon believe my brother ne'er
In being, too!

Torcular. You cannot wonder more to find me here,
Than I do to find myself.

Nassurat. Come, unbind, unbind! this matter's answered.

2nd Judge. Hold!
They are not free: the law exacts the same
For breach of prison, that it did before.

Orsabrin. There is no 'scaping out of Fortune's hands.
Dost hear! hast never a trick for this?

Tamoren. Doubt me not; I have without at my command,
Those which never fail'd me;
And it shall cost many a life yet, sir,
Ere yours be lost.

Enter Prince, Philatel, *from above*

Stramador, Peridor, Reginella, *meet them below*

Prince. Stramador,
You have been a stranger here of late.

Stramador. Peruse
This paper, sir: you'll find there was good reason for't.

Prince. How!
Old Tamoren's brother, captain of the thieves,
That have infested thus our country!
Reginella, too, the heir of that fear'd family!
A happy and a strange discovery!

Tamoren. Peridor and Reginella!
The villain has betray'd me.

Reginella. 'Tis Orsabrin :
They have kept their words.
Orsabrin. Reginella !
She was a woman, then. O, let me go !
Gaoler. You do forget, sure, what you are.
Orsabrin. I do indeed : O, to unriddle now !
Stramador. And to this man you owe it, sir :
You find an engagement to him there ;
And I must hope you'll make me just to him.
Prince. He does deserve it ; seize on him.
Tamoren. Nay, then, all truths must out.
That I am lost, and forfeit to the law,
I do confess ; yet, since to save this prince——
Prince. Prince !
Orsabrin. Our Mephostophilus is mad.
Tamoren. Yes, Prince,
This is the Orsabrin.
Orsabrin. Ha !
Tamoren. So long ago supposed lost—your brother, sir.
Fetch in there Ardellan and Piramont.

Enter ARDELLAN *and* PIRAMONT

Nassurat. What mad planet rules this day !
Ardellan and Piramont !
Orsabrin. The devil's wanton,
And abuses all mankind to-day.
Tamoren. These faces are well known to all Francelians !
Now let them tell the rest.
Piramont. My noble master living ! found in Francelia !
Ardellan. The gods have satisfied our tedious hopes.
Philatel. Some imposture !
Orsabrin. A new design of Fortune :
I dare not trust it.
Tamoren. Why speak you not ?
Piramont. I am so full of joy, it will not out.
Know, ye Francelians,
When Sanborne, fatal field, was fought,
So desperate were the hopes of Orsabrin,
That 'twas thought fit to send away this prince,
And give him safety in another clime ;
That, spite of an ill day, an Orsabrin
Might be preserv'd alive. Thus you all know.
To Garradan's chief charge he was committed ;

Who, when our bark by pirates was surpris'd
(For so it was), was slain i' th' first encounter :
Since that,
We have been forc'd to wait on Fortune's pleasure.
And, sir,
That all this time we kept you from the knowledge
Of yourself, your pardon. It was our zeal that err'd,
Which did conclude it would be prejudicial.
Ardellan. My lords, you look as if you doubted still.
If Piramont and I be lost unto
Your memory, your hands, I hope, are not.
Here's our commission : there's the diamond elephant,
That, which our prince's sons are ever known by,
Which we, to keep him undiscovered,
Tore from his riband in that fatal day
When we were made prisoners.
And here are those that took us, who can witness
All circumstances, both how and when, time and place ;
With whom we ever since have liv'd by force :
For on no kingdom, friend unto Francelia,
Did fortune ever land us, since that hour,
Nor gave us means to let our country know
He liv'd.
Tamoren. These very truths,
When they could have no ends (for they believ'd
Him lost), I did receive from them before ;
Which gave me now the boldness to appear
Here, where I'm lost by law.

Shouts within. { *Long live Prince Orsabrin !*
Long live Prince Orsabrin !

Nassurat. Pellegrin, let's second this : right or wrong, 'tis best for us.
Pellegrin. Observe, observe !
Prince. What shouts are those ?
Stramador. Soldiers of Tamoren's,
The first : the second was the people's, who
Much press to see their long-lost prince.
Philatel. Sir, 'tis most evident, and all agrees.
This was his colour'd hair,
His hair, though altered much with time.
You wear too strange a face upon this news.
Sir, you have found a brother :
I, Torcular : the kingdom, happiness ;

For here the plague of robberies will end.
It is a glorious day.
Prince. It is indeed! I am amaz'd, not sad;
Wonder does keep the passage so, nothing will out.
Brother (for so my kinder stars will have it),
I here receive you as the bounty of
The gods—a blessing I did not expect.
And, in return to them, this day Francelia
Ever shall keep holy.
Orsabrin. Fortune, by much abusing me, has so
Dulled my faith, I cannot credit anything.
I know not how to own such happiness.
Prince. Let not your doubts lessen your joys:
If you have had disasters heretofore,
They were but given to heighten what's to come.
Nassurat. Here's as strange a turn, as if 'twere the fifth act in a play!
Pellegrin. I'm sure 'tis a good turn for us.
Orsabrin. Sir,
Why stands that lady so neglected there,
That does deserve to be the business
Of mankind? O ye gods, since you'll be kind
And bountiful, let it be here.
As fearfully as jealous husbands ask
After some secrets, which they dare not know;
Or as forbidden lovers meet i' th' night,
Come I to thee (and 'tis no ill sign this;
Since flames, when they burn highest, tremble most),
O, should she now deny me!
Reginella. I know not perfectly what all this means;
But I do find some happiness is near,
And I am pleas'd, because I see you are.
Orsabrin. She understands me not!—
Prince. He seems t' have passion for her.
Tamoren. Sir, in my dark commands these flames broke out
Equally violent, at first sight; and 'twas
The hope I had to reconcile myself.
Orsabrin. It is a holy magic, that will make
Of you and I but one.
Reginella. Anything that you would ask me, sure I might grant.
Orsabrin. Hark, gentlemen, she does consent:
What wants there else?

Peridor. My hopes grow cold ; I have undone myself. [*Aside*

Prince. Nothing :
We all join in this : the long-liv'd feud
Between the families here dies. This day
The hymenæal torches shall burn bright,—
So bright, that they shall dim the light of all
That went before. See, Sabrina too !

Enter SABRINA

Tamoren. Sir, I must have much of pardon,
Not for myself alone, but for all mine.

Prince. Rise ! hadst thou not deserv'd what now thou su'st for,
This day should know no clouds.

[*Peridor kneels to Tamoren*

Tamoren. Taught by the Prince's mercy, I forgive too.

Sabrina. Frighted hither, sir ! [*To Samorat*
They told me you would not accept the Prince's mercy.

Samorat. Art thou not further yet in thy intelligence ?
See, thy brother lives !

Sabrina. My brother !

Torcular. And 'tis the least of wonders has fall'n out.

Orsabrin. Yes, such a one as you are, fair ; [*To Reginella, who looks at Sabrina*] and you
Shall be acquainted.

Samorat. [*To Philatel and Torcular*] O, could your hate, my lords, now ;
Or [*to the Prince*] your love die !

Philatel. Thy merit has prevail'd
With me.

Torcular. And me.

Prince. And has almost with me.
Samorat,
Thou dost not doubt thy mistress' constancy ?

Samorat. No, sir.

Prince. Then I will beg of her,
That, till the sun returns to visit us,
She will not give away herself for ever. Although
My hopes are faint, yet I would have 'em hopes ;
And, in such jolly hours as now attend us,
I would not be a desperate thing, one made
Up wholly of despair.

Sabrina. You, that so freely gave me Samorat's life,
Which was in danger, most justly, justly, may
Be suffer'd to attempt upon my love,
Which is in none.

Prince. What says my noble rival ?

Samorat. Sir,
Y'are kind in this, and wisely do provide
I should not surfeit ; for here is happiness
Enough besides, to last the sun's return.

Nassurat. You and I are but savers with all this, Pellegrin : but, by the Lord, 'tis well we came off as we did : all was at stake.

Prince. Come, no more whispers here :
Let's in, and there unriddle to each other ;
For I have much to ask.

Orsabrin. A life ! a friend ! a brother ! and a mistress !

O, what a day was here ! Gently, my joys, distil,
Lest you should break the vessel you should fill.

EPILOGUE

AND how, and how, in faith—a pretty plot;
And smartly carried through too, was it not?
And the devils, how? well; and the fighting?
Well too;—— a fool, and't had been just old writing.
O, what a monster-wit must that man have,
That could please all which now their twelvepence gave!
High characters (cries one); and he would see
Things that ne'er were, nor are, nor ne'er will be.
Romances, cries easy souls; and then they swear
The play's well writ, though scarce a good line's there.
The women—O, if Stephen should be kill'd,
Or miss the lady, how the plot is spill'd!
And into how many pieces a poor play
Is taken still before the second day,
Like a strange beauty newly come to court!
And, to say truth, good faith, 'tis all the sport.
One will like all the ill things in a play,
Another some o' th' good, but the wrong way;
So that from one poor play there comes t'arise
At several tables several comedies.
The ill is only here, that 't may fall out
In plays as faces; and who goes about
To take asunder, oft destroys (we know)
What altogether made a pretty show.

BRENNORALT.

A Tragedy.

Preſented at the Private Houſe in Black-Fryers, by His *Majeſties* ſervants.

WRITTEN

By Sir JOHN SUCKLING.

LONDON,
Printed for *Humphrey Moſeley*, and are to be ſold at his ſhop, at the Signe of the Princes Armes in St *Pauls* Churchyard.
MDCXLVI.

Dramatis Personæ

SIGISMOND, King of Poland.

MIESTA, MELIDOR, A Lord, } councillors to the King.

BRENNORALT, a discontent.

DORAN, his friend.

VILLANOR, GRAINEVERT, MARINEL, } cavaliers and officers under Brennoralt.

STRATHEMAN.

FRESOLIN, brother to Francelia.

IPHIGENE, young Palatine of Plocence.

PALATINE OF MENSECK, Governor, one of the chief rebels.

PALATINE OF TROCK, a rebel.

ALMERIN, a gallant rebel.

MORAT, his lieutenant-colonel.

FRANCELIA, the Governor's daughter.

ORILLA, a waiting-woman to Francelia.

RAGUELIN, a servant in the Governor's house, but spy to Brennoralt.

Gaoler. Guard. Soldiers.

THE SCENE, POLAND.

BRENNORALT

ACT I

Scene I

Enter Brennoralt *and* Doran

Bren. I say, the Court is but a narrow circuit,
Though something elevate above the common ;
A kind of ants' nest in the great wild field,
O'ercharg'd with multitudes of quick inhabitants
Who still
Are miserably busied to get in
What the loose foot of prodigality
As fast does throw abroad.

Dor. Good !
A most eternal place of low affronts,
And then as low submissions.

Bren. Right.
High cowards in revenges 'mongst themselves,
And only valiant when they mischief others.

Dor. Stars that would have no names,
But for the ills they threaten in conjunction.

Bren. A race of shallow and unskilful pilots,
Which do misguide the ship even in the calm,
And in great storms serve but as weight to sink it.
More, prithee, more: [*alarum within*] 'tis music to my melancholy.

Enter Soldier

Sol. My lord,
A cloud of dust and men the sentinels from
The east gate discover ; and, as they guess, the storm
Bends this way.

Bren. Let it be.

Sol. My lord ?

Bren. Let it be.
I will not fight to-day : bid Stratheman
Draw to the trenches. On, prithee, on ! on !

Dor. The king
Employs a company of formal beards,
Men who have no other proofs of their long lives
But that they are old.
Bren. Right;
And, if they are wise, 'tis for themselves, not others,
As old men ever are. [*Alarum*

Enter another Soldier

2nd Sol. Coronel, Coronel,
The enemy's at hand, kills all the sentries.
Young Almerin leads them on again.
Bren. Let him lead them off again.
2nd Sol. Coronel?
Bren. Be gone! If th' art afraid, go hide thyself.
2nd Sol. What a devil ails he? [*Exit*
Bren. This Almerin's the ague of the camp:
He shakes it once a day.
Dor. He's the ill conscience rather;
He never lets it rest. Would I were at home again!
'Sfoot, we lie here i' th' trenches, as if it were
For a wind to carry us into th' other world.
Every hour we expect—I'll no more on't!
Bren. Prithee!
Dor. Not I, by heaven!
Bren. What, man! the worst is but fair death.
Dor. And what will that amount to? a fair epitaph,
A fine account! I'll home, I swear.

Enter STRATHEMAN

Str. Arm, arm, my lord, and show yourself! all's lost else.
Dor. Why so?
Str. The rebels, like an unruly flood,
Roll o'er the trenches, and throw down all before them.
Bren. Ha!
Str. We cannot make a stand.
Bren. He would outrival me in honour too,
As well as love; but that he must not do.
Help me, Stratheman. [*Puts on armour*
The danger now grows worthy of our swords;
And, O Doran, I would to heaven there were
No other storms than the worst tempest here! [*Exeunt*

SCENE II

Enter MARINEL, *throwing down one he carries*

Mar. There !
The sun's the neatest surgeon I know, and th' honestest.
If thou recoverest, why, so : if not, the cure's paid—they have maul'd us.

Enter GRAINEVERT, *with another upon his back*

Gra. A curse light on this powder ! It stays valour, ere it's half-way on its journey. What a disadvantage fight we upon in this age ! He that did well heretofore had the broad fair day to show it in, witnesses enough. We must believe one another : 'tis night, when we begin. Eternal smoke and sulphur smalky—by this hand, I can bear with thee no longer ! How now ? dead, as I live ! Stol'n away just as he us'd to wench. Well, go thy ways : for a quiet drinker and dier, I shall never know thy fellow. [*Searches his pockets*] These trifles, too, about thee ? There was never an honester poor wretch born, I think. Look i' th' t'other pocket, too—hum ! Marinel ?

Mar. Who's that ?

Gra. 'Tis I : how goes matters ?

Mar. Scurvily enough ;
Yet, since our Colonel came, th'ave got no ground
Of us—a weak sculler against wind and tide
Would have done as much. Hark !
This way the torrent bears. [*Exeunt*

Enter FRESOLIN, ALMERIN, *and* Rebels

Fre. The villains all have left us.

Alm. Would they had left
Their fears behind them ! but come, since we must——

Enter BRENNORALT, DORAN, STRATHEMAN, *with* Soldiers

Bren. Ho !
Stratheman, skirt on the left hand with the horse,
And get betwixt these and that body : they're
New rallied up for rescue. [*Brennoralt charges through*

Dor. Th'are ours.
I do not see my game yet. [*Exeunt*

A shout within. *Re-enter* BRENNORALT, STRATHEMAN, MARINEL

Bren. What shout is that?
Str. They have taken Almerin, my lord.
Bren. Almerin? the devil thank 'em for't!
When I had hunted hard all day, and now
At length unherded the proud deer, the curs
Have snatch'd him up.
Sound a retreat: there's nothing now behind.
Who saw Doran?
Str. Shall we bring Almerin in?
Bren. No; gazing is low triumph;
Convey him fairly to the king; he fought
It fairly.

Re-enter DORAN

Dor. What youth was that whom you bestrid, my lord,
And sav'd from all our swords to-day? Was he
Not of the enemy?
Bren. It may be so.
Str. The governor's son, Fresolin, his mistress' brother.
[*In Doran's ear*
Bren. No matter who. 'Tis pity the rough hand
Of war should early courages destroy,
Before they bud, and show themselves i' th' heat
Of action.
Mar. I threw, my lord, a youth upon a bank,
Which seeking, after the retreat, I found
Dead, and a woman—the pretty daughter of
The forester, Lucilia.
Bren. See, see, Doran, a sad experiment!
Woman's the cowardli'st and coldest thing
The world brings forth: yet love, as fire works water,
Makes it boil o'er, and do things contrary
To 'ts proper nature. I should shed a tear,
Could I tell how! Ah, poor Lucilia!
Thou didst for me what did as ill become thee.
Pray, see her gently bury'd.
Boy, send the surgeon to the tent—I bleed.
What lousy cottages th'ave given our souls!
Each petty storm shakes them into disorder;
And't costs more pains to patch them up again,
Than they are worth by much. I'm weary of
The tenement. [*Exeunt*

Scene III

Enter Villanor, Grainevert, Marinel, *and* Stratheman

Gra. Villanor! welcome, welcome, whence camest thou?
Vil. Look,
I wear the king's highway still on my boots.
Gra. A pretty riding phrase—and how, and how?
Ladies cheap?
Vil. Faith, reasonable; those toys were never dear,
Thou know'st: a little time and industry
They'll cost, but, in good faith, not much: some few
There are, that set themselves at mighty rates.
Gra. Which we o' th' wise pass by, as things o'ervalued
In the market. Is't not so?
Vil. Y'have said, sir. Hark you,
Your friend and rival's married, has obtained
The long-lov'd lady, and is such an ass after't.
Gra. Hum! 'tis ever so. The motions of married people are as of other naturals—violent gentlemen to the place, and calm in it.
Mar. We know this too, and yet we must be fooling.
Gra. Faith, women are the baggage of life: they are troublesome,
And hinder us in the great march; and yet
We cannot be without 'em.
Mar. You speak very well
And soldier-like.
Gra. What?
Thou art a wit too, I warrant, in our absence?
Vil. Hum! No, no, a poor pretender,
A candidate or so,—'gainst the next Sessions—
Wit enough to laugh at you here.
Gra. Like enough;
Valour's a crime the wise have still reproached
Unto the valiant, and the fools too.
Vil. *Raillerie à part*, Grainevert, what accommodation shall we find here?
Gra. Clean straw, sweetheart, and meat—when thou canst get it.
Vil. Hum! straw?
Gra. Yes, that's all will be betwixt incest;
You and your mother Earth must lie together.
Vil. Prithee, let us be serious; will this last?

How goes affairs ?

Gra. Well.

Vil. But well ?

Gra. Faith,
'Tis now upon the turning of the balance ;
A most equal business
Betwixt rebellion and loyalty.

Vil. What dost mean ?

Gra. Why ! which shall be the virtue, and which the vice.

Vil. How the devil can that be ?

Gra. O, success is a rare paint, hides all the ugliness.

Vil. Prithee, what's the quarrel ?

Gra. Nay, for that excuse us. Ask the children of peace ; they have the leisure to study it ; we know nothing of it : liberty, they say.

Vil. 'Sfoot, let the king make an act that any man may be unmarried again : there's liberty for them ! a race of half-witted fellows quarrel about freedom, and all that while allow the bonds of matrimony !

Gra. You speak very well, sir.

Enter KING, Lords, BRENNORALT

Mar. Soft, the king and council.

Gra. Look, they follow after, like tired spaniels quest sometimes for company, that is, concur ; and that's their business.

Mar. They are as weary of this sport as a young unthrift of's land ; any bargain to be rid on't. Can you blame them ? Who's that ?

Gra. Brennoralt, our brave Coronel : a discontent, but what of that ? who is not ?

Vil. His face speaks him one.

Gra. Thou art i' th' right : he looks still as if he were saying to Fortune, 'Huswife, go about your business !' Come, let's retire to Barathen's tent. Taste a bottle, and speak bold truths ; that's our way now.

[*Exeunt. Manent King and Lords*

Miesta. Think not of pardon, sir ;
Rigour and mercy us'd in states uncertainly,
And in ill times, look not like th' effects
Of virtue, but necessity. Nor will
They thank your goodness, but your fears.

Mel. My lords,
Revenge in princes should be still imperfect :

It is then handsom'st, when the king comes to
Reduce, not ruin.
Bren. Who puts but on the face of punishing,
And only gently cuts, but prunes rebellion :
He makes that flourish which he would destroy.
Who would not be a rebel, when the hopes
Are vast, the fears but small ?
Mel. Why, I would not,
Nor you, my lord, nor you, nor any here.
Fear keeps low spirits only in ; the brave
Do get above it when they do resolve.
Such punishments, in infancy of war,
Make men more desperate, not the more yielding.
The common people are a kind of flies :
They're caught with honey, not with wormwood, sir.
Severity exasp'rates the stirr'd humour ;
And state-distempers turns into diseases.
Bren. The gods forbid great Poland's state should be
Such as it dares not take right physic ! Quarter
To rebels ? Sir, when you give that to them,
Give that to me which they deserve. I would
Not live to see it.
3rd Lord. Turn o'er your own and others chronicles,
And you shall find, great sir,
'That nothing makes a civil war long-liv'd,
But ransom and returning back the brands,
Which unextinct kindled still fiercer fires.'
Mi. Mercy, bestow'd on those that do dispute
With swords, does lose the angel's face it has,
And is not mercy, sir, but policy
With a weak vizard on.
King. Y'have met my thoughts,
My lords ; nor will it need larger debate.
To-morrow, in the sight of the besieg'd,
The rebel dies. Miesta, 'tis your care.
The mercy of heav'n may be offended so,
That it cannot forgive : mortals' much more,
Which is not infinite, my lords. [*Exeunt*

Scene IV

Enter Iphigene, Almerin, *as in prison*

Iph. O Almerin ! would we had never known
The ruffle of the world ! but were again

By Stolden banks in happy solitude ;
When thou and I, shepherd and shepherdess
So oft by turns, as often still have wish'd,
That we as eas'ly could have chang'd our sex,
As clothes. But, alas ! all those innocent joys,
Like glorious mornings, are retir'd into
Dark sullen clouds, before we knew to value
What we had.

Alm. [*to himself*]. Fame and victory are light
Huswifes, that throw themselves into the arms,
Not of the valiant, but the foıtunate.
To be ta'en thus !

Iph. Almerin !

Alm. Nipp'd i' th' bud
Of honour !

Iph. My lord !

Alm. Foil'd ! and by the man
That does pretend unto Francelia !

Iph. What is't you do, my Almerin ? sit still,
And quarrel with the winds, because there is
A shipwreck, tow'rds, and never think of saving
The bark ?

Alm. The bark ? What should we do with that,
When the rich freight is lost, my name in arms ?

Iph. Who knows
What prizes are behind, if you attend
And wait a second voyage ?

Alm. Never, never !
There are no second voyages in this ;
The wounds of honour do admit no cure.

Iph. Those slight ones which misfortune gives must needs,
Else why should mortals value it at all ?
For who would toil to treasure up a wealth,
Which weak inconstancy did keep, or might
Dispose of ?

Enter Melidor

Iph. Oh, my lord, what news ?

Mel. As ill
As your own fears could give you :
The council has decreed him sudden death ;
And all the ways to mercy are block'd up.

[*She weeps and sighs*

Alm. My Iphigene !

This was a misbecoming piece of love :
Women would manage a disaster better.
[*Iphigene weeps and sighs again*
Again ? thou art unkind !
Thy goodness is so great it makes thee faulty :
For, while thou think'st to take the trouble from me,
Thou givest me more by giving me thine too.
Iph. Alas ! I am indeed an useless trifle,
A dull, dull thing ; for, could I now do anything
But grieve and pity, I might help. My thoughts
Labour to find a way ; but, like to birds
In cages, though they never rest, they aıe
But where they did set out at first.

Enter GAOLER

Gao. My lords, your pardon. The prisoner must retire.
I have receiv'd an order from the king
Denies access to any.
Iph. He cannot be
So great a tyrant.
Alm. I thank him ; nor can
He use me ill enough. I only grieve
That I must die in debt—a bankrupt ! Such
Thy love hath made me : my dear Iphigene,
Farewell. It is no time for ceremony.
Show me the way I must. [*Exit Almerin and Gaoler*
Iph. Grief strove with such disorder to get out,
It stopp'd the passage, and sent back my words
That were already on the place.
Mel. Stay, there
Is yet a way.
Iph. Oh, speak it !
Mel. But there is
Danger in't, Iphigene—to thee high danger.
Iph. Fright children in the dark with that, and let
Me know it. There is no such thing in nature,
If Almerin be lost.
Mel. Thus then : you must
Be taken pris'ner too, and by exchange
Save Almerin. [*Aside*
Iph. How can that be ? [*Aside*
Mel. Why—— [*He studies, then calls to the Gaoler*]
Step in,

Re-enter GAOLER

And pray him set his hand, about
This distance ; his seal, too—— [*Shows him a writing*
Gao. If't be no more——
Mel. Tell him that Iphigene and I desire it. [*Exit Gaoler*
I'll send by Strathocles his servant
A letter to Morat thus sign'd and seal'd,
That shall inform the sudden execution ;
Command him, as the only means
To save his life, to sally out this night
Upon his quarters, and endeavour prisoners.
Name you as most secure and slightest guarded,
Best pledge of safety ; but charge him that he kill
Not any, if it be avoidable ;
Lest 't should enrage the king yet more, and make
His death more certain.

Re-enter GAOLER *with the writing*

Gao. He understands you not, he says, but he
Has sent it.
Mel. So.
Iph. But should Morat mistrust now, or this miscarry ?
Mel. Come,
Leave it to me : I'll take the pilot's part,
And reach the port, or perish in the art. [*Exeunt*

ACT II

SCENE I

Enter ALMERIN, *in prison*

Alm. Sleep is as nice as woman : the more I court it,
The more it flies me. Thy elder brother will
Be kinder yet : unsent-for death will come.
To-morrow ! well, what can to-morrow do ?
'Twill cure the sense
Of honour lost : I and my discontents
Shall rest together. What hurt is there in this ?
But death against the will
Is but a slovenly kind of potion ;
And, though prescrib'd by heaven, it goes against
Men's stomachs.

So does it at fourscore too, when the soul's mew'd up
In narrow darkness, neither sees nor hears.
Pish, 'tis mere fondness in our nature,
A certain clownish cowardice, that still
Would stay at home, and dares not venture into
Foreign countries, though better than its own!
Ha, what countries? for we receive descriptions
Of th' other world from our divines, as blind
Men take relation of this from us.
My thoughts lead me into the dark, and there
They'll leave me. I'll no more on't. Within! [*Knocks*

Enter GUARD

Alm. Some paper and a light! I'll write to th' king,
Defy him, and provoke a quick despatch.
I would not hold this ling'ring doubtful state
So long again, for all that hope can give.

Enter three of the GUARD *with paper and ink*

That sword does tempt me strangely: [*Writing*
Were't in my hands, 'twere worth th' other two.
But then the guard? it sleeps or drinks; maybe
To contrive it so that, if I should not pass,—
Why, if I fall in't, 'tis better yet than pageantry,
A scaffold and spectators; more soldier-like—
[*One of the Guard peeps over his shoulder*
Uncivil villain, read my letter! [*Seizes his sword*
1st Guard. Not I, not I, my lord.
Alm. Deny it too?
Guard. Murder, murder!
Guard. Arm, arm! [*Guard run out*
Alm. I'll follow, give the alarm with them.
'Tis least suspicious. Arm, arm, arm! [*Exit*

Enter SOLDIERS, *running over the stage, one throwing away his arms*

All. The enemy, the enemy!
Sol. Let them come, let them come, let them come!

Re-enter ALMERIN

Alm. I hear fresh noise: the camp's in great disorder.
Where am I now? 'tis strangely dark.
Goddess without eyes,
Be thou my guide, for blindness and sight
Are equal sense, of equal use, this night. [*Exit*

SCENE II

Enter GRAINEVERT, STRATHEMAN, VILLANOR, MARINEL

Gra. Trouble not thyself, child of discontent :
'Twill take no hurt, I warrant thee ; the State
Is but a little drunk, and when it has spew'd
Up that, that made it so, it will be well
Again—there's my opinion in short.
Mar. Th' art i' th' right. The State's a pretty fore-handed State,
And will do reason hereafter. Let's drink,
And talk no more on't.
All. A good motion, a good motion ! let's drink.
Vil. Ay, ay, let's drink again.
Str. Come, to a mistress !
Gra. Agreed. Name, name !
Vil. Anybody. Vermilia !
Gra. Away with it.

She's pretty to walk with,
And witty to talk with,
And pleasant too to think on :
But the best use of all
Is, her health is a stale,
And helps us to make us drink on.

Str. Excellent. Gentlemen, if you say the word,
We'll vaunt credit, and affect high pleasure ; shall we ?
Vil. Ay, ay, let's do that.
Str. What think ye of the sacrifice now ?
Mar. Come, we'll ha't ; for trickling tears are vain.
Vil. The sacrifice ? what's that ?
Str. Child of ignorance, 'tis a camp-health,
An *à-la-mode* one. Grainevert, begin it.
Gra. Come, give it me.
Let me see which of them this rose will serve.
[*Pins up a rose.*
Hum, hum, hum !

Bright star o' th' lower orb, twinkling inviter,
Which draw'st as well as eyes, but sett'st men righter :
For who at thee begins, comes to the place
Sooner than he that sets out at the face :
Eyes are seducing lights, that the good women know,
And hang out these a nearer way to show.

Mar. Fine and pathetical! Come, Villanor.
Vil. What's the matter?
Mar. Come, your liquor and your stanzas!
Lines, lines!
Vil. Of what?
Mar. Why,
Of anything your mistress has given you.
Vil. Gentlemen,
She never gave me anything but a box
O' th' ear for offering to kiss her once.
Str. Of that box then.
Mar. Ay, ay, that box, of that box!
Vil. Since it must be, give me the poison then.
[*Drinks and spits*

That box, fair mistress, which thou gavest to me,
In human guess is like to cost me three,
Three cups of wine and verses six:
The wine will down; but verse for rhyme still sticks:
By which you all may easily, gentles, know,
I am a better drinker than a Po——

Enter DORAN

Mar. Doran! Doran!
Gra. *A hall, a hall*
To welcome our friend!
For some liquor call;
A new or fresh face
Must not alter our pace,
But make us still drink the quicker:
Wine, wine! O 'tis divine!
Come, fill it unto our brother:
What's at the tongue's end,
It forth does send,
And will not a syllable smother.
Then
It unlocks the breast,
And throws out the rest,
And learns us to know each other.
Wine! wine!

Dor. Mad lads, have you been here ever since?
Str. Yes, faith: thou seest the worst of us. We debauch
In discipline. Four-and-twenty hours is

The time : Baruthen had the watch to-night ;
To-morrow 'twill be at my tent.
Dor. Good ! and d'you know what has fall'n out to-night ?
Str. Yes, Grainevert and my lieutenant-coronel ;
But they are friends again.
Dor. Pish, pish ! The young Palatine of Plocence
And his grave guardian—surpris'd to-night,
Carry'd by the enemy out of his quarters.
Gra. As a chicken by a kite out of a back-side,
Was't not so ?
Dor. Is that all ?
Gra. Yes.
My coronel did not love him : he eats sweetmeats
Upon a march too.
Dor. Well—hark ye, worse yet !
Almerin's gone ! forced the court of guard
Where he was a prisoner, and has made an escape !
Gra. So pale and spiritless a wretch
Drew Priam's curtain in the dead of night,
And told him half his Troy was burnt.
He was of my mind : I would have done so myself.
Dor. Well,
There is high suspicions abroad : ye shall
See strange discoveries i' the council of war.
Gra. What council ?
Dor. One called this morning. Y'are all sent to.
Gra. I will put on clean linen, and speak wisely.
Vil. 'Sfoot, we'll have a round first.
Gra. By all means, sir.

Sings

Come, let the State stay,
And drink away ;
There is no business above it :
It warms the cold brain,
Makes us speak in high strain ;
He's a fool that does not approve it.
The Macedon youth
Left behind him this truth,
That nothing is done with much thinking :
He drank and he fought,
Till he had what he sought ;
The world was his own by good drinking. [*Exeunt*

SCENE III

Enter GENERAL OF THE REBELS, PALATINES OF TROCK AND MENSECK, FRANCELIA, ALMERIN, IPHIGENE

Gen. As your friend,
My lord, he has the privilege of ours,
And may enjoy a liberty we would
Deny to enemies.
Alm. I thank your excellence. O Iphigene,
He does not know
That thou the nobler part of friendship hold'st,
And dost oblige, while I can but acknowledge.
Men. Opportunity to statesmen
Is as the just degree of heat to chymists ;
It perfects all the work : and in this pris'ner
'Tis offered. We now are there, where men
Should still begin. To treat upon advantage,
The Palatine of Trock, and Menseck, with Almerin,
Shall to the king :
Petitions shall be drawn, humble in form,
But such for matter
As the bold Macedonian youth would send
To men he did despise for luxury.
The first begets opinion of the world,
Which looks not far, but on the outside dwells :
Th' other enforces courage in our own ;
For bold demands must boldly be maintained.
Trock. Let all go on still in the public name,
But keep an ear open to particular offers.
Liberty and public good are like great olios—
Must have the upper end still of our tables,
Though they are but for show.
Fran. Would I had ne'er seen this shape ! 't has poison in't.
Yet where dwells good, if ill inhabits there ?
Mens. Press much religion ;
For, though we dress the scruples for the multitude,
And for ourselves reserve th' advantages
(It being much pretext), yet it is necessary ;
For things of faith are so abstruse and nice,
They will admit dispute eternally.
So, howsoe'er other demands appear,
These never can be proved unreasonable :

The subject being of so fine a nature,
It not submits itself to sense, but 'scapes
The trials which conclude all common doubts.
Fran. My lord, you use me as ill painters paint,
Who, while they labour to make faces fair,
Neglect to make them like.
Iph. Madam,
There is no shipwreck of your virtues near,
That you should throw away any of all
Your excellences to save the dearest, modesty.
Gen. If they
Proceed with us, we can retreat unto
Our expositions and the people's votes.
If they
Refuse us wholly, then we plead the king's
Besieg'd, blocked up so straitly by some few,
Relief can find no way to enter to
The king, or to get out to us.
Exclaim against it loud, till the Polonians
Think it high injustice, and wish us better yet.
Then easily do we rise unto our ends,
And will become their envy through their pity.
At worst you may confirm our party there,
Increase it too. There is one Brennoralt;
Men call him gallant, but a discontent:
My cousin the king hath us'd him ill. Him a handsome
Whisper will draw. The afternoon shall perfect
What we have loosely now resolv'd.
Iph. If in discourse of beauty
(So large an empire) I do wander, it will
Become your goodness, madam, to set me right,
And, in a country, where you yourself is queen,
Not suffer strangers lose themselves.
Gen. What, making revenges, Palatine,
And taking prisoners fair ladies' hearts?
Iph. Yes, my lord,
And have no better fortune in this war
Than in the other; for, while I think to take,
I am surpris'd myself.
Fran. Dissembler, would thou wert! [*Aside*
Mens. You are a courtier, my lord.
The Palatine of Plocence, Almerin,
Will grace the hymenæals:
And that they may be while his stay is here,

I'll court my lord in absence ; take off for you
The little strangenesses virgins wear at first——
Look to the Palatine ! [*Iphigene swoons*
Mor. How is't, my dearest Iphigene ? [*Aside*
Iph. Not well, I would retire.
Gen. A qualm ?
Lord. His colour stole away ; sank down as water
In a weather-glass pressed by a warm hand.
Mens. A cordial of kind looks——

Enter a Trumpet *blinded*

From the king !
Mor. Let us withdraw, and hear him. [*Exeunt*

SCENE IV

Enter BRENNORALT, DORAN, RAGUELIN

Dor. Yes, to be married ! What, are you mute now ?
Bren. Thou cam'st too hastily upon me, put'st
So close the colours to mine eye, I could
Not see. It is impossible.
Dor. Impossible ?
If 'twere impossible, it should be otherwise ;
What can you imagine there of constancy,
Where 'tis so much their nature to love change,
That, when they say but what they are, they excuse
Themselves for what they do ?
Bren. She hardly knows him yet, in such an instant.
Dor. O, you know not how fire flies, *when it does catch*
Light matter, woman.
Bren. No more of that ! She is yet
The most precious thing in all my thoughts.
If it be so,
I am a lost thing in the world, Doran. [*Studies*
Dor. How ?
Bren. Thou wilt in vain persuade me to be other.
Life, which to others is a good, that they
Enjoy, to me will be an evil, I
Shall suffer in.
Dor. Look on another face : that's present remedy.
Bren. How ill thou dost conclude !
'Cause there are pestilent airs, which kill men suddenly
In health, must there be sovereign, as suddenly
To cure in sickness ? 't never was in nature. [*Exit*

He enters again hastily

I was a fool to think death only kept
The doors of ill-paid love, when or disdain
Or spite could let me out as well !
Dor. Right ;
Were I as you, it should no more trouble me
To free myself of love than to spit out
That which made me sick.
Bren. I'll tell her so, that she may laugh at me,
As at a prisoner threat'ning his guard
He will break loose, and so is made the faster.
She hath charms.—— [*Studies*
Doran can fetch in a rebellious heart,
E'en while it is conspiring liberty.—
O, she hath all
The virtues of her sex, and not the vices ;
Chaste and unsullied as first op'ning lilies
Or untouch'd buds.
Dor. Chaste ? why, do you honour me,
Because I throw myself not off a precipice ?
'Tis her ruin to be otherwise.
Though we blame those that kill themselves, my lord,
We praise not him that keeps himself alive,
And deserves nothing.
Bren. And 'tis the least.
She does triumph, when she does but appear :
I have as many rivals as beholders.
Dor. All that increases but our jealousies ;
If you have now such qualms for that you have not,
What will you have for that you shall possess ?
Bren. Dull heretic !
Know I have these, because I have not her.
When I have her, I shall have these no more.
Her fancy now, her virtue then, will govern ;
And, as I use to watch with doubtful eye
The wavering needle in the best sundial,
Till it has settled, then the trouble's o'er,
Because I know, when it is fix'd, it's true :
So here my doubts are all afore me. Sure,
Doran, crown'd conquerors are but the types
Of lovers, which enjoy, and really
Possess what th' other have in dreams ! I'll send
A challenge to him.

Dor. Do, and be thought a madman! To what purpose?
If she love him, she will but hate you more.
Lovers in favour, Brennoralt,
Are gamesters in good fortune; the more you set them,
The more they get.
Bren. I'll see her, then, this night; by Heaven, I will!
Dor. Where? in the citadel?
Bren. Know what, and why!
Dor. [*aside*]. He raves. [*Aloud*] Brennoralt!
Bren. Let me alone!
I conjure thee, by the discretion
Left betwixt us—that's thine;
For mine's devour'd by injuries of fortune——
Leave me to myself.
Dor. I have done.
Bren. Is there such a passage
As thou hast told me of into the castle?
Rag. There is, my lord.
Bren. And dar'st thou let me in?
Rag. If you, my lord, will venture.
Bren. There are no sentries near it?
Rag. None.
Bren. How to the chamber afterward?
Rag. Her woman.
Bren. What's she?
Rag. A wicket to my lady's secrets,
One that stands up to marriage with me.
Bren. There! [*Flings him a purse*
Upon thy life be secret!
Rag. Else all punishment to ingratitude!
Bren. Enough.
I am a storm within till I am there.
O Doran,
That that which is so pleasant to behold
Should be such pain within!
Dor. Poor Brennoralt!
Thou art the martyr of a thousand tyrants:
Love, honour, and ambition reign by turns,
And show their power upon thee.
Bren. Why, let them! I'm still Brennoralt. 'Ev'n kings
Themselves are by their servants rul'd sometimes:
Let their own slaves govern them at odd hours,
Yet not subject their persons or their powers.' [*Exeunt*

ACT III

SCENE I

Enter IPHIGENE, *disguised as before, as in a garden*

Iph. What have I got by changing place,
But as a wretch which ventures to the wars,
Seeking the misery with pain abroad,
He found, but wisely thought h' had left at home?
Fortune, thou hast no tyranny beyond
This usage. [*Weeps*
Would I had never hop'd,
Or had betimes despair'd! let never in
The gentle thief, or kept him but a guest,
Not made him lord of all!
Tempests of wind thus (as my storms of grief
Carry my tears, which should relieve my heart)
Have hurried to the thankless ocean clouds
And showers, that needed not at all the courtesy,
When the poor plains have languish'd for the want,
And almost burnt asunder.
I'll have this statue's place, and undertake
At my own charge to keep the water full. [*Lies down*

Enter FRANCELIA

Fran. These fond impressions grow too strong upon me.
They were at first without design or end,
Like the first elements, that know not what
And why they act, and yet produce strange things——
Poor innocent desires, journeying they know
Not whither; but now they promise to themselves
Strange things, grow insolent, threaten no rest
Till they be satisfy'd.
What difference was between these lords!
The one made love, as if he by assault
Would take my heart, so forc'd it to defence;
While t'other blew it up with secret mines,
And left no place for it. Here he is!
Tears steal, too, from his eyes,
As if not daring to be known to pass
That way.
Make it good, cunning grief: thou know'st thou couldst
Not dress thyself in any other looks.
To make thee lovely.

Iph. [*spying her*]. Francelia !
If, through the ignorance of places, I
Have intruded on your privacies, found out
Forbidden paths, 'tis fit you pardon, madam ;
For 'tis my melancholy, not I, offends.
Fran. So great a melancholy would well become
Mischances, such as time could not repair.
Those of the war are but the petty cures
Of every coming hour.
Iph. [*aside*]. Why
Should I not tell her all ? since 'tis in her
To save my life ? Who knows, but she may be
Gallant so far, as to undo herself
To make another happy ?
[*Aloud*] Madam,
The accidents of war contribute least
To my sad thoughts (if any such I have)—
Imprisonment can never be,
Where the place holds what we must love ; and yet——
Fran. My lord ?
Iph. In this imprisonment——
Fran. Proceed,
My lord.
Iph. I dare not, madam.
Fran. I see.
I do disturb you, and enter upon secrets,
Which when I know, I cannot serve you in them.
Iph. O, most of any ! You are the cause of all.
Fran. I, my lord ?
Iph. You, madam, you alone !
Fran. [*aside*]. Alas, that 'tis so soon to understand !
Iph. Must not you marry Almerin ?
Fran. They tell me 'tis design'd.
Iph. If he have you, I am for ever lost.
Fran. Lost !
The heavens forbid they should design so ill ;
Or, when they shall, that I should be the cause !
Iph. [*aside*]. Ha !
Her eyes are strangely kind : she prompts me excellently.
Stars, be propitious : and I am safe !—
A way I not expected.
Fran. [*aside*]. His passion labours for vent.
Iph. Is there a hope you will not give yourself
To Almerin ?

Fran. My lord, this air is common :
The walks within are pleasanter. [*Exit*
Iph. Invitation !
God of desires, be kind, and fill me now
With language, such thou lend'st thy favourites,
When thou wouldst give them easy victories ;
And I forgive thee all thy cruelties. [*Exit after her*

Scene II

Enter Palatine of Trock, and Menseck, Almerin, Brennoralt, Lords

Mens. Consider, too, that those
Who are necessitated to use violence
Have first been violent by necessity.
Pal. But still you judge not right
Of the prerogative ; 'For oft it stands
With pow'r and law, as with our faith and reason :
It is not all against that is above,'
My lord.
2nd Lord. You Lithuanians had of all least reason ;
For, would the king be unjust to you, he cannot,
Where there's so little to be had.
Alm. Where there is least, there's liberty, my lord ;
And 'tis more injury to pull hairs from
The bald, than from the bushy heads. [*They go off talking*
Pal. Brennoralt, a word ! [*He pulls Brennoralt*
My lord, the world hath cast its eye upon you,
And mark'd you out one of the foremost men.
Y' have busied fame the earliest of any,
And send her still on errands.
Much of the bravery of your nation
Has taken up its lodging in you ; and gallant men
But copy from you.
Bren. 'Tis goodly language this : what would it mean ?
Pal. The Lithuanians wish you well, and wonder
So much desert should be so ill rewarded.
Bren. Good.
Pal. While all the gifts the crown is mistress of
Are plac'd upon the empty.
Bren. Still I take you not.
Pal. Then, to be plain, our army would be proud of you ;
Pay the neglected scores of merit double.

All that you hold here of command, and what
Your fortune in this Sigismund has suffer'd,
Repair, and make it fairer than at first.
Bren. How?
Than nothing? Lord! trifle below ill language!
How came it in thy heart to tempt my honour?
Trock. My lord?
Bren. Dost think, 'cause I am angry with
The king and state sometimes, I am fallen out
With virtue and myself?
Draw! draw! or by goodness——
Trock. What means your lordship?
Bren. Draw, I say!
He that would think me a villain, is one; and I
Do wear this toy to purge the world of such.

Enter KING OF POLAND, Lords, MELIDOR, MIESTA

They've sav'd thee. Wert thou good-natur'd,
Thou wouldst love the king the better during life.
King. If they be just, they call for gracious answers;
Speedy, howe'er, we promise.
[*They all kiss the King's hand*
All. Long live great Sigismund!
Bren. The Lithuanians, sir,
Are of the wilder sort of creatures, must
Be rid with cavilons and with harsh curbs.
And, since the war can only make them tried,
What can be used but swords? where men have fall'n
From not respecting royalty, unto
A liberty of offending it, what though
Their numbers possibly equal yours, sir;
And now, forc'd by necessity, like cats
In narrow rooms, they fly up in your face?
Think you rebellion and loyalty
Are empty names? and that in subjects' hearts
They don't both give and take away the courage?
Shall we believe there is no difference
In good and bad? that there's no punishment
Or no protection? forbid it, heaven!
If, when great Poland's honour, safety too,
Hangs in dispute, we should not draw our swords,
Why were we ever taught to wear 'em, sir?
Mi. This late commotion in your kingdom, sir,
Is like a growing wen upon the face,

Which as we cannot look on but with trouble,
So take't away we cannot but with danger.
War there hath foulest face, and I most fear it,
Where the pretence is fair'st. Religion
And liberty, most specious names, they urge ;
Which, like the bills of subtle mountebanks,
Fill'd with great promises of curing all,
Though by the wise pass'd by as common cosenage,
Yet by th' unknowing multitude they're still
Admir'd and flock'd unto.

King. Is there no way
To disabuse them ?

Mel. All is now too late.
' The vulgar in religion are like
Unknown lands ; those that first possess them have
them.'
Then, sir, consider, justness of cause is nothing :
When things are risen to the point they are,
'Tis either not examin'd or believed
Among the warlike.
The better cause the Grecians had of yore :
Yet were the gods themselves divided in't ;
And the foul ravisher found as good protection
As the much injur'd husband.
Nor are you, sir, assur'd of all behind you ;
For, though your person in your subjects' hearts
Stands highly honour'd and belov'd, yet are
There certain acts of state, which men call grievances,
Abroad ; and, though they bare them in the times
Of peace, yet will they now perchance seek to
Be free, and throw them off. ' For know, dread sir,
The common people are much like the sea,
That suffers things to fall and sink unto
The bottom in a calm, which, in a storm
Stirr'd and enrag'd, it lifts, and does keep up.'
Then time distempers cures more safely, sir,
Than physic does, or instant letting-blood :
Religion now is a young mistress there,
For which each man will fight and die at least ;
Let it alone a while, and 'twill become
A kind of marry'd wife : people will be
Content to live with it in quietness,
If that at least may be. My voice is therefore, sir,
For peace.

Mens. Were, sir, the question simply war or peace,
It were no more than shortly to be ask'd,
Whether we would be well or ill;
Since war the sickness of the kingdom is,
And peace the health. But here I do conceive
'Twill rather lie, whether we had not better
Endure sharp sickness for a time, to enjoy
A perfect strength, than have it languish on us;
For peace and war in an incestuous line
Have still begot each other.
Those men that highly now have broke all laws,—
The great one only 'tis 'twixt man and man—
What safety can they promise, though you give it?
Will they not still suspect, and justly too,
That all those civil bonds new-made should be
Broken again to them? So, being still
In fears and jealousies themselves, you must
Infect the people; 'for in such a case
The private safety is the public trouble.'
Nor will they ever want pretext; 'since he
That will maintain it with his sword he's injur'd,
May say't at any time.'
Then, sir, as terrible as war appears,
My vote is for't; nor shall I ever care,
How ugly my physician's face shall be,
So he can do the cure.

Lord. In vent'ring physic, I think, sir, none so much
Considers the doctor's face as his own body.
To keep on foot the war with all your wants
Is to let blood, and take strong potions
In dangerous sickness.

King. I see, and wonder not to find, my lords,
This difference in opinion: the subject's large;
Nor can we there too much dispute, where, when
We err, 'tis at a kingdom's charges. Peace
And war are in themselves indifferent;
And time doth stamp them either good or bad:
But here the place is much considerable.
'War in our own is like to too much heat
Within, it makes the body sick: when in
Another country, 'tis but exercise;
Conveys that heat abroad, and gives it health.'
To that I bend my thoughts, but leave it to
Our greater council, which we now assemble:

Meantime, exchange of pris'ners only we
Assent unto.
Lord. Nothing of truce, sir ?
King. No : we'll not take up
Quiet at int'rest : perfect peace or nothing.
'Cessations for short times in war are like
Small fits of health in desp'rate maladies ;
Which, while the instant pain seems to abate,
Flatters into debauch and worse estate.' [*Exeunt*

Scene III

Enter Iphigene, *as leading to her chamber* Francelia, Servants *with lights,* Morat, *and another* Soldier

Iph. I have not left myself a fair retreat,
And must be now the blest object of your love,
Or subject of your scorn.
Fran. I fear some treachery,
And that mine eyes have given intelligence.
Unless you knew there would be weak defence,
You durst not think of taking in a heart,
As soon as you set down before it.
Iph. [*in a whisper*]. Condemn my love not of such fond ambition,
It aims not at a conquest, but exchange,
Francelia. [*In a whisper*
Mor. They're very great in this short time. [*Aside*
Sol. 'Tis ever so.
Young and handsome are made acquaintances in nature ; so
When they meet, they have the less to do. It is
For age or ugliness to make approaches,
And keep a distance. [*Aside*
Iph. When I shall see other perfection,
Which at the best will be but other vanity,
Not more I shall not love it.
Fran. 'Tis still one step not to despair, my lord.
[*Exeunt Iphigene, Francelia, and Servants*
Mor. Dost think he will fight ?
Sol. Troth, it may be not.
Nature, in those fine pieces, does as painters ;
Hangs out a pleasant excellence that takes
The eye, which is indeed

But a coarse canvas in the naked truth,
Or some slight stuff.

Mor. I have a great mind to taste him.

Sol. Fie! a prisoner?

Mor. By this hand, if I thought
He courted my coronel's mistress in earnest!

Re-enter Iphigene, *a* Waiting-woman *coming after her*

Wom. [*to Iph.*] My lord,
My lord, my lady thinks the jessamine walks
Will be the finer: the freshness of th' morning
Takes off the strength o' th' heat, she says.

Iph. 'Tis well. [*Exit*

Mor. Mew! do it so?
I suspect vildly. We'll follow him, and see
If he be so far qualified towards a soldier,
As to drink a crash in's chamber.

Enter Raguelin: *he pulls the Waiting-woman back*

Rag. What are these keys?

Wom. Hark you, I dare not do it.

Rag. How?

Wom. My lady will find——

Rag. Scruples? Are my hopes
Become your fears? There was no other way
I should be anything in this lewd world;
And now—'sfoot, I know she longs to see him too.

Wom. Does she?

Rag. Do you think he would desire it else?

Wom. Ay, but——

Rag. Why, let me secure it all.
I'll say I found the keys, or stole them. Come.

Wom. Well, if you ruin all now—here, these enter the garden from the works; that, the privy walks; and that, the back stairs. Then you know my chamber?

Rag. Yes, I know your chamber. [*Exeunt*

Scene IV

Enter Brennoralt

Bren. He comes not.
One wise thought more, and I return. I cannot
In this act separate the foolish from

The bold so far, but still it tastes o' th' rash.
Why, let it taste! it tastes of love too; and
To all actions 't gives a pretty relish, that——

Enter RAGUELIN

Rag. My lord?
Bren. O, here!
Rag. 'Sfoot, y'are upon our sentries;
Move on this hand. [*Exeunt*

Enter again BRENNORALT *and* RAGUELIN

Bren. Where are we now?
Rag. Entering part of the fort:
Your lordship must be wet a little. [*Exeunt*

They enter again

Bren. Why,
Are there here no guards?
Rag. There needs none: you presently
Must pass a place, where one's an army in
Defence, it is so steep and strait.
Bren. 'Tis well.
Rag. These are the steps of danger. Look to your way,
My lord.
Bren. I do not find such difficulty.
Wait me hereabouts. [*Exit Raguelin*

Enter FRANCELIA, *as in a bed, asleep;* BRENNORALT *draws the curtains*

So misers look upon their gold, which, while
They joy to see, they fear to lose; the pleasure
O' the sight scarce equalling the jealousy
Of being dispossess'd by others.
Her face is like the Milky Way i' th' sky,
A meeting of gentle lights without name.
Heavens!
Shall this fresh ornament of the world, this precious
Loveliness pass, with other common things,
Amongst the wastes of time? What pity 'twere!
Fran. [*waking*] Bless me!
Is it a vision, or Brennoralt?
Bren. Brennoralt, lady.
Fran. Brennoralt? innocence guard me!
What is't you have done, my lord?
Bren. Alas! I were

In too good estate if I knew what I did.
But why ask you, madam ?
Fran. It much amazes me
To think how you came hither, and what could bring you
T'endanger thus my honour and your own life !
Nothing but saving of my brother could make
Me now preserve you.
Bren. Reproach me not the follies you yourself
Make me commit.
I am reduc'd to such extremity,
That Love himself (high tyrant as he is),
If he could see, would pity me.
Fran. I understand you not.
Bren. Would heaven you did, for 'tis a pain to tell you :
I come t' accuse you of injustice, madam !
You first begot my passion, and was
Content (at least you seem'd so) it should live ;
Yet since would ne'er contribute unto it,
Not look upon't ; as if you had desired
Its being for no other end, but for
The pleasure of its ruin.
Fran. Why do you labour thus, to make me guilty of
An injury to you—to you, which, when
It is one, all mankind is alike engag'd,
And must have quarrel to me ?
Bren. I have done ill ; you chide me justly, madam.
I'll lay't not on you, but on my wretched self ;
For I am taught that heavenly bodies
Are not malicious in their influence,
But by the disposition of the subject.
They tell me you must marry Almerin ?
Sure, such excellency ought to be
The recompense of virtue, not the sacrifice
Of parents' wisdom. Should it not, madam ?
Fran. 'Twould injure me were it thought otherwise.
Bren. And shall he have you then, that knew you yesterday ?
Is there in martyrdom no juster way,
But he, that holds a finger in the fire
A little time, should have the crown from them,
That have endur'd the flame with constancy ?
Fran. If the discovery will ease your thoughts,

My lord, know Almerin is as the man
I never saw.
Bren. You do not marry then ?
Condemned men thus hear, and thus receive
Reprieves. One question more, and I am gone :
Is there to latitude of eternity
A hope for Brennoralt ?
Fran. My lord ?
Bren. Have I
A place at all, when you do think of men ?
Fran. My lord, a high one : I must be singular,
Did I not value you. The world does set
Great rates upon you ; and you have first deserv'd them.
Bren. Is this all ?
Fran. All.
Bren. O, be less kind, or kinder :
Give me more pity or more cruelty,
Francelia ! I cannot live with this, nor die.
Fran. I fear, my lord, you must not hope beyond it.
Bren. Not hope ? [*Views himself*
This, sure, is not the body to this soul :
It was mistaken, shuffled in through haste.
Why else should that have so much love, and this
Want loveliness to make that love receiv'd ? [*He studies*
I will raise
Honour to a point it never was—do things
Of such a virtuous greatness she shall love me.
She shall : I will deserve her, though I have her not.
There's something yet in that.
Madam, will't please you, pardon my offence ?——
O Fates !
That I must call thus my affection !
Fran. I will do anything, so you will think
Of me and of yourself, my lord, and how
Your stay endangers both.
Bren. Alas !
Your pardon is more necessary to
My life, than life to me. But I am gone.
Blessings, such as my wishes for you in
Their extasies could never reach, fall on you !
May ev'rything contribute to preserve
That exc'lence (my destruction), till't meet joys
In love, great as the torments I have in't ! [*Exit*

ACT IV

SCENE I

Enter BRENNORALT

Bren. Why so, 'tis well. Fortune, I thank thee still.
I dare not call thee villain neither : 'twas
Plotted from the first, that's certain ; it looks that way.
Hum !
Caught in a trap. Here's something yet to trust to.
[*To his sword*
This was the entry, these the stairs ;
But whither afterwards ?
He that is sure to perish on the land
May quit the nicety of card and compass ;
And safe, to his discretion, put to sea :
He shall have my hand to't. [*Exit*

Enter RAGUELIN *and* ORILLA *the waiting-woman*

Rag. Look ! by this light, 'tis day.

Ori. Not by this ; by t'other 'tis indeed.

Rag. Thou art such another piece of temptation. My lord raves by this time. A hundred to one, the sentinels will discover us too : then I do pay for night-watch.

Ori. Fie upon thee ! thou art as fearful as a young colt. Bogglest at everything, fool ? As if lovers had consider'd hours ! I'll peep in. [*She peeps*

Rag. I am as weary of this wench as if I were married to her. She hangs upon me like an ape upon a horse. She's as common, too, as a barber's glass ; conscienc'd, too, like a dy-dapper !

Ori. There's nobody within : my lady sleeps this hour at least.

Rag. Good, the devil's even with me : not be an honest man neither. What course now ?

Re-enter BRENNORALT *and a* Guard

1*st Sol.* Nay, sir, we shall order you now.

Bren. Dogs !

Enter FRESOLIN

Fre. What tumult's this ?—ha ! Brennoralt ! 'tis he
In spite of his disguise : what makes he here ?
He's lost for ever, if he be discover'd ;
How now, companions, why do you use my friend thus ?

Sol. Your friend, my lord ? if he be your friend, h'as
Used us as ill. H' has played the devil amongst us :
Six of our men are surgeons' work this month.
We found him climbing the walls.

2nd Sol. He had no word neither,
Nor any language but a blow.

Fre. You will be doing these wild things, my lord.
Good faith,
Ye are to blame ; if y' had desir'd to view the walls
Or trenches, 'twas but speaking : we are not nice.
I would myself have waited on you :
Th' are the new outworks you would see perchance.
Boy, bring me
Black Tempest round about and the grey Barbary :
A trumpet come along too !
My lord, we'll take the nearer way and privater
Here through the sally-port.

Bren. What a devil is this ?
Sure I dream. [*Exeunt. Manent Guard*

Sol. Now you are so officious !

2nd Sol. Death ! could I guess he was a friend ?

Sol. 'Twas ever to be thought : how should he come
There else ?

2nd Sol. Friend or no friend, he might have left us
Something to pay the surgeon with. Grant me that,
Or I'll beat you to't. [*Exeunt*

Scene II

Enter Fresolin *and* Brennoralt

Fre. Brennoralt,
Start not : I pay thee back a life I owe thee,
And bless my stars they gave me power to do't ;
The debt lay heavy on me.
A horse waits you there, a trumpet too, which you
May keep, lest he should prate. No ceremony,
'Tis dangerous.

Bren. Thou hast astonish'd me :
Thy youth hath triumphed in one single act
O'er all the age can boast ; and I will stay
To tell thee so, were they now firing all
Their cannons on me. Farewell ! gallant Fresolin,
And may reward, great as thy virtue, crown thee !
[*Exeunt divers ways*

SCENE III

Enter IPHIGENE *and* FRANCELIA

Fran. A peace will come, and then you must be gone,
And whether, when you once are got upon the wing,
You will not stoop to what shall rise, before ye
Fly to some lure with more temptation garnish'd,
Is a sad question.
Iph. Can you have doubts, and I not fears? By this
The readiest and the sweetest oath [*kisses her*], I swear
I cannot so secure myself of you,
But in my absence I shall be in pain.
I have cast up what it will be to stand
The governor's anger, and, which is more hard,
The love of Almerin. I hold thee now
But by thy own free grant—a slight security!
Alas! it may fall out, giving thyself,
Not knowing thine own worth or want of mine;
Thou mayst, like kings deceiv'd, resume the gift
On better knowledge back.
Fran. If I so easily change,
I was not worth your love; and by the loss
You'll gain.
Iph. But, when y'are irrecoverably gone,
'Twill be slight comfort to persuade myself
You had a fault, when all that fault must be
But want of love to me; and that again
Find in my much defect so much excuse,
That it will have no worse name than discretion,
If unconcern'd [you] do cast it up—I must
Have more assurance.
Fran. You have too much already,
And sure, my lord, you wonder, while I blush,
At such a growth in young affections.
Iph. Why should I wonder, madam?
Love, that from two breasts sucks, must of a child
Quickly become a giant.
Dunces in love stay at the alphabet:
The inspir'd know all before, and do begin
Still higher.

Enter WAITING-WOMAN

Wom. Madam,
Almerin return'd has sent to kiss your hands.
I told him you were busy.

Fran. Must I, my lord, be busy?
I may be civil, though not kind. Tell him
I wait him in the gallery.

Iph. [*whispers*]. May I not kiss your hand this night?

Fran. The world is full of jealous eyes, my lord;
And, were they all lock'd up, you are a spy,
Once enter'd in my chamber at strange hours.

Iph. The virtue of Francelia is too safe
To need those little arts of preservation.
Thus to divide ourselves, is to distrust ourselves.
A cherubin despatches not on earth
Th' affairs of heaven with greater innocence
Than I will visit; 'tis but to take a leave—
I beg.

Fran. When you are going, my lord. [*Exeunt*

Enter ALMERIN, MORAT

Alm. Pish! Thou liest, thou liest.
I know he plays with womankind, not loves it.
Thou art impertinent.

Mor. 'Tis the camp-talk, my lord, though.

Alm. The camp's an ass; let me hear no more on't.
[*Exeunt talking*

SCENE IV

Enter GRAINEVERT, VILLANOR, *and* MARINEL

Gra. And shall we have peace? I am
No sooner sober but the state is so too.
If't be thy will, a truce for a moneth only.
I long to refresh my eyes, by this hand;
They have been so tir'd with looking upon faces
Of this country.

Vil. And shall the Donazella
To whom we wish so well-a
Look babies again in our eyes-a?

Gra. Ah!
A sprightly girl above fifteen, that melts,
When a man but takes her by the hand; eyes full
And quick; with breath sweet as double violets,
And wholesome as dying leaves of strawberries;
Thick silken eyebrows, high upon the forehead;
And cheeks mingled with pale streaks of red,
Such as the blushing morning never wore.

Vil. Oh, my chops, my chops!

Gra. With narrow mouth, small teeth, and lips swelling,
As if she pouted——
Vil. Hold, hold, hold!
Gra. Hair curling, and cover'd, like buds of marjoram;
Part tied in negligence, part loosely flowing——
Mar. Tyrant, tyrant, tyrant!
Gra. In a pink-colour taffeta petticoat,
Lac'd smock-sleeves dangling! This vision stol'n
From her own bed, and rustling into one's chamber!
Vil. O good Grainevert, good Grainevert!
Gra. With a wax candle in her hand, looking
As if she had lost her way, at twelve at night.
Mar. Oh, any hour, any hour!
Gra. Now I think on't, by this hand, I'll marry, and be long-liv'd.
Vil. Long-liv'd! how?

Gra. Oh, he that has a wife eats with an appetite; h'as a very good stomach to't first. This living at large is very destructive. Variety is like rare sauces; provokes too far, and draws on surfeits more than th' other.

Enter Doran

Dor. So;
Is this a time to fool in?
Gra. What's the matter?
Dor. Draw out your choice men
And away to your Coronel immediately.
There's work towards, my boys, there's work.
Gra. Art in earnest?
Dor. By this light.
Gra. There's something in that yet.

This moiety war,
Twilight,
Neither night nor day:
Pox upon it!
A storm is worth a thousand
Of your calm;
There's more variety in it. [*Exeunt*

Scene V

Enter Almerin *and* Francelia, *as talking earnestly*

Alm. Madam, that shows the greatness of my passion.
Fran. The imperfection rather: jealousy's

No better sign of love, my lord, than fevers are
Of life : they show there is a being, though
Impair'd and perishing ; and that, affection,
But sick and in disorder. I like't not.
Your servant. [*Exit*

Alm. So short and sour ? the change is visible.

Enter Iphigene

Iph. Dear Almerin, welcome, y' have been absent long.
Alm. Not very long.
Iph. To me it hath appear'd so.
What says our camp ? am I not blamed there ?
Alm. They wonder——
Iph. While we smile.
How have you found the king inclining ?
Alm. Well.
The treaty is not broken, nor holds it. Things
Are where they were : 't has a kind of face of peace.
You, my lord, may, when you please, return.
Iph. I, Almerin ?
Alm. Yes, my lord,
I'll give you an escape.
Iph. 'Tis least in my desires.
Alm. Hum !
Iph. Such prisons are beyond all liberty.
Alm. Is't possible ?
Iph. Seems it strange to you ?
Alm. No,
Not at all. What, you find the ladies kind ?
Iph. [*smiles*]. Civil.
Alm. You make love well too, they say, my lord.
Iph. Pass my time.
Alm. Address unto Francelia ?
Iph. Visit her.
Alm. D'you know she is my mistress, Palatine ?
Iph. Ha ?
Alm. D'you know she is my mistress ?
Iph. I have been told so.
Alm. And do you court her then ?
Iph. [*smiles*]. Why,
If I saw the enemy first, would you not charge ?
Alm. [*aside*]. He does allow it too, by Heaven !
Laughs at me too. [*Aloud*] Thou filcher of a heart,

False as thy title to Francelia,
Or as thy friendship, which with this [*draws*] I do
Throw by. Draw !
Iph. What do you mean ?
Alm. I see
The cunning now of all thy love, and why
Thou cam'st so timely kind, suffering surprise.
Draw !
Iph. I will not draw. Kill me ;
And I shall have no trouble in my death,
Knowing it is your pleasure ;
As I shall have no pleasure in my life,
Knowing 'tis your trouble.
Alm. Oh, poor —— I look'd for this.
I knew th' wouldst find 'twas easier to do
A wrong than justify it. But——
Iph. I will not fight. Hear me !
If I love you not more than I love her ;
If I do love her more than for your sake,
Heaven strangely punish me.
Alm. Take heed how thou
Dost play with heaven !
Iph. By all that's just, and fair
And good ; by all that you hold dear, and men
Hold great, I never had lascivious thought,
Or e'er did action that might call in doubt
My love to Almerin.
Alm. That tongue can charm me into anything.
I do believe't : prithee, be wiser then.
Give me no further cause of jealousy ;
Hurt not mine honour more, and I am well.
Iph. But well ? Of all
Our passions, I wonder nature made
The worst, foul jealousy, her favourite.
And, if it be not so, why took she care,
That everything should give the monster nourishment,
And left us nothing to destroy it with ?
Alm. Prithee, no more ; thou plead'st so cunningly,
I fear I shall be made the guilty, and need
Thy pardon.
Iph. If you could read my heart, yould wou.
I will be gone to-morrow, if that will satisfy.
Indeed,

I shall not rest until my innocence
Be made as plain as objects to the sense.
Alm. Come,
You shall not go, I'll think upon't no more.
'Distrusts ruin not friendship,
But build it fairer than it was before.' [*Exeunt*

SCENE VI

Enter BRENNORALT, Captains, STRATHEMAN, DORAN

Bren. No more but ten from every company;
For many hands are thieves,
And rob the glory, while they take their share.
How goes the night?
Str. Half spent, my lord:
We shall have straight the moon's weaker light.
Bren. 'Tis time, then. Call in the officers.

Enter Officers

Friends, if you were men that must be talk'd
Into courage, I had not chosen you.
Danger with its vizard oft before this time
Y' have look'd upon, and outfac'd it too:
We are to do the trick again—that's all.
Here—— [*Draws his sword*
And yet we will not swear;
For he, that shrinks in such an action,
Is damn'd without the help of perjury.
Doran, if from the virgin-tow'r thou spiest
A flame, such as the east sends forth about
The time the day should break, go tell the king
I hold the castle for him: bid him come on
With all his force; and he shall find a victory
So cheap, 'twill lose the value. If I fall,
The world has lost a thing it us'd not well;
And I, a thing I car'd not for—that world.
Str. Lead us on, Coronel; if we do not fight
Like——
Bren. No like! we'll be ourselves' similitude;
And time shall say, when it would tell that men
Did well, they fought like us. [*Exeunt*

ACT V

SCENE I

Enter BRENNORALT *and* STRATHEMAN

Bren. What made thee stop?
Str. One in's falling sickness
Had a fit which choked the passage; but all is well.
Softly, we are near the place. [*Exeunt*

Alarum within, and fight; then enter ALMERIN *in his nightgown*

Alm. What noise is here to-night? Something on fire?
What, ho!
Send to the virgin-tower; there is disorder thereabouts.

Enter Soldiers

Sol. All's lost, all's lost!
The enemy's upon the place of arms;
And is by this time master of that and of the tower.
Alm. Thou liest! [*Strikes him*

Enter MORAT

Mor. Save yourself, my lord, and haste unto the camp;
Ruin gets in on every side.
Alm. There's something in it, when this fellow flies.
Villains, my arms! I'll see what devil, reigns. [*Exeunt*

SCENE II

Enter IPHIGENE *and* FRANCELIA

Iph. Look, the day breaks!
Fran. You think I'll be so kind
As swear it does not now? Indeed, I will not.
Iph. Will you
Not send me neither your picture, when y'are gone?
That, when my eye is famish'd for a look,
It may have where to feed,
And to the painted feast invite my heart.
Fran. Here, take this virgin bracelet of my hair,
And if, like other men, thou shalt hereafter
Throw it with negligence
'Mongst the records of thy weak female conquests;

Laugh at the kind words and mystical contrivement;
If such a time shall come,
Know I am sighing then thy absence, Iphigene,
And weeping o'er the false but pleasing image.

Enter ALMERIN

Alm. Francelia, Francelia,
Rise, rise, and save thyself! the enemy
That does not know thy worth, may else destroy it.
[*Throws open the door*
Ha! mine eyes grow sick:
A plague has through them stol'n into my heart,
And I grow dizzy! Feet, lead me off again,
Without the knowledge of my body! I
Shall act, I know not what else. [*Exit*
Fran. How came he in?
Dear Iphigene, we are betray'd!
Let's raise the castle, lest he should return.
Iph. That were to make all public. Fear not;
I'll satisfy his anger: I can do it.
Fran. Yes, with some quarrel!
And bring my honour and my love in danger.

Re-enter ALMERIN

Look, he returns; and wrecks of fury,
Like hurried clouds over the face of heaven
Before a tempest, in his looks appear.
Alm. If they would question what our rage doth act,
And make it sin, they would not thus provoke men.
I am too tame.
For, if they live, I shall be pointed at.
Here I denounce a war to all the world;
And thus begin it. [*Runs at Iphigene*
Iph. What hast thou done? [*She falls*
Fran. Ah me, help, help! [*Almerin wounds her*
Iph. Hold!
Alm. 'Tis too late.
Iph. [*aside*]. My fond deceits involve the innocent.
Rather than she shall suffer, I will discover
All.
Alm. Ha! what
Will he discover?
Iph. That which shall make thee curse
The blindness of thy rage—I am a woman!

Alm. Ha, ha, ha! brave and bold!
Because thy perjury deceived me once,
And sav'd thy life, thou think'st to escape again.
Impostor, thus thou shalt—— [*Runs at her*
Iph. Oh, hold! I have enough.
Had I hope of life, thou shouldst not have this secret.
Fran. What will it be now?
Iph. My father, having long desir'd
A son to heir his great possessions,
And in six births successively deceived,
Made a rash vow—O, how rash vows are punished!—
That, if the burthen then my mother went with
Prov'd not a male, he ne'er would know her more.
Then was unhappy Iphigene brought forth,
And by the women's kindness nam'd a boy,
And since so bred—a cruel pity, as
It hath fallen out. If now thou find'st that, which
Thou thought'st a friendship in me, love, forget it.
It was my joy—and—death. [*She faints*
Alm. For curiosity
I'll save thee, if I can, and know the end,
If't be but loss of blood—
Breasts!
By all that's good, a woman! Iphigene!
Iph. I thank thee, for I was fall'n asleep before
I had despatch'd. Sweetest of all thy sex,
Francelia, forgive me now: my love
Unto this man, and fear to lose him, taught me
A fatal cunning, made me court you and
My own destruction.
Fran. I am amaz'd.
Alm. And can it be, O mockery of heaven?
To let me see what my soul often wish'd,
And make't my punishment—a punishment
That, were I old in sins, were yet too great!
Iph. Would you have lov'd me, then? Pray, say you would:
For I, like testy sick men at their death,
Would know no news but health from the physician.
Alm. Canst thou doubt that,
That hast so often seen me extasi'd
When thou wert dress'd like woman,
Unwilling ever to believe thee man?
Iph. I have enough.

Alm. Heavens!
What thing shall I appear unto the world?
Here might my ignorance find some excuse,
But, there,
I was distracted. None, but one enrag'd
With anger to a savageness, would e'er
Have drawn a sword upon such gentle sweetness.
Be kind, and kill me—kill me, one of you!
Kill me, if't be but to preserve my wits.
Dear Iphigene, take thy revenge, it will
Not misbecome thy sex at all; for 'tis
An act of pity, not of cruelty,
Thus to despatch a miserable man.
Fran. And thou wouldst be more miserable yet,
While, like a bird made prisoner by itself,
Thou beat'st and beat'st thyself 'gainst everything,
And dost pass by that which should let thee out.
Alm. Is it my fault,
Or heaven's? Fortune, when she would play upon me,
Like ill musicians, wound me up so high,
That I must crack sooner than move in tune.
Fran. Still you rave;
While we for want of present help may perish.
Alm. Right.
A surgeon! I'll go find one instantly.
The enemy too!—I had forgot!
O, what fatality govern'd this night! [*Exit*
Fran. How like an unthrift's case will mine be now?
For all the wealth he loses shifts but's place;
And still the world enjoys it: and so will 't you,
Sweet Iphigene, though I possess you not.
Iph. What excellence of nature's this! Have you
So perfectly forgiv'n already, as to
Consider me a loss? I doubt which sex
I shall be happier in. Climates of friendship
Are not less pleasant, 'cause they are less scorching,
Than those of love; and under them we'll live:
Such precious links of that we'll tie our souls
Together with, that the chains of the other
Shall be gross fetters to it.
Fran. But I fear
I cannot stay the making. O, would you
Had never undeceiv'd me! for I had died

With pleasure, believing I had been your martyr.
Now——

Iph. She looks pale! Francelia!

Fran. I cannot stay:
A hasty summons hurries me away,
And—gives—no—— [*She dies*

Iph. She's gone,
She's gone! Life, like a dial's hand, hath stol'n
From the fair figure, ere it was perceiv'd.

[*A noise within. Enter Soldiers. She thinks them Almerin*

What will become of me? Too late, too late
Y'are come: you may persuade wild birds, that wing
The air, into a cage, as soon as call
Her wand'ring spirits back.
Ha!
Those are strange faces: there's a horror in them;
And, if I stay, I shall be taken for
The murtherer. O, in what straits they move,
That wander 'twixt death, fears, and hopes of love! [*Exit*

Scene III

Enter Brennoralt, Grainevert, Soldiers

Bren. Forbear, upon your lives,
The place! There dwells Divinity within it.
All else the castle holds is lawful prize,
Your valour's wages: this I claim as mine.
Guard you the door.

Grd. Coronel, shall you use all the women yourself?

Bren. Away! 'tis unseasonable.

[*They retire: he draws the curtain*

Awake, fair saint, and bless thy poor idolater.
Ha! pale? And cold? And dead?
The sweetest guest fled—murdered, by heaven!
The purple streams not dry yet!
Some villain has broke in before me,
Robb'd all my hopes; but I will find him out,
And kick his soul to hell. I'll do't.

[*Dragging out Iphigene*] Speak!

Iph. What should I say?

Bren. Speak, or by all——

Iph. Alas! I do confess

Myself th' unfortunate cause.

Bren. O, d'you so? Hadst thou been cause of all the plagues
That vex mankind, thou'dst been an innocent
To what thou art: thou shalt not think repentance.
[*He kills her*

Iph. O, thou wert too sudden, and—— [*She dies*

Bren. Was I so?
The lustful youth would sure have spoil'd her honour;
Which finding highly guarded, rage, and fear
To be reveal'd, counsell'd this villainy.
Is there no more of them? [*Exit*

Enter ALMERIN

Alm. Not enter?
Yes, dog, through thee! Ha! a corpse laid out,
Instead of Iphigene! Francelia dead too!
Where shall I begin to curse?

Re-enter BRENNORALT

Bren. Here, if he were thy friend!

Alm. Brennoralt!
A gallant sword could ne'er have come
In better time.

Bren. I have a good one for thee,
If that will serve the turn.

Alm. I long to try it. That sight doth make me desperate;
Sick of myself and the world.

Bren. Didst value him?
A greater villain did I never kill.

Alm. Kill?

Bren. Yes.

Alm. Art sure of it?

Bren. Maybe, I do not wake.

Alm. Th'ast taken then
A guilt off from me, would have weigh'd down my sword,
Weak'ned me to low resistance:
I should have made no sports, hadst thou conceal'd it.
Know, Brennoralt, thy sword is stain'd in excellence,
Great as the world could boast.

Bren. Ha, ha!
How thou'rt abus'd! Look there, there lies the excellence
Thou speak'st of! Murd'red: by him too; he did

Confess he was the cause.
Alm. O innocence
Ill understood, and much worse us'd! She was,
Alas, by accident! but I—I was
The cause in deed.
Bren. I will believe thee too,
And kill thee; destroy all causes, till I make
A stop in nature;
For to what purpose should she work again?
Alm. Bravely then!
The title of a kingdom is a trifle
To our quarrel, sir. Know by sad mistake
I kill'd thy mistress, Brennoralt; and thou
Kill'dst mine.
Bren. Thine?
Alm. Yes, that Iphigene,
Though shown as man unto the world, was woman,
Excellent woman!
Bren. I understand no riddles; guard thee.
[*Fight and pause*
Alm. O, could they now look down and see,
How we two strive which first should give revenge,
They would forgive us something of the crime.
Hold! prithee, give me leave
To satisfy a curiosity—
I never kissed my Iphigene as woman.
[*Kisses Iphigene and rises*
Bren. Thou motion'st well, nor have I taken leave.
[*Kisses Francelia*
It keeps a sweetness yet,
As stils from roses when the flowers are gone. [*Rises*
Alm. Even so have two faint pilgrims, scorch'd with heat,
Unto some neighbour fountain stepp'd aside,
Kneel'd first, then laid their warm lips to the nymph,
And from her coldness took fresh life again,
As we do now.
Bren. Let's on our journey, if thou art refresh'd.
Alm. Come! and, if there be a place reserv'd
For height'ned spirits better than other,
May that which wearies first of ours have it!
[*Fight a good while; Almerin falls*
Bren. If I grow weary, laugh at me, that's all.
Alm. Brave souls above, which will

Be, sure, inquisitive for news from earth,
Shall get no other but that thou art brave.

Enter King, Stratheman, Lords, Menseck

Str. To preserve some ladies, as we guess'd !
King. Still gallant, Brennoralt ? thy sword not sheath'd yet ?
Busy still ?
Bren. Revenging, sir,
The foulest murder ever blasted ears,
Committed here by Almerin and Iphigene !
Alm. [*reviving*]. False, false ! the first-created purity
Was not more innocent than Iphigene.
Bren. Lives he again ?
Alm. Stay, thou much-wearied guest,
Till I have thrown a truth amongst them—
We shall look black else to posterity.
King. What says he ?
Lord. Something concerning this he labours to
Discover.
Alm. Know, it was I that kill'd Francelia,
I alone !
Mens. O barbarous return of my civilities.
Was it thy hand ?
Alm. Hear and forgive me, Menseck. Ent'ring this morning
Hastily, with resolution to preserve
The fair Francelia, I found a thief
Stealing the treasure (as I thought) belong'd to me.
Wild in my mind, as ruin'd in my honour,
In much mistaken rage I wounded both.
Then (O, too late !)
I found my error, found Iphigene a woman,
Acting stol'n love, to make her own love safe,
And all my jealousies impossible.
Whilst I ran out to bring them cure,
Francelia dies, and Iphigene found here—
I can no more. [*Dies*
King. Most strange and intricate !
Iphigene a woman ?
Mel. With this story I am guiltily acquainted,
The first concealments, since her love, and all
The ways to it, I have been trusted with ;
But, sir, my grief, join'd with the instant business,

Begs a deferment.
King. I am amaz'd, till I do hear it out.
But, i' th' meantime, lest in these mists
Merit should lose itself, these forfeitures
Of Trock and Menseck, Brennoralt, are thine.
Bren. A princely gift! But, sir, it comes too late.
Like sunbeams on the blasted blossoms, do
Your favours fall: you should have given me this,
When't might have rais'd me in men's thoughts, and made
Me equal to Francelia's love. I have
No end, since she is not.
Back to my private life I will return.
'Cattle, though weary, can trudge homewards after.'
King. This melancholy time must cure. Come, take
The bodies up, and lead the prisoners on.
Triumph and funerals must walk together;
Cypress and laurel twin'd make up one chaplet.
For we have got
The day; but bought it at so dear a rate,
The victory itself's unfortunate. [*Exeunt*

The
SAD ONE.

A
TRAGEDY

BY
S[r] JOHN SUCKLING.

London
Printed for Humphrey Mosely at the Prince's
Arms in St Pauls Churchyard.
1659.

TO THE READER

I HOPE I shall not need to crave your pardon for publishing this dramatic piece of Sir John Suckling (imperfect, I cannot say, but rather unfinish'd), there being a kind of perfection even in the most deficient fragments of this incomparable author. To evince that this copy was a faithful transcript from his own handwriting, I have said enough in my former epistle; and I thought it much better to send it into the world in the same state I found it, without the least addition, than procure it supplied by any other pen, which had not been less preposterous than the finishing of Venus' picture, so skilfully begun by Apelles, by some other hand. Nor are we without a sufficient precedent in works of this nature, and relating to an author, who confessedly is reputed the glory of the English stage (whereby you'll know I mean Ben Jonson), and in a play also of somewhat resembling name, *The Sad Shepherd*, extant in his third volume, which, though it wants two entire Acts, was nevertheless judg'd a piece of too much worth to be laid aside by the learned and honorable Sir [K. D.] who published that volume. We have also in print (written by the same hand) the very beginning only (for it amounts not to one full scene) of a tragedy called *Mortimer*; so that we find the same fate to have hapned to the works of two of the most celebrated and happy wits of this nation. Now, as it is to have been wish'd that this tragedy had come whole and compleat to public view, so is it some happiness that there is so much of it preserved; it being true of our author what Dr. Donne said of a famous artist of his time—

A HAND OR EYE
BY HILLIARD DRAWN, IS WORTH A HISTORY
BY A WORSE PAINTER MADE.

I shall add no more, but only say (with some just confidence) that I could not have answer'd myself, to the world, if I had suppressed this tragedy, and therefore may hope for some favour by its publication. Farewell.

H. M.

THE ARGUMENT INTRODUCING TO THE FOLLOWING SCENES

SICILY had been a long time tormented with civil wars, and the crown was still in dispute, till Aldebrand, getting the upper hand in a set battle, establish'd himself in the throne, and gave a period to all those troubles in shew only; for the old factions were set on foot again shortly after, and the house of the Floretties and the Cleonaxes strove now as much who should be most powerful with the king, as before who should make him. In conclusion, the favour of Aldebrand inclining to the Cleonaxes, and by degrees resting wholly upon them, the Floretties took arms, but in a set field lost all. The father and the son being both taken prisoners, the one was banish'd, the other condemned suddenly to lose his head.

Thus far the author drew the curtain; the rest of the plot is wrapt up in the following scenes.

Dramatis Personæ

ALDEBRAND, King of Sicily.
CLEONAX senior, his treasurer.
CLEONAX junior, son of the former.
BELLAMINO, favourite of pleasure, and cousin to Cleonax.
CLARIMONT, an old lord.
CLARIMONT junior.
FIDELIO, friend to Clarimont.
FLORELIO, a lord married to Francelia.
FLORELIO junior, his brother.
LORENZO, an ambitious courtier.
PARMENIO, his supposed creature.
DROLLIO, } two courtiers.
LEPIDO, }
DOCO DISCOPIO, one that pretends to be a great statesman.
SIGNIOR MULTECARNI, the poet.
PETRUCHIO, servant to Florelio.
Ambassador from Spain.
Actors.
AMASIA, queen to Aldebrand.
FRANCELIA, daughter to Clarimont.
Keeper.

THE SCENE, SICILY.

THE SAD ONE

ACT I

Scene I

Enter old Clarimont *in prison, in his nightgown ; his Servant following him*

Condemn'd unheard ! Just heavens, it cannot be !
Why, tyranny itself could do no more :
The pale ghosts of Tiberius and Nero
Would blush to see an act so foul and horrid,
So full of black ingratitude as this !
'Twas I that set the crown upon his head,
And bid him live king of his enemies,
When he durst hardly hope it :
And does he thus requite me ? Now I see,
Who by the compass of his merit sails,
May guide his fraught of hopes in seasons fair
And calm ; but, when storms come,
All his good deeds, with his good days, must perish.
O my unhappy stars ! [*Beats his breast*

Ser. My lord, let not a fruitless passion
Make you to die less man than you have lived.

Clar. Who art thou ?

Ser. I was lately one, my lord,
Of the vast crowd that waited on your fortunes ;
But am now become the whole train : the rest have left you.

Clar. Prithee, do thou leave me too. [*Servant exit*
The clap o' th' vulgar and loud popular applause
Are not the echo of our acts, but Fortune's.
Great men but dials are, which, when the sun
Is gone or hides his face, are hardly look'd upon.
But yesterday I was time's minister :
On me the whole court gaz'd, as at
Some comet set in Cassiopeia's chair :
Who but old Clarimont could with nods create,

And with a speaking eye command bare heads
And knees. But now—— [*Beats his breast again*
Greatness is but the shadow of the beams
Of prince's favours, nourish'd in extremes;
First taught to creep, and feed on hopes, to live
Upon the glance, and humbly to observe
Each under-minion, till its own desire
Work itself near enough to set itself on fire.
[*Studies a little*
Fain would I make my audit up with heaven,
For 'tis a large one; but the small, vain hopes,
Which yet I have of life and of revenge,
Smother these thoughts within me
Faster than they are born.

Enter FIDELIO *disguised like a friar*

A ghostly father!
My minutes are but few, I see by this.
Sir, you are welcome:
I was but now considering how to die,
And, trust me, I do find it something hard.
I shall extremely need some such good help
As yours to do it well.
Fid. Faith, my lord, divines do hold
The way to die well is to live well first.
[*Discovers himself*
Clar. Fidelio!
Fid. Not too loud: there's danger in't.
The king has promised life; but none as ye
Must know't: the enemies are too potent,
And must be soft'ned by degrees.
Clar. Why, then,
I see he hath not quite forgot pass'd services.
Fid. Not too much of that:
This is not gratitude; or, if it be, it does
As thankfulness in great ones use[s] to do;
It looks asquint, and seems to turn to favours,
But regards new ends.
Clar. Prithee, unriddle.
Fid. Why, to be short, it is your daughter's beauty,
Not your merit.
Clar. My fears prompt me too quick:
She's not turned whore, is she?
Fid. No; but her honesty is so strait beset,

That, if she be not victualled well within,
And have some sudden succours, she will, I fear,
Ere long surrender.

Clar. O Fidelio,
When kings do tempt, th' had need be angels that
Endure the shock, not women.

Fid. 'Tis true, my lord.
Yet let not uncertain fears create new griefs.
Doubt is of all the sharpest passion,
And often turns distempers to diseases.
Collect yourself, and be assur'd my zeal
Shall watch abroad; and, when I may reveal
Myself your servant, I'll not do't in breath,
But with the adventure of my life or death.

Clar. O, you are noble, sir, I know't, and mean
To hope the best. Farewell. [*Exeunt*

Enter LORENZO *and his father, with servants, whispering together and frowning. They pass over the stage, and exeunt*

SCENE II

Enter LORENZO *solus, as going to prison*

Arm'd with the love of sovereignty and revenge,
I'll ravish fortune, and all engines try,
That heaven or hell have yet discovered;
But I will scale my end, and plant desire
As high as any thought durst e'er aspire.
The dotage of the king shall not secure thee,
Poor old man!
Clarimont, I come: this night our quarrel ends!
Nothing but death could ever make us friends.
[*Knocks at the prison door*

Enter the Keeper

Where's old Clarimont?

Keep. In's bed, my lord.

Lor. In's grave, thou wouldst have said.

Keep. Must he then die to-night?

Lor. The king will have it so:
He fears the people love him, and to save
His life may prove tumultuous.

Keep. Poor gentleman! how quick
Is fate come on him! how sudden is all woe!

Bad days have wings ; the good on crutches go.
My lord,
Will't please you walk into that private chamber ?
The executioner shall straight be here.
[*Lorenzo goes forth, murders him within, enters again*

Lor. You must be sure to keep it secret now.
Perchance the king, to try your honesty,
And blind his daughter's eyes, will send to ask
Of's welfare.

Keep. O my lord !

Lor. Nay, I know you understand.
Farewell. [*Turns back again*
One thing I had forgot : if any ask
What groan that was, say 'tis an usual thing
Against great men's deaths to hear a noise at midnight.
So now, royal lecher, set you safe !
'Tis your death must secure my life ; I'll on !
Danger is but a bug-word ; my barque shall through,
Did mountains of black horrors me surround.
When fortunes hang in doubt,
Bravely to dare is bravely to get out.

ACT II

Scene I

Enter Lorenzo, Parmenio *attending*

All leave the chamber ! If any come, I'm busy.
Parmenio, be nigher—nigher yet.
What dar'st thou do to make thy master king,
Thyself a favourite ?

Par. 'Tis something blunt, my lord. [*Studies.*] Why, I dare do—
That which I dare not speak.

Lor. By all my hopes, spoke like the man I want !
'Twould be lost time to use much circumstance
To thee : shall we this night despatch the king ?

Par. This minute, were he my father !
He's not the first, nor shall he be the last.

Lor. Soul of my soul ! My better angel sure
Foresaw my wants, and sent thee hither.
Parmenio,

There's none but he stands 'twixt a crown and me.
The cloud that interpos'd betwixt my hopes before
Is, like a vapour, fall'n, and seen no more.
The house of Clarimont is lost : the king
Has sent one son to banishment, and I
Have sent the father.

Par. How, sir, you have not murdered him ! [*Starts*

Lor. Why ?

Par. Nothing, my lord ;
Only I'm sorry I had no hand in't.
'Sdeath, hath the villain killed him ? [*Aside*

Lor. O, thou art jealous ! Thy hand comes well enough.
This night I have determined that soon,
Ere the royal blood's a-tilt, you shall to horse.
'Tis easy to outride——

Par. Imagination itself, my lord !

Lor. For then report will say thou kill'dst him.
No matter.

Par. O, none at all, my lord.

Lor. When I am king, I can restore at ease.

Par. True, my lord.
What, if your excellence cast out, when I'm gone,
That Clarimont's youngest son did this, and took
His flight upon't. His discontent's known well
Enough to make of a suspicion
A most received truth.
Besides, wheresoev'r I go, I'll swear 'twas he.

Lor. By Jove, most rare ! when I am king, I shall
Be poorer than I am, by giving thee
Thy due. Away ! let's lose no time in words :
We're both resolv'd to put this cause to swords.
I'll to the king : thou to prepare for night.
Four hours hence, wait me in the gallery. [*Exeunt*

Scene II

Enter young Clarimont *solus*

Break, heart, and burst ! My father murdered,
And in the midst of all his hopes of life !
Methinks I see millions of furies stand,
Ready to catch my rage's sacrifice.
O, for a man that could invent more plagues

Than hell could hold! I have conceiv'd of wrong,
And am grown great already.
O sweet revenge, I humbly thee entreat,
Be my grief's midwife! let the mother die,
So thou bring'st forth her long'd-for progeny.
Methinks I feel the villain grow within me,
And spread through all my veins.
How I could murder now, poison or stab!
My head is full of mischief. Sulphur and flaming pitch
Shall be but mercy to those deaths I'll give. [*Exit*

Scene III

Enter the King, *with* Fidelio

Fid. Though it be not safe for subjects
To pry into the secrets of their prince,
Much less to question about them, yet
The implicit faith of blind obedience,
Poison'd with pleasing oft—and 't like your majesty,
Why do you court this lady thus?
King. Why dost thou ask?
Fid. I know 'tis insolence to make reply:
Yet hear me as the echo of the court, great sir;
They call your last-giv'n mercy and those favours
But fairer ends to lust.
King. The zeal hath got thy pardon. [*Stares upon him*
No more!
He that does offer to give direction
To his prince, is full of pride, not of discretion. [*Exit*
Fid. So,
To give kings good advice, may show, I see,
Men faithful, but not wise. I'm honest yet,
And I do fare the worst for't. O, the court!
There humours reign, and merits only serve
To mock with idle hopes those best deserve. [*Exit*

Scene IV

Enter Francelia, Bellamino

Fran. Sir, leave your compliment!
Methinks the sweetest speech is that that's meant.

Bel. Wrong not
My love, best creature, so to think my words
Are not the true ambassadors of my heart.
By thy fair self, I swear, Nature has been
Too partial in robbing heaven and earth
To give you all——
Fran. Their weaknesses you mean,
And I confess, my lord——
Bel. Their richest graces,
Sweetest! O, do not rack me thus! I love:
Can you give love again?
Fran. Yes, any love
That you dare ask, or I dare give, my lord.
Bel. O, but, fair lady, love must have no bounds:
It pines in prison.
Fran. O, but, my lord, hot loves,
If not contain'd, like fiery meteors,
Promise no good to others, and are themselves
Consum'd.

Enter the KING, *and* Lords *attending*

Bel. O, leave me not in doubt's distracting trance.
King. How, my boy? what, courting?
Bel. No, sir.
King. What was he doing then, Francelia?
Fran. So please your grace,
He was i' th' midst of all your praises, when
Your highness ent'red.
Bel. [*Aside.*] Hum! there's yet some hope then.
King. O, you are glad we are come, then! That discourse
Was tedious.
Fran. No, my lord;
I should have been well pleas'd to have heard him longer.
King. You are grown a courtier, fair one! Sileo,
Are the coaches ready?
Sil. Yes, and 't please your majesty.
King. Come,
We'll abroad then: this day invites us forth.
Where's our queen? [*Exeunt*

SCENE V

Enter young CLARIMONT, FIDELIO, *and young* FLORELIO

Clar. Then, with a pause fill'd up with sighs,
Ask him how strong his guards are ; but, above all,
Be sure t' apply inflaming corrosives :
Screw up his anger to the height, and make
His fears be double.
Officious friends and mediation
May else prove remedies.
Fid. Enough. If we
Do fail to act our parts to th' life in's tragedy,
May all those horrors that do threaten him
Fall upon us ! Farewell. [*Exeunt*
Clar. So, my revenge
Flies high : the villain first shall kill his father ;
And, while his hands are hot i' th' blood, this sword
Shall pierce him. Murder'd he shall sink quick to hell :
I will not give him leave t' unload himself
Of one poor single sin of thought ;
But, lest he should wake out
Of's great security, and shun his fate,
I will rock him on.
Mischiefs are like the cockatrice's eye :
If they see first, they kill ; if seen, they die. [*Exit*

ACT III

SCENE I

Enter KING, *young* FLORELIO, *and* FIDELIO

King. And must the villain kill me too ?
Flo. This very night.
King. Why, 'tis not possible :
What would he have had more ? He had my heart,
And might have had all but the name of king.
O, heaven had tied so strict a friendship, we
Could not part with 't : I durst have thought that I
Had merited fidelity from him.
Fid. O my lord, let ne'er so many drops,
Sweet as the morning dew, fall on the sea,

The brinish water turns them all to salt.
Where there's an ocean of ingratitude,
Favours must needs be lost.

King. Thou speak'st but truth. Who does to merit trust,
But writes an obligation in the dust.
Your counsels now my faithful life preserve,
Is there a way for pardon ?

Fid. Faith, sir,
It would pollute mercy to use it here.
The fact's so foul, it calls itself for death.

King. And it shall have it.
Traitor's enough ; but, when ungrateful comes,
It stops the mouth of pity.
Go, take our guards, and apprehend him straight.

Flo. Soft, great sir ! 'Twere fit
Your justice should consider what way is made :
If you shall apprehend him for treason unborn,
And which he only did intend,
Foolish report, which never was i' th' right,
May clear his guiltiness, and censure majesty.
If you'd permit him to approach the chamber,
(Yet who'ld advise treason should come so near ?)
You would take him in the act, and leave no place
For foul suspicion. Then, if your grace
Sent for his father,
And kept him with pretence of business by you,
Till he became the witness of th' attempt,
Envy itself could have no cause to bark.

King. Thou art my oracle : I cannot tell
Whether my debt be greater to thy faith
Or to thy counsel. Go and watch abroad,
And let these cares wait upon fate and me.
The captain of the guard 'twere fit you sounded ;
He may do mischief. Florelio, you
Shall to his father : the rest is mine to manage.
[*Exeunt Florelio and Fidelio*
These men are honest, and must be rewarded ;
They do deserve it. 'Tis most rare to find
A greatness that enjoys true friends ;
For commonly it makes us fear'd and hated.
The one doth breed offence : th' other leaves naked.
Let the impartial eye but look upon
All we call ours, and then again behold

The many hungry eyes of expectation
That wait upon our bounty, and it shall find
That we have scarce enough to keep men's hopes up,
We are rich if we can purchase friends.
Thrones, though they advance their glory ne'er so high,
Are but the seats of fear and misery. [*Exit*

Scene II

Enter Parmenio *and* Lorenzo

Par. In deep security, my lord,
The lady's at one window courted ;
The king, with Florelio and the favourite,
Contriving of a masque, which he must never see !
Lor. Good ! which he must never see.
O, thou dost hug my fates ! How I am ravish'd
To think upon ensuing joys ! Parmenio,
He's dead already.
Par. Six hours ago, my lord, you cannot think
How much ado I had to keep myself
From saying, 'And 't shall please your majesty,'
I' th' open presence to you. Methinks, one while
I see your highness sit like Jupiter
In state, with all the petty gods about you ;
And then
Again, in a more tempting shape than was
The shower of gold, lie in some Danae's lap,
More wanton than Europa's bull. Another time,
With some great train, as if you went to battle,
Rock'd in a downy coach, go take the air, and have
The thronging city, crowded into a handful,
Looking along to bless your eyes, and striving
Who shall cry loudest, 'God bless your majesty !'
Lor. And all the while thou, like my Ganymede,
Shalt taste ambrosia with me, while the petty gods
Burst with repining at thy happiness.
Thou shalt dispose of all, create, displace,
Be call'd my boy, revel and masque, what not ?
O, for one
Half-year I will not speak unto the people :
Take you that office, keep that part for yours.
O, how I long for night ! Thou canst not name
The pleasure could make the time not tedious.

Away unto thy watch, and, when the king's
A-bed, be here.

Par. I shall, my lord—and 't please your majesty,
I shall. [*Exeunt*

SCENE III

Enter the QUEEN AMASIA, BELLAMINO *her favourite,* DROLLIO, *Attendants*

Bel. What is the matter, madam, that the court
Is in such clouds to-night?
The king feigns mirth and freeness; but withal
Flashes of fury make escapes.

Queen. 'Tis strange,
My lord, you should not know.

Bel. Faith, madam, I
Know nothing.

Queen. Troth, nor I; but I suspect.
The clock no sooner struck, but all the statesmen
Started, as if they had been to run a race,
And the king told me 'twere fit I took my rest.
There's something in't; but these designs of state
We women know no more than our own fate.
To turn our talk—faith, my lord, where lies
That beauty, that so captivates you all?
She has a graceful garb, 'tis true.

Bel. Who, madam? Francelia?
O, she has a dainty foot and daintier hand,
An eye, round as a globe, and black as jet,
So full of majesty and life, that when
It most denies, it most invites.

Queen. These parts she has indeed; but is here all?

Bel. All? heaven forbid!
Her hair's so preciously fair and soft,
That, were she fall'n into some river, and
In danger, one would make a conscience
To save her life, for fear of spoiling it.
Her lips are gently swelled, like unto
Some blushing cherry, that hath newly tasted
The dew from heaven; and her cheeks——

Queen. Hold, hold, my lord!
All this is poetry: a painter could
Not flatter more. To my eye, now,
She is so slender! She's scarce, I think, a span
About i' th' middle.

Bel. O madam! you must think
Wise Nature, of such rich mould as she was fram'd,
Would make as little waste as could be!
Queen. So, so.
What think you of the upper part o' th' nose, then;
Does it not look as, if it did give way,
The eyes should shortly have an interview?
Bel. You're too severe a critic, madam: so good
A wit as yours could make, where there were any,
All bless'd perfections. After all,
Next to your highness, I'm resolved to think
She is chiefest beauty.
Queen. Not next to me, my lord!
Now I am sure you flatter; but 'tis too late
To chide you for it. Good-night. [*Exeunt*

Scene IV

Enter the King *going to bed*, Cleonax, *Lords*, *Attendants*

King. Good-night to all. Lord Cleonax,
A word in private! [*They whisper.*] Take away the light,
And shut the door. [*Exeunt King and Cleonax*

Enter Parmenio *and* Lorenzo

Lor. Is the king gone to bed?
Par. An hour ago, my lord.
Lor. What if he should not be asleep yet?
Par. No matter; ere his tongue can speak, our swords
Shall kill. What, though he call us traitors?
'Twill be his last, and may be pardoned.
Come, sir, bravely on! fear's worse than death:
You're lord of all, or not of your own breath.
Lor. Nay, if I fear, may I not live! Follow.

[*The King calls out, 'Treason!' Old Cleonax, rising to go out at the door to call for help, is met by his son, who took him for the King, and killed him: Lorenzo is presently of set purpose run through by Parmenio*

Scene V

Enter the King *in his nightgown, Lords, Attendants*

King. Trust me, most sad and strange!
A flood of grief beats at my eyes for vent.

Poor Cleonax, I'm truly sorry for thee.
Lords. So are we all.
King. This accident
Commands our pity ; but what is done, is done.
Let it not be as yet divulged.
Remove the corpse, and let it be the care
Of thee, Florelio, to see his burial
Honourable and private. Good thanks to all the rest.
Clarimont, stay you with me. [*Exeunt Lords, etc.*
The traitor's dead by Parmenio ; but you must know
There's one yet lives within me. I love, Clarimont !
Clar. That passion of all others, sir, heaven
Easiliest pardons : he lives not, sure, that loves not.
King. Ay, but my love's not pure ; 'tis great, not good,
Clarimont. I love—Francelia !
Clar. Take heed of unchaste fires, great sir ;
They mischief, sir. Forget her, faith, forget her.
Such fits as these are ever cur'd like agues—
Best when they are most starved.
If you shall give them their desired fuel,
They'll not be quench'd with ease ;
And it is ever seen (heaven keep my sovereign !)
The house they're bred in feels them first and ever.
King. Clarimont, thou wert ne'er in love ;
Thou art philosophical, and wouldst have reason
Guide where it was never yet companion.
Thou show'st thy want of love, but helpst not mine.
Counsel is now too late ;
It's like smith's water flung upon the coals,
Which more inflames. Here.
Thou twice hast sav'd my life, if thou now speed'st ;
Go to Francelia, and present
This jewel to her, and withal my love. [*Gives him a jewel*
Do't with thy best of language and respect.
Fair means at first we'll use ;
But foul shall come, if she the fair refuse.
Good-night, and good success.
Clar. Obedience is the best of what I am :
Your will's my law, sir. [*Exit.*] Why, then, it must be.
Was there no woman in the court to feed
Thy lust with, but my sister ; and none to be
The bawd, but I ?
Couldst thou not think of any other way
To express thy greatness, but by doing me wrong ?

My father's angry ghost, I see, is not full
Appeased yet. [*Studies*
Why should I make of murther thus begun
A massacre ?
He did my father right in his revenge :
Ay, but he wrong'd him first ; and yet, who knows
But it was justice to attempt by force ?
The removal of
Great favourites, though enemies to th' state,
Is not so warrantable—I'm in a maze.
Something I'll do, but what I cannot tell :
I fear the worst ; lust never ended well. [*Exit*

ACT IV

Scene I

Enter Francelia *and* Bellamino

Fran. Fie, leave this importunity, my lord !
I shall yield else, by this kiss I shall.
Bel. By this, and this, and this, thou shalt !
Heavens, what a breath is here ! Thy father fed
On musk and amber, when he begot thee, sure !
The wanton air,
Chaf'd by the hot scents of Arabic spices,
Is nothing nigh so sweet :
The ambrosia, the gods themselves were drunk with,
Dwells on thy lips.

Enter Florelio, *senior, behind*

Fran. Come, come, you flatter, 'tis on yours, my lord.
Bel. On mine ? Alas, Nature gave us the prickles,
You the roses, but meant that they should grow together.
[*Kisses again*
Fran. So, so : what, if the King or Florelio saw ye ?
Bel. What, if they did ? I can fear nothing now
But surfeits.
Come, we lose time, my fairest, do we not ? [*Kisses her again*
This is the minute.
Flo. By heaven,
This is not fair, madam.
Fran. Wonder strikes me dumb. [*Exit*
Flo. How does she kiss, favourite ?

Bel. Who, my lord ?
Flo. My wife, my lord. Draw, draw, or by all my hopes,
My rage will make me turn a murderer.
Bel. Not so easily. [*They fight*
Flo. Hold, let's breathe : why should I do him right,
Who has done me such wrong,
Or die for her that will not live for me ? [*Puts up*
Go, enjoy her ! [*Offers to go out*
Bel. Soft ! [*Pulls him back.*] You have stol'n a secret here,
That you must give again, or take my life.
Draw !
Flo. Prithee, disturb me not.
Bel. No,
Unless you promise never to disclose
What you have here discover'd, this must be
The passage. [*Stands betwixt the door and Florelio*
Flo. Hum !
I will be mute, credit me : I will not speak one word.
[*Offers to go out again*
Bel. Nay [*pulls him back*], you must swear it too.
Flo. If I must, I must.
By heaven and by my honour, how tame a thing
A cuckold is ! [*Exit*
Bel. 'Sdeath,
Why did I let him go ? We can no more
Subsist together than fire and water.
One of us two must die ;
And, charity tells me, better he than I.
But how ?
It is not for my honour to kill him basely ;
Nor is it for hers to kill him otherwise.
Th' whole court will guess the quarrel, if it be a duel.
[*Studies again*
It is decreed. No matter which way, so he fall :
Mine, in respect of hers, are no respects at all. [*Exit*

SCENE II

Enter DOCO DISCOPIO *and* DROLLIO

Doc. Abused, grossly abused !
A base affront, believe it, Drollio !
Drol. Why, what's the matter, signior ?

Doc. Why, do you hear nothing ?
Drol. No. Why, what should it be ?
Doc. Pisaro is the man.
Drol. Fie, fie ! it cannot be ;
The state could not commit so great an oversight.
Neglect a man of merit for Pisaro !
Fie, fie !
Doc. Want of judgment, Drollio.
An unlearned council : I ever told you so ;
Never more heads, nor never less wit, believe't.
Drol. Say you so, signior ? that's hard. What say you to
Diano ?
Doc. Alas, an ordinary brain !
Talks and talks, it's true, but speaks more than he is :
Believe't betwixt you and I, a mere prattler.
There's Falorio, too ; why, he cannot read his own hand :
Vasquez cannot speak sense without two days' premeditation. Sillio, Vechio, Caronnio—all stones in their head !
Drol. If I
Should tell these lords now, signior, what you say,
It might cost an ear or so.
Doc. Ay. Why, there's another abuse i' th' state : a man
Shall have his ears cut off for speaking a truth.
A sick government, Drollio, and a weak one, believe't.
It never thriv'd, since Spain and we grew so great.
There is a mystery in that too, Drollio :
I will know all before they have any more
Of my money——
Drol. Peace, signior ! The king ! [*Exeunt*

Enter the King, Queen, Lords, *an* Ambassador *from Spain, who has his audience. After which the* King *goes out talking with* Fidelio ; *the rest follow. Then enter the two brothers* Florelio ; *the elder speaks earnestly*

Flor. sen. I prithee,
Leave me : by all that's good, thou canst not know it.
Why shouldst thou thus in vain torment thyself
And me ? [*They whisper*
Flor. jun. Well, I guess ; and 'tis enough.
[*Exit. The elder Florelio goes out at another door*

SCENE III

Enter CLARIMONT *and* FRANCELIA

Fran. Think not, good sir,
Your elegant enforcements can seduce
My weaker innocence :
It's a resolution grounded ; and sooner
Shall the fixed orbs be lifted off their hinges,
Than I be mov'd to any act that bears
The name of foul. You know the way you came, sir.

Clar. Is this all the respect the king shall have ?
No, you would do well to clothe this harsh denial
In better language.

Fran. You may please to say,
I owe my life unto my sovereign,
And should be proud to pay it in at any
Warning, were it ne'er so short. But, for my chastity,
It doth so much concern another, I can
By no means part with it. So, fare you well, sir. [*Exit*

Clar. By heaven, a saint, no woman !
Sure, she was born o' th' virtues of her mother,
Not of her vices. The whole sex may come
To be thought well of for her sake. I long
To meet Florelio :
My joy is not complete, till I have cured
His jealousies as well as mine. [*Exit*

Enter FLORELIO *and a* Boy

Flor. There was
A time when snakes and adders had no being ;
When the poor infant-world had no worse reptiles
Than were the melon and the strawberry !
Those were the golden times of innocence.
There were no kings then, nor no lustful peers,
No smooth-fac'd favourites, nor no cuckolds, sure.
O,
How happy is that man, whose humbler thoughts
Kept him from court ; who never yet was taught
The glorious way unto damnation !
Who never did aspire
Further than the cool shades of quiet rest !
How have the heavens his lower wishes bless'd !
Sleep makes his labours sweet, and innocence

Does his mean fortunes truly recompense:
He feels no hot loves, nor no palsy-fears,
No fits of filthy lusts, or of pale jealousies:
He wants, it's true, our clothes, our masks, our diet,
And wants our cares, our fears, and our disquiets.
But this
Is all but raving, and does distemper more.
I'll sleep. [*Lies all along on the ground.*] Boy, sing the song I gave you.

A Song to a Lute

Hast thou seen the down i' th' air,
when wanton blasts have tost it;
Or the ship on the sea,
when ruder waves have crost it?
Hast thou mark'd the crocodile's weeping,
or the fox's sleeping?
Or hast view'd the peacock in his pride,
or the dove by his bride,
when he courts for his lechery?
O, so fickle, O, so vain, O, so false, so false is she!

Flor. Good boy, leave me! [*Boy exit*

Re-enter Clarimont

Clar. How now, Florelio, melancholy?
Flor. No, I was studying.
Prithee, resolve me, whether it be better to
Maintain a strong, implicit faith, that can
By no means be opprest?
Or, falling to the bottom at the first,
Arm'd with disdain and with contempts, to scorn the worst?
Clar. This is a subtle one; but why studying about this?
Flor. Faith, I would find a good receipt for the head-ache,
That's all.
Clar. Hum,
I know now whereabouts you are. No more on't!
I'm come to clear those doubts— Your wife is chaste,
Chaste as the turtle-dove.
Flor. Ha, ha, ha!
Clar. Ha!
Why do you laugh? I know she is: 'tis not

So many hours, since I tempted her
With all my eloquence, and for the king,
Yet found her cold as ice.
Flor. Ha, ha, ha !
Clar. You do not well to tempt a friend : you do
Forget she is my sister.
Flor. I would I ne'er had known you had one.
Clar. You'll give a reason now for this.
Flor. None.
Clar. By all that's good, since our dear father left us,
We are become his scorn ; look you, sir,
I dare maintain it. [*Draws*
Flor. But I dare not. Put up, put up, young man,
When thou hast known a woman, thou wilt be tamer.
[*Exit*
Clar. Ha ! what should this mean ? I know
He's valiant, wise, discreet ; and what of that ?
Passion,
When it hath got the bit, doth ofttimes throw
The rider. Yet why should I be peremptory ?
She may, for ought I know, be yet unchaste
With some unworthy groom. [*Studies.*] What, if I stole
Into some corner, and heard her at confession ?
'Twould not be amiss ; for souls at such a time,
Like ships in tempests, throw out all they have.
And, now I think on't, her trial shall be quick.
Friend, I'll do thee right :
Come on't what will, she dies, if she be light. [*Exit*

SCENE IV

Enter SIGNIOR MULTECARNI *the* Poet, *and two of the* Actors

Mul. Well, if there be no remedy, one must act two parts. Roselio shall be the fool and the lord, and Tisso the citizen and the cuckold.

1 *Act.* That cannot be, signior : you know, one still comes in, when the other goes out.

Mul. By Jove, 'tis true. Let me see, we'll contrive it : the lord and the usurer, the citizen and the politician ; and, sure, they never are together. But who shall act the honest lawyer ? 'tis a hard part, that !

2 *Act.* And a tedious one ! It's admired you would

put it in, squire; and 'tis against your own rules to represent anything on the stage that cannot be.

Mul. Why, dost think 'tis impossible for a lawyer to be honest?

1 *Act.* As 'tis for a lord treasurer to be poor, or for a king not to be cozened. There's little Robin, in debt within these three years, grown fat and full by the trade; and then there's Borachio, an unknown man, got it all by speaking loud and bawling. Believe it, sir, they have no more conscience than an inn-keeper.

Mul. I grant you all this: an old cook and a good will please all palates. There's that for the young tapers of the law: then there's a bawdy jest or two extraordinary for the ladies; and, when it comes to be acted in private, I'll have a jerk at the state for the country gentlemen. If it does not take, my masters, it lies not upon me: I have provided well; and, if the stomach of the times be naught, the fault's not in the meat or in the cook. Come, let's find out Lepido, and dine at the Mermaid. Come, let us have one rouse, my Joves, in Aristippus: we shall conceive the better afterwards.

Act. Agreed, agreed. [*Exeunt singing*

Come, come away to the tavern, I say;
For now at home is washing-day.
Leave your prittle-prattle, let's have a pottle:
We are not so wise as Aristotle.

SCENE V

Enter CLARIMONT *and* FLORELIO *senior.*

Clar. By heaven,
She's false, false as the tears of crocodiles,
Or what is yet more feign'd, I do confess.
Your pardon, Florelio, come, pray, your pardon;
Perchance I may deserve it.
Flor. You have it, so has she;
Would heaven would do it as easily as I.
Clar. Heaven cannot do so foul an act. She has——
O, she has done too much! And, should not I
See justice done, the gods would punish me.
Brother, clear up!
The world shall not be one day elder, ere
I see thy injuries revenged.

This night the king will revel and be gamesome :
He will change beds with thee. Deny him not,
And leave the rest to me.
Flor. Thy youth, I see, doth put thee on too fast :
Thou hast too much of passion, gentle brother.
Think'st thou the death of a poor lustful king
Or peer can give me ease ?
No ; for, if it could,
My hand durst go as far that way as thine.
Had she been chaste, there had no tempters been ;
Or, if there had, I had not thought it sin.
Draw not thy sword at all, I do beseech thee ;
'Twill not deserve one drop of noble blood.
Forget it, do, for my sake.
Clar. May heaven forget me then !
Where is the courage of thy house become ?
When didst thou cease to be thyself ? Shall two
Brave families be wrong'd—most basely wrong'd—
And shall we tamely, like philosophers,
Dispute it without reasons ?
First may I live the scorn of all the world,
Then die forgotten ! No, no ;
Were there as many actors in thy wrong,
As does the vast stage of the world now bear,
Not one should 'scape my rage : I and my ghost
Would persecute them all.
By all our ties, of love, of brother, friend ;
By what thou hold'st most dear, I do conjure thee
To leave this work to me ;
And, if e'er thou canst think
That I present thee not a full revenge,
Then take it out on me.
Flor. Thy zeal hath overcome me :
What wouldst thou have me do ?
Clar. Nothing but this.
Obey the king in all he shall desire,
And let your servants be at my dispose
This night. One of your faithful'st confidants
Send hither presently.
Flor. Well, I shall ; but what
You'll do, heaven knows : I know not, nor will I.
It is enough that I, against my will,
Am made a passive instrument of ill.
Farewell. [*Exit*

Clar. So there is but this : the wanton king this night
Thinks to embrace my sister : his bed shall prove
His grave ; his own favourite shall make it so.
I have persuaded him
She yields, and this night doth expect him : he,
To make sure o' th' husband, by my advice, as if
He did intend some jest, means to change lodgings
With wrong'd Florelio the favourite.

Enter Petruchio

O Petruchio, welcome ! You have other clothes ;
These I should borrow for a little while :
In masquing times disguises are in fashion.
I have a pretty plot in hand ;
And, if it take, 'twill be some crowns in thy way.
Pet. I shall pray hard it may, sir ;
My clothes, howsoever, are at your service.
Clar. And I
At yours, Petruchio. But you must be dumb
And secret now.
Pet. As any statue, sir.
Clar. Come, then, let us about it ! [*Exeunt*

ACT V

Scene I

Enter Lepido *and* Drollio

Drol. A rare masque, no doubt ; who contriv'd it ?
Lep. Marry, he that says 'tis good, howsoe'er he has made it,
Signior Multecarni.
Drol. Who, the poet-laureat ?
Lep. The same.
Drol. O, then, 'twere blasphemy to speak against it.
What, are we full
Of Cupids ? Do we sail upon the vast,
And re-sail, and fetch the masque from the clouds ?
Lep. Away, critic ! thou never understood'st him.
Drol. Troth, I confess it ; but my comfort is,
Others are troubled with the same disease,
'Tis epidemical, Lepido ; take't on my word.
And so let's in, and see how things go forward. [*Exeunt*

Scene II

Enter Francelia *alone, weeping*

Fran. Swell on, my griefs ; and O, ye gentler tears,
Drop still, and never cease to fall till you
Become a boundless ocean, then drown
The source that sent you out,
And hide Francelia from her husband's sight,
Her wronged husband's !
O, could my Florelio but see
How all hot flames within me are gone forth,
Sure he would love again ! Yet sure he would not !
Heavens,
How just you are, and, O, how wicked I am !
My heart beats thick,
As if my end were nigh ; and would it were !
A better time death cannot take.
An absolution I have had, and have confest
My unchaste love unto my ghostly father.
My peace is made above ; but here below ?—
What mak'st thou here, Petruchio ?

Enter Clarimont *like to Petruchio*

Clar. [*aside*]. She weeps : the whore repents perchance.
[*Aloud*] Madam,
It is my master's pleasure that this night
You keep your chamber.
Fran. Thy voice and countenance are not the same ;
They tell me that thy master is displeas'd.
Clar. Madam, it may be so ; but that to me
Is as unknown as is the new-found world.
I am his servant, and obey commands.
Fran. And so am I. I pr'ythee tell him so ;
I will not stir. [*Exit*
Clar. How cunning is the devil in a woman's shape !
He had almost again persuaded me
To have become her brother.

Enter Servant.

Ser. Petruchio,
The favourite is lighted at the door,
And asks to see my lady.
Clar. My lady is retired : where is he ? [*Exit Servant*
This to my heart's desire falls out.

Enter Bellamino *the favourite*

Bel. Where is Francelia ?
Clar. My lord,
She is not well, and craves your lordship's pardon.
Bel. What, sick upon
A masque-night, and when the king sends for her ?
Come, come, that must not be : which way is she ?
[*Clarimont steps to him, and whispers. He starts*
By heaven !
Clar. By heaven !
Nor will she ever see you more, if he—
Bel. I understand you—I am Bellamino—
If e'er he see the morning. I had decreed it ;
Nor should he have surviv'd three days, had he
Been ne'er so silent. This night's his last, Petruchio :
This arm shall make it so ; I will not trust
My brother with the act.
Clar. Nobly resolv'd !
But how or where, my lord ?
Bel. No matter where.
Rather than fail, I'll make the presence chamber
Be the place of execution.
Clar. Still nobly !
But, my lord——
Bel. 'But' again, Petruchio ?
Clar. And again, my lord.
No, no, my lady loves you well, but loves
Her honour too ; and there are ways (I hope)
To keep the one, and yet not lose the other.
Do not I know my lady lies alone,
And will feign herself sick this night, and all
On purpose too ? am not I to let you
Into her chamber,
And to give out, the fact once done, that he
Killed himself ?——

[*The play ends here imperfectly.*]

LETTERS
To divers Eminent
PERSONAGES:
Written on several Occasions,

By

Sir JOHN SUCKLING.

Printed by his owne Copy.

LONDON,
Printed by *Ruth Raworth* for *Humphrey Moseley*, and are to be sold at his shop at the signe of the *Princes Arms* in S. *Pauls* Church-yard. 1646

LETTERS

I

Fortune and Love have ever been so incompatible, that it is no wonder (Madam) if, having had so much of the one for you, I have ever found so little of the other for myself. Coming to town (and having rid as if I had brought intelligence of a new-landed enemy to the State), I find you gone the day before, and with you (Madam) all that is considerable upon the place; for, though you have left behind you faces whose beauties might well excuse perjury in others, yet in me they cannot, since, to the making that no sin, Love's casuists have most rationally resolved that she for whom we forsake ought to be handsomer than the forsaken, which would be here impossible. So that now a gallery, hung with Titian's or Vandike's hand, and a chamber filled with living excellence, are the same things to me; and the use that I shall make of that sex now will be no other than that which the wiser sort of Catholiques do of pictures—at the highest, they but serve to raise my devotion to you. Should a great beauty now resolve to take me in (as that is all they think belongs to it) with the artillery of her eyes, it would be as vain as for a thief to set upon a new-robbed passenger. You (Madam) have my heart already; nor can you use it unkindly but with some injustice, since (besides that it left a good service to wait on you) it was never known to stay so long or so willingly before with any. After all, the wages will not be high, for it hath been brought up under Platonicks, and knows no other way of being paid for service than by being commanded more; which truth when you doubt, you have but to send to its master and

Your humble Servant,

J. S.

II

A Dissuasion from Love

Jack,

Though your disease be in the number of those that are better cured with time than precept, yet, since it is lawful for every man to practise upon them that are forsaken and given over (which I take to be your state), I will adventure to prescribe to you ; and of the innocence of the physic you shall not need to doubt, since I can assure you I take it daily myself.

To begin methodically, I should enjoin you travel ; for absence doth in a kind remove the cause (removing the object), and answers the physician's first recipez, vomiting and purging ; but this would be too harsh, and indeed not agreeing to my way. I therefore advise you to see her as often as you can ; for (besides that the rarity of visits endears them) this may bring you to surprise her, and to discover little defects which, though they cure not absolutely, yet they qualify the fury of the fever. As near as you can, let it be unseasonably, when she is in sickness and disorder ; for that will let you know she is mortal, and a woman, and the last would be enough to a wise man. If you could draw her to discourse of things she understands not, it would not be amiss.

Contrive yourself often into the company of the cried-up beauties ; for if you read but one book, it will be no wonder if you speak or write that style : variety will breed distraction, and that will be a kind of diverting the humour.

I would not have you deny yourself the little things, for these agues are easier cured with surfeits than abstinence ; rather (if you can) taste all, for that (as an old author saith) will let you see—

That the thing for which we woo
Is not worth so much ado.

But since that here would be impossible, you must be content to take it where you can get it. And this for your comfort I must tell you (Jack) that mistress and woman differ no otherwise than Frontiniack and ordinary grapes ; which though a man loves never so well, yet, if he surfeit of the last, he will care but little for the first.

I would have you leave that foolish humour (Jack) of saying you are not in love with her, and pretending you care not for her ; for smothered fires are dangerous, and malicious humours are best and safest vented and breathed out. Continue your affection to your rival still : that will secure you from one way of loving, which is in spite ; and preserve your friendship with her woman, for who knows but she may help you to the remedy ?

A jolly glass and right company would much conduce to the cure ; for though in the Scripture (by the way, it is but Apocrypha) woman is resolved stronger than wine, yet whether it will be so or not, when wit is joined to it, may prove a fresh question.

Marrying (as our friend the late ambassador hath wittily observed) would certainly cure it ; but that is a kind of live pigeons laid to the soles of the feet, a last remedy, and (to say truth) worse than the disease.

But (Jack) I remember I promised you a letter, not a treaty. I now expect you should be just ; and as I have shewed you how to get out of love, so you (according to our bargain) should teach me how to get into it. I know you have but one way, and will prescribe me now to look upon Mistress Howard ; but for that I must tell you aforehand that it is in love as in antipathy—the capers which will make my Lord of Dorset go from the table, another man will eat up. And (Jack) if you would make a visit to Bedlam, you shall find that there are rarely two there mad for the same thing.

Your humble Servant.

III

Though (Madam) I have ever hitherto believed play to be a thing in itself as merely indifferent as religion to a statesman, or love made in a privy-chamber ; yet hearing you have resolved it otherwise for me, my faith shall alter without becoming more learned upon it, or once knowing why it should do so. So great and just a sovereignty is that your reason hath above all others, that mine must be a rebel to itself, should it not obey thus easily ; and, indeed, all the infallibility of judgment we poor Protestants have, is at this time wholly in your hands.

The loss of a mistress (which kills men only in romances, and is still digested with the first meat we eat after it) had yet in me raised up so much passion, and so just a quarrel (as I thought) to Fortune for it, that I could not but tempt her to do me right upon the first occasion ; yet (Madam) has it not made me so desperate, but that I can sit down a loser both of that time and money too, when there shall be the least fear of losing you.

And now, since I know your ladyship is too wise to suppose to yourself impossibilities, and therefore cannot think of such a thing as of making me absolutely good, it will not be without some impatience that I shall attend to know what sin you will be pleased to assign me in the room of this : something that has less danger about it, I conceive it would be ; and therefore, if you please (Madam), let it not be women, for, to say truth, it is a diet I cannot yet relish, otherwise than men do that on which they surfeited last.

Your humblest Servant,
J. S.

IV

Madam,

Before this instant I did not believe Warwickshire the other world, or that Milcot walks had been the blessed shades. At my arrival here I am saluted by all as risen from the dead, and have had joy given me preposterously and as impertinently as they give it to men who marry where they do not love. If I should now die in earnest, my friends have nothing to pay me, for they have discharged the rites of funeral sorrow beforehand. Nor do I take it ill that report, which made Richard the Second alive so often after he was dead, should kill me as often when I am alive. The advantage is on my side. The only quarrel I have is, that they have made use of the whole Book of Martyrs upon me; and without all question, the first Christians under the great persecutions suffered not in 500 years so many several ways as I have done in six days in this lewd town. This (Madam) may seem strange unto you now, who know the company I was in; and certainly, if at that time I had departed this transitory world, it had been a way they had never thought on; and this epitaph of the Spaniard's (changing the names) would better have become my gravestone than any other my friends the poets would have found out for me:

Epitaph.

Here lies Don Alonzo,
Slain by a wound received under
His left Pap,
The Orifice of which was so
Small, no Chirurgeon could
Discover it.
Reader,
If thou wouldst avoid so strange
A Death,
Look not upon Lucinda's eyes.

Now all this discourse of dying (Madam) is but to let you know how dangerous a thing it is to be long from London, especially in a place which is concluded out of the world. If you are not to be frighted hither, I hope you are to be persuaded ; and if good sermons, or good plays, new braveries, or fresh wit, revels (Madam), masques that are to be, have any rhetoric about them, here they are, I assure you, in perfection, without asking leave of the provinces beyond seas, or the assent of ——. I write not this that you should think I value these pleasures above those of Milcot ; for I must here protest, I prefer the single tabor and pipe in the great hall, far above them; and were there no more belonging to a journey than riding so many miles (would my affairs conspire with my desires) your ladyship should find there, not at the bottom of a letter,

Madam,
Your humble Servant.

V

Madam,

I thank Heaven we live in an age in which the widows wear colours, and in a country where the women that lose their husbands may be trusted with poison, knives, and all the burning coals in Europe, notwithstanding the precedent of Sophonisba and Portia. Considering the estate you are in now, I should reasonably imagine meaner physicians than Seneca or Cicero might administer comfort. It is so far from me to imagine this accident should surprise you, that, in my opinion, it should not make you wonder, it being not strange at all that a man who hath lived ill all his time in a house should break a window, or steal away in the night through an unusual postern. You are now free ; and what matter is it to a prisoner whether the fetters be taken off the ordinary way or not ? If instead of putting off handsomely the chain of matrimony, he hath rudely broke it, 'tis at his own charge, nor should it cost you a tear. Nothing (Madam) has worse mien than counterfeit sorrow ; and you must have the height of woman's art to make yours appear other, especially when the spectators shall consider all the story.

The sword that is placed betwixt a contracted princess and an ambassador was as much a husband ; and the only difference was that that sword, laid in the bed, allowed one to supply its place. This husband denied all, like a false crow set up in a garden, which keeps others from the fruit it cannot taste itself. I would not have you so much as enquire whether it were with his garters or his cloak-bag strings, nor engage yourself to fresh sighs by hearing new relations.

The Spanish princess Leonina (whom Balzac delivers the ornament of the last age) was wise; who, hearing a post was sent to tell her her husband was dead, and knowing the secretary was in the way for that purpose, sent to stay the post till the arrival of the secretary, that she might not be obliged to shed tears twice. Of ill things the less we know the better. Curiosity would here be as vain as if a cuckold should inquire whether it were upon the couch or a bed, and whether the cavalier pulled off his spurs first or not.

I must confess it is a just subject for our sorrow to hear of any that does quit his station without his leave that placed him there; and yet, as ill a mien as this act has, 'twas *a-la-Romansci*, as you may see by a line of Master Shakespeare's who, bringing in Titinius after a lost battle, speaking to his sword, and bidding it find out his heart, adds—

> 'By your leave, gods, this [is] a Roman's part.'

'Tis true, I think cloak-bag strings were not then so much in fashion; but to those that are not swordmen the way is not so despicable; and, for mine own part, I assure you Christianity highly governs me in the minute in which I do not wish with all my heart, that all the discontents in his majesty's three kingdoms would find out this very way of satisfying themselves and the world.

I. S.

VI

Sir,

Since the settling of your family would certainly much conduce to the settling of your mind (the care of the one being the trouble of the other), I cannot but reckon it in the number of my misfortunes, that my affairs deny me the content I should take to serve you in it.

It would be too late now for me (I suppose) to advance or confirm you in those good resolutions I left you in, being confident your own reason hath been so just to you, as long before this to have represented a necessity of redeeming time and fame, and of taking a handsome revenge upon yourself for the injuries you would have done yourself.

Change, I confess (to them that think all at once) must needs be strange, and to you hateful, whom first your own nature, and then custom, another nature, have brought to delight in those narrow and uncouth ways we found you in. You must therefore consider that you have entered into one of those near conjunctions of which death is the only honourable divorce, and that you have now to please another as well as yourself; who, though she be a woman, and by the patent she hath from nature hath liberty to do simply, yet can she never be so strongly bribed against herself as to betray at once all her hopes and ends, and for your sake resolve to live miserably. Examples of such loving folly our times afford but few; and in those there are, you shall find the stock of love to have been greater, and their strengths richer to maintain it, than is to be feared yours can be.

Woman (besides the trouble) has ever been thought a rent-charge; and though through the vain curiosity of man it has often been inclosed, yet has it seldom been brought to improve or become profitable. It faring with married men for the most part, as with those that at great charges wall in grounds and plant, who cheaper might have eaten melons elsewhere, than in their own gardens cucumbers. The ruins that either time, sickness, or the melancholy you shall give her, shall bring, must all be made up at your cost; for that thing a husband is but tenant for life in what he holds, and is bound to leave the place tenantable to the next that shall take it. To conclude, a young woman is a hawk upon her wings; and if she be handsome, she is the more subject to go out at check. Falconers, that can but seldom spring right game, should still have something about them to take them down with. The lure to which all stoop in this world is either garnished with profit or pleasure; and when you cannot throw her the one, you must be content to shew out the other. This I speak not out of a desire to increase your fears, which are already but too many, but out of a hope that, when you know the worst, you will at once leap into the river, and swim through handsomely, and not (weather-beaten with the divers blasts of irresolution) stand shivering upon the brink.

Doubts and fears are, of all, the sharpest passions, and are still turning distempers to diseases. Through these false opticks 'tis, all that you see is, like evening shadows, disproportionable to the truth, and strangely longer than the true substance. These (when a handsome way of living, and expense suitable to your fortune, is represented to you) makes you in their stead see want and beggary, thrusting upon your judgment impossibilities for likelihoods, which they with ease may do, since (as Solomon saith) they betray the succours that reason offers.

'Tis true that all here below is but diversified folly, and that the little things we laugh at children for, we do but act ourselves in great; yet is there difference of lunacy; and, of the two, I had much rather be mad with him that (when he had nothing) thought all the ships that came into the haven his, than with you who (when you have so much coming in) think you have nothing. This fear of losing all in you is the ill issue of a worse parent, desire of getting, in you; so that, if you would not be passion-rent, you must cease to be covetous. Money in your hand is like the conjurer's devil, which while you think you have, that has you.

The rich talent that God hath given, or rather lent you, you have hid up in a napkin; and man knows no difference betwixt that and treasures kept by ill spirits, but that yours is the harder to come by. To the guarding of these golden apples, of necessity must be kept those never sleeping dragons, Fear, Jealousy, Distrust, and the like; so that you are come to moralize Æsop, and his fables of beasts are become prophecies of you; for, while you have catched at the shadow, uncertain riches, you have lost the substance, true content.

The desire I have ye should be yet yourself, and that your friends should have occasion to bless the providence of misfortune, has made me take the boldness to give you your own character, and to show you yourself out of your own glass; and though all this tells you but where you are, yet it is some part of a cure to have searched the wound. And for this time we must be content to do like travellers, who first find out the place, and then the nearest way.

VII

My Noble Lord,

Your humble servant had the honour to receive from your hand a letter, and had the grace upon the sight of it to blush. I but then found my own negligence, and but now could have the opportunity to ask pardon for it. We have ever since been upon a march, and the places we are come to have afforded rather blood than ink; and of all things, sheets have been the hardest to come by, specially those of paper. If these few lines shall have the happiness to kiss your hand, they can assure that he that sent them knows none to whom he owes more obligation than to your lordship, and to whom he would more willingly pay it; and that it must be no less than necessity itself that can hinder him from often presenting it. Germany hath no whit altered me: I am still the humble servant of my Lord —— that I was, and when I cease to be so, I must cease to be

John Suckling.

VIII

Since you can breathe no one desire that was not mine before it was yours—or full as soon (for hearts united never knew divided wishes)—I must chide you (dear princess) not thank you, for your present, and (if at least I knew how) be angry with you for sending him a blush, who needs must blush because you sent him one. If you are conscious of much, what am I then, who guilty am of all you can pretend to, and something more—unworthiness? But why should you at all (heart of my heart) disturb the happiness you have so newly given me, or make love feed on doubts, that never yet could thrive on such a diet? *If I have granted your request!* Oh! Why will you ever say that you have studied me, and give so great an interest to the contrary? That wretched *if* speaks as if I would refuse what you desire, or could—both which are equally impossible. My dear princess, there needs no new approaches where the breach is made already; nor must you ever ask anywhere, but of your fair self, for anything that shall concern

Your humble Servant.

IX

My dearest Princess,

But that I know I love you more than ever any did any, and that yet I hate myself because I can love you no more, I should now most unsatisfied dispatch away this messenger.

The little that I can write to what I would, makes me think writing a dull commerce, and then—how can I choose but wish myself with you to say the rest? My dear dear, think what merit, virtue, beauty, what and how far Aglaura, with all her charms, can oblige; and so far and something more I am.

Your humble Servant.

X

A letter to a friend to dissuade him from marrying a widow which he had formerly been in love with, and quitted.

At this time when no hot planet fires the blood, and when the lunaticks of Bedlam themselves are trusted abroad, that you should run mad, is (Sir) not so much a subject for your friends' pity as their wonder. 'Tis true, love is a natural distemper, a kind of small pocks. Every one either hath had it, or is to expect it, and the sooner the better.

Thus far you are excused. But having been well cured of a fever, to court a relapse, to make love the second time in the same place, is (not to flatter you) neither better nor worse than to fall into a quagmire by chance, and ride into it afterwards on purpose. 'Tis not love (Tom) that doth the mischief, but constancy; for love is of the nature of a burning-glass, which, kept still in one place, fireth: changed often, it doth nothing—a kind of glowing coal which, with shifting from hand to hand, a man easily endures. But then to marry (Tom)! Why, thou hadst better to live honest. Love, thou knowest, is blind; what will he do when he

An answer to the letter.

Cease to wonder (honest Jack) and give me leave to pity thee, who labourest to condemn that which thou confessest natural, and the sooner had the better.

Thus far there needs no excuse, unless it be on thy behalf, who stylest second thoughts (which are by all allowed the best) a relapse, and talkest of a quagmire where no man ever stuck fast, and accusest constancy of mischief in what is natural, and advisedly undertaken.

'Tis confessed that love changed often doth nothing—nay, 'tis nothing; for love and change are incompatible; but where it is kept fixed to its first object, though it burn not, yet it warms and cherisheth, so as it needs no transplantation or change of soil to make it fruitful; and certainly, if love be natural, to marry is the best recipe for living honest.

Yes, I know what marriage is, and know you know it not, by terming it the dearest way of curing love; for certainly there goes more charge to the keeping of a stable full of horses, than one only steed; and much of vanity is therein besides, when, be the errand what it will, this one steed shall serve your turn as well

hath fetters on, thinkest thou ?

Dost thou know what marriage is ? 'Tis curing of love the dearest way, or waking a losing gamester out of a winning dream, and after a long expectation of a strange banquet, a presentation of a homely meal. Alas ! (Tom) love seeds when it runs up to matrimony, and is good for nothing. Like some fruit-trees, it must be transplanted, if thou wouldst have it active, and bring forth anything.

Thou now perchance hast vowed all that can be vowed to any one face, and thinkest thou hast left nothing unsaid to it ; do but make love to another, and if thou art not suddenly furnished with new language and fresh oaths, I will conclude Cupid hath used thee worse than ever he did any of his train.

After all this, to marry a widow, a kind of chew'd meat ! What a fantastical stomach hast thou, that canst not eat of a dish till another man hath cut of it ! Who would wash after another, when he might have fresh water, enough for asking ?

Life is sometimes a long journey. To be tied to ride upon one beast still, and that half tired to thy hand too ! Think upon that (Tom).

Well, if thou must needs marry (as who can tell to what height thou hast as twenty more. Oh, if you could serve your steed so !

Marriage turns pleasing dreams to ravishing realities, which out-do what fancy or expectation can frame unto themselves.

That love doth seed when it runs into matrimony, is undoubted truth ; how else should it increase and multiply, which is its greatest blessing ?

'Tis not the want of love, nor Cupid's fault, if every day afford not new language and new ways of expressing affection : it rather may be caused through an excess of joy, which oftentimes strikes dumb.

These things considered, I will marry ; nay, and to prove the second paradox false, I'll marry a widow, who is rather the chewer than thing chewed. How strangely fantastical is he who will be an hour in plucking on a strait-boot, when he may be forthwith furnished with enough that will come on easily, and do him as much credit and better service ? Wine, when first broached, drinks not half so well as after a while drawing. Would you not think him a madman who, whilst he might fair and easily ride on the beaten roadway, should trouble himself with breaking up of gaps ? A well-wayed horse will safely convey thee to thy journey's

sinned ?), let it be a maid, and no widow; for (as a modern author hath wittily resolved in this case) 'tis better (if a man must be in prison) to lie in a private room than in the hole.

end, when an unbacked filly may by chance give thee a fall. 'Tis prince-like to marry a widow, for 'tis to have a taster.

'Tis true, life may prove a long journey ; and so, believe me, it must do—a very long one too, before the beast you talk of prove tir'd. Think you upon that (Jack).

Thus, Jack, thou seest my well-ta'en resolution of marrying, and that a widow, not a maid ; to which I am much induced out of what Pythagoras saith (in his *2da Sect. cuniculorum*) that it is better lying in the hole than sitting in the stocks.

XI

When I receive your lines (my dear princess) and find there expressions of a passion ; though reason and my own immerit tell me it must not be for me, yet is the cosenage so pleasing to me, that I (bribed by my own desires) believe them still before the other. Then do I glory that my virgin love has stayed for such an object to fix upon, and think how good the stars were to me that kept me from quenching those flames (youth or wild love furnished me withal) in common and ordinary waters, and reserved me a sacrifice for your eyes. While thought thus smiles and solaces himself within me, cruel remembrance breaks in upon our retirements, and tells so sad a story that (trust me) I forget all that pleased fancy said before, and turns my thoughts to where I left you. Then I consider that storms neither know courtship nor pity, and that those rude blasts will often make you a prisoner this winter, if they do no worse.

While I here enjoy fresh diversion, you make the sufferings more by having leisure to consider them ; nor have I now any way left me to make mine equal with them, but by often considering that they are not so ; for the thought that I cannot be with you to bear my share is more intolerable to me than if I had borne more. But I was only born to number hours, and not enjoy them—yet can I never think myself unfortunate, while I can write myself

Aglaura,
Her humble Servant.

XII

When I consider (my dear princess) that I have no other pretence to your favours than that which all men have to the original of beauty, light; which we enjoy, not that it is the inheritance of our eyes, but because things most excellent cannot restrain themselves, but are ours, as they are diffusively good; then do I find the justness of your quarrel, and cannot but blush to think what I do owe, but much more to think what I do pay, since I have made the principal so great, by sending in so little interest.

When you have received this humble confession, you will not, I hope, conceive me one that would (though upon your bidding) enjoy myself, while there is such a thing in the world as

Aglaura,
Her humble Servant,
J.S.

XIII

So much (dear ——) was I ever yours, since I had first the honour to know you, and consequently so little myself, since I had the unhappiness to part with you, that you yourself (dear) without what I would say, cannot but have been so just as to have imagined the welcome of your own letters; though indeed they have but removed me from one rack to set me on another—from fears and doubts I had about me of your welfare, to an unquietness within myself, till I have deserv'd this intelligence.

How pleasingly troublesome thought and remembrance have been to me, since I left you, I am no more able now to express, than another to have them so. You only could make every place you came in worth the thinking of; and I do think those places worthy my thought only, because you made them so. But I am to leave them, and I shall do't the willinger, because the gamester still is so much in me, as that I love not to be told too often of my losses. Yet every place will be alike, since every good object will do the same. Variety of beauty and of faces (quick underminers of constancy to others) to me will be but pillars to support it, since, when they please me most, I most shall think of you.

In spite of all philosophy, it will be hottest in my climate when my sun is farthest off; and in spite of all reason, I proclaim that I am not myself, but when I am

Yours wholly.

XIV

Though desire in those that love be still like too much sail in a storm, and man cannot so easily strike, or take all in when he pleases; yet (dearest princess) be it never so hard, when you shall think it dangerous, I shall not make it difficult, though— well, love is love, and air is air; and (though you are a miracle yourself) yet do not I believe that you can work any. Without it I am confident you can never make these two, thus different in themselves, one and the self-same thing; when you shall, it will be some small furtherance towards it, that you have

Your humble Servant,

J. S.

Who so truly loves the fair Aglaura, that he will never know desire, at least not entertain it, that brings not letters of recommendation from her, or first a fair passport.

XV

My Dear Dear,

Think I have kissed your letter to nothing, and now know not what to answer; or that, now I am answering, I am kissing you to nothing, and know not how to go on! For, you must pardon, I must hate all I send you here, because it expresses nothing in respect of what it leaves behind with me. And oh! why should I write then? Why should I not come myself? Those tyrants, business, honour, and necessity, what have they to do with you and I? Why should we not do love's commands before theirs, whose sovereignty is but usurped upon us? Shall we not smell to roses 'cause others do look on, or gather them 'cause there are prickles, and something that would hinder us? Dear, I fain would, and know no hindrance but what must come from you; and why should any come? since 'tis not I, but you, must be sensible how much time we lose, it being long time since I was not myself, but

Yours.

XVI

Dear Princess,

Finding the date of your letter so young, and having an assurance from —— who at the same time heard from Mr. —— that all our letters have been delivered at [B.], I cannot but imagine some ill mistake, and that you have not received any at all. Faith I have none in Welsh man ; and though fear and suspicion look often so far that they oversee the right, yet when love holds the candle, they seldom do mistake so much. My dearest princess, I shall long, next hearing you are well, to hear that they are safe; for though I can never be ashamed to be found an idolater to such a shrine as yours, yet since the world is full of profane eyes, the best way, sure, is to keep all mysteries from them, and to let privacy be (what indeed it is) the best part of devotion. So thinks,

My D. D. P.,

Your humble Servant.

XVII

Since the inferior orbs move but by the first, without all question desires and hopes in me are to be govern'd still by you, as they by it. What mean these fears, then, dear princess ?

Though planets wander, yet is the sphere that carries them the same still ; and though wishes in me may be extravagant, yet he in whom they make their motion is, you know, my dear princess,

Yours and wholly to be disposed of by you.

And till we hear from you, though (according to the form of concluding a letter) we should now rest, we cannot.

XVIII

Fair Princess,

If parting be a sin (as sure it is) what then to part from you ? If to extenuate an ill be to increase it, what then now to excuse it by a letter ? That which we would allege to lessen it, with you perchance has added to the guilt already, which is our sudden leaving you. Abruptness is an eloquence in parting, when spinning out of time is but the weaving of new sorrow. And thus we thought ; yet not being able to distinguish of our own acts, the fear we may have sinn'd farther than we think of has made us send to you, to know whether it be mortal or not.

XIX

For the two Excellent Sisters

Though I conceive you (ladies) so much at leisure that you may read anything, yet since the stories of the town are merely amorous, and sound nothing but love, I cannot, without betraying my own judgment, make them news for Wales. Nor can it be less improper to transport them to you, than for the king to send my Lord of C—— over ambassador this winter into Greenland.

It would want faith in so cold a country as Anglesey, to say that your cousin Duchess, for the quenching of some foolish flames about her, has endured quietly the loss of much of the king's favour, of many of her houses, and of most of her friends.

Whether the disfigurement that travel or sickness has bestowed upon B. W. be thought so great by the Lady of the Isle as 'tis by others, and whether the alteration of his face has bred a change in her mind, it never troubles you, ladies. What old loves are decay'd, or what new ones are sprung up in their room; whether this lady be too discreet, or that cavalier not secret enough, are things that concern the inhabitants of Anglesey not at all. A fair day is better welcome and more news than all that can be said in this kind; and for all that I know now, the devil's chimney is on fire, or his pot seething over, and all North Wales not able to stay the fury of it. Perchance while I write this, a great black cloud is sailing from Mistress Thomas's bleak mountains over to Baron-Hill, there to disgorge itself with what the sea or worse places fed it with before.

It may be, the honest banks about you turn bankrupt too, and break; and the sea, like an angry creditor, seizes upon all, and hath no pity, because he has been put off so long from time to time. For variety (and it is not impossible), some boisterous wind flings up the hangings; and thinking to do as much to your clothes, finds a resistance, and so departs, but first breaks all the windows about the house for it in revenge.

These things, now, we that live in London cannot help, and they are as great news to men that sit in boxes at Black-Friars, as the affairs of love to flannel-weavers.

For my own part, I think I have made a great compliment when I have wished myself with you, and more than I dare make good in winter; and yet there is none would venture farther for such a happiness than

Your humble Servant.

XX

The Wine-drinkers to the Water-drinkers, greeting :

Whereas by your ambassador, two days since sent unto us, we understand that you have lately had a plot to surprise or (to speak more properly) to take the waters, and in it have not only a little miscarried, but also met with such difficulties, that unless you be speedily relieved, you are like to suffer in the adventure ; we, as well out of pity to you, as out of care to our state and commonwealth (knowing that women have ever been held necessary, and that nothing relisheth so well after wine), have so far taken it into our consideration, that we have neglected no means, since we heard of it first, that might be for your contents or the good of the cause ; and therefore to that purpose we have had divers meetings at the Bear at the Bridge-foot, and now at length have resolved to dispatch to you one of our cabinet-council, Colonel Young, with some slight forces of canary, and some few of sherry, which no doubt will stand you in good stead, if they do not mutiny and grow too headstrong for their commander. Him Captain Puff of Barton shall follow with all expedition, with two or three regiments of claret ; Monsieur de Granville, commonly called Lieutenant Strutt, shall lead up the rear of Rhenish and white. These succours, thus timely sent, we are confident will be sufficient to hold the enemy in play, and, till we hear from you again, we shall not think of a fresh supply. For the waters (though perchance they have driven you into some extremities, and divers times forc'd their passages through some of your best guarded places), yet have they, if our intelligence fail us not, hitherto had the worst of it still, and evermore at length plainly run away from you.

Given under our hands at the Bear,
This fourth of July.

XXI

Since joy (the thing we all so court) is but our hopes stripped of our fears, pardon me if I be still pressing at it, and, like those that are curious to know their fortunes aforehand, desire to be satisfied, though it displeases me afterward. To this gentleman (who has as much insight as the t'other wanted eyesight) I have committed the particulars, which would too much swell a letter. If they shall not please you, 'tis but fresh subject still for repentance ; nor ever did that make me quarrel with anything but my own stars. To swear new oaths from this place were but to weaken the credit of those I have sworn in another. If heaven be to forgive you now for not believing of them then (as sure as it was a sin) heaven forgive me now for swearing of them then (for that was double sin). More than I am I cannot be, nor list,

Yours,

I. S.

I am not so ill a Protestant as to believe in merit, yet if you please to give answer under your own hand, such as I shall for ever rely upon, if I have not deserv'd it already, it is not impossible but I may.

XXII

To a Cousin (who still loved young girls, and when they came to be marriageable, quitted them, and fell in love with fresh), at his father's request, who desired he might be persuaded out of the humour, and marry.

Honest Charles,

Were there not fools enow before in the common-wealth of lovers, but that thou must bring up a new sect ? Why delighted with the first knots of roses, and when they come to blow, can satisfy the sense, and do the end of their creation, dost not care for them ? Is there nothing in this foolish transitory world that thou canst find out to set thy heart upon, but that which has newly left off making of dirt-pies, and is but preparing itself for loam and a green sickness ? Seriously (Charles) and without ceremony, 'tis very foolish, and to love widows is as tolerable an humour, and as justifiable as thine ; for beasts that have been rid off their legs are as much for a man's use as colts that are unway'd, and will not go at all. Why the devil such young things ? Before these understand what thou wouldst have, others would have granted. Thou dost not marry them neither, nor anything else. 'Sfoot, it is the story of the jack-an-apes and the partridges : thou starest after a beauty till it is lost to thee ; and then lett'st out another, and starest after that till it is gone too ! Never considering that it is here as in the Thames, and that while it runs up in the middle, it runs down on the sides ; while thou contemplat'st the coming-in tide and flow of beauty, that it ebbs with thee, and that thy youth goes out at the same time. After all this, too, she thou now art cast upon will have much ado to avoid being ugly. Pox on't, men will say thou wert benighted, and wert glad of any inn! Well (Charles) there is another way, if you could find it out. Women are like melons; too green or too ripe are worth nothing: you must try till you find a right one. Taste all—but hark you (Charles) you shall not need to eat of all; for one is sufficient for a surfeit:

Your most humble Servant.

I should have persuaded you to marriage; but, to deal ingenuously, I am a little out of arguments that way at this present. 'Tis honourable, there's no question on't; but what more, in good faith I cannot readily tell.

XXIII

Madam,

To tell you that neither my misfortunes nor my sins did draw from me ever so many sighs as my departure from you has done, and that there are yet tears in mine eyes left undried for it; or that melancholy has so deeply seized me, that colds and diseases hereafter shall not need above half their force to destroy me, would be, I know, superfluous and vain, since so great a goodness as yours cannot but have out-believed already what I can write.

He never knew you that will not think the loss of your company greater than the Imperialists can all this time the loss of all their companies; and he shall never know you that can think it greater than I, who, though I never had neither wisdom nor wit enough to admire you to your worth, yet had my judgment ever so much right in it as to admire you above all. And thus he says that dares swear he is

Your most devoted Servant.

XXIV

Madam,

The distrust I have had of not being able to write to you anything which might pay the charge of reading, has persuaded me to forbear kissing your hands at this distance. So, like women that grow proud because they are chaste, I thought I might be negligent because I was not troublesome; and, were I not safe in your goodness, I should be (madam) in your judgment, which is too just to value little observances, or think them necessary to the right honouring my lady.

Your ladyship, I make no doubt, will take into consideration that superstition hath ever been fuller of ceremony than the true worship. When it shall concern any part of your real service, and I not throw by all respects whatsoever to manifest my devotion, take what revenge you please. Undo me, madam : resume my best place and title, and let me be no longer

Your humble Servant.

XXV

Madam,

By the same reason the ancients made no sacrifice to death, should your ladyship send me no letters, since there has been no return on my side. But the truth is, the place affords nothing : all our days are (as the women here) alike, and the difference of *Fair* does rarely show itself, such great state do beauty and the sun keep in these parts. I keep company with my own horses (madam) to avoid that of the men ; and by this you may guess how great an enemy to my living contentedly my lady is, whose conversation has brought me to so fine a diet that, wheresoever I go, I must starve : all days are tedious, companies troublesome, and books themselves (feasts heretofore) no relish in them. Finding you to be the cause of all this, excuse me (madam) if I resent, and continue peremptory in the resolution I have taken to be,

Madam, during life,
Your humblest Servant.

XXVI

Madam,

But that I know your goodness is not mercenary, and that you receive thanks, either with as much trouble as men ill news, or with as much wonder as virgins unexpected love, this letter should be full of them. A strange, proud return you may think I make you (madam) when I tell you, it is not from everybody I would be thus obliged ; and that, if I thought you did me not these favours because you love me, I should not love you because you do me these favours. This is not language for one in affliction, I confess, and upon whom, it may be, at this present a cloud is breaking ; but finding not within myself I have deserved that storm, I will not make it greater by apprehending it.

After all, lest (madam) you should think I take your favours as tribute, to my great grief I here declare, that the services I shall be able to render you will be no longer presents, but payments of debts, since I can do nothing for you hereafter which I was not obliged to do before.

Madam,

Your most humble and faithful Servant.

XXVII

My Noble Friend,

That you have overcome the danger of the land and of the sea is news most welcome to us, and with no less joy received amongst us than if the King of Sweden had the second time overcome Tilly, and again passed the Meine and the Rhine. Nor do we in this look more upon ourselves and private interests than on the public, since in your safety both were comprised; and though you had not had about you the affairs and secrets of state, yet to have left your own person upon the way had been half to undo our poor island, and the loss must have been lamented with the tears of a whole kingdom.

But you are now beyond all our fears, and have nothing to take heed on yourself but fair ladies. A pretty point of security, and such a one as all Germany cannot afford. We here converse with northern beauties, that had never heat enough to kindle a spark in any man's breast, where heaven had been first so merciful as to put in a reasonable soul.

There is nothing either fair or good in this part of the world, and I cannot name the thing can give me any content, but the thought that you enjoy enough otherwhere; I having ever been, since I had the first honour to know you,

Yours, more than his own.

XXVIII

My Lord,

To persuade one that has newly shipwracked upon a coast to imbark suddenly for the same place again, or your lordship to seek that content you now enjoy in the innocence of a solitude among the disorders and troubles of a court, were, I think, a thing the king himself (and majesty is no ill orator) would find some difficulty to do; and yet, when I consider that great soul of yours, like a spider, working all inwards, and sending forth nothing but, like the cloistered schoolmen's divinity, threads fine and unprofitable—if I thought you would not suspect my being serious all this while; for what I should now say, I would tell you that I cannot but be as bold with you as your ague is, and for a little time, whether you will or not, entertain you scurvily.

When I consider you look (to me) like ——, I cannot but think it as odd a thing as if I should see Vandike with all his fine colours and pencils about him, his frame, and right light, and everything in order, and yet his hands tied behind him; and your lordship must excuse me, if upon it I be as bold.

The wisest men and greatest states have made no scruple to make use of brave men whom they had laid by with some disgrace; nor have those brave men, so laid by, made scruple, or thought it a disgrace, to serve again when they were called to it afterwards.

These general motives of the state and common good I will not so much as once offer up to your lordship's consideration, though, as 'tis fit, they have still the upper end. Yet, like great olios, they rather make a show than provoke appetite. There are two things which I shall not be ashamed to propound to you as ends, since the greater part of the wise men of the world have not been ashamed to make them theirs, and, if any has been found to contemn them, it hath been strongly to be suspected that either they could not easily attain to them, or else that the readiest way to attain to them was to contemn them. These two are honour and wealth; and though you stand possessed of both of them, yet is the first in your hands like a sword which, if not through negligence, by mischance hath taken rust, and needs a little clearing, and it would be much handsomer a present to posterity, if you yourself in your lifetime wipe it off.

For your estate (which, it may be, had been more, had it not been too much), though it is true that it is so far from being contemptible that it is nobly competent, yet must it be content to undergo the same fate greater states (common-wealths themselves) have been and are subject to; which is, when it comes to be divided in itself, not to be considerable. Both honour and estate are too fair and sweet flowers to be without prickles, or to be gathered without some scratches.

And now, my lord, I know you have nothing to urge but a kind of incapability in yourself to the service of this state, when indeed you have made the only bar you have by imagining you have one.

I confess (though) had vice so large an empire in the court as heretofore it has had, or were the times so dangerous that to the living well there wise conduct were more necessary than virtue itself, your lordship would have reason (with Æsop's country mouse) to undervalue all change of condition, since a quiet mediocrity is still to be preferred before a troubled superfluity. But these things are now no more ; and if at any time they have threatened that horizon, like great clouds, either they are fallen of themselves to the ground, or else, upon the appearing of the sun (such a prince as ours is) they have vanished, and left behind them clear and fair days. To descend to parts, envy is so lessened, that it is almost lost into virtuous emulation, every man trusting the king's judgment so far, that he knows no better measure of his own merit than his reward. The little word behind the back, and undoing whisper, which, like pulling of a sheet-rope at sea, slackens the sail, and makes the gallantest ship stand still--that that heretofore made the faulty and the innocent alike guilty, is a thing, I believe, now so forgot, or at least so unpractised, that those that are the worst have leisure to grow good, before any will take notice they have been otherwise, or at least divulge it.

'Tis true, faction there is ; but 'tis as true, that it is as winds are, to clear and keep places free from corruption, the oppositions being as harmless as that of the meeting tides under the bridge, whose encounter makes it but more easy for him that is to pass. To be a little pleasant in my instances : the very women have suffered reformation, and wear through the whole court their faces as little disguised now as an honest man's actions should be ; and if there be any have suffered themselves to be gained by their servants, their ignorance of what they granted may well excuse them from the shame of what they did. So that it is more than possible to be great and good ; and we may safely conclude, if there be some that are not so exact, as much as they fall short of it just so much they have gone from the great original, God, and from the best copies of him on earth, the king and the queen.

To conclude : if those accidents or disasters which make men grow less in the world (as some such, my lord, have happened to you) were inevitable as death, or, when they were once entered upon us, there were no cure for them, examples of others would satisfy me for yours ; but since there have been that have delivered themselves from their ills, either by their good fortune or virtue, 'twould trouble me that my friends should not be found in that number, as much as if one should bring me a catalogue of those that truly honoured my Lord of ——, and I should not find among the first

Your humble Servant.

XXIX

To Mr. Henry German, in the beginning of Parliament, 1640.

That it is fit for the King to do something extraordinary at this present, is not only the opinion of the wise, but the expectation. Men observe him more now than at other times: for Majesty in an eclipse, like the Sun, draws eyes, that would not so much as have looked towards it, if it had shined out and appeared like itself. To lie still now would at the best shew but a calmness of mind, not a magnanimity: since in matter of government, to think well at any time (much less in a very active) is little better than to dream well. Nor must he stay to act till his people desire, because 'tis thought nothing relishes else: for therefore hath nothing relished with them, because the King hath for the most part stayed till they have desired; done nothing but what either they have, or were petitioning for. But that the King should do, will not be so much the question, as what he should do. And certainly for a King to have right counsel given him is at all times strange, and at this present impossible. His party for the most part (I would that were modestly said and it were not all) have so much to do for their own preservation, that they cannot (without breaking a law in nature) intend another's. Those that have courage have not perchance innocence, and so dare not shew themselves in the King's business; and if they have innocence, they want parts to make themselves considerable; so consequently the things they undertake. Then in Court, they give much counsel, as they believe the King inclined, determine his good by his desires, which is a kind of setting the Sun by the dial—interest, which cannot err, by passion, which may.

In going about to shew the King a cure, a man should first plainly shew him the disease. But to Kings, as to some kind of patients, it is not always proper to tell how ill they be; and it is too like a country clown, not to shew the way unless he know from whence, and discourse of things before.

Kings may be mistaken, and Counsellors corrupted, but true interest alone (saith *Monsieur de Rohan*) cannot err. It were not amiss then to find out the interest; for setting down right principles before conclusions is weighing the scales before we deal out the commodity.

Certainly the great interest of the King is *a union with his people*, and whosoever hath told him otherwise (as the Scripture saith of the devil) was a seducer from the first. If there ever had been any one Prince in the whole world, that made a felicity in this life, and left fair fame after death, without the love of his subjects, there were some colour to despise it.

There was not among all our princes a greater courtier of the people than Richard the third ; not so much out of fear as out of wisdom. And shall the worst of our Kings have striven for that, and shall not the best ? it being an angelical thing to gain love.

There are two things in which the people expect to be satisfied, Religion and Justice ; nor can this be done by any little acts, but by royal and kingly resolutions.

If any shall think that by dividing the factions (a good rule at other times) he shall master the rest now, he will be strangely deceived ; for in the beginning of things that would do much, but not when whole Kingdomes are resolved. Of those now that lead these parties, if you could take off the major number, the lesser would govern, and do the same things still. Nay, if you could take off all, they would set up one and follow him.

And of how great consequence it is for the King to resume this right and be the author himself, let any body judge ; since (as *Cumneus* said) those that have the art to please the people, have commonly the power to raise them.

To do things so that there shall remain no jealousy is very necessary, and is no more than really reforming, that is, pleasing them. For to do things that shall grieve hereafter, and yet pretend love, amongst lovers themselves, where there is the easiest faith, will not be accepted. It will not be enough for the King to do what they desire, but he must do something more—I mean by doing more, doing something of his own, as throwing away things they call not for, or giving things they expected not. And when they see the King doing the same things with them, it will take away all thought and apprehension, that he thinks the things they have done already ill.

Now if the King ends the differences, and takes away suspect for the future, the case will fall out to be no worse, than when two duellists enter the field, where the worsted party (the other having no ill opinion of him) hath his sword given him again without further hurt, after he is in the other's power. But otherwise it is not safe to imagine what may follow, for the people are naturally not valiant, and not much Cavalier. Now it is the nature of cowards to hurt where they can receive none. They will not be content (while they fear and have the upper hand) to fetter only royalty, but perchance (as timorous spirits use) will not think themselves safe while that is at all. And possibly this is the present state of things.

In this great work (at least to make it appear perfect and lasting to the kingdom) it is necessary the Queen really join : for if she stand aloof, there will be still suspicions, it being a received opinion in the world, that she hath a great interest in the King's favour and power. And, to invite her, she is to consider with her self, whether such great virtues and eminent excellencies (though they be highly admired and valued by those that know her), ought to rest satisfied with so narrow a payment as the estimation of a few, and whether it be not more proper for a great Queen to arrive at universal honour and love than private esteem and value ?

Then, how becoming a work for the sweetness and softness of her sex is composing of differences and uniting hearts : and how proper for a Queen, reconciling King and people !

There is but one thing remains, which whispered abroad busies the King's mind much (if not disturbs it) in the midst of these great resolutions ; and that is the preservation of some servants, whom he thinks somewhat hardly torn from him of late, which is of so tender a nature, I shall rather propound something about it than resolve it.

The first *Quære* will be whether, as things now stand (kingdoms in the balance) the King is not to follow nature, where the conservation of the more general commands and governs the less : as iron by particular sympathy sticks to the loadstone, but yet, if it be joined with a great body of iron, it quits those particular affections to the loadstone, and moves with the other to the greater, the common country.

The second will be whether, if he could preserve those ministers, they can be of any use to him hereafter ? Since no man is served with a greater prejudice, than he that employs suspected instruments, or not beloved, though able and deserving in themselves.

The third is, whether to preserve them there be any other way than for the King to be first right with his people ? Since the rule in philosophy must ever hold good : *nihil dat, quod non habet.* Before the King have power to save, he must have power.

Lastly, whether the way to preserve this power be not to give it away ? For the people of England have ever been like wantons, which pull and tug as long as the princes pulled with them, as you may see in Henry the third, King John, Edward the second, and indeed all the troublesome and unfortunate reigns. But when they have let it go, they come and put it into their hands again, that they may play on, as you may see in Queen Elizabeth.

I will conclude with a prayer (not that I think it needs at this present : prayers are to keep us from what may be, as well as to preserve us from what is), that the King be neither too insensible of what is without him, nor too resolved from what is within him. To be sick of a dangerous sickness and find no pain cannot but be with loss of understanding ('tis an aphorism of Hippocrates).

And on the other side Opiniastry is a sullen Porter, and (as it was wittily said of Constancy) shuts out oftentimes better things than it lets in.

LETTERS

to

SEVERAL PERSONS

of

HONOR.

BY

S^R JOHN SUCKLING.

LONDON:
Printed for *Humphrey Moseley* at the Prince's Arms in St *Pauls* Churchyard. 1659.

LETTERS

XXX

My Lord,

But that you do and say things in Scotland now (my lord) unfit for a good subject to hear, I should have hoped your lordship, by a true relation of the passages there, would have disabused your humble servant here. Distance and men's fears have so enlarged the truth, and so disproportioned everything about the town, that we have made the little troop of discontents a gallant army, and already measure no Scotchman but by his evening shadow.

We hear say you have taken livery and seisin of Northumberland, and there are that give in Cumberland for quietness sake, and are content to think it part of Scotland, because it is so barren. London scriveners begin to wish they had St. Michael-Mount's-men's security for the borderers they have standing bound in their shops; and the Witheringtons' and Howards' estates are already freely disposed to the needier rebels. Much of this part of the world is in agues, but not all, my lord; there are that have read the chronicles, and they find the English oftener marched into Edenburgh than the Scots into London.

Your old friend, Alderman —— (a learned bard, and a great in-seer into times), saith it is a boil broken out in the breech of the kingdom, and that when it is ripe, it will heal of itself. Others use a handsomer similitude, and compare Scotland to a hive of swarming bees which they say the king watches to reduce them for the better. There is a saucy kind of intelligence about the town, of ten thousand pounds that should be sent by my Lord M—— for redemption of affairs there; but this the wiser sort suspects, for, besides that his majesty buys his own again, they say none but the king would give so much for it.

Some are scandalized at the word of union, and protest they find no resemblance betwixt this new Covenant and our Saviour's. Others wonder why they would make use of religion rather than their poverty for the cause of their mutining, since the one is ever suspected, and the other none would have disputed.

In short, while one part of the town is in whisper and serious, the other part smiles. I therefore desire your lordship to send me word in what state things stand there, that I may know of which side to be. But I beseech you think it not any inbred love to mischief that I now send to enquire how rebellion prospers, but impute it to a certain foolish and greedy curiosity in man's nature of news, and remember that he that hath this disease about him is

Your humble Servant.

XXXI

Good Mr. Alderman,

It is most true (I confess) that we do say things here unfit for you to hear there, and for this very reason I will forbear particulars. But this I do (Mr. Alderman) not so much out of fear for myself as care for you ; for though you write in the present tense, and use the particle *now*, which is a kind of an exclusive word, yet it is well enough known a Scotchman at all times might speak what an Englishman durst not hear. It seems (sir) strange to me, that in the beginning of your letter you give us the name of rebels, when none are more his majesty's most humble subjects than we, as in the front of our petitions and messages most plainly appears. True it is, that in case the king will not do what we would have him, we have provided arms, and have persuaded those here, and sent to others abroad to assist us ; but that we have at any time denied ourselves to be his most faithful subjects (by your favour, Mr. Alderman) I think will hardly appear. For the taking of livery and seisin of Northumberland (if there be any such thing) neither you nor my Lord —— ought to be troubled at it, for that is a business belongs to the law, and upon a trial had here in Edenburgh before any of the Covenant, no question but there will be a speedy end of it. The thing I most wonder at is, that our old friend should be so much mistaken as to call Scotland the breech of the kingdom, since you know that is a part of all the rest most subject, and is still put to endure the lash, so that in all likelihood it should rather be your country than ours.

For your simily of the bees, and reducing us to the better, you may assure his majesty from me that it will not quit cost ; for both his predecessors and himself have found sufficiently that, hived or unhived, we yield not much honey.

Now, sir, for our new Covenant's having relation to the other, you must know that, though it is not absolutely alike in all, yet in some things it doth not disagree, and in this especially it suits—that there is but little care taken for settling High Commission Courts in either.

The last scruple that troubles you is, why in this case we have made use of religion (which every one is apt to doubt) rather than poverty (which no man would have disputed); and to say truth in this, I was something unsatisfied myself, until I had spoken with one of the learneder of the Covenant, who told me that he had observed very few to thrive by publishing their poverty, but a great many by pretending religion. And now I doubt not but I have in part satisfied your curiosity. There remains only that I give you my opinion concerning which party you ought to be of, and according to the friendship that is betwixt us, I will deal plainly with you, that if you had no more to lose than some of us have, this would be no ill side (for you see how God hath blessed the Hollanders). But, as you are, London is no ill place; for, should you bring your money hither, the temptation would be too strong for the men, and like a hungry man brought to a strange table, we should fall to, without much inquiring whose the meat was.

XXXII

An Answer to a Gentleman that sent to inquire after the Scottish business

Sir,

That you may receive an account of the Scottish business, and why there hath been such irresolution and alteration about the levies lately, it is fit you know that this northern storm (like a new disease) hath so far posed the doctors of state that as yet they have not given it a name, though perchance they all firmly believe it to be rebellion. And therefore (sir) it is no wonder if these do here as the learned in physick, who, when they know not certainly the grief, prescribe medicines sometimes too strong, sometimes too weak. The truth is, we here consider the Scottish affair much after the rate the mortals do the moon: the simpler think it no bigger than a bushel, and some (too wise) imagine it a vast world, with strange things undiscovered in it—certainly two ill ways of casting it up, since the first would make us too secure, the other too fearful. I confess, I know not how to meet it in the middle, or set it right; nor do I think you have, since I should believe the question to be rather *A King or no*

King there, than *A Bishop or no Bishop*. In great mutinies or insurrections of this nature pretentions speciously conscionable were never wanting, and indeed are necessary ; for rebellion is itself so ugly, that did it not put on the vizard of religion, it would fright rather than draw people to it, and being drawn, it could not hold them without it.

Imaginary cords, that seem to fasten man to heaven, have tied things here below surer together than any other obligation. If it be liberty of conscience they ask, 'tis a foolish request, since they have it already, and must have it in despite of power. For as Theoderic the Goth said to the Jews, *Nemo cogitur credere invitus*. If the exercise of that liberty, 'tis dangerous ; for not three men are of the same opinion in all, and then each family must have a war within itself. Look upon their long preparations (and consider withal prophecy is sealed, and therefore they could not foretell this book should be sent unto them), and you will conclude they rather employed Conscience, than Conscience employed them. Enquire after their leaders, and you will hardly find them apostles, or men of such sanctity that they should order religion. Lesley himself (if his story were searched) would certainly be found one who, because he could not live well there, took up a trade of killing men abroad, and now is returned, for Christ's sake, to kill men at home. If you will have my opinion, I think their quarrel to the king is that which they may have to the sun : he doth not warm and visit them as much as others. God and nature have placed them in the shade, and they are angry with the King of England for it. To conclude, this is the case : the great and wise Husbandman hath planted the beasts in out-fields, and they would break hedges to come into the garden. This is the belief of

Your humble Servant.

XXXIII

Sir,

We are at length arrived at that river, about the uneven running of which my friend Mr. William Shakespeare makes Henry Hotspur quarrel so highly with his fellow-rebels, and for his sake I have been something curious to consider the scantlet of ground that angry monsieur would have had in, but cannot find it could deserve his choler, nor any of the other side ours, did not the king think it did. The account I shall now give you of the war will be but imperfect, since I conceive it to be in the state that part of the four and twenty hours is in, which we can neither call night nor day. I should judge it dawning towards earnest, did not the Lords Covenanters' letters to our Lords here something divide me. So (sir) you may now imagine us walking up and down the banks of Tweed like the Tower lions in their cages, leaving the people to think what we would do if we were let loose. The enemy is not yet much visible : (it may be, it is the fault of the climate, which brings men as slowly forwards as plants :) but it gives us fears that the men of peace will draw all this to a dumb show, and so destroy a handsome opportunity, which was now offered, of producing glorious matter for future chronicle.

These are but conjectures, sir. The last part of my letter I reserve for a great and known truth, which is, that I am (sir)

Your most humble Servant, &c.

XXXIV

My Lord,

At this instant it is grown a calm greater than the storm, and if you will believe the soldier, worse. Good arms and horses are already cheap, and there is nothing risen in value but a Scotchman. Whether it be (my lord) the word *native*, or the king's good nature, we know not ; but we find they really have that mercy on earth which we do but hope for from heaven ; nor can they sin so fast as they are forgiven.

Some (and not unreasonably) perchance will imagine that this may invite good subjects to be ill, and that, as the sun melts ice but hardens clay, majesty, when it softens rebellion, may make allegiance stubborn. If (my lord) they shall more straitly now besiege the king's ear, and more boldly ingross suits, posterity must tell this miracle, that there went an army from the south, of which there was not one man lost, nor any man taken prisoner but the king.

All we have to raise the present joys above the future fears is, that we know majesty hath not swallowed down so severe pills as it was thought necessity would prescribe for the purging and setting itself right.

Your humble Servant.

XXXV

Sir,

The little stops or progresses which either love of the public, private fears, niceties of honour, or jealousy have caused in the treaty now on foot, arrive at me so slowly, that unless I had one of Mr. Davenant's Barbary pigeons (and he now employs them all, he says, himself for the queen's use) I durst not venture to send them, sir, to you, lest, coming to your hands so late, you should call for the map to see whether my quarters were in England or in Barbary. The truth is, I am no first favourite to any Lord of Secrets at this time ; but when they come from Council, attend the short turn with those that are, and, as in discharge of pieces, see a whisper go off some good space of time before I hear it, so satisfy my thirst of novelty from the stream, not from the fountain.

Our very thoughts are hardly news ; and while I now intend to write you other men's (for my own are not worthy of knowledge), it is not without some fear that they have already sent them to Whitehall themselves.

There are, sir, here that have an opinion, necessity, not good nature, produced this treaty, and that the same necessity which made them thus wise for peace will make them as desperate for war, if it succeed not suddenly.

Some conceive little distrusts among themselves will facilitate the work, and that the danger, now grown nearer, will divide the body, by persuading each man to look to his own particular safety. So we see men in ships, while there is hope, assist each other ; but when the wrack grows visible, leave the common care, and consult only their own escape.

There are some imagine this treaty of either side is not so much to beget a good peace as a good cause, and that the subject could do no less than humbly petition, not to appear a rebel, nor the king no less than graciously to hear those petitions, not to appear a tyrant, and that when one party shall be found unreasonable, the other will be thought excusable.

J. S.

XXXVI

Sir,

I send to you now to know how we do here, for in my Lady Kent's well-being much of ours consists. If I am the last, you must impute it to the tenderness of my fears, which durst not inquire into so great a misfortune, or to the coming of bad news, which ever comes latest thither, whither it knows it shall be most unwelcome. For I confess, the report of so great a sickness as my Lady Kent's would give me more trouble than half the sex, although amongst the rest a mistress or two took their fortunes ; and though such excellence cannot change but for the better, yet you must excuse us that enjoy the benefit of her conversation here, if we are content Heaven should only give her the blessing of the Old Testament, and for a while defer those of the New. The only comfort I have had in the midst of variety of reports hath been that I have seen nothing of extraordinary in the elements of late, and I conceived it but reasonable that so general an ill, as my Lady Kent's death would be, should be proclaimed by no less than what foretells the evil of great princes or the beginning of great plagues. When so unlucky a minute shall arrive, I would conclude the virtuous and better sort of people have lost some of their power and credit above, and that the sins are more particularly punished of him that is

Her much obliged,
And, sir,
Your most humble Servant,
J. S.

XXXVII

Ladies,

The opinion of things is the measure of their value, as was wisely said of a niece of Queen Gorbuduke's. Know then that, if another than the coronet had received this script, he would not perchance have valued it so highly. The Sybil leaves had not so much consultation about them, nor were they half so chargeable as these are like to be. We have first sent them to Secretary Cook, imagining nothing but a state key could unlock those mysteries. Now we are in quest of an Arabic figure-caster, for as much of it as we conceive is Chaldee or Syriac. The coronet believes there are noble things in it; but what Beaumont said of worth wrapped up in rivelled skin he saith of this—Who would go in to fetch it out? Indeed the opinions about it have been different: some thought it a little against the state, others a ballad with the pictures the wrong way; and the most discreet have guessed it to be a collection of charms and spells, and have adventured to cut it into bracelets, to be distributed and worn by poor people as remedies against cramps and toothaches—only we will preserve the faces. And for Mistress Delana's, we do not despair but Vandike may be able to copy it. Threescore pounds we have offered, and I think fourscore will tempt him. For Mistress T. there are in that certain *je ne scay quoys*, which none but those that have studied it can discover, and Sir Anthony shall hold his hand till Mr. H. comes to town. This is all the favour can be done in this business by

Your humble Servant,
J. S.

XXXVIII

Sir,

Lest you think I had not as perfectly forgot you as you glory to have done me, let these lines assure you that, if at any time I think of you, it is with as much scorn as you vainly hitherto may have supposed 't has been with affection. A certain general compassion in me, and pity of poor follies, of which number I take this to be one—a triumph, where there has been no conquest, has persuaded me to let you know this much.

And now, if that you have had so much faith as that you could believe a thing so impossible, as that of my loving of you, would you but reduce yourself to believe a thing so reasonable as that there never was any such matter, you would make me step into a belief that you never yet had the good thoughts of

J. S.

XXXIX

There was (O seldom-happy word of *was!*) a time when I was not Mountferrat; and sure there was a time too, when all was handsome in my heart, for you were there (dear princess), and filled the place alone. *Were* there—O wretched word again! and should you leave that lodging, more wretched than Mountferrat needs must be

Your humble Servant,

J. S.

XL

To T. C.

Though writing be as tedious to me as no doubt reading will be to thee, yet considering that I shall drive that trade thou speak'st of to the Indies, and for my beads and rattles have a return of gold and pearl, I am content for thy sake, and in private, thus to do penance in a sheet.

Know then, dear Carew, that at eleven last night, flowing as much with love as thou hast ebbed, thy letter found me out. I read, considered, and admired; and did conclude at last, that Horseley air did excel the waters of the Bath, just so much as love is a more noble disease than the pox.

No wonder if the Countesses think time lost till they be there. Who would not be, where such cures flow? The care thou hast of me, that I should traffick right, draws me by way of gratitude to persuade thee to bottle us some of that, and send it hither to town. Thy returns will be quicker than those to the Indies ; nor need'st thou fear a vent, since the disease is epidemical.

One thing more : who knows (wouldst thou be curious in the search), but thou mayest find an air of contrary virtue about thy house, which may, as this destroys, so that create affection ? If thou couldst,

The lady of High-gate then should embrace
The disease of the stomach, and the word of disgrace.
Gredeline and grass-green
Shall sometimes be seen,
Its arms to intwine
About the woodbine.

In honest prose thus : we would carry ourselves first, and then our friends manage all the little loves at Court, make more Tower work, and be the Duke of B. of our age, which without it we shall never be. Think on't, therefore, and be assured that, if thou join'st me in the patent with thee, in the height of all my greatness I will be thine, all but what belongs to Desdemonna, which is just as I mean to venture at thy horse-race Saturday come seven-night.

J. S.

XLI

It is none of the least discourtesies money hath done us mortals, the making things, easy in themselves and natural, difficult. Young and handsome people would have come together without half this trouble, if that had never been. This would tell you, madam, that the offer, having nothing about it of new, begot in our young lover very little of anything else, but melancholy, which, notwithstanding, I could easily perceive grew rather from a fear of his father's mind, than a care of satisfying his own. That persuaded me to throw in all, and add the last reserve, which fortunately turned the scale, the cavalier setting a greater rate, and truly, upon the kindness of it, than upon the thing, and in that showed the courtesy of his judgment, as well as his ability. The uncle is no less satisfied than the nephew, and both are confident to draw to the same thoughts, to whom, as it was fit, I have left the office.

And now, madam, you may safely conclude the cause to be removed out of Pluto's court into Cupid's—from the God of Moneys to the God of Love who, if he break not off old customers, will quickly dispatch them, since he seldom delays those that have pass'd their trials in the other place.

Your humble Servant,

J. S.

AN ACCOUNT OF RELIGION BY REASON.

A Discourse upon Occasion presented to the Earl of DORSET.

By

Sir JOHN SUCKLING.

Printed by his owne copy.

Lucret. pag. 227. *Tentat enim dubiam mentem rationis egestas.*

LONDON,
Printed by *Ruth Raworth* for *Humphrey Moseley*, and are to be sold at his shop at the signe of the *Princes Arms* in S. *Pauls* Church-yard. 1646.

THE EPISTLE

I SEND you here (my lord) that discourse enlarged, which frighted the lady into a cold sweat, and which had like to have made me an atheist at court, and your lordship no very good Christian. I am not ignorant that the fear of Socinianism at this time renders every man, that offers to give an account of religion by reason, suspected to have none at all; yet I have made no scruple to run that hazard, not knowing why a man should not use the best weapon his Creator hath given him for his defence. That faith was by the apostles both highly exalted and severely enjoined, is known to every man, and this upon excellent grounds; for it was both the easiest and best way of converting, the other being tedious and almost useless, for but few among thousands are capable of it, and those few not capable at all times of their life, judgment being required. Yet the best servant our Saviour ever had upon earth was so far from neglecting or contemning reason, that his epistles were admired even by those that embraced not the truths he delivered. And, indeed, had the fathers of the Church only bid men believe, and not told them why, they had slept now unsainted in their graves, and as much benighted with oblivion as the ordinary parish-priests of their own age.

That man is deceivable is true, but what part within him is not likelier than his reason? For as Manilius said—

Nam neque decipitur ratio nec decipit unquam.

And how unlikely is it that that which gives us the prerogative above other creatures, and wholly entitles us to future happiness, should be laid aside, and not used to the acquiring of it!

But by this time (my lord) you find how apt those which have nothing to do themselves are to give others trouble. I shall only therefore let you know that your commands to my Lord of Middlesex are performed; and that when you have fresh ones, you cannot place them where they will be more willingly received, than by

Your humble Servant,
John Suckling.

BATH, *Sept.* 2.

A DISCOURSE OF RELIGION

AMONG the truths (my lord) which we receive, none more reasonably commands our belief than those which by all men at all times have been assented to. In this number, and highest, I place this great one, that there is a Deity; which the whole world hath been so eager to embrace, that rather than it would have none at all, it hath too often been contented with a very mean one.

That there should be a great Disposer and Orderer of things, a wise Rewarder and Punisher of good and evil, hath appeared so equitable to men, that by instinct they have concluded it necessary. Nature (which doth nothing in vain) having so far imprinted it in us all that, should the envy of predecessors deny the secret to succeeders, they yet would find it out. Of all those little ladders with which we scale heaven, and climb up to our Maker, that seems to me not the worst, of which man is the first step. For but by examining how I, that could contribute nothing to mine own being, should be here, I come to ask the same question for my father, and so am led in a direct line to a last Producer, that must be more than man; for if man made man, why died not I when my father died? since, according to that maxim of the philosophers, the cause taken away, the effect does not remain. Or, if the first man gave himself being, why hath he it not still? since it were unreasonable to imagine anything could have power to give itself life, that had no power to continue it. That there is then a God, will not be so much the dispute, as what this God is, or how to be worshipped, is that which hath troubled poor mortals from the first; nor are they yet in quiet. So great has been the diversity, that some have almost thought God was no less delighted with variety in his service than he was pleased with it in his works. It would not be amiss to take a survey of the world from its cradle, and, with Varro, divide it into three ages—the Unknown, the Fabulous, and the Historical.

The first was a black night, and discovered nothing; the second was a weak and glimmering light, representing things imperfectly and falsely; the last (more clear) left handsome monuments to posterity. The unknown I place in the age before the Flood, for that deluge swept away things as well as men, and left not so much as footsteps to trace them by. The fabulous began after the Flood; in this time godheads were cheap, and men, not knowing where to choose better, made deities one of another. Where this ended, the historical took beginning; for men began to ingrave in pillars, and to commit to letters, as it were by joint consent; for the three great epochs or terms of accompt were all established within the space of thirty years, the Grecians reckoning from their Olympiads, the Romans from the building of their city, and the Babylonians from their King Salmonassar. To bring into the scale with Christian religion anything out of the first age we cannot, because we know nothing of it.

And the second was so fabulous, that those which took it up afterwards smiled at it as ridiculous and false (which, though, was easier for them to do than to show a true). In the historical, it improved and grew more refined; but here the fathers entered the field, and so clearly gained the victory, that I should say nothing in it, did I not know it still to be the opinion of good wits that the particular religion of Christians has added little to the general religion of the world. Let us take it, then, in its perfecter estate, and look upon it in that age, which was made glorious by the bringing forth of so many admirable spirits; and this was about the eightieth Olympiad, in the year of the world 3480; for in the space of an 100 years flourished almost all that Greece could boast of—Socrates, Plato, Aristotle, Architas, Isocrates, Pythagoras, Epicurus, Heraclitus, Xenophon, Zeno, Anaxagoras, Democritus, Demosthenes, Parmenides, Zenocrates, Theophrastes, Empedocles, Tymæus, with divers others, orators and poets. Or rather (for they had their religion one from another, and not much different), let us take a view of it in that century in which Nature (as it were to oppose the Grecian insolence) brought forth that happy birth of Roman wits—Varro, Cicero, Cæsar, Livie, Salust, Virgil, Horace, Vitruvius, Ovid, Pliny, Cato, Marcus Brutus; and this was from Quintus Servilius his consulship to that of Augustus, 270 years after the other. And to say truth, a great part of our religion, either directly or indirectly hath been professed by heathens, which I conceive not so much an exprobation to it as a confirmation, it being no derogating from truth to be warranted by common consent.

First, then, the creation of the world is delivered almost the same in the Phœnician stories with that in Moses ; from this the Grecians had their Chaos, and Ovid the beginning of his *Metamorphosis*. That all things were made by God was held by Plato and others ; that darkness was before light, by Thales ; that the stars were made by God, by Aratus ; that life was infused into things by the breath of God, Virgil ; that man was made of dust, Hesiod and Homer ; that the first life of man was in simplicity and nakedness, the Ægyptians taught ; and from thence the poets had their Golden Age. That in the first times men's lives lasted a thousand years, Berosus and others ; that something divine was seen amongst men till that the greatness of our sins gave them cause to remove, Catullus ; and this he that writes the story of Columbus reports from the Indians, of a great deluge, almost all. But to the main they hold one God ; and though multiplicity hath been laid to their charge, yet certainly the clearer spirits understood these petty gods as things, not as deities : second causes, and several virtues of the great power : by Neptune, water ; Juno, air ; by Dispater, earth ; by Vulcan, fire ; and sometimes one god signified many things, as Jupiter the whole world, the whole heaven ; and sometimes many gods one thing, as Ceres, Juno Magna, the earth. They concluded those to be vices which we do ; nor was there much difference in their virtues, only Christians have made ready belief the highest, which they would hardly allow to be any. They held rewards for the good, and punishments for the ill ; had their Elysium and their hell ; and that they thought the pains eternal there, is evident in that they believed from thence was no return. They proportioned sufferings hereafter to offences here ; as in Tantalus, Sisyphus, and others, among which that of conscience (the worm that never dies) was one, as in the vulture's gnawing of Prometheus' heart, and Virgil's ugliest of Furies thundering in Pirithous' ear, was not obscurely shown ; and, yet nearer us, they held the number of the elect to be but small, and that there should be a last day, in which the world should perish by fire. Lastly, they had their priests, temples, altars.

We have seen now the parallel ; let us inquire whether those things they seem to have in common with us, we have not in a more excellent manner, and whether the rest, in which we differ from all the world, we take not up with reason. To begin, then, with their Jupiter (for all before were but little stealths from Moses' works)—how much more like a deity are the actions our stories declare our God to have done, than what the ethnick authors deliver of theirs ? How excellently elevated are our descriptions of Him, theirs looking as if they knew what power only by their fears, as their statues erected to him declare! for when he was Capitolinus, he appeared with thunder; when Latiaris, besmeared with blood; when Feretrius, yet more terrible. We may guess what their conceptions were by the worship they gave him. How full of cruelty were their sacrifices! it being received almost through the whole world, that gods were pleased with the blood of men; and this custom neither the Grecian wisdom nor Roman civility abolished, as appears by sacrifices to Bacchus.

Then the ceremonies of Liber Pater and Ceres, how obscene! and those days, which were set apart for the honour of the gods, celebrated with such shows as Cato himself was ashamed to be present at. On the contrary, our services are such as not only Cato, but God Himself, may be there: we worship Him that is the purest Spirit, in purity of spirit; and did we not believe what the Scriptures deliver from Himself, yet would our reason persuade us that such an essence could not be pleased with the blood of beasts, or delighted with the steam of fat; and in this particular Christians have gone beyond all others except the Mahometans, besides whom there has been no nation that had not sacrifice, and was not guilty of this pious cruelty.

That we have the same virtues with them is very true; but who can deny that those virtues have received additions from Christianity, conducing to men's better living together? Revenge of injuries Moses both took himself and allowed by the law to others; Cicero and Aristotle placed it in virtue's quarter. We extol patient bearing of injuries; and what quiet the one, what trouble the other, would give the world, let the indifferent judge. Their justice only took care that men should not do wrong; ours, that they should not think it, the very coveting severely forbidden; and this holds, too, in chastity, desire of a woman unlawfully being as much a breach of the commandment as their enjoying, which showed not only the Christian's care, but wisdom to prevent ill, who provided to destroy it, where it was weakest, in the cradle, and declared He was no less than a God which gave them these laws; for had He been but man, He never would have provided or taken care for what He could not look into, the hearts of men, and what He could not punish, their thoughts. What charity can be produced answerable to that of Christians? Look upon the primitive times, and you shall find that (as if the whole world had been but a private family) they sent from province to province, and from places far distant, to relieve them they never saw nor knew.

Now for the happiness which they proposed : if they take it as the heathens understood it, it was an Elysium, a place of blessed shades, at best but a handsome retirement from the troubles of this world ; if according to the duller Jews, feastings and banquetings (for it is evident that the Sadducees, who were great observers of the Mosaical law, had but faint thoughts of anything to come), there being in Moses' books no promises but of temporal blessings, and (if any) an obscure mention of eternity. The Mahometans are no less sensual, making the renewing of youth, high feasts, a woman with great eyes, and dressed up with a little more fancy, the last and best good.

Then the hell—how gentle with the heathens ! but the rolling of a stone, filling of a sieve with water, sitting before banquets and not daring to touch them, exercising the trade and businesses they had on earth : with the Mahometans, but a purgatory acted in the grave, some pains inflicted by a bad angel, and those qualified and mitigated too by an assisting good one. Now, for the Jews, as they had no hopes, so they had no fears ; so that if we consider it rightly, neither their punishments were great enough to deter them from doing ill, nor their rewards high enough to invite men to strictness of life ; for, since every man is able to make as good a heaven of his own, it were unreasonable to persuade him to quit that certain happiness for an uncertainty ; whereas Christians, with as much more noble consideration both in their heaven and hell, took care not only for the body but the soul, and for both above man's apprehension.

The strangest, though most epidemical, disease of all religions has been an imagination men have had that the imposing painful and difficult things upon themselves was the best way to appease the Deity, grossly thinking the chief service and delight of the Creator to consist in the tortures and sufferings of the creature. How laden with chargeable and unnecessary ceremonies the Jews were, their feasts, circumcisions, sacrifices, great Sabbaths and little Sabbaths, fasts, burials, indeed almost all their worship, sufficiently declare ; and that the Mahometans are much more infected appears by the cutting of the præpuces, wearing iron rings in the skin of their foreparts, lancing themselves with knives, putting out their eyes upon the sight of their prophet's tomb, and the like. Of these last we can shew no patterns amongst us ; for though there be such a thing as whipping of the body, yet it is but in some parts of Christendom, and there perchance too more smiled at than practised. Our religion teaches us to bear afflictions patiently when they fall upon us, but not to force them upon ourselves; for we believe the God we serve wise enough to choose His own service, and therefore presume not to add to His commands. With the Jews, it is true, we have something in common, but rather the names than things, our fasts being more the medicines of the body than the punishments of it; spiritual, as our Sabbaths; both good men's delight, not their trouble.

But, lest this discourse should swell into a greatness such as would make it look rather like a defence, which I have laboured to get, than an accompt which I always carry about me, I will now briefly examine whether we believe not with reason those things we have different from the rest of the world. First, then, for the persuasion of the truth of them in general, let us consider what they were that conveyed them to us: men (of all the world) the most unlikely to plot the cozenage of others, being themselves but simple people, without ends, without designs: seeking neither honour, riches, nor pleasure, but suffering (under the contrary) ignominy, poverty, and misery: enduring death itself, nay, courting it; all which are things distasteful to nature, and such as none but men strangely assured would have undergone. Had they feigned a story, certainly they would not in it have registered their own faults, nor delivered Him, whom they propounded as a God, ignominiously crucified. Add to this the progress their doctrine made abroad, miraculous above all other either before or since: other religions were brought in with the sword, power forcing a custom, which by degrees usurped the place of truth, this even power itself opposing; for the Romans (contrary to their custom, which entertained all religions kindly) persecuted this, which by its own strength so possessed the hearts of men, that no age, sex, or condition refused to lay down life for it. A thing so rare in other religions that, among the heathens, Socrates was the sole martyr; and the Jews (unless of some few under Manasses and Antiochus) have not to boast of any. If we cast our eyes upon the healing of the blind, curing the lame, redeeming from the grave, and but with a touch or word, we must conclude them done by more than humane power, and if by any other, by no ill: these busy not themselves so much about the good of man; and this religion not only forbids by precept the worship of wicked spirits, but in fact destroys it wheresoever it comes. Now, as it is clear by authors impartial (as being no Christians) that strange things were done, so it is plain they were done without imposture. Delusions shun the light; these were all acted openly, the very enemies both of the Master and disciples daily looking on. But let us descend to those more principal particulars which so much trouble the curious wits : these I take to be the Incarnation, Passion, Resurrection, and Trinity.

For the first, that man should be made without man, why should we wonder more at it in that time of the world, than in the beginning ? Much easier, certainly, it was here, because nearer the natural way, woman being a more prepared matter than earth. Those great truths and mysteries of salvation would never have been received without miracles ; and where could they more opportunely be shown than at His entrance into the world, where they might give credit to His following actions and doctrine ? So far it is from being against my reason to think Him thus born, that it would be against it to believe Him otherwise, it being not fit that the Son of God should be produced like the race of men. That humane nature may be assumed by a deity, the enemy of Christians, Julian, confirms, and instances (himself) in Æsculapius, whom he will have descend from heaven in mortal shape, to teach us here below the art of physick. Lastly, that God has lived with men, has been the general fancy of all nations, every particular having this tradition, that the Deity at some time or other conversed amongst men. Nor is it contrary to reason to believe Him residing in glory above, and yet incarnate here. So, in man himself, the soul is in heaven when it remains in the flesh, for it reacheth with its eye the sun : why may not God then, being in heaven, be at the same time with us in the flesh ? since the soul without the body would be able to do much more than with it, and God much more than the soul, being the soul of the soul. But it may be urged as more abstruse, how all in heaven, and all in earth ? Observe man speaking (as you have done seeing). Is not the same speech, at the instant it is uttered, all in every place ? Receives not each particular ear alike the whole ? and shall not God be much more ubiquitary than the voice of man ? For the Passion (to let alone the necessity of satisfying divine justice this way, which, whosoever reads more particularly our divines, shall find rationally enforced), we find the heathen had something near to this (though as in the rest, .mperfect), for they sacrificed single men for the sins of the whole city or country. Porphyrius, having laid this foundation, that the supreme happiness of the soul is to see God, and that it cannot see Him unpurified, concludes that there must be a way for the cleansing of mankind ; and proceeding to find it out, he tells that arts and sciences serve but to set our wits right in the knowledge of things, and cleanse us not enough to come to God. The like judgment he gives of purging by theurgy, and by the mysteries of the sun; because those things extend but to some few, whereas this cleansing ought to be universal for the benefit of all mankind : in the end resolves, that this cannot be done but by one of the three In-beings, which is the word they use to express the Trinity by. Let us see what the divinest of the heathens (and his master Plato) delivers to admiration, and as it were prophetically, to this purpose. That a truly just man be shown (saith he) it is necessary that he be spoiled of his ornaments, so that he must be accounted by others a wicked man, be scoffed at, put in prison, beaten, nay, be crucified ; and certainly for Him that was to appear the highest example of patience, it was necessary to undergo the highest trial of it, which was an undeserved death.

Concerning the Resurrection, I conceive the difficulty to lie not so much upon our Lord as us, it being with easy reason imagined, that He, which can make a body, can lay it down and take it up again. There is something more that urges and presses us ; for in our estate we promise ourselves hereafter, there will be no need of food, copulation, or excrement : to what purpose should we have a mouth, belly, or less comely parts ? it being strange to imagine God to have created man, for a moment of time, a body consisting of particulars which should be useless to all eternity. Besides, why should we desire to carry that along with us which we are ashamed of here, and which we find so great a trouble, that very wise men (were it not forbidden) would throw it off before it were worn out ? To this I should answer that, as the body is partner in well or ill doing, so it is but just it should share in the rewards or punishments hereafter ; and though by reason of sin we blush at it here, yet when that shall cease to be, why we should be more ashamed than our first parents were, or some in the last discovered parts of the world are now, I cannot understand. Who knows but these unsightly parts shall remain for good use, and that, putting us in mind of our imperfect estate here, they shall serve to increase our content and happiness there ? What kind of thing a glorified body shall be, how changed, how refined, who knows ? Nor is it the meanest invitement to me now to think that my estate there is above my capacity here. There remains that which does not only quarrel with the likelihood of a resurrection, but with the possibility ; alleging that man, corrupted into dust, is scattered almost into infinite, or devoured by an irrational creature; goes into aliment, and grows part of it; then that creature, perchance, is made like food to another: and truly, did we doubt God's power, or not think Him omnipotent, this were a labyrinth we should be lost in. But it were hard, when we see every petty chymick in his little shop bring into one body things of the same kind, though scattered and disordered, that we should not allow the great Maker of all things to do the same in His own Universe.

There remains only the mystery of the Trinity, to the difficulty of which the poverty and narrowness of words have made no small addition.

St. Austin plainly says the word person was taken up by the Church for want of a better. Nature, substance, essence, hypostasis, suppositum, and persona have caused sharp disputes amongst the doctors; at length they are contented to let the three first and three last signify the same thing. By all of them is understood something complete, perfect, and singular; in this only they differ, that nature, substance, essence, are communicable *ad quid* and *ut quo* (as they call it). The other are not at all; but enough of this. Those that were the immediate conveyers of it to us wrapt it not up in any of these terms. We then hold God to be one and but one, it being gross to imagine two Omnipotents, for then neither would be so; yet since this good is perfectly good, and perfect goodness cannot be without perfect love, nor perfect love without communication, nor to an unequal or created, for then it must be inordinate, we conclude a Second Coeternal, though Begotten; nor are these contrary (though they seem to be so) even in created substances, that one thing may come from another, and yet that, from whence it comes, not be before that which comes from it, as in the sun and light. But in these high mysteries similitudes may be the best arguments. In metaphysicks they tell us, that to the constituting of every being there is a *posse sui esse*, from whence there is a *sapientia sui esse;* and from these two proceedeth an *amor sui esse:* and though these three be distinct, yet they may make up one perfect being. Again, and more familiarly, there is a hidden original of waters in the earth; from this a spring flows up; and of these proceeds a stream: this is but one essence, which knows neither a before nor an after, but in order—and that, too, according to our considering of it: the head of a spring is not a head but in respect of the spring; for if something flowed not from it, it were not original; nor the spring a spring, if it did not flow from something; nor the stream a stream but in respect of both. Now, all these three are but one water, and though one is not the other, yet they can hardly be considered one without the other. Now, though I know this is so far from a demonstration, that it is but an imperfect instance (perfect being impossible of infinite by finite things), yet there is a resemblance great enough to let us see the possibility. And here the eye of reason needed no more the spectacles of faith, than for these things of which we make sympathy the cause, as in the load-stone, or antipathy, of which every man almost gives instance from his own nature; nor is it here so great a wonder that we should be ignorant; for this is distant and removed from sense, these near and subject to it; and it were stranger for me to conclude that God did not work *ad extra*, thus one and distinct within Himself, because I cannot conceive how begotten, how proceeding, than if a clown should say the hand of a watch did not move because he could not give an account of the wheels within. So far is it from being unreasonable, because I do not understand it, that it would be unreasonable I should. For why should a created substance comprehend an uncreated; a circumscribed and limited, an uncircumscribed and unlimited? And this I observe in those great lovers and lords of reason, quoted by the fathers, Zoroastres, Trismegistus, Plato, Numenius, Plotinus, Proclus, Amelius, and Avicen, that when they spoke of this mystery of the Trinity, of which all writ something, and some almost as plainly as Christians themselves, that they discussed it not as they did other things, but delivered them as oracles which they had received themselves, without dispute.

Thus much of Christian profession compared with others. I should now shew which (compared within itself) ought to be preferred; but this is the work of every pen, perhaps to the prejudice of religion itself. This excuse (though) it has, that (like the chief empire), having nothing to conquer, no other religion to oppose or dispute against, it hath been forced to admit of civil wars, and suffer under its own excellency.

APPENDIX

The following letter, in Suckling's handwriting, is among the Domestic State Papers in the Public Record Office (Charles I., vol. ccxvi., No. 4). It was printed by Mr. W. C. Hazlitt in his edition of Suckling's works, with a facsimile of the signature and date. In the present edition it is printed from the editor's own copy of the original. The spelling has been modernized, save in the case of proper names and of two or three characteristic words. The passages printed in italics are in cipher in the original, in which the translation has been interlined. One ciphered word has been left without explanation by the translator.

The letter is interesting for the information which it affords with regard to English diplomacy during the most critical period of the Thirty Years' War, and with respect to Suckling's return from his expedition as a volunteer in the Lutheran army. Sir Henry Vane, Comptroller of the Household, had gone in 1631 on a mission to Gustavus Adolphus to ask his help for the dispossessed Elector Palatine, and had spent the winter at Mainz, Gustavus's headquarters. Here Suckling, who had taken part in the campaign of 1631, probably met him. Suckling returned to England in the spring of 1632, and arrived in London on Tuesday, May 1, the day before this letter was written. It was addressed evidently to Sir Henry Vane, and gives an account of Suckling's reception by the King and by the Lord Treasurer, Sir Richard Weston, then Baron Weston of Neyland, created Earl of Portland in 1633. Clarendon's long account of Lord Portland (*History of the Rebellion*, ed. 1705, i. 47-55) is emphatic as regards his haughty and jealous temper, and his more than suspected leaning to Spain and the Roman interest, which this letter corroborates. Gustavus had entered on his spring campaign, and his advance on Munich had been secured by the capture of Donauwörth at the beginning of April. In February the Emperor Ferdinand had concluded an alliance with Philip IV. of Spain ; and, later, a Spanish force, at the invitation of the Chapter of Trier, had entered the Archbishopric of Trier, and, pressing on from the Moselle to the Rhine, captured Speyer in the Palatinate. Wallenstein had been induced, on extraordinary terms, to get an army together; the final agreement had been made in April, and when this letter was written Wallenstein was already moving on Prague from his headquarters at Znaim in Moravia. The allusion to the Landgrave of Hesse's defeat is not very clear: William, Landgrave of Hesse-Cassel, was Gustavus's most steadfast supporter in the Rhenish territory, and probably had attempted to check the Spanish advance on the Palatinate. For English policy (1630-1635) with respect to a Spanish alliance, as criticized in this letter, see *Cambridge Modern History*, vol. iv., 1906, pp. 275, 276.

Sir Henry Vane's negotiations with Gustavus were not successful: England had not enough money to offer. Sir Henry's son, afterwards the famous Sir Henry Vane of Commonwealth times, had been attached to the English Embassy at Vienna, and had returned to England shortly before Suckling. Of the other persons referred to, Maxfield and Murray were gentlemen of the King's bedchamber, William Murray being created Earl of Dysart in 1643. Sir Isaac Wake was English Ambassador at Paris in 1631-32; he died in 1632. Sir Thomas Roe, a personal friend of Charles I.'s sister, the Electress Palatine, was employed throughout the period in missions on behalf of the Protestant cause, and, as Ambassador to the Sublime Porte, had prevented an alliance between the Emperor and the Sultan in 1628; presumably his friends regarded his influence with Gustavus as likely to be injured by Vane. 'My Lord Marquis' is James, Third Marquess of Hamilton, the leader of the English volunteers in the Lutheran army; he appears to have been at Mainz with Gustavus, while his troops, or a remnant of them, remained with David Leslie in Silesia. 'Jacob Ashley' is Sir Jacob, afterwards Baron, Astley, who, in spite of his advanced years, did good service with the King in the Civil War. 'My Lord of Middlesex' was, of course, Suckling's uncle, Lionel Cranfield, who at this time occupied no official position. The sense of the passage implies that, by 'my Lord Vane,' Suckling referred to the younger Henry, though neither he nor his father were peers.

The allusion to the appointment of a Cofferer of the Household is obvious, but who actually received that appointment at this time the editor has not discovered. 'Pharneses'' case is doubtful: the allusion is certainly to one of the House of

Farnese, and may be a historical reference to Alexander, Prince of Parma, famous in the statesmanship of Philip II.'s reign.

'Right Honourable,

'What my journey through France afforded your Lordship had in haste from Dover by the way of Antwerp. On Tuesday I arrived at court, and came soon enough to find the face of it extremely changed, looking asquint upon you in Germany, as well as upon all us that were sent from thence. The fault at first I laid upon the night and my own bad eyes, but the next day made it clear and plain. The packet to my Lord Treasurer I presented first, and the taking of Donawart, *who both to the bearer and the news showed alike indifferent, something cool, if not cold perchance,* his garb. From thence I went to the King, and made my way by Maxfeild, Murrey being not there. His Majesty was well content the King was still victorious, but took it not so hot as those of France; nor did he at first conceive of it of so great importance. The bedchamber men were most of them there, and the King spoke loud: that little, therefore, I had to say to him from Sir Isaack Wake and your Lordship, I reserved for a more private audience, that I might see something more into the King's mind. Mr. Murrey would have had it been the next morning, but I deferred it a day, and, having seen my Lord of Middlesex, and spoken with your son, I found, as I conceived, the reason of what I so much wondered at, and a better way than otherwise perchance I had taken. Before, therefore, I went to the King, I attended my Lord Treasurer, and told him that by more particular command I was more specially to wait upon his Lordship, that I was to speak to the King that morning, but was come before to kiss his Lordship's hands; *and, having in a manner repeated what I was to say, because I knew that which I had both* from you and Sir Isaack Wake *was something too much Sweden and monarchy, I mingled with it the* noise of the Spaniards passing the Mosell, the confirmation of the Landgrave of Hessen's defeat, and the voted forces of Wallesten (of which I conceived by circumstance you writ nothing), *all which more specially he commanded me to represent to his Majesty.* In the conclusion I told him that, if there were *any thing in what I had said that could seem less fit to his Lordship, or any thing besides that his Lordship* could think *more fit,* I stood there ready to be disposed of by him. Upon which he imbraced me, thanked your Lordship more especially for that address, promised to send away presently to you, and willed me to attend while he came to the King, that he might present me; which he did. The King was very well pleased and satisfied, much better than he was at my first appearing. He questioned me much and about many things; resolved for a dispatch, *but seemed to refer it to my Lord Treasurer:* he conceived you had . . . already, but yet should have more since you required them. Thus things have passed in shew well in this last act. *By the dispatch itself you will easily judge whether really be intended or no, if, after all this delay, it be full and without reserves, the fears of all those that honour you and serve you are at an end.* Howsoever, though there be some, yet the *next from you* (I conceive) will take them all away. The disposal of the Coferer's place after *this manner makes the world think that there is some staggering in the friendship betwixt my Lord Treasurer and you, if not a breach;* and those that are of *Sir Thomas Roe's cabinet* would persuade that you were *sent over to undo the affairs of the King of Swede and your own.* Many that *really wish you well* begin to imagine that you shall *be kept there longer than you would.* If there be any such thing, the causes certainly will be these. First, *your greatness with my Lord Marquis, and your too strict intelligence* one with another, which is *here represented to the full.* And howsoever your Lordship *thinks things are reconciled betwixt my Lord Treasurer and him,* yet they say otherwise here, and the effects speak no less. *No man dares think well of him here;* and, by what your son and I have observed, it is easy to believe *the King's ears himself has been a little too open to the reports. I do him all the service I can,* where I find it may do any good, though I know Jacob Ashley *has lost himself about the same thing.*

'That which may in a second place be considerable will be *your too lively representations, making the King of Swede to outway the Emperor* more than they will allow him here to do; and, indeed, your Lordship's case in this is not much unlike that of Pharneses, for *where you are they thought you too much a Spaniard, and here they think you all much a Spaniard.* Then, again, the women *take it ill that your son should be a statesman before theirs, and my Lady Weston* has let fall in a manner so much to my Lord Vane. Besides, which I conceive has more importance, *larger instructions were by him carried to the King than to my Lord Treasurer, and sooner.* Last of all, whether your Lordship's clerks have in your absence followed your directions or no, or whether they have behaved themselves ill or well, in the issuing out and disposing of moneys, I cannot tell; but I suspect a *sinister report* has been made of all. Your person would certainly be necessary here; and I make no doubt your wisdom will find out the quickest and best way for it, unless you yourself (as it well may be after all this) know that all the world on this side of the seas are in errors. That which makes me any way stagger in my hopes of your sudden coming home, is, that the King *of Suede* knows too well that, England satisfied in the demands of the *Palatinate*, and things at a full point concerning that particular, *this crown will no longer make court to him, and after it he must expect no great matters from hence*. Besides, France, which in show pretends to go along with us, really perchance intends nothing less, since there is nothing but that of the Palatinate *that can keep Spain and us from tying a more strict knot together*, and nothing but that that [*sic*] *has kept us so long asunder*. And the ill will be that, if his *Majesty of Suede make larger progress and be more fortunate*, we shall here fear *him as too great*, or *he himself will be more difficult: if he be less successful, we shall not conclude with him, as too weak*. And now, my Lord, your Lordship has what we talk here. I am not peremptory that things are so, as I have here represented them; but I am certain they are thought to be so. Your Lordship's better judgment will resolve it, and, I am more than confident, will yet bring everything to its right place. You have many here that can do more towards it, but none that more sincerely wishes it than

'Your humble servant,

'Jo. Sucklinge.'

'*May 2d*, 1632,
'Whitehall.

'If your Lordship would please to think it fit to send at random (and by any messengers rather than none) the news, it would not certainly be amiss.'

NOTES ON POEMS

PAGE

7. On New-Year's Day, 1640.

The year is 1641, N.S. Strafford had been impeached in the preceding November, Laud in December. In a few months the discovery of the Army Plot brought Suckling's career in England to a close.

9. A Session of the Poets.

'Sessions' is the form printed in the earliest three editions. The date is probably about 1637, the year of Ben Jonson's death. Rochester imitated this poem about 1683 in his *Trial of the Poets for the Bays*. Another imitation is Sheffield's *Election of a Poet Laureat*, 1719.

l. 10. *There was*] *There* 1646, 1658.

Selden] Aubrey, *Brief Lives*, ed. Clark, 1898, ii. 223, refers to this passage and to two examples of Selden's poetical skill, one of which, prefixed to Ben Jonson's works (Gifford's one vol. edition, pp. 81, 82), is a copy of Latin hendecasyllabics. The 'sessions' is open to critics as well as to poets.

l. 11. *Wenman*] *Weniman* 1646, 1658; *Wainman* 1648. For the form 'Wainman,' *cf.* Clarendon, *Hist. Reb.*, ed. 1707, ii. 575, and an erasure in Aubrey, *loc. cit.*, i. 151. Sir Francis Wenman 'of Caswell, in Witney parish,' is enumerated by Aubrey among the 'learned gentlemen of the country' who gathered round Falkland at Great Tew. Lady Wenman, on the same authority, was a niece of George Sandys, the next poet on the list. Hazlitt mentions a Thomas Wenman, author of the *Legend of Mary, Queen of Scots*, published from MS., 1810.

l. 12. *Sands*] Aubrey, *loc. cit.*, ii. 212, quotes the register of Sandys' burial at Boxley in 1644, 'poetarum Anglorum sui sæculi facile princeps.' Sandys' poetry was confined mainly to translations.

PAGE

9. l. 12. *Townsend*] See Carew's Poems in *Muses' Library*, p. 104, and Mr. Vincent's note. Lord Herbert of Cherbury mentions, as his companion abroad in 1608, 'Mr. Aurelian Townsend, a gentleman that spoke the languages of French, Italian, and Spanish in great perfection.'

l. 13. *Digby*] Sir Kenelm Digby, 1603-65, 'a gentleman absolute in all numbers' (Jonson, *Eupheme*, 1633); called by a competent scholar 'the Mirandula of his age' (Aubrey, *loc. cit.*, i. 225). See Howell to Sir Thomas Lake, 3 July, 1629, on translations of Martial, x. 47, submitted to Digby's judgment (*Epp. Ho-El.*, i., § 5, No. 25).

Shillingsworth] In spite of Hazlitt's opinion to the contrary, it is probable that William Chillingworth, 'the most intimate and beloved favourite' of Falkland (Aubrey, *loc. cit.*, i. 151), takes his place here with so many of Falkland's circle among the 'wits of the town.' Hobbes bore testimony to his wit (*ibid.*, i. 370, 173): his epitaph at Chichester, by Archdeacon Whitby, reckons him as 'omni Literarum genere celeberrimus.'

l. 15. *Lucan's translator*] Thomas May, 1595-1650, famous for his *History of the Parliament of England*, 1647. His translation of the *Pharsalia* appeared in 1627, and was followed in 1630 by an original continuation of the poem to the death of Julius Cæsar, and, in 1640, by a Latin version of the same, highly praised by Clarendon. Mr. Fleay (*Biograph. Chron. Eng. Drama*, ii. 84) attributes to him, on doubtful grounds, the famous tragedy of *Nero*. He certainly wrote plays in early life, and published other translations and historical poems. His reputation with his contemporaries was doubtful: 'A handsome man, debaucht *ad omnia*' (Aubrey, ii. 56). This judgment, passed at second-hand, was qualified by Aubrey in a later note. Wood, however, added charges of atheism. Marvell, *Tom May's Death*, calls him "Most servile wit, and mercenary pen. Polydore, Lucan, Alan, Vandal, Goth, Malignant poet and historian both.' Clarendon speaks on the whole in his favour.

PAGE

9. ll. 15, 16. *he That makes*, etc.] Hazlitt suggests that this is Francis Quarles.

l. 17. *Selwin*] This person, like the Bartlets immediately after, has left no traces which make identification certain—probably one of the Selwyns of Matson, near Gloucester, and an ancestor of Horace Walpole's witty friend, George Selwyn.

Waller] *Walter*, 1646, 1658.

Bartlets] The editor of the 1836 edition mentioned William Bartlet, the independent minister (d. 1682), but doubted whether he was alluded to in this passage.

l. 18. *Jack Vaughan*] Probably John Vaughan of the Inner Temple, Selden's friend and executor, who became Lord Chief Justice of the Common Pleas in 1668.

Porter] Endymion Porter, famous as a friend and patron of poets. D'Avenant inscribed *The Wits* 'to the Chiefly Belov'd of all that are ingenious and noble, Endymion Porter of His Majesty's Bed-chamber': see Maidment and Logan's ed. of D'Avenant's dramatic works, ii. 112-15. Thomas May dedicated to him his *Antigone*. Five of Herrick's *Hesperides* are addressed to him: see especially Nos. 117, 1072. Porter's own verse included an elegy on Donne, printed in the 1633 ed. of Donne's poems.

10. ll. 19-27. *Cf.* the picture of Jonson's self-commendation in Howell, *Epp. Ho-El.*, ii., No. 13, dated 5 April, 1636. Suckling may have had this incident in mind, if the 'T. Ca.' of Howell's letter is the poet Carew, as is usually supposed. If so, the date of these verses is fixed between April, 1636, and Jonson's death, 6 Aug., 1637. *Cf.* also the portrait of Jonson as Multecarni in *The Sad One*, Acts IV. and V.

l. 26. *hoped*] *hopes* 1646, 1658.

l. 36. *New Inn*] Jonson's *New Inn*, acted 1629, is notorious for its failure, which inspired the disappointed author to the lines, 'Come, leave the loathed stage.'

l. 37. *Tom Carew*] See Mr. Vincent's introduction to Carew's poems, especially pp. xxxiii, xxxiv.

l. 39. *hide-bound*] *hard bound* 1646, 1658.

PAGE

10. l. 45. *cup-bearer's place*] Carew was appointed a sewer to the royal table about 1630.

l. 47. *travelling in France*] See Aubrey, *loc. cit.*, i. 205, 206, where Sir John Mennes's satirical lines are given. Aubrey says that the mischance was got in Westminster: 'travelling in France' is thus merely an allusion to its nature.

l. 52. *precedent*] *President* all early editions. Many parallels may be found for this form—*e.g.*, Shakespeare, *Richard III.*, III. vi. 7 (quarto).

11. l. 63. *Toby Mathews*] Sir Tobie Matthew, son of Tobie Matthew, Archbishop of York. His conversion to Romanism brought him the reputation of a dangerous intriguer: Fuller, *Church History*, lib. xi., sect. i., § 76, expresses the common Protestant estimate of his character. Harrington, quoted in *Dict. Nat. Biog.*, esteemed him 'likely for learning, memory, sharpness of wit, and sweetness of behaviour.' Bacon, whose Essays and Wisdom of the Ancients he translated into Italian, is said to have added his Essay on Friendship to the rest at his request and in his honour. His favour at court was largely due to Lady Carlisle's friendship: his panegyric on her character, published with a volume of his letters in 1660, had been seen in MS. as early as 1637, the presumptive date of this poem.

l. 64. *ear*] *ears* all early editions.

l. 66. *Lady Carlisle*] Lady Lucy Percy, daughter of Henry, ninth Earl of Northumberland, and second wife of James Hay, first Earl of Carlisle of the second creation. Her political intrigues are matter of history; and it will be remembered that Browning made her the chief female character of his *Strafford*. She was a patroness of poets: Waller, Herrick, and D'Avenant addressed verses to her when she was in mourning for her husband; she was Carew's Lucinda; and *cf.* the dialogue between Suckling and Carew, pp. 21, 22. Sir Tobie Matthew writes of her: 'Her wit being most eminent among the rest of her great abilities, she affects the conversation of the persons who are most famed for it'; and again he calls her 'too lofty and dignified to be capable of friendship, and

PAGE

having too great a heart to be susceptible of love.' For the criticism, half admiring, half scandalized, of a younger woman, see Dorothy Osborne's letters, ed. Parry, pp. 171, 180.

11. l. 83. *Wat Montague*] Second son of Henry Montagu, first Earl of Manchester. He became a Romanist in 1635, was banished in 1649, and became Abbot, first of Nanteuil, then of St. Martin's in Pontoise. His pastoral (l. 86) was *The Shepherd's Paradise*, acted in 1632-33 by the Queen and the Maids of Honour before Charles I. It was printed in 1659. See Maidment and Logan's D'Avenant, i. 283, for a letter by John Pory, dated 3 Jan., 1633, in which this masque is mentioned.

l. 92. *little Cid*] Aubrey, *loc. cit.*, ii. 209, has a note on Richard Sackville, fifth Earl of Dorset, relative to his father, the fourth Earl: ''Twas he that translated *The Cid*, a French comoedie, into English about 1640.' The translation of Corneille's *Cid*, the first part of which appeared in 1637, was actually by Joseph Rutter, tutor to the Earl. Aubrey's informant was Samuel Butler. Sackville, in 1637, was only in his fifteenth year; but, the year after, he contributed verses to *Jonsonius Virbius*. Did Suckling know of Rutter's authorship, or was Sackville, the supposed author, here called 'little' on the ground of his youth?

l. 95. *Murray*] Hazlitt says 'William Murray.' Possibly William Murray, gentleman of the bedchamber, created Earl of Dysart in 1643. He is mentioned in the letter printed in the Appendix. The allusion here is not clear.

12. l. 97. *Hales*] The 'ever-memorable' John Hales, fellow of Eton, to whom Suckling addressed an epistle, pp. 27, 28 below. Aubrey, *loc. cit.*, i. 278-281, quotes these lines inaccurately to support the statement: 'He was a generall scolar, and I beleeve a good poet.'

l. 102. *He was of late*, etc.] Aubrey, *loc. cit.*, i. 150, 151. mentions Falkland's addiction to Socinianism, and says: 'He was the first Socinian in England.' In another place, he ascribes this priority to Hales. Aubrey had been informed that Falkland was responsible for the title of *Jonsonius Virbius*, in

PAGE

which he had verses ; but ' Dr. Earles '—*i.e.*, Earle —' would not allow him to be a good poet, though a great witt ; he writt not a smoth verse, but a greate deal of sense.'

12. l. 107. *Davenant*] D'Avenant, as a young man about town, was probably hostile to members of the City Council. During the Civil War (Aubrey, *loc. cit.*, i. 206-208) he took prisoner two aldermen of York, who afterwards were instrumental in saving his life.

12-14. LOVE'S WORLD.

The annotator who signs himself ' W. W.' remarks on the mixture of childish conceit with beauty in this poem. The idea of man's heart or soul as a microcosm of the world at large was well-worn in Suckling's time. Donne especially had used it ; *cf. The Dissolution* (ed. Chambers, i. 69) : ' My fire of passion, sighs of air, Water of tears, and earthy sad despair, Which my materials be ' ; *Holy Sonnets*, v. (*ibid.*, i. 159) : ' I am a little world made cunningly Of elements,' etc.

14. SONNETS : I.

In the early editions, these so-called sonnets are preceded by the song, ' Why so pale and wan, fond lover,' which is sung in *Aglaura*, Act IV., and will be found there in the present volume.

l. 10. *Am still*] *And still* 1658.

15. SONNETS : II.

l. 12. *Lik'd*] *Like't* 1646, 1648, 1658.

16. SONNETS : III.

l. 1. Suckling's opening is obviously inspired by the famous beginning of Donne's *Love's Deity* (*loc. cit.*, i. 56). A similar opening to a poem by James Greene, called *Girls' Dreams*, is mentioned in a note quoted by Hazlitt.

l. 26. *Philoclea*] In Sidney's *Arcadia*, the Thracian Prince Pyrocles falls in love with the Arcadian Princess Philoclea, and, disguised as an Amazon, obtains admission to the country retirement of her parents, Basilius and Gynecia. Cecropia, sister-in-law of Basilius, wishes to marry Philoclea to her son Amphialus, and, out of spite to Basilius

PAGE

carries her off with her sister Pamela and the pretended Amazon. In the end, Philoclea is wedded to Pyrocles; and Amphialus, in the later continuation of the story, marries Helen, Queen of Corinth.

17. To the Lord Lepington.

Henry Carey, son of Sir Robert Carey, Earl of Monmouth, was known by his father's second title of Baron Leppington from the creation of the earldom in 1626 to his succession to it in 1639. A list of translations by this noble author is given by Wood, *Ath. Ox.*, ed. Bliss, iii. 516. He married in 1620 Suckling's first cousin, Martha Cranfield, eldest daughter of the future Earl of Middlesex. His translation of the *Ritratto del Privato Politico Christiano* (1635) of Virgilio, Marchese di Malvezzi, appeared in 1637. See Carew's complimentary verses in Mr. Vincent's ed. of Carew, p. 131, and the editor's note, p. 254. Suckling's and Carew's verses, with others by D'Avenant, Aurelian Townshend, and Sir Francis Wortley, appeared before the second ed. of the translation, 1638. Another translation, by T. Powel, was published in 1647: see H. Vaughan, *Olor Iscanus* (ed. Chambers, 1896, i. 97). Malvezzi (whom Dr. Jessopp, in an article on Carey in *Dict. Nat. Biog.*, vol. ix., wrongly calls Valezzi) was ambassador to London from Philip IV. of Spain. Milton, *Of Reformation in England*, lib. ii., mentions 'their Malvezzi, that can cut Tacitus into slivers and slits.'

ll. 1, 2. W. W. quotes Byron: 'And 'tis some praise in peers to write at all.'

18. Against Fruition.

See Cowley's poem on the same theme (*Poems*, ed. Waller, 1905, pp. 98, 99) Waller's answer to Suckling, with which this poem is printed with some variants of reading, will be found in Mr. Drury's ed. of Waller, 1893, pp. 116-119.

l. 19. *whate'er before th' have been*] Early eds. read *t'have*. Mr. Drury modernizes to *they've*, as in Chalmers, *Eng. Poets*, vi. 494; but Waller's reading, which Mr. Drury notes, was *what e'retofore hath been*.

PAGE

18. l. 20. *sights*] *scenes* Waller. This variant has not been mentioned by Mr. Drury, who notes all the rest.

'THERE NEVER YET,' etc.] W. W.'s note is as follows: 'This poem is remarkable for ease and sprightliness, the true characteristics of Sir J. Suckling's verse, and may therefore be taken as a fair specimen of his powers. Suckling seems to have been intimately acquainted with the female heart; he praises, ridicules, and adores the sex in the same breath. The germs of thought in some of Moore's most beautiful lyrics may be found in this ode.'

19. l. 10. *to jet in general*] *Cf. Twelfth Night*, II., v. 36.

l. 15. *It is because*, etc.] 1648; *It is because the loadstone yet was never brought* 1646, 1658, etc.; *It is because near the loadstone yet 'twas never brought*, Hazlitt. It seems probable that what Suckling wrote was, *It is because to th' loadstone yet 'twas never brought*, and that a misprint in the first edition brought about the subsequent introduction of *near*.

TO MY FRIEND WILL. DAVENANT.

The two pieces addressed to D'Avenant were prefixed to D'Avenant's collected poems in 1638. *Madagascar*, printed 1635, was dedicated to Henry Jermyn, afterwards Earl of St. Albans. Aubrey, *loc. cit.*, i. 205, calls Jermyn and Endymion Porter D'Avenant's 'two Mecaenasses.' D'Avenant had become poet laureate in 1637.

20. TO MY FRIEND WILL. D'AVENANT, ON HIS OTHER POEMS.

l. 3. *the great lord of it*] The phrase recalls Carew's epicede on Donne: 'Here lies a king that ruled, as he thought fit, The universal monarchy of wit.' *Cf.* ll. 49, 50 of the same poem: 'Since to the awe of thy imperious wit Our troublesome language bends,' etc. Donne died in 1631.

'LOVE, REASON, HATE'] The game of barley-break, which furnishes the idea of these verses, is explained in the last eclogue of Sidney's *Arcadia*, lib. i. It was played by three couples: the middle couple was said to be 'in hell,' and had to catch the other couples. The catching pair were not allowed to separate till they had succeeded; while the other pairs, if hard pressed, were

PAGE

allowed to 'break' or separate, from which the game derived the second part of its name. When all had been caught, new couples were formed, and the pair which failed to occupy one of the ends of the ground was 'in hell.' 'Barley' may be derived from the fact that the game was often played in a cornfield: in Scotland, where one person caught the rest, and the rest, as caught, helped him, it was known as 'barla-bracks about the stacks.' Or 'barley' may be from a Scottish corruption of the cry 'parley.' For examples, see Nares' *Glossary*, and *New English Dict.*, *s.v.*

21. UPON MY LADY CARLISLE'S WALKING IN HAMPTON COURT GARDEN.

See note on *A Session of the Poets*, l. 60. T. C., of course, is Thomas Carew. W. W. has a long note here on the general tendencies of poetry in the age, and says of Carew: 'He, like his friend Suckling, was ambitious of being ranked among the metaphysical poets, but fortunately had not power to attain it.'

l. 8. *bean-blossoms*] *Cf.* Coleridge, *The Eolian Harp*, ll. 9, 10: 'How exquisite the scents Snatched from yon bean-field.' See also *Aglaura*, I. v. 88.

23. AGAINST ABSENCE.

ll. 17, 18. In ll. 9, 10 of the immediately preceding poem, Suckling expresses the somewhat contrary opinion that sense is essential to intelligence.

24. A SUPPLEMENT, ETC.

See Shakespeare, *Lucrece*, ll. 386, etc. W. W. writes: 'The continuation is equal to the first part.'

l. 11. *this pretty perdue*] Lucrece's hand is 'sentinelle perdue' of her body—*i.e.*, as Littré explains the word, 'sentinelle postée dans un lieu très-avancé.'' W. J. Craig, on *King Lear*, IV., vii. 35 (Arden ed. 1901), quotes English uses of the word from Fletcher and Tourneur. *Cf. Goblins*, III. iv. below.

25. ''TIS NOW SINCE I SAT DOWN'] W. W. says: 'In this poem Suckling seems to have succeeded completely in what is called the metaphysical style of poetry.' For the metaphor of a siege, *cf.* the

next poem, ll. 29-35; the lines upon A. M., pp. 61, 62 below; Cowley, *Against Fruition*, ll. 9, 10.

25. l. 5. *Made my approaches*] W. W. quotes (inaccurately) Byron, *To Thyrza*, st. 8: 'Ours too the glance none saw beside,' etc., as an apparent imitation of this stanza. There is a general likeness of thought; but the imitation is not obvious.

26. l. 19. *Praising*] *Praying* 1658.

l. 35. *That giant*] 'The giant, Honour,' is personified by Carew, *The Rapture*, ll. 3-9: see note in Mr. Vincent's ed., p. 246. Honour is reproached again by Suckling, *Upon the Black Spots worn by my Lady D. E.*, ll. 7, 8.

UPON MY LORD BROHALL'S WEDDING.

Roger Boyle, Baron Broghill, younger son of the first Earl of Cork, married in 1641 Lady Margaret Howard, third daughter of the second Earl of Suffolk. Lord Broghill was created Earl of Orrery in 1650. Aubrey, *loc. cit.*, i.,118, prints a funeral sermon on his sister, Lady Warwick, in which Lord Orrery is described as 'that great poet, great statesman, great soldier, and great everything which merits the name of great and good.' Cowley (*Poems*, ed. Waller, 1905, pp. 406-409) wrote an Ode, 'Upon Occasion of a Copy of Verses of my Lord Broghills.' For Broghill's' heroic romance, *Parthenissa* (first six vols., 1654; complete ed., 1665), see the able summary in Raleigh, *English Novel*, pp. 93-96, and Dorothy Osborne's Letters, ed. Parry, pp. 230-232. For his rimed tragedies, all probably composed after the Restoration, see A. W. Ward, *English Dram. Lit.*, new ed., 1899, iii. 340-345, and notices in Pepys' Diary, 13 Aug., 1664, 19 Oct., 1667, 8 Dec., 1668, and Evelyn's Diary, 18 Oct., 1668. Dryden dedicated to Lord Orrery *The Rival Ladies*, 1664 (Works, ed. Scott and Saintsbury, 1882, iii. 129-139). Jack Bond, Suckling's interlocutor in this dialogue, is mentioned again below in the verses to John Hales, l. 10.

27. l. 9. *differ but*] 1658, a better reading than the simple *differ* of 1646.

l. 17. *A sprig of willow*] 'The Willow, worne of forlorne paramours' (Spenser, *Faerie Queene*, I., i. 9).

PAGE

See Brand, *Popular Antiquities*, i. 121, 122. *Cf.* among many instances, *Much Ado about Nothing*, II., i. 194-199; the song in *Othello*, IV., iii. 41 *ff*., and Percy, *Reliques*, ser. i., lib. ii., No. 8; Fletcher, *Night-Walker*, c. 1638, I., i.; Herrick, *Hesperides*, 263; and the pun on the subject in G. Meredith, *The Egoist*, 1879, ch. xxxiv.

27. ll. 27, 28. *gipsies' knots . . . fast and loose*] *Cf. Antony and Cleopatra*, IV., xii. 29; Jonson, *Gipsies Metamorphosed*, 1621: 'I'll shew you the slight of our Ptolemy's knot, It is, and 'tis not.' The game of 'fast and loose' was a favourite with dishonest vagabonds. The cheat tied up a leathern belt or thong into a number of deceptive folds; and the gull was given a knife, and asked to pierce the folded belt in the centre, which he usually failed to do. There is an allusion to the thong and knife in *Merry Wives of Windsor*, II., ii. 19. *New Eng. Dict.* quotes Donne, *Sermon* lxxxv.: 'Never ask wrangling Controverters that make Gypsie-knots of Mariages;—ask thy Conscience, and that will tell thee that thou wast married till death should depart you.' Mr. Ivor B. John has an elaborate note on 'fast and loose,' with reference to *King John*, III., i. 242 (Arden ed. 1907).

l. 36. *hearts*] *harts* 1658.

'Whether these lines,' etc.] This epistle is addressed to John Hales, Fellow of Eton: see note on *A Session of the Poets*, l. 91. The mention of Socinus here corroborates the Socinian tradition associated with Hales' name. It is known, however, that the Socinian tracts with which Hales has been credited were the work of Continental writers.

28. ll. 21, 22. *The sweat of learned Jonson's brain*] The likeness to Milton, *L'Allegro*, 131-34, need not be designed, although, if the date of most of these poems be taken into account, Milton's poem preceded these lines by some years.

l. 23. *hackney-coach*] John Taylor, *Old Parr*, 1635, quoted by *New Eng. Dict.*, gives a notice of hackney-coaches in the reigns of the first two Stewarts. Coaches 'have increased . . . by the multitudes of Hackney or hired Coaches; but they never swarmed so thick to pester the streets, as they doe now, till the yeare 1605.'

29. Against Fruition.

l. 5. *camelion*] *Cf. Two Gentlemen of Verona*, II., iv. 26; *Hamlet*, III., ii. 98. For the tradition, see Ovid, *Metamm.*, xv. 411: 'Id quoque, quod ventis animal nutritur et aura, Protinus assimulat tetigit quoscumque colores.' Sir Thomas Browne, *Pseud. Epid.*, iii. 21, discusses the legend at length.

A Ballad upon a Wedding.

See note above, *Upon my Lord Brohall's Wedding*. The wedding took place in 1641: *New Eng. Dict.* quotes ll. 19-21 from G. H., *Witts' Recreations*, 1640 (? O.S.), in which the poem appeared, 'accompanied by a woodcut of two ploughmen or rustics, the one narrating, the other listening' (Hazlitt). W. W. pronounces the ballad Suckling's '*opus magnum;* indeed, for grace and simplicity it stands unrivalled in the whole compass of ancient or modern poetry.' Hazlitt mentions lines called 'Three merry boys of Kent,' occurring in *Folly in Print, or a Book of Rhymes*, 1667, to the tune of an old song beginning thus, 'I rode from England into France' (*cf.* opening of *Cantilena Politico-Jocunda* below), or to the tune of Sir John Suckling's Ballad; and lines to the tune of 'I tell thee, Dick, where I have been,' in Patrick Carey's *Trivia*, 1651. 'Dick' is usually identified with Lovelace.

ll. 7-9. *At Charing Cross . . . stairs*] Northampton House, built by Henry Howard, Earl of Northampton, in James I.'s reign, passed, on his death in 1614, to his nephew, Thomas, Earl of Suffolk, grandfather to the bride of this poem. It was now known as Suffolk House. In 1642, the year after this wedding, the bride's sister, Elizabeth, married Algernon, tenth Earl of Northumberland, and brought the house into her husband's family, in which it remained, as Northumberland House, till its destruction in 1874. The 'place where we do sell our hay' is the Haymarket: Hazlitt says that his uncle, Mr. Reynell, who died in 1892, at the age of ninety-three, told him

PAGE

'that he remembered hay sold there in his early days.'

30. l. 19. *Course-a-Park*] A country game, akin to Barley-break, and not unlike Kiss-in-the-ring. See W. Browne, *Britannia's Pastorals*, I., iii. 25: 'Or that he cours'd a park with females fraught, Which would not run except they might be caught.' *New Eng. Dict.* quotes Teonge's Diary, 1675, ed. 1825, p. 112: 'Like boys and gyrles at course-a-packe, or barly breakes.'

l. 31. *The maid*] Hazlitt cites the opinion of an anonymous commentator, that 'Moore's description of Lilias (*sic*) in *The Loves of the Angels* appears to be an imitation of Suckling.' The resemblance, if there be any, is of the most general kind. W. W., commenting on the 'bashful tenderness' of the bride at l. 49, remarks that Suckling's 'portraits of female beauty are not so finished as those of Moore and Byron; but they possess greater attraction, because he gives only a glimpse, and leaves the rest to fancy. Indeed, Homer, in describing the peerless Helen, leaves it almost entirely to the imagination, which is the great secret of poetry.' Suckling mentions presumably Lady Margaret Howard in his letter to Jack [? Bond] headed 'A Dissuasion from Love' (see p. 301): 'I know you have but one way' —*i.e.*, of teaching the art of getting into love,— 'and will prescribe me not to look upon Mistress Howard.'

l. 32. *Whitson-ale*] See Brand, *Pop. Antt.*, i. 276-284. The surplus of these feasts, supplied by parochial contributions, was devoted to repairs, etc., connected with the church fabric or furniture. Thus an inscription on the ringing-gallery at Cawston, Norfolk, records 'what good ale this work made'; and another, on the 'bachelors' loft' before the south chapel of the chancel at Thorpe-le-Soken, Essex, states that part of the expense was defrayed by 'alys.'

l. 34. *kindly ripe*] Ripe after its nature, and so thoroughly ripe. The latest example of this use of 'kindly' cited by *New Eng. Dict.* is *Romeo and Juliet*, II., iv. 59.

PAGE

30. l. 38. *they*] *he* 1648.

l. 50. *so nice*] *nice* 1646, 1648, 1658.

l. 59. *Katherne pear*] 'A small and early variety of pear' (*New Eng. Dict.*). *Cf.* Gay, *Shepherd's Week*, 1714, Wednesday, l. 56; Crabbe, *Tales of the Hall*, 1819, x. 598, 599: ''Twas not the lighter red, that partly streaks The Catherine pear, that brighten'd o'er her cheeks.'

31. l. 75. *purely*] Halliwell notes the use as East Anglian, and quotes Miège's *French Dict.*, 1688: 'Ortolan . . . sings purely, and is good to eat.'

ll. 91-96. In the 1648 and some later editions, this stanza, with the two halves inverted, is placed after the stanza which ends at l. 78.

l. 94. *Passion o' me*] *Passion oh me!* all early edd.

32. l. 107. *Whilst*] *Till* 1646, 1658.

l. 120. *God b'w'ye*] *God B'w'y'* 1648; *Good Boy!* 1646, 1658.

l. 127. *out; and now*] *out and out* 1646, 1658.

l. 128. *do*] *do't* 1646, 1658.

'My dearest rival'] *Cf.* the poem *To His Rival*, below, pp. 35, 36; and see the advice in letter ii. (p. 300): 'Continue your affection to your rival still: that will secure you from one way of loving, which is in spite.'

l. 10. *Or*] *Or else* 1658.

33. Song.

l. 1. *whosoever*] *whatsoever* 1658. There is a parody of this song in the *Poetry of the Anti-Jacobin*.

35. Upon Two Sisters.

l. 4. *Or the nice points*] So all the editions; but, to make sense, we should read *As the nice points*.

l. 6. This line is wanting. Hazlitt supplied it thus: *As . . . and Aglaura are*.

To His Rival.

l. 2. *creep where't cannot go*] Suckling uses this proverbial phrase below, in the lines *Upon Sir John Laurence's bringing Water . . . to Witten*.

36. l. 11. *like clocks*] This simile is also used above, in the second of the three 'sonnets,' and in the lines 'That none beguiled be,' p. 25.

PAGE

36. ll. 29, 30. *But ev'ry smile,* etc.] W. W. writes: 'These two lines are very beautiful. The rest of the poem is hardly above mediocrity, but two such lines do not recompense us for a mass of base matter.'

l. 33. *too many*] *to many* 1646.

37. FAREWELL TO LOVE.

W. W.'s note is: 'This ode is inferior to none of his writings for nature and simplicity, but it partakes of all their faults.'

l. 1. *Well, shadow'd*] *Well-shadow'd* early edd.

ll. 11-15. *As he,* etc.] *Cf.* Donne's famous song: 'Go and catch a falling star'; and his Epithalamion for Lord Somerset, 1613, stanza 10: 'As he that sees a star fall, runs apace, And finds a jelly in the place.' Mr. Chambers, in his ed. of Donne (i. 221, 222), cites parallels. For superstitions regarding the origin of star-jelly or witches' butter (*Nostoc commune*), see Brand, *Pop. Antt.*, iii. 404, 405.

ll. 26-30. See Burton, *Anat. Mel.*, iii., sect. 2, memb. 5. subs. iii. (ed. Shilleto, 1896, iii. 245), for similar methods of curing love by imagination, especially his quotation from Chrysostom.

38. l. 31. *gum*] *Gun* 1646, 1648.

l. 33. *hair, 't*] *heart,* old edd.; *hair,* Hazlitt. The right reading is obvious.

l. 35. *the hay*] See Sir John Davies, *Orchestra,* 1594, l. 64: 'He taught them Rounds and winding Heyes to tread'; *Love's Labour's Lost,* V., i. 161, with H. C. Hart's note in Arden ed., 1906; and the 'report' song 'Shall we go dance the hay?' in *England's Helicon,* 1600 (ed. Bullen, 1899, p. 243).

l. 41. *methinks*] *me think* 1658.

l. 44. *Checks*] Hazlitt; *Check,* early edd. The metaphor is from hawking: see *Twelfth Night,* II., v. 125; III., i. 71.

ll. 46, 47. *They . . . These*] It seems more natural to read *These . . . They,* and suppose the usual reading to be an accidental transposition of the earlier editors.

45. THE INVOCATION.

l. 1. *Cf. The Expostulation,* below: 'Ye juster deities, That pity lovers' miseries.'

PAGE

A Poem with the Answer.

For 'Sir Toby Matthews' see note on *A Session of the Poets*, l. 63.

47. Love Turned to Hatred.

The opening lines recall Drayton's famous sonnet (*Idea*, lxi.) : 'Since there's no help,' etc.

l. 9. *I'll hate so perfectly*] *Cf.* Donne, Satire II., ll. 1, 2 : 'Sir, though—I thank God for it—I do hate Perfectly all this town.'

The Careless Lover.

l. 6. *know it*] *knows it*, early edd.

ll. 15, etc. *Cf.* the fifth stanza of the song 'Honest lover,' above.

48. ll. 19, 20. *And when*, etc.] *Cf.* the seventeenth stanza of the *Ballad upon a Wedding*, above.

l. 23. *Blackfriars*] The private theatre, where Suckling's plays were produced.

l. 25. *pathless grove*] *Cf. Against Absence*, above, l. 32.

50. To a Lady, etc.

The editor of 1836 notes that Cibber, in the *Lives of the Poets* published under his name, considered these to be Suckling's best lines. With the contrary opinion of the editor most readers will be in harmony.

l. 2. *muff*] *Cf. To His Rival*, above, l. 31. See Fairholt, *Costume in England*, ed. Dillon, ii. 291, where the first instance quoted is from Jonson, *Cynthia's Revels*, 1601, II., i. : 'She always wears a muff if you be remembered.' The earlier term for a muff seems to have been a snuffkin : Fairholt gives the variants snuftkin, snoskin. The muff was much used by dandies after the Restoration (*ibid.*, i. 353, 354). The literary *locus classicus* for the muff is, of course, the episode in the inn at Upton-on-Severn in Fielding's *Tom Jones*.

l. 11. *nice*] *Cf.* stanza 17 of *Love's World*, above : 'Extremely cold, extremely nice.'

The Guiltless Inconstant.

l. 5. *Each wanton eye*] *Cf.* stanza 5 of *Farewell to Love*, above.

PAGE

50. l. 12. *gesture . . . grace*] *Cf. Upon Two Sisters*, above, l. 22.

51. LOVE'S REPRESENTATION.

l. 1. *head*] *hand*, early edd.

l. 6. *No hope*] *Chose hope* 1709 ; *In hope*, Hazlitt.

52. l. 33. *beamy fetters*] *Cf.* the stanzas on Lucrece, above, l. 19 : 'Her beams, which some dull men call'd hair.'

SONG.

l. 4. *setting up his rest*] *Cf. Romeo and Juliet*, IV., v. 6, and see Nares' explanation of the phrase, *s.v. rest.*

53. UPON THE BLACK SPOTS WORN BY MY LADY D. E.

Hazlitt asks : 'Could this be the Dorothy Enion who married Thomas Stanley the poet ?' The lady referred to by Suckling is obviously a nobleman's daughter, possibly an Egerton.

56. DESDAIN.

l. 2. *serments*] *servens* 1658.
vents] *vent*, early edd.

l. 6. *Entendez*] 1709 ; *N'tendez*, earlier editions.

l. 15. *Ni le rompre*] *In le rompre* 1646, 1648, 1658.

l. 16. *Ni d'estre*] *In d'estre* 1658.
perfide] *perfite*, early edd.

l. 18. *vous obliger*] *nous obliger* 1658.

l. 20. *Des vœux*] *Du vous* 1658.

57. LUTEA ALLISON.

The 1709 ed. calls this poem *Lutea Allanson*, obviously an error.

58. PERJURY EXCUSED.

l. 7. *And I have bound*, etc.] He refers to the *Farewell to Love* above.

l. 14. After this poem, in the early editions, occurs the song 'Hast thou seen the down in the air,' which is printed in *The Sad One*, IV. iii.

UPON THE FIRST SIGHT OF MY LADY SEYMOUR.

There were several ladies at the Stewart Court who bore this title. Francis, younger brother of

William, Earl of Hertford, and afterwards first Duke of Somerset, was created Baron Seymour of Trowbridge in 1641, and was twice married. Sir Edward Seymour of Berry Pomeroy, second baronet, married Dorothy, daughter of Sir Henry Killigrew; while Anne, daughter of Richard, Earl of Dorset, was widow of Sir Edward Seymour, elder brother of the future Duke of Somerset. One of three ladies may be thus intended.

59. UPON L. M. WEEPING.

L. M. is printed by Hazlitt, L(ady) M(iddlesex). It is impossible to identify her with certainty. Suckling's maternal uncle, Lionel Cranfield, married as his second wife in 1621, Anne, daughter of James Bret, Esq., of Hoby, Leicestershire.

61. HIS DREAM.

l. 16. *Arabick spices*] *Cf.* the passage in *Sad One*, IV. i., which begins, 'Thy father fed On musk and amber,' etc.

63. UPON SIR JOHN LAURENCE'S, ETC.

Witten is Whitton in the parish of Twickenham, the seat of Suckling's uncle, Lord Middlesex.

l. 8. *For love will creep*] *Cf.* the opening of the poem *To His Rival* above.

A BARBER.

l. 8. *great Sweden's force*] This allusion suggests a fairly early date for the poem. The exploits of Gustavus Adolphus in the Thirty Years' War took place between 1630 and 1632.

64, 65. A PEDLAR OF SMALLWARES.

The ladies whose initials are given in this poem cannot be identified with any certainty. L. W. may be Lady Weston. Sir Jerome Weston, styled Baron Weston of Neyland in 1634, succeeded his father, the famous Lord Treasurer, as second Earl of Portland in 1635. His wife was Lady Frances Stewart, second daughter of Esmé, Duke of Lennox, whom he married in 1632. This, at any rate, supplies a date-limit for the poem; but, even so, it is simply matter of conjecture.

PAGE

65. An Answer to Some Verses, etc.

l. 6. *herse*] The frame of wood or metal on which the pall was suspended above a coffin or tomb.

66. l. 19. *barbed steed*] A horse fully caparisoned for battle: *cf. Rich. III.*, I. i. 10, and note citing parallel passages in Arden ed. of play.

68. Song.

l. 20. *promont*] Nares gives an instance of this form from the tragedy of *Hoffman*, 1631: 'Ile to yon promont's top, and there survey What shipwrackt passengers the Belgique sea Casts from her fomy entrailes by mischance.'

69. Detraction Execrated.

l. 29. *correspondency*] *correspondence had* 1709; *correspondence*, Hazlitt.

l. 36. *lose't*] Hazlitt; *lost* 1646, and other early edd.; *loos'd* 1709.

70. Song.

l. 20. *The gentle and quick approaches*] *Cf.* second stanza of ''Tis now since I sat down,' etc.

71-73. Cantilena Politico-Jocunda.

This was first printed by Hazlitt from Harl. MS. 367, where no author's name is given to it. On the endorsement is a note in the handwriting of Sir Henry Ellis, principal librarian of the British Museum, 1827-36, attributing it to Suckling. The date of the piece is usually assigned to about 1623, from the apparent mention of the Duc de Luynes, who died at Montauban in 1622. Some of the allusions, however, seem to point to a rather later date. In any case, Suckling's authorship is by no means certain, and may be left an open question. In the present edition, the poem has been carefully collated with the original MS.

73, 74. Verses.

Printed by Hazlitt from a transcript by Dyce, communicated to *Notes and Queries*, 1st ser., vol. i., from a small volume of English poetry, temp.

PAGE

Charles I. In that volume they were headed 'Sir John Suckling's Verses.'

74, 75. SIR JOHN SUCKLING'S ANSWER.

Printed by Hazlitt from Ashmole MS. 36, f. 54. It seems to have been written in answer to some satirical doggerel by Sir John Mennes on Suckling's preparations for the Scottish war. The allusion to Lashly refers, of course, to the Scottish general Leslie, who afterwards led the Scottish army to victory at Newburn.

NOTES ON AGLAURA

85. ACT I., SCENE I.

l. 8. *as it were one's own*] *as 'twere ones owne* 1646, 1648; *as 'twere his owne* 1658.

l. 22. [*is*] *fest'red*] *festred* 1646, etc.

86. SCENE II.

l. 3. *carbonadoes*] '*Carbonade*: a carbonadoe, a rasher on the coals; also a flash over the face, which fetcheth the flesh with it' (Cotgrave). *Cf. All's Well that Ends Well*, IV., iv. 107. The faces of the soldiers without are so slashed that they are more like rashers cut crosswise before boiling, than like faces.

87. l. 21. *chemists, blowing still the coals*] *Cf.* Jonson, *Alchemist*, ii. 1: 'His fire-drake, His Lungs, his Zephyrus, he that puffs his coals.'

SCENE III.

l. 2. [*to*] *sin*] Hazlitt; *sin* 1646, etc.

89. SCENE IV.

l. 11. *Platonic ladies' hearts*] Howell (3 June, 1634) mentions the new fashion of Platonic love at court, and the prospect of a masque on the subject. D'Avenant's *Temple of Love* was acted by the Queen, Maids of Honour, etc., on Shrove Tuesday, 1634-35: see Preface to *The Platonic Lovers* (D'Avenant's Works, ed. Maidment and Logan, 1872, ii. 3-5), and *cf.* Goblins, IV., ii., below. Cowley, in *The Mistress*, has two poems on this

PAGE

subject—viz., *Platonick Love* (*Poems*, ed. Wailer, pp. 75, 76), and *Answer to the Platonicks* (*ibid.*, pp. 80, 81).

91. SCENE V.

l. 30. *the ascending*] Hazlitt; *ascending* 1646, etc.

92. l. 38. *court*] *Courts* 1658.

l. 47. *imp*] 'In hawking, to insert a new feather in place of a broken one' [Halliwell), as *Rich. II.*, II., i. 292. Massinger uses the metaphor of imping feathers to the wings of time in three places (*Renegado*, V., viii.; *Roman Actor*, V., ii.; *Great Duke of Florence*, I., i.). O.E. *impan*=to graft: thus subst. *imp*=a shoot or scion. See *Piers the Plowman*, B-text, V., 136 *ff.*: 'I was sum-tyme a frere, And þe couentes Gardyner . for to graffe *ympes;* On limitours and listres . lesynges I *ymped*, Tyl þei bere leues of low speche . lordes to plese.'

l. 52. *Think you*, etc.] This speech is almost identical with the poem *Against Fruition*, ll. 7-12. Semanthe's next speech is repeated from the same poem.

l. 61. [*and*] *that*] Hazlitt; *that* 1646, etc.

l. 66. *Flesh'd*] Given their first taste of blood: see *Rich. III.*, IV., iii. 6, and note thereon in Arden edition of the play (1907).

93. l. 78. *curiosity*] Fastidiousness, as *King Lear*, I., i. 6; I., ii. 4. So 'curious' in this play: 'curious heraldry' (II., iii.); 'curious posterity' (III., ii.), 'curious studiers' (IV., i.).

l. 88. *bean's first blossoms*] Suckling uses this image again in the poem on Lady Carlisle.

l. 109. *They keep me fasting*] *Cf. Against Fruition*, l. 22.

98. ACT II., SCENE I.

l. 29. *'Tis misery's happiness*, etc.] *Cf.* John of Gaunt's words in *Rich. II.*, I., iii. 292, 293: 'gnarling sorrow hath less power to bite The man that mocks at it and sets it light.'

l. 41. *King?* etc.] *Cf.* Amintor's words in Beaumont and Fletcher, *Maid's Tragedy*, II., i.: 'Oh, thou hast nam'd a word, that wipes away All thoughts revengeful! In that sacred name, 'The King,' there lies a terror. What frail man Dares lift his hand against it ?' So also Lucio, in D'Avenant's *Cruel Brother*, 1630, Act V., shrinks from murdering the Duke : 'Furnish us, sweet heaven, with some Instinct ! Inspire remorse, or we accuse Thy skillfulness to predestine us a Prince, Murdering whom thou didst anoint our Sovereign.'

l. 42. *cancel that high bond*] The phrase is used by Shakespeare, *Macbeth*, III., ii. 49 ; *Rich. III.*, IV., iv. 77 ; *Cymbeline*, V., iv. 29. Suckling appears to echo it here, without reflecting on the sense in which Shakespeare always uses it.

99. l. 66. *Diana's nunnery*] *Cf. Mids. Night's Dream*, I., i. 68-78, etc.

100. SCENE II.

l. 15. *The gracious glance*, etc.] *Cf.* stanza 2 of the lyric beginning ''Tis now since I sat down,' etc. The same lyric is recalled in Orsames' speech below, beginning, 'Well, if she hold out,' etc.

l. 30. *Could do*] *would do* 1646, 1648.

101. l. 68. *one disguise*] 1658. This should be *own disguise*, as 1646.

SCENE III.

l. 12. *Man* (*Nature's heir*), etc.] *Cf.* Edmund's sentiment in *King Lear*, I., ii. : 'Thou, Nature, art my goddess,' etc.

102. l. 16. *does impart*] *doth impart* 1658.

l. 42. *addition*] Added greatness or importance : *cf. Goblins*, V., ii. : 'There can be no addition to you, sir, By his death,' and see *Troilus and Cressida*, IV., v. 141. For another common use of the word, implying a title added to a name, see *Othello*, IV., i. 106.

l. 49. *they keep not for me*] *they keep not from me* 1646, 1658.

103. l. 69. *trouch-man*] Interpreter, go-between : Arab. *tardjemân*, Span. *trujaman*, Mod. Eng. *dragoman*. *Cf.* Peele, *Polyhymnia*, 1590 (ed. Dyce, p. 569) : 'And having by his truch-man [old edd., trounch-man] pardon craved.'

l. 81. *False as a falling star*] *Cf. Farewell to Love*, stanza 3.

l. 85. [*is*] *more*] Hazlitt.

PAGE

104. l. 91. *is borrow'd*] *it borrowes* 1648. *It* is the right reading.

l. 94. *Chalking*] So all the editions. 'Caulking' seems to be the word intended; but 'choking' is also possible.

106. SCENE V.

l. 22. *the new love*] *I.e.*, the new Platonic fashion: *cf.* Scene II., 'the new religion in love.'

110. ACT III., SCENE II.

l. 117. *envious penury*] Hateful, malicious, penury: *cf. Rom. and Jul.*, III., ii. 40; *Rich. III.*, I., iv. 37.

111. l. 150. *pretty*] 1658; *petty* 1646, 1648.

l. 158. *witty*] *Cf. Rich. III.*, IV., ii. 42.

l. 164. *advance—*] Ziriff means 'advance (*i.e.*, heighten) our joy': the same sentiment occurs in *Rom. and Jul.*, III., v. 52. He breaks off, however, to finish the scene by a general reflexion on the subject of joy.

112. ACT IV., SCENE I.

l. 6. *as good pictures*, etc.] Hazlitt notes the reference to portraits by Titian and other great masters: 'at whatever point you place yourself, they seem to be fixing their eyes on you.'

l. 20. *the lions*] *I.e.*, the lions in the Tower, for which see Stow, *Survey of London*, ed. Morley, p. 76. *Cf.* Slender on the bears at Bankside, *Merry Wives*, I., i. 306 *ff*.

l. 34. *rack*] All early edd. have *wrack*.

113. l. 40. *close*] secret, as *Meas. for Meas.*, IV., iii. 123.

l. 57. *sicklied o'er*, etc.] A reminiscence of *Hamlet*, III., i. 84, 85.

114. l. 86. *for those*] *for these* 1658.

SCENE II.

l. 8. *bittern*] *Bittorne* 1646, 1658; *bittorns* 1648.

reed] Halliwell gives an East Anglian use of this word, meaning 'a very small wood.' The sense intended here seems to be 'a marshy plantation.'

115. l. 47. *the Courteous Reader*] In allusion to this familiar phrase in the preface of a book.

116. SCENE III.

l. 4. *slight*] 1709. Early edd. have *sleight*.

PAGE

118. SCENE IV.

l. 7. *For were it in my power*] W. W. calls attention to a similar idea in one of Moore's songs: "Though the heart would break with more, It could not live with less.'

l. 10. *'Twould*] *I would* 1658; and early edd. of the poems, in which this song is included—obviously a wrong reading.

119. l. 26. *the mainspring, Hope*] *Cf.* stanza 2 of the lyric, 'That none beguiled be,' etc.

121. l. 137. *Ziriff, despatch! Away!*] *Ziriff, dispatch away* —1646; Zir. *Despatch. Away!* 1658.

123. SCENE V.

l. 36. *the honest swain*] The simile may be a reminiscence of *Winter's Tale*, III., iii.

l. 55. *Two fixed stars*, etc.] *Cf.* 1 *Hen. IV.*, V., iv. 65.

124. l. 63. *Ye mighty powers*] *Cf. The Invocation*, l. 1.

l. 64. *fond boy*] *Cf.* similar addresses to love at the opening of Sonnet II., and the song, 'I prithee spare me.'

ACT V., SCENE I.

l. 5. *Th' inheritance*] The realm, possession: *cf.* 'inherit' in *Tempest*, IV., i. 154; and 'inheritor' in D'Avenant, *Wits*, IV., i.: 'A free inheritor Of ev'ry modest, or voluptuous wish, That young desires can breathe.'

125. l. 24. *So*] *Lo* 1658.

l. 36. *Basely! and tamely—*] *Basely and tamely!—* 1658.

126. l. 62. *and star'd*, etc.] *Cf.* 'mortal-staring' in *Rich. III.*, V., iii. 90. This passage seems to throw light on that disputed epithet.

127. l. 96. *shape*] So all edd.; but *shapes* is probably the reading intended.

128. SCENE II.

l. 56. *For ever?* etc.] Ziriff's meditations on eternity have a general likeness to Hamlet's in *Hamlet*, III., i. and those of Claudio in *Meas. for Meas.*, III., i.

129. l. 93. *Poor bankrupt heart*] *Cf. Rom. and Jul.*, III., ii. 57.

PAGE

130. SCENE III.

l. 4. *private retir'd ones*] *Cf.* Donne's last sermon: 'That private and retired man, that thought himself his own for ever.'

ll. 7, 8. *the great prince in prison*] The allusion is to Donne's famous phrase in *The Ecstacy*, ll. 65-68: 'So must pure lovers' souls descend To affections, and to faculties, Which sense may reach and apprehend, Else a great prince in prison lies.'

l. 20. *In me you shall see*, etc.] *Cf. Hamlet*, III., iv. 19, 20.

l. 28. *the great load*, etc.] *Cf. Hamlet*, III., i. 76, 77.

131. l. 38. *They're Thread*] Thread is Clotho, the spinner; Time is Atropos, the inflexible; Chance is Lachesis, the disposer of lots. *Cf.* D'Avenant, *Albovine*, Act IV: 'Have you of late Been gossipping with the grim Stygian dames, And seen their scissors gall my vital thread?'

132. l. 92. *sins full blown*] *Cf.* Hamlet, III., iii. 81; I., iv. 76.

134. l. 183. *this arrest*] *Cf. Hamlet*, V., ii. 347, 348.

135. l. 187. *the story*] *a story* 1658.

aft. l. 190. bearing in] 'tearing in' is the general reading of the early edd.

l. 197. *so torn a state*] *Cf.* 'the gored state,' *King Lear*, V., iii. 320.

NOTES ON THE GOBLINS

163. PROLOGUE.

l. 21. *'less that his boots*] *lest that his boots* 1658. Hazlitt, who omits *that his* calls attention to a passage from a work by Fabian Phillips (*Antiquity . . . of Præ-emption, and Pourveyance for the King*, 1663), in which the fashion of wearing boots is referred to as having been general towards the end of the reign of James I.,' when the Spanish Ambassador, the Conde of Gondomar, could pleasantly relate, when he went home into Spain, that all the citizens of London were booted, and ready, as he thought, to go out of town.'

167. ACT I., SCENE I.

l. 90. *screech-owls*] The foreboding cry of the screech-owl is referred to by Shakespeare, *Mids. Night's Dream*, V., i. 383-85; *Macbeth*, II., ii. 3, 16.

PAGE

168. l. 99. *'Twas at his circle*] *Cf.* the 'hallowed verge' of the conjurors in 2 *Hen. VI.*, I., iv. 25; and see D'Avenant, *Wits*, V., iii.: 'Conjurors in a circle, That have rais'd up a wrong spirit.'

169. l. 140. *Tamorens*] 1648. The other early edd. have here and at Scene III., l. 18, the wrong reading, *Samorats.*

170. SCENE II.

l. 8. *Sedgly curse*] *Cf.* Fletcher, *Woman's Prize*, V. ii.: 'A Sedgly curse light on him; which is, Pedro, "The fiend ride through him booted and spurr'd, with a scythe at his back!"' Sedgley is in Staffordshire, between Dudley and Wolverhampton; but Massinger, *City Madam*, II., ii., gives a Scottish origin to the curse.

l. 9. *neck*] So all eds., but *back* is the right reading.

171. SCENE III.

l. 42. *ship*] *ships* 1646, 1648.

l. 43. *To reel*, etc.] *Cf.* Psalm cvii. 27.

172. l. 55. And for the blue] *Cf.* D'Avenant, *Cruel Brother*, 1630, Act II: 'His eyes . . . are crept into his head, Encircled with the weakly colour blue.'

l. 57. Pinch him, pinch him] Printed as a stage-direction by all early eds. Collier claimed the words as part of the text, on the ground of 'the repetition and the sense (to say nothing of the measure which is very irregular).'

SCENE IV.

l. 5. *Will he foin*] Steevens refers to *Merry Wives of Windsor*, II., iii. 24: see note by H. C. Hart in Arden ed. of that play. Another note in Dodsley's ed. of *The Goblins* refers to *Return from Parnassus*, I., ii.: 'Then royster doyster in his oylie tearmes, Cutts, thrusts, and foynes at whomesoever he meets.'

l. 8. Topo] Italian for 'a rat.' *Cf.* Hamlet's cry, 'How now! a rat?'—*Hamlet*, III., iv. 24.

174. l. 62. *venter*] So all edd.

175. ACT II., SCENE I.

l. 16. *a Platonic*] See notes to *Aglaura*.

l. 25. *well* (*rid*)] Text in Dodsley. Early edd. omit *rid*.

PAGE

179. SCENE II.

l. 14. *villany's*] Dodsley. Early eds. have *villany*.

l. 15. in her closet] into her closet 1658.

l. 22. *an army such*] 1709; *an Armie, such* 1646; *an Army' such* 1648; *an Armie such* 1658. Dodsley, etc., read *an army of such*.

l. 27. *Base!*] *Cf.* Iolas' exclamation, 'Basely and tamely——' in *Aglaura*, V., i.

180. ACT III., SCENE I.

Enter Peridor, etc.] Enter Thieves (all early edd.).

l. 9. speak] speaks (Dodsley).

l. 18. *gaudy day*] In Dodsley there is a long quotation from Blount's *Glossographia*, 1656, which mentions one derivation of the phrase from a certain Judge Gawdy. The true derivation is from *gandium*, 'because, to say truth, they are days of joy, as bringing good cheer to the hungry student.' *Cf. Ant. and Cleo.*, III., xiii. 183; D'Avenant, *Albovine*, Act. IV: 'Phœbus' car . . . who smiles, and seems to prophesy A gaudy day.' See also Halliwell, *s.v. gaudy*.

181. l. 38. *rule*] *rules* 1646, 1648.

182. SCENE II.

l. 21. *an eye of white*] 'An eye is a small shade of colour' (Steevens). He refers to *Tempest*, II., i. 55.

l. 29. Some drink, etc.] In Dodsley, this line is printed as part of Nassurat's speech. It clearly forms the first line of the catch, which in 1646 and 1658 is given to Nassurat alone. The first stanza recalls Iago's catch in *Othello*, II., iii.

l. 36. The Prince of Darkness, etc.] *Cf. King Lear*, III., iv., 148, 149; in the same play, IV., i. 63, Mahu is defined as the fiend of stealing. The note in Dodsley assumes that the catch was much older than Suckling's time, and that Edgar, in *King Lear*, alluded to it, 'unless the present performance were written from the hints in *King Lear*.' It is generally agreed that Shakespeare found the names of Edgar's fiends in Harsnet's *Declaration of Popish Impostures*, 1603. In the present case,

PAGE

it seems almost certain that these lines do not form the end of the catch, as they are printed in all the editions, but are quoted by Nassurat at the gaoler in a spirit of derision.

182. l. 37. Mahu, Mahu] 1648, 1709; Mahu, Mohu 1646, 1658.

l. 39. *as if you*] 1709; *as you* 1646, etc.

l. 40. *an* O yes] A crier of a court, who prefaces his proclamations with the word *Oyez*, corrupted into *O yes*. Steevens points out the propriety of the comparison in the case of a man whose jaws, like the gaoler's, are extended by a gag. *Cf. Merry Wives*, V., v. 45.

183. l. 51. *excellent*] *an excellent* 1648, 1709.

l. 53. *That Ann*, etc.] A familiar 'play-end' from *Rich. III.*, IV., ii. 52, 58, loosely quoted.

l. 55. *rogue in buckram*] Another Shakespearean tag. See 1 *Hen. IV.*, II., iv. 213, etc.

let me bite thee] Steevens refers to *Rom. and Jul.*, II., iv. 81, and Jonson, *Alchemist*, II., iii. Dowden explains 'bite thee by the ear' (*Rom. and Jul.*, *u.s.*, Arden ed.) as 'a sign of fondness,' as one horse bites the ear of another.

l. 57. *the ballad, too*] *the ballad do*, Dodsley. The allusion is to the *Session of the Poets*.

l. 58. foutre for the Guise] 'A proverbial expression during the League' (Steevens). This and the two lines following seem to be tags from some bombastic popular play.

l. 59. accrue] *accrew*, early edd.; *agree*, Dodsley.

l. 61. *I'll tickle you*] *Cf.* 1 *Hen. IV.*, II., iv. 489.

old ends] *Cf. Rich. III.*, I., iii. 337.

185. SCENE IV.

l. 9. *perdues*] See note on Suckling's *Supplement to Lucrece*, l. 11. Here the word means simply 'sentinels in ambush.'

186. SCENE VI.

l. 2. *Maybe*] *May it be* 1646, 1658.

SCENE VII.

l. 14. *Court ladies*] *Cf.* Molière, *Festin de Pierre*, I., i.: 'Dame, demoiselle, bourgeoise, paysanne, il ne trouve rien de trop chaud ni de trop froid pour

PAGE

lui'; and Leporello's song in *Don Giovanni*: 'Madamina, il catalogo è questo.'

186. l. 16. *termers*] Steevens explains as 'ladies who only visit the city in *term-time—i.e.*, when the courts of justice are open, and young lawyers are willing to qualify their dry studies with female dalliance.' Cut-purses who haunted the law-courts were also called 'termers': see Decker, *Bel-man of London*, 1608 (ed. Smeaton, p. 147): 'Some of these *Boote-halers* are called *Termers*, and they ply Westminster Hall.'

187. l. 44. *Fie, fie*, etc.] *Cf.* 2 *Hen. IV.*, II., iv. 283, 284.

l. 53. *one of Fortune's fools*] Steevens quoted *Rom. and Jul.*, III., i. 141, and referred to *Meas. for Meas.*, III., i. 11. In both these cases, Steevens and Johnson discovered an allusion to the Fool of the moralities. The next line defines the meaning sufficiently.

188. l. 71. Peridor. *I like not this*] 1646, 1658 omit 'Peridor.'

189. l. 94. *for like myself*, etc.] *Cf. Tempest*, III., i. 48 *ff.* Reginella, on Dryden's authority, is an 'open imitation' of Miranda.

l. 107. *I'll bring thee*, etc.] One recalls 'that smooth song which was made by Kit Marlowe,' and hummed by Sir Hugh Evans in the field near Frogmore: see *Passionate Pilgrim*, No. xx.

190. l. 143. *coal-staff*] See Nares, *s.v.* Colestaff: 'A strong pole on which men carried a burden between them—originally, perhaps, of coals. Sometimes written *colt-staff*,' as in the quotation added by Nares from *Arden of Feversham*. The punishment of the poet was given, according to Ray (quoted by Halliwell, *s.v.* Stang), to misdemeanants in certain Cambridge colleges, by their fellow-undergraduates, 'to *stang* scholars in Christmas being to cause them to ride on a colt-staff or pole for missing of chapel.' The stang or coltstaff was the pole used in such colleges for the conveyance of casks of beer from and to the buttery. Mr. R. F. Scott, in his short monograph on St. John's College, Cambridge (pp. 4, 5), notes that the passages by which the college kitchen is approached from the Hall and from the lane outside the buildings are still known as

PAGE

the Stankard or Staincoat, and that the place where the Stang was kept was called the Stangate Hole.

190. ACT IV., SCENE I.

l. 6. *saucer-ey'd devil*] In *King Lear*, IV., vi. 70, the eyes of the fiend described by Edgar to Gloucester were 'two full moons.'

191. l. 21. *O O S*] So all the editions. Samorat's sighs and their depth attract the attention of his more talkative companions.

l. 23. *enjoying*] *enjoyning* 1646, 1658.

l. 35. as out of his study] omitted 1648, 1709. *A sort of his study* 1658.

l. 49. *fall out*] *will fall out*, Dodsley.

192. l. 60. Nassurat. *Thou hast*] 1648. The speech is printed as a continuation of that of Pellegrin, in 1646, 1658. Collier noted the alteration in the 1696 ed., but evidently had not seen 1648.

l. 63. *with every light*] *ere 'tis light*, Dodsley.

l. 83. *the head of the bass-viol*] *Cf. Com. of Errors*, IV., iii. 23.

193. l. 114. *laver*] *laveer* is the more correct form. Collier explains: 'To *tack*, or *make boards* against the wind,' and quotes Dryden, *Astræa Redux*, l. 65. The word is used by D'Avenant and Lovelace; and Clarendon uses the substantive 'laveerer.' See below, Scene III.

194. SCENE II.

l. 7. *first-created light*] *Cf.* Milton, *Sams. Ag.* 83.

195. l. 49. *lead*] Dodsley. Early eds. have *load*, which probably should be read.

SCENE III.

l. 13. *muscadine*] Or muscadel, wine grown from the grape called the muscat of Alexandria: 'Vinum muscatum, quod moschi odorem referat.' (Minsheu, quoted by Nares). Burton, *Anat. Mel.*, i., sect. 2, mem. 2, subs. 1, mentions muscadine among the 'black wines, overhot, compound, strong thick drinks,' as hurtful to persons of a certain temperament. See Howell, *Epp. Ho-El.*, i., § iv., lett. 28.

196. l. 23. *training to a pace*] *straining to a pace* 1648.

PAGE

197. ll. 51, 52. *Farewell*, etc.] Quoted, without strict accuracy, from *Othello*, III., iii. 349-50.

SCENE IV.

l. 21. *a cramp*] *Cf. Tempest*, V., i. 286; IV., i. 261.

198. l. 45. *Querer per solo Querer*] *Carer per so lo carer* (old edd.). Sir Richard Fanshawe, Ambassador at Madrid, translated a play by Antonio de Mendoza (d. 1639), which appeared in 1628, and bore this title (' Love for Love's sake '). The original play must be referred to here, as the translation was not made till after Suckling's death, and was not printed until 1671; and the point of the passage is that the writer for whom the poet asks is already dead. The passage is of some interest, as showing English interest in Spanish drama, and fixing the date of production of *The Goblins* at a point after Mendoza's death in 1639.

l. 52. *empresses*] *emp'rors*, Dodsley. This reading receives no support from the early eds., and the long quotation given by the editors from *Tamburlaine* loses its point. Suckling's allusion is probably to 1 *Tamburlaine*, III., iii. where Zenocrate addresses Zabina as 'Disdainful Turkess and unreverend boss.'

l. 54. *the 'Bold Beauchamps'*] See induction to Beaumont and Fletcher, *Knight of Burning Pestle*: 'My husband hath promised me any time this twelvemonth, to carry me to the Bold Beauchamps.' In the surreptitious 2 *Hudibras*, 1663, Heywood is credited with the authorship of this popular play, now lost (Fleay, *Biog. Chron. Eng. Drama*). Dodsley's editors mention the old proverb, 'as bold as Beauchamp,' and quote Drayton, *Poly-Olbion*, xviii. 255-59, where the origin of the adage is referred to 'that brave and god-like brood of *Beuchamps*,' Earls of Warwick. See also Middleton, *A Mad World, my Masters*, 1608, Act V.: 'Being every man well hors'd like a bold Beacham.'

l. 55. *'England's Joy'*] A patriotic play, now lost, attributed to Richard Vennard or Vennar. It was acted in dumb-show. The plot, 'to be played at the Swan, this 6th Nov. 1602,' is preserved in a broadside in the library of the Society of Antiquaries. See Jonson, *Masque of Augurs*, 1622 : 'That famous matter of England's Joy in six hundred and three' ; *Love Restored :* ''Slight, a fine trick ! a piece of England's Joy, this !' Dodsley's editors quote John Taylor, *A Cast over the Water . . . given gratis to Will Fennor, the Rimer*, 1615 : 'And poor old Vennor, that plaine dealing man, Who acted "England's Joy" first at the Swan, Paid eight crowns for the writing of these things, Besides the covers and the silken strings.'

198. l. 57. *A Briton*] A British patriotic piece. Collier rightly rejects Steevens' theory that Nicholas Breton is indicated here as the author of *England's Joy*, and as a friend of Shakespeare.

200. SCENE V.

l. 36. *last*] *last night*, Dodsley.
l. 48. *shows*] *flows*, Dodsley.
l. 51. *goodliest*] *godli'st* 1646.

201. ACT V., SCENE I.

l. 26. *soldiers' habits*] *habits* omitted 1646, 1658.
l. 29. *gaberdines*] Nares gives, *s.v.*, 'A coarse cloak or mantle,' and derives from Spanish *gabardina*, a long cloak, cassock. 'Gabardine. A rough Irish mantle or horseman's cloak, a long cassock' (Blount, *Glossographia*). In Arden ed. *Merchant of Venice*, I., iii, 112 [113], Mr. C. K. Pooler gives a passage from Barnabe Riche : 'Disguised like a right porter with a long gaberdine downe to the calf of his legges.'
l. 41. *secret of the prison-house*] An echo of *Hamlet*, I., v. 14.

202. SCENE II.

l. 2. *Not look on*] *nor looke of* 1646, 1658.
languishes] *she languishes* 1648, 1709.
l. 11. *O, nothing less !*] Hazlitt reads *O* [*no, he'll die*]. *Nothing less*.
l. 12. *censure*] *sentence*, Dodsley.
l. 15. *a secretary*] Dodsley's editors suppose this to allude to 'the Queen of Scots' case and Davison's

PAGE

disgrace, in compliment to the Stuarts.' It seems hardly likely that this allusion to an event of fifty years before would be readily understood by Suckling's audience.

203. l. 47. *regain*] Dodsley; *again* 1646, etc., possibly the right reading.

l. 49. *fair*] *fair one* 1648, 1709.

l. 64. *thy favours*] *any favours*, Dodsley.

204. SCENE III.

l. 8. *the prince*] *the King* 1646, 1658.

205. SCENE IV.

l. 7. *has*] *'Has* 1648, 1709. *'Thas*, Dodsley.

l. 9. *pass*] Dodsley; *pass by* 1646. etc.

206. l. 46. *the point of honour*] *Cf.* dialogue in Scene II. above, between Sabrina and the Prince.

l. 59. *his anger*] *this anger* early eds.

207. SCENE V.

l. 15. *strange*] *strict*, Dodsley.

l. 35. *what mistake*] *what a mistake*, Dodsley.

208. l. 71. *save*] *save you*, Dodsley.

209. l. 91. *questioned*] demanded, made requisition of. *Cf.* Henry VIII., I., i. 12.

l. 98. *ne'er*] 1709; *Neere* 1646, 1648, 1658. Philatel means that he would as soon believe that Torcular had never lived, as that he was alive.

l. 117. *have infested*] Dodsley; *has infested* 1646, etc.

210. l. 125. *was a woman*] *is a woman*, Dodsley.

l. 136. *Mephostophilus*] So all early edd. Orsabrin refers to Tamoren. 'Mephostophilus' in *Merry Wives*, I., i. 132, is a term of abuse, borrowed from the devil in Marlowe's *Faustus*.

l. 152. *Sanborne, fatal*] *Sanborn' fatal*, Dodsley.

211. l. 176. *time*] *both time*, Dodsley.

l. 196. *hair, though*] So Hazlitt; but 1649, etc., have *air though*, and Dodsley reads *air, though*. Possibly a bad pun was intended.

l. 199. *kingdom*] 1648; *Kingdomes* 1646, 1658.

212. l. 204. *kinder*] *kindred*, Dodsley.

l. 233. *commands*] regions under my command.

213. l. 243. *all join*] 1648; *all will join* 1646.

PAGE

215. Epilogue, l. 4. *old*] *Cf.* North's Plutarch, *Alex. Great* (ed. Rouse, vol. vii., p. 80) : 'At this feast there was old drinking.' The adjective is purely intensitive.

BRENNORALT

NOTE ON TITLE.

The quarto edition of this play, published during Suckling's lifetime, bears the title, *The Discontented Colonell.* The date of production was probably 1640 : allusions to the Scottish Rebellion point to this date. *Aglaura* had been produced by Suckling at great expense in 1638 ; and the first edition of the play had shown the same ostentation and extravagance. Nothing appears to be known of the production of *The Goblins ;* but it seems probable that all Suckling's dramatic attempts were produced within the inclusive dates 1638-1640.

Dramatis Personæ.

In the quarto the following variations occur : *Miessa* for *Miesta, Granivert* for *Grainevert, Strathman* for *Stratheman, Menser* for *Menseck.*

NOTES ON BRENNORALT

220. ACT I., SCENE I.

l. 30. *they are old*] *th'art old* 1658.

l. 34. *Coronel*] The form in all the early edd.

l. 52. *A fine account !*] *Cf.* Falstaff's words on Shrewsbury field, 1 *Henry IV.*, V., i. : 'A trim reckoning ! . . . Honour is a mere scutcheon."

221. SCENE II.

l. 10. *smalky*] 1648 : *Smalke* the rest.

l. 15. *was never*] *never was* 1658.

l. 19. *goes matters*] *go the matters* 1658.

222. l. 65. *cottages*] *Cf.* Waller, *Last Verses*, l. 13 : 'The soul's dark cottage, battered and decayed' ; and l. 33 of same poem : 'old tenement'; *Of Divine Love,* vi. 31, 32 : 'The soul contending to that light to flee From her dark cell.'

PAGE

223. SCENE III.

l. 12. *rival's*] *the Rivals* early edd.

l. 29. Raillerie à part] *Raillery apart* 1709.

224. l. 56. *spaniels*] All early eds. have *spannels.*

l. 57. *concur*] *Cf.* the pun in Calverley's *Cock and the Bull*, l. 4 : 'As we curtail the already cur-tail'd cur.'

225. SCENE IV.

l. 2. *ruffle*] *Cf.* Shakespeare, *Lover's Complaint*, l. 58 : 'A blusterer, that the ruffle knew Of court, of city.' The substantive is metaphorical; *cf.* the verb, 'the bleak winds Do sorely ruffle' in *King Lear*, II., iv. 304.

226. l. 8. *Like glorious mornings*] *Cf.* metaphor in Shakespeare, Sonnets 33, 34.

228. l. 74. *the sudden execution*] *Cf. Richard III.*, I., iii. 346.

ACT II., SCENE I.

l. 2. *Thy elder brother*] See Hesiod, *Theog.*, 211, 212 : Νὺξ δ' ἔτεκε στυγερόν τε Μόρον καὶ Κῆρα μέλαιναν | καὶ θάνατον, τέκε δ' ὕπνον, ἔτικτε δὲ φῦλον Ὀνείρων. Homer, *Il.*, xvi. 672, makes Death and Sleep twins. *Cf.* Shelley, *Qu. Mab*, ll. 1, 2 : 'How wonderful is Death—Death, and his brother Sleep !'

229. l. 18. *what countries ?*] *Cf. Hamlet*, III., i. 79, 80.

l. 37. *Arm, arm, arm !*] The earlier eds. give this as a stage direction.

230. SCENE II.

l. 17. stale] decoy. *Cf. Tempest*, IV., i. 187.

l. 23. *trickling tears*] This same play-end is quoted by Falstaff, 1 *Henry IV.*, II., iv. 431.

l. 28. Pins up a rose] See Newton, *Herball to the Bible*, 1587, quoted by Brand, *Pop. Antt.*, ii. 346, 347 : 'When pleasaunt and merry companions doe friendly meete together to make goode cheere, as soone as their feast or banket is ended, they give faithfull promise mutually one to another, that whatsoever hath been merrily spoken by any in that assembly, should be wrapped up in silence, and not to be carried out of the doores.

For the assurance and performance whereof, the tearme which they use is, that all things there saide must be taken as spoken *under the rose.* Whereupon *they use in their parlours and dining roomes to hang roses over their tables*, to put the companie in memorie of secresie and not rashly or indiscreetly to clatter and blab out what they heare.' Lloyd's Dictionary, quoted *ibid.*, 346 *n.*, gives the following lines : 'Est rosa flos Veneris, cujus quo furta laterent Harpocrati matris dona dicavit amor. Inde rosam mensis hospes suspendit amicis, convivæ ut sub ea dicta tacenda sciant.'

231. l. 71. *We debauch*, etc.] Early edd. have *We—debauch—in discipline.* Stratheman has some difficulty in getting his words out.

232. l. 78. *Plocence*] Hazlitt prints throughout as *Florence.* The name is obviously intended to recall some Polish name, probably Plock.

l. 81. *back-side*] Halliwell explains as 'the barton, or any premises at the back of a house.' Thus the 'back-side' of Trinity Hall at Cambridge was the portion of the college buildings occupied by the stables, etc.

ll. 89-91. *So pale*, etc.] A free quotation from 2 *Hen. IV.* I., i. 70-73.

l. 106. The Macedon youth] See North's Plutarch, *Alex. Great* (ed. Rouse, vii. 225) : 'Be that this prince did exceed in drinking, yet that notwithstanding, wine must not drown nor bury so many excellent vertues that do shine in him in time of peace and war.'

233. Scene III.

Iphigene] Hazlitt adds [disguised].

l. 18. *the bold Macedonian youth*] The allusion is to the rebukes which Alexander administered to his friends who 'became very dissolute and licentious in diet and life.' See North's Plutarch, *u.s.*, vii. 65, 66 : 'And how I pray you, can a man take pain to dress his own horse, or to make clean his lance or helmet, that for slothful curiosity's sake, disdaineth to rub his own body with his fingers ?' etc.

PAGE

233. l. 26. *olios*] Hazlitt reads *aloes* wrongly, as also in Letter xxviii. (p. 320): 'These general motives of the state and common good . . . have still the upper end. Yet, like great olios, they rather make a show than provoke appetite.' An olio is a dish of stewed meat of various kinds. *Cf.* Lovelace, *On Sanazar's being honoured,* etc., 'for, to rise high, Commend this Olio of this Lord 'tis fit.'

l. 31. *Press much religion*] The source of Menseck's arguments will be found in Machiavelli, *Il Principe*, cap. 18.

234. l. 48. *the dearest, modesty*] *Cf. Tempest,* III., i. 53, 54.

l. 68. *wander*] *wonder* 1646.

l. 72. *revenges*] *revenge* 1658.

235. SCENE IV.

l. 23. *pestilent airs*] *Cf.* 'taking airs' in *King Lear,* II., iv. 166.

237. l. 69. *set*] challenge. *Cf. Rich. II.*, IV., i. 57.

238. ACT III., SCENE I.

ll. 17, 18. *I'll have this statue's place,* etc.] *Cf.* Donne, *Twickenham Garden,* stanza 2: 'Make me a mandrake, so I may grow here, Or a stone fountain weeping out my year.'

240. SCENE II.

l. 5. '*For oft it stands,*' etc.] This, and other statements placed within inverted commas, seem to be drawn from some common source of maxims; or the commas may simply be intended to call attention to their gnomic character.

l. 16. *its eye*] *his eye* 1658.

241. l. 53. *cavilons*] So the early edd. Hazlitt prints *cavezous* for the right reading *cavezons;* and *cavilons* may be a misprint for *cavisons.* The cavezon (Sp. *cabezón*) is a nose-band, used in breaking-in horses.

243. l. 151. *our own*] *country,* two lines below, is understood.

244. SCENE III.

l. 6. *taking in a heart*] Suckling's favourite metaphor of a siege. *Cf.* the lines ''Tis now since I sat down,' etc.

PAGE

245. l. 34. *Mew!*] Morat's contemptuous comment on the dialogue which he has overheard.

l. 35. *vildly*] vilely (an intensitive use). The folio of 1623 has 'vild' in *Tempest*, I., ii. 358.

l. 37. *crash*] carouse. Halliwell and Nares explain as 'entertainment' or 'feast.'

l. 38. *What are these*] 1648. The right reading is *Where are those* 1646, etc.

l. 49. *the works*] the outworks of the castle. See Clarendon, *Hist. Reb.*, bk. vii., of the siege of Bristol: 'The Works were so good, that they must expect to lose very many men.'

246. Scene IV.

l. 4. *o'th'rash*] 1658. The other editions have *a'th'rash.*

247. l. 60. *heavenly bodies*] On the co-operation supposed to exist between a man's genius and his horoscope, see North's Plutarch, *Antonius*. An Egyptian soothsayer warned Antony to abandon Octavius, 'for thy demon said he (that is to say, the good angel and spirit that keepeth thee) is afraid of his: and being courageous and high when he is alone, becometh fearful and timorous when he cometh near unto the other.'

l. 64. *excellency*] 1658. The other editions have *excellence.*

l. 71. *the crown*] *Cf.* Sonnet iii., stanza 5: 'Some bays, perchance, or myrtle bough,' etc.

249. Act IV., Scene I.

l. 16. *pay*] *pray* 1658.

ll. 18, 19. *consider'd hours*] *Cf.* 'consider'd time,' *Hamlet*, II., ii. 81.

l. 23. *dy-dapper*] *Cf. Ven. and Adonis*, ll. 86, 87; Beaumont and Fletcher, *Woman-Hater*, IV., ii.: 'The misery of man may fitly be compared to a didapper, who, when she is under water, past our sight, and indeed can seem no more to us, rises again, shakes but herself, and is the same she was.'

250. l. 37. *word*] *i.e.*, pass-word.

l. 46. *Black Tempest*] *Cf.* 'white Surrey,' *Rich. III.*, V., iii. 64.

PAGE

251. SCENE III.

Iphigene] It should be remembered that Iphigene is still in disguise.

l. 3. *You will not stoop*, etc.] *Cf.* Petruchio's simile, *Tam. of the Shrew*, IV., i. 193 *ff*.

l. 27. [*you*] Hazlitt. Early edd. omit.

252. l. 42. *the gallery*] The long state-room often found in the larger houses of the sixteenth and early seventeenth centuries, frequently occupying the whole length of the upper floor of a house, as at Montacute House, Somerset, or of a wing, as at Drayton House, Northants, and Haddon Hall, Derbyshire. *Cf.* Webster, *Duchess of Malfi*, I., i. : 'You must attend my lady in the gallery'; D'Avenant, *Wits*, Act V. : 'This key conveys you through the chancel to The house-gallery.' See also *Sad One*, II., i.

l. 50. *cherubin*] For this French singular of 'cherub' *cf. Othello*, IV., ii. 63; *Tempest*, I., i. 152. It is found in Chaucer, *Cant. Tales*, Prol., 624.

SCENE IV.

l. 3. *moneth*] All the early editions have this old form.

l. 8. *well-a*] *Cf.* Autolycus' songs in *Winter's Tale*, IV., iii. 132-35; IV., iv. 321 *ff*. The same drawling rhyme is used throughout the satiric poem called *A Letter sent by Sir John Suckling from France*, etc., 1641.

l. 9. *Look babies*] Nares explains: 'to look closely or amorously into the eyes, so as to see the figures reflected in them.' *Cf.* Sidney, *Astrophel and Stella*, sonnet 11 : 'So, when thou saw'st in Nature's cabinet Stella, thou straight look'st babies in her eyes'; Beaumont and Fletcher, *Woman-Hater*, III., i. : 'I cannot think I shall become a coxcomb, To ha' . . . Mine eyes look'd babies in.'

l. 11. *above*] Hazlitt reads *about*, but suggests *not above*. But *above* here probably = upwards of—*i.e.*, getting on for fifteen.

253. l. 25. *taffeta*] *Cf.* 1 *Hen. IV.*, I., ii. 11.

l. 27. *rustling into*] 1648; *rustling in* 1646, etc., probably right.

PAGE

253. l. 46. *moiety*] Used adjectivally : half-and-half, neither one thing nor the other.

255. Scene V.

l. 65. *monster*] *Cf. Othello*, III., iii. 166

257. Act V., Scene I.

l. 6. *virgin-tower*] Either virgin because it had never been taken, which is more probable from the context ; or less probably, because it contained the women's rooms, as the 'mayden's tower' in Surrey's poem on his imprisonment at Windsor.

258. Scene II.

l. 31. *wrecks*] *I.e.*, wracks.

ll. 44, 45. *My fond . . . suffer*] Hazlitt. These lines have been carelessly transposed in the earlier eds. ; for a similar transposition *cf.* the first folio reading of *Rich. III.*, IV., iv. 52, 53.

259. l. 51. *deceived*] 'Having been' is, of course, understood. A somewhat similar ellipse occurs in *Rich. III.*, I., iii. 213, 214.

260. l. 118. *fatality*] *Cf.* Romeo's apprehensions, *Rom. and Jul.*, I., iv. 106.

263. Scene III.

l. 56. *A stop in nature*] Probably an echo of *Ant. and Cleo.*, II., ii. 221-23.

l. 79. *the nymph*] *Cf.* Crashaw's well-known epigram : 'Nympha pudica Deum vidit et erubuit.'

264. l. 98. *thou much-wearied guest*] Almerin addresses his soul, the tenant of its 'dark cottage, battered and decayed."

l. 100. *black else*] 1648. The rest have *back else.*

265. l. 130. *gift*] 1648. The rest have *guilt.*

NOTES ON THE SAD ONE

273. Act I., Scene I.

l. 11. *fraught*] *Cf. Othello*, III., iii. 449.

l. 27. *Cassiopeia's chair*] *Cf.* Lovelace, *On Sanazar's being honoured*, etc. : 'Then seat her in *Cassiopeia's* Chair, As now you're in your Coach.'

PAGE

275. ll. 69, 70. *Doubt . . . diseases*] *Cf.* Iago's warning in *Othello*, III., iii. 326 *ff*.

SCENE II.

The dumb-show of the inter-scene recalls the use of this stage-device in the class of play on which *The Sad One* is modelled. *Cf.* Webster, *White Devil*, II., iii. where the conjuror shows Brachiano the deaths of his duchess and of Camillo; *Duchess of Malfi*, III., iv.

276. l. 28. *great men's deaths*] 1709. The other eds. have *great men's death.* Hazlitt reads [*a*] *great man's death.*

a noise at midnight] *Cf.* the mysterious noises at Duncan's death, *Macbeth*, II., iii. 59 *ff*.

278. ACT II., SCENE II.

ll. 6, 7. *I have conceiv'd,* etc.] *Cf. Othello*, V., ii. 55, 56.

l 14. *Sulphur,* etc.] Recalls the tortures invented by the mock-fiends in *Goblins*, III., i.

SCENE III.

l. 20. *There humours,* etc.] *Cf.* the complaints of Brennoralt and Doran in *Brennoralt*, III., i.

280. SCENE V.

l. 3. *corrosives*] *Cf.* 2 *Hen. VI.*, III., ii. 403; Beaumont and Fletcher, *Elder Brother*, V., i.: 'the surgeon, That did apply those burning corrosives.'

ll. 14, 15. *I will not give him,* etc.] *Cf. Hamlet*, II., iii. where Hamlet determines to kill his uncle 'about some act That has no relish of salvation in't.'

l. 19. *cockatrice's eye*] *Cf. Rom. and Jul.*, III., ii. 47. Numerous other references occur in the dramatists to this superstition, for which see Sir Thos. Browne, *Pseud. Epid.*, lib. iii., cap. 7.

284. ACT III., SCENE III.

l. 36. *waste*] For the pun *cf.* 2 *Hen. IV.*, I., ii. 160, 162.

l. 42. *where there were any*] Hazlitt suggests *Were there not any.*

PAGE

285. SCENE V.

l. 15. *he lives not, sure, that loves not*] The same sentiment is finely expressed by Thackeray in the concluding chapter of *Esmond*, and the passage beginning 'Sure, *omnia vincit Amor*.'

286. ACT IV., SCENE I.

l. 5. *amber*] *Cf.* George Herbert's lines on the words *My Master*, stanza 1: 'as ambergris leaves a rich scent Unto the taster.'

288. SCENE II.

l. 25. *his ears cut off*] Hazlitt sees an allusion to Prynne, whose ears were cut off in 1634: he lost the remainder of them in 1637. Burton's ears were cut off in 1636. These dates may point, at any rate, to the earliest date at which this fragment may have been written. The words, spoken by a character like Doco Discopio, imply no admiration on Suckling's part for Prynne and his friends. The lines which follow contain an obvious allusion to English politics.

289. SCENE III.

l. 19. *vices*] *nieces* early edd.

290. l. 47. Hast thou seen, etc.] The song is an imitation of Jonson's beautiful lines on Charis.

291. l. 95. *groom*] *Cf. Tam. of the Shrew*, IV., i. 128, for this general use of the word to signify 'low-born person.'

SCENE IV.

Signior Multecarni] The character is intended to caricature Ben Jonson, whose great size is referred to in the name. His fondness for set types of character, or 'humours,' is touched in the opening lines of the scene. As Jonson died in 1637, the fragment must have been written by then.

ll. 8, 9. *the honest lawyer*] Hazlitt assumes an allusion to a play called *The Honest Lawyer*, by S. S., printed 1616. This seems unnecessary.

l. 10. *admired*] *I.e.*, wondered.

PAGE

292\. l. 15. *lord treasurer*] The allusions in this speech may all be to particular persons. Suckling had dealings with Lord Treasurer Weston (see the letter from the State Papers printed in the Appendix), and may here be making a satirical allusion to him.

l. 26. *If it does not take*, etc.] *Cf.* below, v. 1 : 'Marry, he that says 'tis good,' etc. Jonson presented *Cynthia's Revels* to the public with the scornful line, 'By G——, 'tis good ; and, if you like't, you may.'

l. 30. *Aristippus*] A kind of wine, according to Nares, who quotes Middleton : 'O for a bowl of fat canary, Rich Aristippus, sparkling sherry.'

294\. Scene V.

l. 65. *should*] Hazlitt reads the preferable *would.*

Act V., Scene I.

l. 7. *the vast*] *Cf. Pericles*, I., i. 1.

NOTES ON LETTERS, Etc.

297\. The title-page in the edition of 1648 bears the name of Thomas Warren instead of that of Ruth Raworth. No printer's name is given in the title-page of 1658.

299\. I.

Hazlitt heads this letter [*To Aglaura*(?)]

ll. 3, 4. *to town*] *to the Town* 1658.

ll. 17, 18. *take me in*] *Cf.* the dialogue *Upon my Lord Brohall's Wedding*, l. 35.

l. 25. *Platonicks*] *Cf. Aglaura*, passim.

II.

Suckling's correspondent was probably Jack Bond ; see the dialogue *Upon my Lord Brohall's Wedding.* The allusion to Mistress Howard seems to indicate that this letter was nearly contemporary with the dialogue, and that its date is therefore 1642.

300\. l. 27. *agues*] *Agents* 1658.

l. 35. *Frontiniack*] *Cf.* Howell, *Epp. Ho.-El.*, bk. ii., No. 54 (ed. Jacobs, p. 457) : '. . . towards the *Alpes* and *Italy*, she [France] hath a luscious rich wine called *Frontiniac*.' The original home of this sweet wine was Frontignan in Languedoc, seven kilometres east of Cette : Howell does not seem to have connected it with this part of France ; for his next sentence tells us expressly that 'in the Country of *Provence* towards the *Pyrenees*, and in *Languedoc*, there are Wines concustable with those of *Spain*.'

300. l. 48. *woman is resolved stronger than wine*] Suckling probably refers to the story of Zorobabel and Darius in 1 Esdras, iii., iv. : see especially iv. 14 *ff*. 'O sirs, is not the king great, and men are many, and wine is strong ? who is it then that ruleth them, or hath the lordship over them ? are they not women ?' etc. (R.V.).

301. l. 51. *the late ambassador*] The allusion is too indefinite to be identified with certainty.

l. 55. *treaty*] treatise.

l. 59. *Mistress Howard*] Possibly the reference is to Lady Margaret Howard, the bride of Lord Broghill, whose wedding forms the subject of Suckling's dialogue in verse with Bond.

l. 60. *in love*] 1648 ; *love* 1646, 1658.

l. 61. *my Lord of Dorset*] Sir Edward Sackville, fourth Earl of Dorset, whose son Richard married Suckling's cousin, Lady Frances Cranfield. The fourth Earl died in 1652.

III.

l. 9. *we poor Protestants*] Suckling probably intends a play on the word 'Protestants,' alluding to the Protestant rejection of infallible authority, and also implying the significance of the word in the sense of 'devoted champion,' as in Herrick's famous lines to Anthea. See also a similar use in the postscript to letter XXI., *infra*.

302. IV.

Hazlitt heads this letter [*To Aglaura*(?)]. Whoever the lady may have been, she had been staying at his uncle's place in Warwickshire, and he writes to her on his return to London.

l. 3. *Milcot*] Milcote, in the Alcester division of Barlichway hundred, co. Warwick, is about three miles

PAGE

S.S.W. of Stratford-on-Avon, and forms part of the parish of Weston-on-Avon in Gloucester diocese. It belonged, with the Manor of Weston, to the Grevilles; but Sir Edward Greville's fifth daughter, who married a Yorkshire knight, Sir Arthur Ingram, of Temple Newsam, parted with the manors to pay her father's debts. The purchaser was Lionel, Earl of Middlesex, Suckling's uncle. On the death of the second Earl without issue the estate passed to his sister, Frances, Countess of Dorset, and so to her descendants, in whose hands it remains to-day. See Dugdale, *Antiquities of Warwickshire*, ed. Thomas, 1730, [ii.], p. 705.

303. V.

Hazlitt suggests with great probability that this letter was addressed to Suckling's sister Martha, whose husband, Sir George Southcote, had deserted her, and committed suicide. She married a second husband, William Clagett, of Isleworth.

l. 5. *precedent*] The old editions have the usual spelling of the day—viz., *president*.

l. 6. *Sophonisba*] Referred to by Suckling as a type of constancy in love, Sonnet iii., stanza 4. Portia is, of course, the daughter of Cato of Utica, and wife of Marcus Brutus.

l. 18. *mien*] *Mine* 1646, etc.

304. l. 29. *Balzac*] Jean-Louis Guez, seigneur de Balzac (1594-1655). The allusion is to the third part of Balzac's *Letters*, No. XIII. (tr. Sir Richard Baker, 1638, p. 27).

l. 40. *mien*] *Mine* 1646, etc.

l. 44. *By your leave*, etc.] *Julius Cæsar*, V., iii. 89.
this [*is*]] *this* 1646, 1648; *'tis* 1658.

305. VI.

l. 39. *a hawk*] *Cf.* the metaphor in *Othello*, III., iii. 260-263: 'If I do prove her haggard,' etc. See also the dialogue *Upon my Lord Brohall's Wedding*, l. 36: 'To hawks, good Jack, and hearts,' etc.

ll. 53, 54. *false opticks*] *Cf.* 'optic glass,' Milton, *P. L.*, i. 288. The simile of 'evening shadows' recalls Antony's description of 'black vesper's pageants,' *Ant. and Cleo.*, IV., xiv. 2 *ff*.

305. l. 60. *they betray*, etc.] *Wisdom of Solomon*, xvii. 12, 13: 'For fear is nothing else but a betraying of the succours which reason offereth. And the expectation from within, being less, counteth the ignorance more than the cause which bringeth the torment.'

306. l. 87. *you are*] Hazlitt adds [*hurt*]. There seems to be some need of such an addition, to explain the metaphor that follows.

VII.

This letter was clearly written by Suckling about 1631, when he was in Germany during the Thirty Years War.

307. VIII.

Hazlitt supposes this letter to be addressed to the lady whom Suckling, in the following and other letters, calls Aglaura. The somewhat wide variety in the dates, where they can be traced, of these letters, and Suckling's elaborately paraded inconstancy in love, make such identification purely conjectural.

ll. 15, 16. *approaches . . . breach*] The old metaphor pursued in the lines ''Tis now since I sat down,' etc.

308. X.

These letters are printed in parallel columns in all editions. Tom, to whom Suckling's letter is addressed, is possibly Thomas Carew; see the dialogue *Upon my Lady Carlisle's Walking*, etc.

309. (ANSWER).

l. 65. *a widow*] 1658; *Widow* 1646, 1648.

310. XI.

l. 12. *turns*] Hazlitt altered to *turn*; but *cruel remembrance* is probably intended to be the subject, though the sentence thereby is rendered very clumsy.

311. XII.

l. 3. *it is*] 1646, 1648; *'tis* 1658.

PAGE

312. XV.

ll. 13 *ff. Dear*, etc.] Printed thus in the early editions: 'Dear —— I fain would—and know no hindrance —but what must come from you—and—why should any come?' The dashes are probably intended to indicate the heat of Suckling's passion: a multiplicity of such dashes, indicative of high tragic feeling, disfigure all the early printed copies of Suckling's plays.

313. XVI.

l. 4. [*B.*] Either Beaumaris or Baron Hill. See note on No. XIX.

l. 6. *Welsh man*] The early editions have *Welch, man*, which somewhat obscures the sense.

XVII.

l. 3. *What . . . princess?*] Early editions have *What . . . then? Dear Princesse.*

XVIII.

l. 8. *not being*] 1646, 1648; *not being all* 1658.

314. XIX.

The 'two Excellent Sisters' are probably those on the subject of whom Suckling wrote the lines 'Believe't, young man'; and one of them is almost certainly the 'dear princess' of Letter XVI., as the allusions to Wales in that letter indicate, and, if so, may further be identified with Suckling's Aglaura. Baron Hill, near Beaumaris, where the sisters were at this time, was the seat of the Bulkeley family, and had been built by Sir Richard Bulkeley, kt., of Cheadle and Beaumaris, constable of Beaumaris Castle. He died in 1621; his son, Sir Richard Bulkeley, kt., of Beaumaris, died in 1635, and was succeeded by Richard Bulkeley, esq., of Beaumaris, his son, who died unmarried in March, 1639-40. The second Sir Richard married Anne, daughter of a Kentish knight, Sir Thomas Wilford, and had by her, in addition to the son just mentioned, two daughters, Margaret and Anne. Margaret married John Bodychen; Anne married, first, Henry Whyte, and, second, Robert Price, bishop of Ferns and Leighlin 1660-66. It is not at all unlikely that

PAGE

these are the sisters addressed by Suckling. The date of the letter may be fixed between the death of the second Sir Richard in 1635, and of his son in 1640. The allusion to the Lady of the Isle is doubtless to the widowed Lady Bulkeley, who subsequently married Sir Thomas Cheadle, kt., who died in 1660. Mistress Thomas may reasonably be identified with Blanch, daughter of Robert Coytmor, of Coytmor (? Coed Mawr), Carnarvonshire, who married Thomas Bulkeley, brother of the second Sir Richard, and was therefore aunt by marriage to the two sisters. Thomas succeeded to his nephew's property in 1640, and was created Viscount Bulkeley of Cashel in 1643. It is impossible to identify B. W. on merely general knowledge. 'Your cousin Duchess' introduces another problem: possibly this is Katherine, Duchess of Buckingham, daughter of the sixth Earl of Rutland, and widow of George Villiers, first Duke of Buckingham. She married Randal Macdonnell, Viscount Dunluce, and afterwards second Earl and first Marquess of Antrim, in 1635. See Clarendon, *Hist. Reb.*, bk. viii. (ed. 1707, vol. ii., pp. 607, 617), for her favour with Charles I., and his opinion that she had forgotten her first husband too soon. Her second marriage and some temporary disgrace at Court in consequence may be referred to here. Suckling was connected with her by marriage, the mothers of the Duke of Buckingham and of Anne Bret, the second wife of Suckling's uncle, Lord Middlesex, being sisters. There is a pedigree of the Bulkeleys in Ormerod's *History of Cheshire*, ed. Helsby, 1882, iii. 628; but this, unfortunately, omits dates of marriages. The letter shows that Suckling was acquainted with Baron Hill, and the magnificent view of the Snowdonian range and the Menai Straits which it commands.

314. l. 6. *my Lord of C——*] This may refer to James Hay, first Earl of Carlisle, husband of the lady whose charms Suckling and other poets celebrated. Lord Carlisle had much experience in foreign embassies. He died in 1636, which suits well with the possible allusion to the Duchess of Buckingham's second marriage, and indicates the date of the letter as 1635-36.

PAGE

314. l. 15. *mind . . . ladies*] Early editions have *mind—it never troubles you—Ladies.*

315. XX.

This letter seems to be written to some of Suckling's friends who had gone to take the waters at Bath. 'Colonel Young' is no doubt Jack Young, afterwards Sir John, whom Aubrey mentions as Suckling's companion on the road to Bath in 1637, and as the victim of a practical joke at Marlborough (*Brief Lives*, ed. Clark, 1898, ii. 242 *ff*.). Aubrey (*ibid*., ii. 13) tells the story that Young paid eighteenpence to have the inscription cut over Ben Jonson's grave. 'Captain Puff of Barton' is evidently a nickname: there may be an inaccurate allusion to 'goodman Puff of Barson' in 2 *Henry IV*., V., iii. 93, 94. 'Monsieur de Granville' may be a real name. The military titles are, of course, Suckling's humorous invention of the moment.

316. XXII.

Charles Suckling, to whom this letter is addressed, was the youngest son of Charles Suckling, esq., of Woodton in Loddon hundred, Norfolk, who was half-brother to the poet's father. He eventually married, and had four daughters.

l. 12. *rid off*] Early editions *ridd of.*

317. l. 33. *ingenuously*] *ingeniously* 1646.

XXIII.

From the allusion to the Imperialists, it would seem that this letter was written by Suckling while he was serving with Hamilton's force under Gustavus Adolphus. The victory of Gustavus at Breitenfeld, near Leipzig (17 September, 1631), is probably referred to. It was computed that about half the Imperialist army were killed or taken prisoners (see account in *Cambridge Mod. Hist.*, iv. 240). If this letter, as well as No. XIX., was written to Aglaura, and if the passion expressed is genuine, the difference in probable date shows that Suckling was capable of a degree of constancy which, in his poems, he feigned to disown.

l. 13. *neither*] 1646, 1658; *any* 1648.

PAGE

318. XXV.

l. 5. *the women here*] *Cf.* the mention of 'northern beauties' in No. XXVII. Probably Nos. XXIV., XXV., and XXVI. were written from Germany, as well as XXIII. and XXVII.

319. XXVII.

This letter was obviously written from Germany in the winter of 1631-32. The victory over Tilly at Breitenfeld took place, as already noted, on 17 September, 1631. Gustavus entered Würzburg, on the Main, on 12 October. On 19 November he left Würzburg, and moved down the banks of the Main in the direction of the Rhine. He took Mainz on 20 December; and on 8 January, 1631-32, Bernard of Weimar took Mannheim. During this time the English troops, under the command of Sir Alexander Leslie, afterwards Earl of Leven, were in Silesia, co-operating with the Elector of Saxony, whose army invaded Bohemia, and took Prague in November. Suckling was doubtless with the rest of his countrymen. He may have been present at Breitenfeld, where the Swedish and Saxon armies were combined against Tilly; but he returned to England before the battle of Lützen (16 November, 1632), at which Gustavus died.

XXVIII.

It is possible that the nobleman to whom this letter was addressed was Lucius Cary, second Viscount Falkland, who succeeded to his peerage in 1633, and was living at Great Tew in scholarly retirement between 1634 and 1639. The passage beginning 'when I consider that great soul of yours,' is peculiarly applicable to Falkland at this period, and the allusion to 'the cloistered schoolman's divinity' is appropriate to those studies which Suckling touched lightly in the *Session of the Poets*, and Clarendon commemorated more seriously (see *Hist. Reb.*, bk. vii., vol. ii., pt. 1, 1706, p. 352). It may again be noted that the *Session of the Poets* was probably written in 1637.

320. l. 28. *olios*] Early editions *Oleoes*. See note on *Brennoralt,* II., iii. 26. In both passages Hazlitt reads *aloes*.

PAGE

320. l. 42. *too much*] 1646, 1658 ; *so much* 1648.

321. l. 65. *man*] *mans* 1648.

ll. 87, 88. *the best copies*, etc.] Suckling's royalism is sufficiently apparent in *Aglaura ;* see note on II., ii. 41. The likeness between *Aglaura*, in some respects, and Beaumont and Fletcher's *Maid's Tragedy* has been remarked already ; and phrases like the present recall Coleridge's often-repeated allusions to what he called the 'hollow extravagance of Beaumont and Fletcher's ultra-royalism.'

322. XXIX.

The title of this letter declares its occasion and purpose. Henry Jermyn, member for Bury St. Edmunds in the Long Parliament, was created Baron Jermyn at Oxford in 1643, and Earl of St. Albans shortly before the Restoration, while he was abroad with Charles II. Implicated, like Suckling, in the first Army plot of 1641, he fled abroad in haste, dressed, as the Parliament noted in their complaints (Clarendon, *Hist. Reb.*, book v., vol. ii., pp. 551, 563), in a black 'Sattin Suit, and white Boots.' His influence with the Queen and Court was great ; and this letter was obviously designed for the eyes of the King and Queen. It appears in this position in all editions of the *Fragmenta Aurea*, but was published separately in quarto form in 1641, under the title, A | COPPY | OF | A LETTER | FOUND IN THE | PRIVY LODGE- | INGS AT *WHITE-HALL*. Hazlitt reprinted the 4to tract, with a few variations of text, in his edition of Suckling, and notes the existence of a French translation, incorporated in a French edition of *Eikon Basilike*, 1649. This letter, in company with other of Suckling's prose works, may be taken as evidence of the more serious and thoughtful side of his character. The text of the early editions of the *Fragmenta Aurea* is reproduced here, and collated with Hazlitt's reprint, to which the various readings in the notes refer, unless otherwise stated.

l. 2. *wise*] *wisest.*

ll. 2, 3. *the expectation. Men*] *their expectation also ; men.*

l. 6. *would at the best shew*] *at least, shewes.*

PAGE

322. l. 8. *less*] *more.*

l. 11. *relishes else*] *relisheth with them lesse.*

l. 12. *hath for the most part*] *for the most part hath.*

ll. 12, 13. *have desired ; done*] *desired, and done.*

ll. 15, 16. *certainly for a King*] *surely for the King.*

l. 16. *is at all times*] *at all times is.*

l. 17. *present*] *time almost.*

l. 18. *that*] *it.*

said . . . all] *spoken . . . all of them.*

l. 21. *innocence*] *innocency* (so also l. 31).

ll. 23, 24. *considerable ; so*] *considerable, and so.*

l. 24. *in Court*] *in the Court.*

l. 25. *inclined*] *is inclined to.*

l. 26. *determine*] *and determine of.*

desires] *desire.*

ll. 29, 30. *first plainly shew*] *first shew.*

l. 31. *always*] *alway.*

tell . . . be] *shew them . . . are.*

l. 32. *it is too like*] *is too much like.*

l. 33. *know from whence*] *know of you first, from whence you come.*

l. 35. *saith* Monsieur de Rohan] *said the Duke of* Rohan. Henri, prince de Léon, and duc de Rohan, the Huguenot general during the French civil war of 1620-29, and the conqueror of the Imperialist army in the Valtelline (1635) He was mortally wounded at the battle of Rheinfelden, where he was serving under Bernard of Weimar, on 28 February, 1637-38. The allusion is to a passage in the preface to a tract, translated into English (1640) by H. H., under the title, 'A Treatise of the Interest of the Princes and States of Christendome,' in which the words run thus : 'The Prince may deceive himselfe, his *Counsell* may be corrupted, but the interest alone can never faile.'

l. 36. *then to find out the*] *therefore to find out this.*

l. 38. *deal out*] *deale for.*

commodity] *commodities.*

l. 39. *the great interest*] *the interest.*

ll. 39, 40. a union with his people] *the union of the people.*

322, 323. ll.40, 41. *the Scripture*] Apparently a recollection of St. John viii. 44 and 1 John iii. 8.

PAGE

323. ll. 41, 42. *there ever had been any one*] *there had beene one.*

ll. 42, 43. *a felicity*] *felicity.*

l. 43. *left fair*] *left a faire.*

l. 45. *courtier*] *Courter.*

l. 47. *of our Kings*] *of Kings.*

l. 50. *There are*] *There bee.*

l. 51. *can this*] *can it.*

l. 52. *royal*] *Reall.*

l. 53. *any shall think*] *any thinke.*

l. 54. *the rest now*] *the rest.*

l. 55. *in the beginning*] *in beginning.*
that would] *it would.*

l. 56. *but not when*] *but when.*

l. 57. *these*] *those.*
could] *would.*

l. 59. after *follow him*] The following passage, from the 1641 tract, is omitted in the *Fragmenta Aurea*: *For as* Cato *said of the* Romans *they were like sheepe, and the way to drive them was in a flocke, for if one would bee extravagant, all the rest would follow; so it will bee here. It will dearely appeare, that neither the person of the* Scottish *or* English *Actours upon the stage are considerable to the great Body of* England, *but the things they undertake, which, done by another hand and sq done that there remaines no jealousie, and leaves them where they were and not much risen in value.* Hazlitt omitted the *and* before *leaves*, thus giving some construction to this concluding slipshod sentence, over which the printer evidently made some mistake. The allusion to Cato (the elder) is from Plutarch: see North's translation, ed. Rouse, 1899, iv. 71: 'He said also that the Romans were like a flock of sheep. For saith he, as every wether when he is alone, doth not obey the shepherd, but when they are all together they one follow another for love of the foremost; even so are you, for when you are together, you are all contented to be led by the noses by such, whose counsel not a man alone of you would use in any private cause of your own.'

l. 61. *this right*] *the right.*
the author] *Authour.*

PAGE

323. ll. 61, 62. *as* Cumneus *said*] *as* Comines *saith*. The quotation is probably a free rendering of a maxim which the editor has failed to identify in the works of Philippe de Commines.

l. 63. *have commonly the power*] *have the power.*

l. 64. *there shall remain*] *there remaine.*

l. 70. *more—I mean*] *more ; for that will show the heartinesse ; I meane.*

l. 71. *things*] *that.*

l. 73. *them, it*] *them, that.*
thought and] *thought or.*

l. 75. *differences*] *difference.*
suspect] *the suspect.*

l. 76. *case*] *cause.*

l. 77. *field, where the*] *field, the.*

l. 79. *further*] *any farther.*
he is] *hee hath beene.*

l. 80. *may follow*] *will follow.*

l. 81. *and not much Cavalier*] *nor not much Cavalliers.*

l. 82. *it is*] *'tis.*
where they can] *when they.*

l. 83. *none. They*] *none, and wound, even the dead ; they.*

324. l. 85. *while that is*] *while it is.*

l. 86. *this is the present state*] *this is now the state.*

l. 88. *the Queen*] *that the Queene.*

l. 89. *suspicions*] *suspition.*

l. 93. *they be*] *shee bee.*

l. 94. *know her*] *know her and are about her.*

l. 96. *a great Queen to arrive*] *a Queene so great to aime.*

l. 98. *Then . . . for*] *Besides . . . of.*

l. 99. *composing*] *compounding.*

l. 101. *thing*] *thing more.*

l. 102. *busies . . . mind much*] *busieth . . . mind.*

l. 104. *whom*] *which.* The allusion is, of course, to the impeachment of Strafford and Laud. Strafford had been committed to the Tower on 11 November.

l. 105. *which is*] *which is a thing.*

l. 109. *more general*] *generall weale.*

l. 110. *by particular*] *in particular.*

l. 111. *but yet, if . . . great*] *but, if . . . greater.*

ll. 112, 113. *other to the greater*] *other the greater body.*

l. 114. *those*] *these.*

l. 117. *instruments*] *Ministers.*

PAGE

324. l. 120. *to be first*] *first to bee.*
l. 121. nihil] nemo.
l. 122. *save*] *preserve.*
l. 124. *Lastly*] *And lastly.*
l. 126. *princes*] *Prince hath.* The right reading is *princes have.*
ll. 127, 128. *in Henry . . ., King John, Edward*] *in King Henry . . . King John, and King Edward.*

325. l. 129. *they . . . go, they come*] *the Princes . . . goe, the people come.*
ll. 129, 130. *into their hands*] *in their hands.*
l. 132. *conclude*] *conclude all.*
ll. 132, 133. *at this present*] *for the present.*
ll. 133, 134. *as to preserve*] *as preserve.*
ll. 134, 135. *be neither too insensible*] *may not bee too unsensible.*
l. 135. *resolved from*] *resolv'd of.*
l. 136. *sickness and find*] *disease and feel.*
l. 137. *but be*] *bee but.*
l. 139. *Opiniastry*] *Opinionistrie.*
l. 140. *it was wittily said*] *is witnessed.*

329. XXX.

This and the remaining letters form the additional prose matter which appeared for the first time in the third edition of *Fragmenta Aurea* (1658), and was printed in subsequent editions. The present letter was probably written early in 1639, after the abolition of Episcopacy and the Court of High Commission by the General Assembly, and during the preparations for the first Bishops' War. Suckling had probably known Sir Alexander Leslie, afterwards the victor of Newburn, during the Thirty Years War (see Letter XXVII.); and this letter, if it is addressed to a real correspondent, might have been addressed to him. Leslie, however, did not receive his peerage till 1641. The Scottish invasion of England, which was supposed to be impending, did not take place till August, 1640. The date of this letter is also that of Nos. XXXI. and XXXII.; and Nos. XXX. and XXXI. must be taken as complementary to each other. See note on No. XXXI.

l. 9. *evening shadow*] *Cf.* the use of the same metaphor in Letter VI.

PAGE

329. ll. 13, 14. *St. Michael-Mount's-men's security*] Some proverb or local custom may be alluded to. But possibly Suckling is merely referring to the heavenly protection, which, according to tradition, was vouchsafed to the 'guarded mount,' as to its parent monastery off the Norman coast.

ll. 15, 16. *Witheringtons' and Howards' estates*] The Widdringtons were one of the oldest families of Northumberland. William Widdrington, knighted in 1642, and created Baron Widdrington of Blankney, co. Lincoln, in 1643, was an active Royalist. He was mortally wounded at the battle of Wigan, 1651; see Clarendon, *Hist. Reb.*, book xiii. (vol. iii., 1706, part 2, pp. 404, 405). Widdrington Castle lies about mid-way between Warkworth and Morpeth. The Howard estates lay in Cumberland. Naworth Castle, near the eastern border of the county, belonged in 1638-39 to Lord William Howard, the famous 'Belted Will,' who died there on 9 October, 1640. Greystoke Castle, near Penrith, was the property of his nephew, Thomas, Earl of Arundel and Surrey. Both castles had come into the possession of the Howards by the marriages of Lord William and his eldest brother with two sisters, co-heiresses of the last Lord Dacre of Gilsland.

ll. 20, 27. *Alderman ——; my Lord M——*] These names cannot be identified with certainty. The Earl of Montrose did not openly desert the Covenant until 1641; but there may have been some rumour of an attempt on his part to buy off his allies.

l. 21. *boil*] *Byle* 1658.

330. XXXI.

This letter may be read in two ways. (1) It may be a genuine answer to Suckling from his correspondent of No. XXX., to which letter it obviously refers. The address, 'Good Mr. Alderman,' repeated below, but abandoned in the subsequent allusion to 'our old friend,' is a reference to the anonymous alderman's diagnosis of the situation, with which Suckling in the main agreed. The simile of the bees is referred to as Suckling's, and the alderman was in no way responsible for it. (2) It may be an imaginative composition of Suckling's own, in which case there can be hardly any doubt but that No. XXX. is on the same footing, and that both were written as a kind of tract to show the two sides of the question from one point of view. It may be argued that the tone of the first and last paragraphs, especially of the last, is ironical rather than openly cynical, and therefore is his and not his correspondent's. The allusion to the Court of High Commission would be consonant with either theory. If the letter is genuine, there would be good reason for withholding its publication till a date twelve or thirteen years later than the first edition of the *Fragmenta Aurea*. But the second theory is the more likely, and the tone of the next letter tends to corroborate it.

331. XXXII.

This may again be a short political tract couched in the form of a letter to an imaginary correspondent. Hazlitt collated it with a copy among the Ashmolean MSS., and notes one or two variations. For the date, see note on No. XXX.

331, 332. ll. 18, 19. *A King or no King*] The allusion is to the title of Beaumont and Fletcher's well-known play.

332. ll. 29, 30. Nemo cogitur, etc.] The quotation is from an edict of Theodoric to the Jews in Genoa, Cassiodorus, *Variarum*, ii. 27: 'Religionem imperare non possumus, quia nemo cogitur ut credat invitus.'

l. 33. *sealed*] Hazlitt printed *ceased*, from MS. Ashmole.

l. 38. *Lesley*] Sir Alexander Leslie, lord-general of the Scottish forces: see note on No. XXX. He had served for thirty years in the Swedish army, and had taken an active part in the campaigns of the Thirty Years War during the life and after the death of Gustavus Adolphus.

l. 47. *the beasts*] Suckling was probably thinking of Ps. lxxx. 13.

XXXIII.

Written, with the two letters following, by Suckling during the Scottish campaign of June, 1639, which ended in the Pacification of Berwick on

PAGE

18 June. Charles I. and his army were at the Birks, near Berwick, on 5 June, while Leslie was at Duns Law. This letter was probably written on or very soon after 5 June. Suckling's appearance in this war was a subject of amusement to his contemporaries, according to Aubrey (*Brief Lives*, ed. Clark, ii. 241, 242). 'Anno Domini 163—, when the expedition was into Scotland, Sir John Suckling, at his owne chardge, raysed a troope of 100 very handsome young proper men, whom he clad in white doubletts and scarlett breeches, and scarlet coates, hatts, and . . . feathers, well horsed, and armed. They say 'twas one of the finest sights in those dayes. But Sir John Menis made a lampoon of it : . . .

'The ladies opened the windows to see
So fine and goodly a sight-a,' &c.

I thinke the lampoon sayes he made an inglorious chardge against the Scotts.'

332. l. 3. *Shakespeare*] See 1 *Henry IV*., III., i. 98 *ff*. 'See how this river comes me cranking in,' etc. The river in Shakespeare was not the Tweed, but the Trent ; and, when Suckling uses the word 'scantlet,' he is thinking of the original 'cantle.'

333. l. 12. *the Lords Covenanters' letters*] The general tenour of the letters to the King's three generals, the Earls of Essex, Arundel, and Holland, is given by Clarendon, book ii. (vol. i., 1705, part i., pp. 119, 120).

XXXIV.

The only military operation in this expedition was Lord Holland's advance to Duns and hasty retreat to Berwick. Clarendon (*u. s.*, p. 121) comments on Charles's approval of the retreat, and the absence of hostilities on either side : his judgment is that Charles, by simply showing the Scots his army, would have gained their submission, 'if he had but Sate still, and been Constant to his own Interest, and positive in Denying their insolent Demands.'

XXXV.

The Pacification of Berwick was signed on 18 June, 1639. 'An Agreement,' says Clarendon (*ibid.*,

PAGE

p. 123), 'was made, if that can be call'd an Agreement in which no body meant what others believ'd he did : " The Armies were to be disbanded ; an Act of Oblivion pass'd ; the King's Forts and Castles to be restored ; and an Assembly and Parliament to be call'd for a full Settlement ; no persons reserv'd for Justice, because no Fault had been committed." ' This letter was written while the negotiations were in progress.

l. 5. *Mr. Davenant's Barbary pigeons*] The usual sources of anecdote with regard to D'Avenant, who had been poet laureate since 1637, are silent as to this form of his versatility. D'Avenant was a constant favourite with Henrietta Maria, and in 1646 carried to Charles at Newcastle-on-Tyne the letter in which she attempted to induce him to abandon the Church of England.

334. XXXVI.

Elizabeth, Countess of Kent, was daughter and co-heiress to Gilbert Talbot, seventh Earl of Shrewsbury. She married Henry Grey, seventh Earl of Kent, who died in 1639. She was said to have married as her second husband John Selden, who was solicitor and steward to the Earl of Kent. See Aubrey, *Brief Lives* (ed. Clark, ii. 220), who calls her 'an ingeniose woman,' and tells us (i. 135 *ff*.) that Samuel Butler, the author of *Hudibras*, waited on her for some years, and attracted the attention of Selden. She died 7 December, 1651, leaving her estate to Selden, who survived her for some three years. Aubrey (ii. 221) says that 'he never owned the mariage . . . till after her death, upon some lawe account. He never kept any servant peculiar, but my ladie's were all at his command ; he lived with her in *Aedibus Carmeliticis* (White Fryers), which was, before the conflagration, a noble dwelling.' It seems highly probable that the present letter is addressed to Selden ; if so, the date must lie between 1639-42, and Selden's executors may have allowed its incorporation among the additional letters of 1658. For Lady Kent's published work, of an unimportant kind, see her life in *Dict. Nat. Biog.*, xxiii. 181.

PAGE

335. ll. 19, 20. *what foretells*, etc.] Shakespeare refers to these two meanings of comets: *Julius Cæsar*, II., ii., 30, 31; *Timon of Athens*, IV., iii., 108-110. Suckling may have had these passages in his mind.

XXXVII.

It is possible that this may be written to the 'two excellent sisters' of No. XIX., and that 'Mistress T.' may be 'Mistress Thomas' of that letter. The allusions are too obscure to be fixed with any certainty; but Suckling appears to have received a letter from the ladies in hieroglyphic or cipher, and to return this answer to it.

l. 3. *a niece of Queen Gorbuduke's*] An imaginary authority. Hazlitt altered *Queen* to *King* without apparent reason.

l. 4. *the coronet*] This seems to be equivalent to 'the cornet,' and to refer to Suckling's position as a cavalry officer. *Cf.* the form 'coronel' for 'colonel,' which occurs so often in *Brennoralt*. Neither 'coronel' nor 'coronet' have any reference to the true derivation of the words of which they are corruptions. If 'coronet' means this, this letter was probably written during the Scottish expedition.

l. 8. *Secretary Cook*] Sir John Coke, Secretary of State 1625-39; 'a man of gravity, who never had quickness from his Cradle; who lov'd the Church well enough as it was twenty years before; and understood nothing that had been done in *Scotland*, and thought that nothing that was, or could be done there, was worth such a Journey as the King had put himself to' (Clarendon, book ii., vol. i., part i., p. 122). Coke, who was then in his seventy-sixth year, was made the scapegoat for the injury done to the King's cause by the Treaty of Berwick, and was dismissed from office. He died in 1644.

l. 10. *figure-caster*] astrologer.

l. 12. *what Beaumont said*] See Francis Beaumont's lines on *The Examination of His Mistress' Perfections*, ll. 21-23 (Chalmers, *Eng. Poets*, 1810, vol. vi., pp. 187, 188): 'Or hadst thou worth wrapt in a rivell'd skin, 'Twere inaccessible; who

PAGE

durst go in To find it out ?' As usual, Suckling quotes *memoriter*.

335. l. 20. *Mistress Delana's*] The allusions to this lady, to Mistress T., and Mr. H., appear to be undiscoverable, in the absence of any certain clues. The meaning of the whole passage is obscure ; but one may conjecture that the 'faces' mentioned were caricatures of Mistress Delana and Mistress T., enclosed in the letter. Vandyck was in England in 1639 ; he went abroad in 1640, and, when he returned, Suckling had fled from the country.

336. XXXIX.

l. 2. *Mountferrat*] Possibly an allusion to the disgraced knight in Fletcher's *Knight of Malta* (written probably in conjunction with Massinger and another). Suckling writes in a spirit of dejection ; and it is conceivable that this letter, which Hazlitt conjectured to be addressed to Aglaura, may have been sent home after his flight abroad.

XL.

This letter, as the text shows, is addressed to Thomas Carew. The allusions are all of a trivial nature ; and most that may be gathered from them is that Carew had been to Bath for his health, and was now staying with his friend Carew Ralegh at West Horsley, between Guildford and Leatherhead. Mr. Vincent has some remarks on Carew's illness (Carew's Poems, in Muses' Library, Introd., pp. xxxi-xxxiii), and on his friendship with Carew Ralegh (*ibid.*, p. 244). Among Howell's letters is a long one to Ralegh on the subject of Sir Walter Ralegh's voyage to Guiana (*Epp. Ho.-El.*, ii. 61, ed. Jacobs, p. 479 *ff.*) : Howell's brother Thomas, afterwards Bishop of Bristol, was rector of West Horsley at one time (*ibid.*, p. 242, and note), and Howell may have met Ralegh in this way. From Carew's poems it is possible to conjecture that the Countesses may be Lady Carlisle and Lady Anglesey ; but we have no proof of this. Carew appears to have been in Scotland during the expedition of 1639, possibly in Suckling's troop. See his lines *To my Friend G. N. from Wrest* (Poems, *u.s.*, p. 120).

PAGE

337. l. 24. *Gredeline*] The name of a colour, apparently equivalent to *gris de lin—i.e.*, flaxen grey. See Dryden, *The Flower and the Leaf*, l. 343, where the form is 'gridelin.' Nares quotes Thomas Killigrew, *The Parson's Wedding*, II., iii. : 'his love (Lord help us !) fades like my gredaline petticoat.' The colours 'gredeline and grass-green' are here symbolical of jealousy.

339. AN ACCOUNT, ETC.

Aubrey, *Brief Lives*, ii. 242-44, tells the story of Suckling's journey to Bath in 1637 with Davenant and Jack Young. 'Sir John came like a young prince for all manner of equipage and convenience, and Sir W. Davenant told me that he had a cart-load of bookes carried downe, and 'twas there, at Bath, that he writt the little tract in his booke about Socinianism. 'Twas as pleasant a journey as ever men had ; in the heighth of a long peace and luxury, and in the venison season.' They spent the second night at Marlborough ; were 'nobly entertained' by Sir Edward Baynton for several days at Bromham House, between Chippenham and Devizes, and then went for a week to Robert Davenant's rectory of West Kington, on the edge of Wiltshire and Gloucestershire, south of Badminton. Aubrey added a memorandum : 'Parson Robert Davenant haz told me that that tract about Socinianisme was writt on the table in the parlour of the parsonage at West Kington.' For Socinianism in England, see notes on *The Session of the Poets* and on the lines to John Hales. The Earl of Dorset was Sir Edward Sackville, fourth Earl (d. 1652), whose son, the fifth Earl, was married to Suckling's cousin, Frances Cranfield. Her father, the Earl of Middlesex, is mentioned in Suckling's preface. Hazlitt notes that a MS. of this essay is among the public records. The motto is taken from Lucretius, v. 1210. The discourse gives ample proof of Suckling's wide reading, and his general, though not always accurate, knowledge of Greek and Latin literature. A few variations occurring in the text of 1658 are given here, but otherwise there is nothing in the discourse

PAGE

which calls for annotation of the type which the letters demand. The language throughout is singularly clear and perspicuous; and the piece contains no allusions which bear either on Suckling's life or the history of his time. The greater number of the references to classical and other authors in the pamphlet are made *memoriter*, and apparently in most cases at second hand.

343. DISCOURSE.

l. 5. *hath*] *had* 1658.

347. l. 186. *so that if*] *If* 1658.

350. l. 306. *In-beings*] *In-beginings* 1658.

351. l. 351. *Universe*] *University* 1658.

l. 380. *a hidden*] *an hidden* 1658.

INDEX TO FIRST LINES

OF POEMS, PROLOGUES AND EPILOGUES, AND LYRICS IN THE PLAYS

THE END